Prentice Hall LITERATURE

PENGUIN EDITION

Reader's Notebook

Teaching Guide

Grade Twelve

PEARSON

Upper Saddle River, New Jersey
Boston, Massachusetts
Chandler, Arizona
Glenview, Illinois
Shoreview, Minnesota

13-digit ISBN: 978-0-13-366688-5
10-digit ISBN: 0-13-366688-3

1 2 3 4 5 6 7 8 9 10   17 16 15 14 13 12 11 10 09 08

Contents

Reader's Notebook

Answers to Part 1

Answers to Part 2

Reader's Notebook Adapted Version

Answers to Part 1

Answers to Part 2

Reader's Notebook English Learner's Version

How to Use the *Reader's Notebooks*

Share the same selection with all your students!

STEP 1

Introduce instruction using *Prentice Hall Literature* Student Edition

- Use the Background information
- Introduce the Literary Analysis and Reading Strategy
- Preview the vocabulary words

STEP 2

Develop instruction with targeted reading support
Choose the *Reader's Notebook* that meets each student's needs

Reader's Notebook
- For average readers
- Full-length selections
- Interactive reading support for all selections
- Vocabulary and pronunciation guides
- All selections on audio CD

Adapted Version
- For struggling readers
- Selection adaptations and authentic text
- Enhanced design for easier readability
- All adapted selections on audio CD

English Learner's Version
- Specialized vocabulary and reading support
- Focus on idioms, colloquialisms, and cultural information
- All adapted selections on audio CD

STEP 3

Conclude instruction using *Prentice Hall Literature* Student Edition

- Present the unabridged selection and instruction in the student edition
- Have students read along with the audio CDs
- Use the scaffolded Critical Reading questions

To the Teacher

As you face the challenge of heterogeneous classes, you will find a wide variety of abilities and strengths among your students. The *Reader's Notebook*, the *Reader's Notebook Adapted Version*, and the *Reader's Notebook English Learner's Version* that accompany your *Prentice Hall Literature* anthology are aimed at students who have difficulty with their grade-level textbook. You can use the *Notebooks* to keep your classes reading the same selections but getting the instruction and reading support at the appropriate level. These books provide extended support for those students who need more guidance with reading skills and strategies, literary analysis, and critical thinking skills.

Factors that Affect Reading Success

Four key factors influence students' ability to achieve reading success. These factors, alone and in combination, determine how well a student will learn, grow, and succeed as a reader. To understand the students in your classroom, consider these factors:

(a) **Kinds of Learners** Consider each student's background, previous learning experiences, and special needs. In addition to students who read fluently at grade level, you may find a mix of the following learning characteristics in your classroom:

- *Students who speak a language other than English at home* Unlike their fully fluent counterparts, these students often speak English only at school. This situation leaves them limited hours in which to learn the grammar, vocabulary, idioms, and other intricacies of English.

- *Students who have recently moved to this country* These students may be highly capable students without the specific language skills to function academically in English.

- *Students with learning disabilities* These students may have cognitive, behavioral, social, or physical challenges that make reading more difficult.

(b) **Kinds of Skills and Instruction** Students' reading ability is influenced by the skills they bring to the task. Students must master the skills of decoding, activating and building prior knowledge, and making connections among experiences and new information. Other factors include a student's knowledge of the English language and vocabulary and a student's ability to apply reading comprehension strategies.

Active reading, including the practice of summarizing, questioning, setting a purpose, and self-monitoring, is key to successful reading. For those students who have not yet developed such skills, your classroom instruction is critical. You should model such skills and encourage students to practice them. Through practice, students should be able to internalize the strategies of active reading.

(c) **Kinds of Texts** Just as students and their backgrounds and skills vary, so do the texts presented in a language arts curriculum. The grade-level language arts classroom curriculum traditionally addresses fiction, nonfiction, poetry, and drama. Each of these forms presents unique challenges to students. Each writer and selection also presents challenges in the difficulty of the concepts addressed or in the coherence of the writing. For example, you may find that students are more comfortable with narratives than with expository writing. Focused reading strategies that you model and reinforce can help students tackle texts that are more dense or difficult for them to master.

(d) **Classroom Environment** The classroom environment affects everything and everyone within it. Research suggests that students learn best in a friendly, respectful setting categorized by these criteria:

- Students feel a sense of safety and order.

- They feel comfortable taking risks.

- They understand the purpose and value of the tasks presented.

- They have high expectations and goals for learning.

- They feel accepted by their teachers and peers.

Students performing below grade level may be especially self-conscious. Therefore, these criteria are key to helping students take full advantage of the opportunities the classroom affords. Set up your classroom as a caring yet on-purpose environment that helps students achieve.

Researchers encourage teachers to be truthful with students about the work it will take to build and master abilities in the language arts. Tell your students that improving reading, writing, speaking, and listening takes a great deal of practice. You need to be prepared to provide direct instruction, guided practice, specific feedback, coaching, and more. Then, encourage your students to understand their responsibilities as active, self-directed learners as well.

The Special Education or Special Needs Student

Your classroom may have a number of special education or special needs students—young people who begin the year three or more years below grade level and yet do not qualify for special education services. Special education and special needs students have difficulty in organizing and categorizing new information during instruction. They may have trouble in the following areas:

Memory

- ordering or arranging information

- classifying information

- grasping a main idea or "big picture"

- using long-term memory to make meaningful connections or connecting to prior knowledge

Attention

- focusing attention on the most important elements of a presentation or a selection

By presenting specific focused strategies and interactive review and extension activities, you can provide these students with full access to the language arts curriculum.

Another category of deficiency in special education readers is the ability to apply learning strategies to a variety of situations. Special education and special needs students often have these weaknesses:

Learning Strategies

- a lack of effective or efficient strategies for completing academic tasks such as taking notes, responding to literature, or writing a focused paragraph

- a limited set of learning strategies from which to draw

- difficulty in self-monitoring—they often don't know which strategies to use or when a strategy is not working

Many of these students are underprepared; their deficiencies are generally based on their lack of experience, not on any biological difference. When these students learn effective strategies, they can improve their academic performance. You need to provide direct instruction to explicitly show them how, when, and why to use each strategy.

Overview of Components for Differentiated Instruction

Prentice Hall Literature: Penguin Edition includes an array of targeted resources for special needs students. Fully integrated, these materials help teachers identify student needs or deficiencies, teach to the varying levels in a classroom, and provide the quality that literature teachers expect.

As your main resource, the *Annotated Teacher's Edition* provides a lesson plan for every selection or selection grouping. In addition to teaching notes and suggestions, the *Annotated Teacher's Edition* also includes cross-references to ancillary material such as the *Reader's Notebook,* the *Reader's Notebook Adapted Version,* and the *Reader's Notebook English Learner's Version.* *Differentiated Instruction* notes help teachers direct lessons to the following groups of students: special needs students, less proficient readers, English learners, gifted and talented students, and advanced readers.

The **Reading Kit** has three parts, each designed to help you address the needs of students with varying ability levels.

- *Part 1: Practice and Assess* includes worksheets for every selection to build reading proficiency.

- *Part 2: Literature-Based Strategies* provides direct instruction to improve students' comprehension and interpretation.

- *Part 3: Classroom Management for Differentiated Instruction* presents research-based, classroom-tested strategies for engaging students of all ability levels in learning activities and class discussions.

Success Tracker is an online intervention system that allows you to monitor progress and intervene before students take your state standardized test.

- *Assess:* Students take a Diagnostic or Benchmark test online.

- *Diagnose:* Based on assessment results, Success Tracker automatically diagnoses student mastery level for each skill tested.

- *Remediate:* Customized assignments are made for each student based on the skills mastered. Assignments can be made automatically or customized by the teacher.

- *Report:* Color-coded reports make it easy for you to monitor progress on your standards.

Several components—**Vocabulary and Reading Warm-Ups, Selection Tests,** and **Graphic Organizer Transparencies**—are offered in two versions, Level A and Level B. This allows you to customize to the individual ability levels of your students.

- *Vocabulary and Reading Warm-Ups* for every selection include word lists, exercises, and reading passages.

- *Selection Tests* for every selection include multiple choice and essay questions.

- *Graphic Organizer Transparencies* support the skills taught in the student edition.

The **Reader's Notebook** is a consumable component. The book contains instructional support for all the selections and the full text of approximately half of the selections from the student book. Questions prompt students to interact with the text by circling, underlining, or marking key details. Write-on lines in the margins also allow for students to answer questions. You can use this book in place of the student book to help students read interactively.

The **Reader's Notebook Adapted Version** is another consumable component. This book uses the same format and contains the same selections as the *Reader's Notebook*. However, the selections are abridged and appear in a larger font size. The questions are targeted toward special education students. You can use this book as a supplement to or in place of the student book for certain selections to enable special education students to experience the same literature and master the same skills as on-level students.

The **Reader's Notebook English Learner's Version** is a third consumable component. This book uses the same format and contains the same selections as the *Reader's Notebook*. Again, the selections are abridged and appear in a larger font size. The questions are targeted toward English learners. This book also contains summaries, in English and seven other languages, of all selections in *Prentice Hall Literature*. You can use this book as a supplement to or in place of the student book for certain selections to enable English learners to experience the same literature and master the same skills as students who are native English speakers.

Listening to Literature Audio CD This component features professional recordings of every selection in the *Reader's Notebook*. To support student reading, you can play the selections, in part or in full, before students read them.

Reader's Notebook Adapted and English Learner's Version Audio Program These components feature professional recordings of every adapted selection in the *Reader's Notebook Adapted* and *English Learner's Versions*. The recordings include the explanatory bridges along with the lines of original text. As with the *Listening to Literature Audio CD*, you can support student reading by playing selections, in part or in full, before students read them.

The Listening to Literature Audio CD and the *Reader's Notebook Adapted and English Learner's Version Audio Program* can be used to support reading fluency. As you play the CDs, have students read along, either silently or aloud.

Spanish/English Summaries Audio CD Audio summaries in both English and Spanish are provided for every selection. You can play these selection summaries for struggling readers, special education students, and English learners before they read the actual texts.

About the *Reader's Notebook*, the *Reader's Notebook Adapted Version*, and the *Reader's Notebook English Learner's Version*

The *Reader's Notebook* is designed to support students who are reading on level or one grade level below level. The *Reader's Notebook Adapted Version* and the *Reader's Notebook English Learner's Version* are designed to support your special needs and special education students.

Part 1: Skills Instruction and Complete Selections (*Reader's Notebook*)

Part 1 will guide students as they interact with the selection from *Prentice Hall Literature*. Skills instruction is included for every selection that appears in *Prentice Hall Literature*. In addition, many of the selections from *Prentice Hall Literature* appear in the *Reader's Notebook* in their entirety. The selections that appear include the more accessible selections, the most frequently taught selections, and many examples of narrative and expository writing.

Part 1: Skills Instruction and Selection Adaptations with Excerpts of Authentic Text (*Reader's Notebook Adapted and English Learner's Versions*)

Part 1 will guide special needs students and English learners as they interact with the selections from *Prentice Hall Literature*. Part 1 in the *Reader's Notebook Adapted Version* and the *Reader's Notebook English Learner's Version* provides larger print summaries of literature selections with passages from the selections.

Prereading pages

The **Before You Read** page in the *Reader's Notebook* and in the *Reader's Notebook Adapted Version* is based on its parallel in *Prentice Hall Literature*. It introduces the same literary element and reading skill addressed in the textbook and provides a graphic organizer to make the information more accessible. The **Before You Read** page in the *Reader's Notebook English Learner's Version* introduces vocabulary words from the selection and provides sentences that enable students to practice using the words. *Getting Ready to Read* provides background information related to the selection and includes questions that serve as discussion starters.

The **Vocabulary Warm-up** and **Reading Warm-up** pages in the *Reader's Notebook Adapted Version* introduce vocabulary words from the selection, provide practice sentences, and offer a reading passage to reinforce vocabulary comprehension.

The **Making Connections** page will help your students get the general idea of the selection and therefore be better equipped to understand it. A written summary, along with an image or illustration, previews the selections before students read. The Note-taking Guide helps students organize the main ideas of the selection, and helps them track their understanding.

Selection pages

The *selection* pages in the *Reader's Notebook* present the selections as they appear in the student edition. The selection pages in the *Reader's Notebook Adapted Version* and the *Reader's Notebook English Learner's Version* present the text in a larger font size. Interspersed among blocks of authentic text, these two Notebooks also provide summaries of episodes or paragraphs to make the selections more accessible to your students.

The *Take Notes* feature provides questions to accompany the selections. These questions make active reading strategies explicit, asking students to look closely at the text to analyze it in a variety of ways. Notes with a pencil icon prompt students to underline, circle, or otherwise note key words, phrases, or details in the selection. Notes with write-on lines offer students an opportunity to respond in the margin to questions or ideas. These notes offer focused support in a number of ways:

Literary Analysis notes provide point-of-use instruction to reinforce the literary element introduced on the *Before You Read* page. By pointing out details or events in the text in which the literary element applies, these notes give students the opportunity to revisit and reinforce their understanding of literature.

Reading Skill notes help students practice the skill introduced on the *Before You Read* page. These notes guide students to understand when, how, and why a skill is helpful.

Stop to Reflect notes ask students to reflect on the selection or on a skill they are using. By encouraging students to solidify their own thinking, these notes help to develop active reading skills.

Reading Check notes help students confirm their comprehension of a selection. These notes help to make explicit a critical strategy of active reading.

Read Fluently notes provide students with concrete, limited practice reading passages aloud with fluency.

THESE INSTRUCTIONAL NOTES ARE SPECIFIC TO THE READER'S NOTEBOOK ENGLISH LEARNER'S VERSION:

Vocabulary Builder notes guide students in understanding prefixes, suffixes, roots, words with multiple meanings, idioms, compound words, contractions, synonyms, antonyms, verb tenses, and difficult sentence construction. In some cases, they explain how specific words are pronounced in English.

Cultural Understanding notes explain an aspect of American culture that might be unfamiliar to English Learners. They may focus on an aspect of popular culture or on an event or a concept of historical significance.

Comprehension Builder notes help students understand significant parts of selections. They may ask students to note important details, summarize sections of text, or make and check predictions.

Fluency Builder notes provide frequent practice in reading passages aloud. They also give students tips and strategies for building fluency.

Post-reading Pages

The **After You Read** pages in the *Reader's Notebook* and in the *Reader's Notebook Adapted Version* ensure students' comprehension of the selection. Written in simple language, they assess students' understanding of the literary element and the reading skill. In addition, they offer a scaffolded guide to support students in an activity based on the writing lesson in the student edition of the grade-level textbook. Students are also provided with additional support for an extension activity based on either the Listening and Speaking activity or the Research and Technology activity in the student edition. The **After You Read** page in *Reader's Notebook English Learner's Version* provides comprehension questions and a graphic organizer as well as discussion and writing prompts. The **After You Read** page in all three versions includes Writing About the Essential Question, which provides questions to help students focus on essential ideas and elements in the selections. It also helps build student vocabulary by using vocabulary that is introduced in the student edition.

Using the *Notebooks*

Classroom Management:

When you are planning lessons for heterogeneous classes, the *Reader's Notebooks* offer you an opportunity to keep all the students in your class reading the same selection and studying the same vocabulary, literary element, and reading strategy but also to get the support they need to succeed. At the outset, assign appropriate *Notebooks* to the students and have them write their names in them. Students very quickly assume ownership as they complete the interactive format of the *Notebooks*. The books become a personalized "response journal" and study guide for tests as they move through the selections.

Here are some planning suggestions for using these books in tandem with the grade-level volume of *Prentice Hall Literature:*

Use the *Annotated Teacher's Edition* and the *Student Edition* of the grade-level textbook as the central text in your classroom. The *Annotated Teacher's Edition* includes *Differentiated Instruction* notes throughout each selection. In addition, it identifies when use of the *Notebooks* is appropriate.

Accountability:

Collect the *Notebooks* at intervals that you choose. For example, you may decide to review students' work in the *Notebooks* once weekly. Have students mark a page completed during that time period with a sticky note, which can be used as a tab. This tab makes it easy for you to open the *Notebook* quickly to the specific page, check for the accuracy and thoroughness of the work on selected questions, and award points or a grade.

Absent students:

Use the *Reader's Notebook* for students who will be absent during discussions or for home-bound students. These students will be in step with the rest of the class in terms of concepts, strategies, and standards covered during their absence.

Teaching The Selections and Informational Texts

The Selections
PRETEACH with the Full Class

Anticipate the reading. Use the *Motivation* activity provided for the selection in the *Annotated Teacher's Edition.* These activities vary and may include discussion questions, anticipation guides, or graphic organizers that will help students focus their attention on the important ideas presented in the selection.

Preview the selection. To help students see the organization of a selection, or to help them get a general idea of the text, lead a quick text pre-reading or "text tour" using the textbook. Focus student attention on the selection title, the art accompanying the text, and any unusual text characteristics. To build connections for students, ask them to identify links between the selection and other works you have presented in class or to find connections to themes, activities, or other related concepts.

Build background. Use the Background information provided in the *Student Edition.* Whether explaining a historical time period, a scientific concept, or details about an idea that may be unfamiliar to students, this instruction presents useful information to help all students place the literature in context.

Build connections. Use the *Connecting to the Literature* feature in the *Student Edition* to help students find relationships between their own life experiences or reading and the selection they are about to read. You may also follow these steps to complete that exercise with the full class:

- Draw students' attention to vocabulary that is central to the ideas presented in the *Connecting to the Literature* material. For example, the text may invite students to think about being an outsider, or showing compassion. Make sure students understand the meaning of such key terms.

- To check students' comprehension of key concepts, have them define the terms in their own words. You may have students work alone or in pairs to accomplish this task. Invite volunteers to share their definitions with the class.

- Then, have students work alone or in pairs to write down two examples of situations, actions, or events that illustrate each key concept. These examples may come from students' personal experiences, their reading, their viewing of television shows or movies, or their imaginations. Invite volunteers to share their work with the class.

Focus vocabulary development. The *Student Edition* provides a list of vocabulary words included in each selection. Instead of attempting to cover all of the vocabulary words you anticipate your students will not know, identify the vocabulary that is most critical to talking and learning about the central concepts. However, for the words you do choose to teach, work to provide more than synonyms and definitions. Using the vocabulary notes in the *Annotated Teacher's Edition,* introduce the essential words in more meaningful contexts: for example, through simple sentences drawing on familiar issues, people, scenarios, and vocabulary. Guide students in internalizing the meanings of key terms through these familiar contexts and ask them to write the definitions in their own words. Look at the following examples of guided vocabulary instruction:

> Point out the word *serene* and explain that it means "calm or peaceful." Then, provide the following scenarios and ask students to determine whether the situations are *serene* or not: an empty beach at sunset *(yes);* a basketball playoff game *(no).* You might also ask students to provide their own examples of *serene* situations.

> Point out the word *interval* and explain that it means "the period of time between two events or points of time." Ask students to identify the interval between Monday and Wednesday *(two days)* and the interval between one Monday and the next Monday *(one week).*

> You might also take the opportunity to teach the prefix *inter-,* meaning "between." Then, discuss with students the following group of words:

> *interview* (a meeting between two or more people);
> *interstate* (between two or more states);
> *international* (between nations);
> *intervene* (to come between two sides in a dispute).

Separate the class to introduce the skills. For average students, introduce the *Literary Analysis* and *Reading Skills* using the instruction in the *Student Edition* and the teaching support in the *Annotated Teacher's Edition.* Have struggling readers, special education students and special needs students put their textbooks aside. Direct these students to the *Notebooks* to begin study of *Literary Analysis* and *Reading Skills.*

PRETEACH Using the *Notebooks*

Introduce skills. All versions of the *Reader's Notebooks* except the *English Learner's* version provide the same literary analysis and reading skills concepts as the *Student Edition.* The *Adapted* version does so with simplified language and basic sentence structures. Use the *Before You Read* page in the *Notebooks* along with teaching support from the *Annotated Teachers' Edition* to introduce the skills to struggling readers, special education students, and special needs students.

Reinforce the key ideas. Use the *Summary* presented on the *Making Connections* page for every selection in the *Notebooks.* The summary will give students a framework to follow for understanding the selection. Use this tool to build familiarity, but do not use it as a replacement for reading.

Introduce note taking. Prepare the students to use the *Note-taking Guide* that appears on the *Making Connections* page for every selection. Each note-taking guide focuses on a specific aspect of the selection. For example, the guide may help students keep track of details in a poem, trace the plot of a story, or track the line of reasoning in an essay. Tell students that taking notes can help them focus their reading and better understand a selection. It will also allow them to gather information that will help them later as they answer questions or write about a particular selection.

Present audio and written summaries. The *Spanish/English Summaries on Audio CD* can reinforce the main idea of a selection and provide extra support for students whose first language is Spanish. In the *Reader's Notebook English Language Learner's Version*, the Summary Translations provide support for students whose first language is Spanish, Haitian Creole, Filipino, Hmong, Chinese, Vietnamese, or Korean.

Provide decoding practice. Because many struggling readers, special education students, and English learners lack strategies for decoding bigger words, give them guided practice with the vocabulary words for the selection. Using the list from the *Student Edition*, model a strategy for decoding polysyllabic words. First, show students how to break the word into parts and then put the parts back together to make a word.

> For the words *mimic* and *frightening*, ask students to draw a line under each word part as they pronounce it.
>
> *mim ic*   *fright en ing*

Using this strategy, you can encourage students to look for familiar word parts and then break the rest of the word down into its consonant and vowel sounds. By building this routine regularly into your preteaching instruction, you reinforce a key reading skill for your students.

Prepare for lesson structure. To build students' ability to complete classroom activities, examine your lesson to see what types of language functions students will need to participate in. Look at these examples:

> If students are being asked to make predictions about upcoming paragraph content in an essay, review the power of transition words that act as signals to meaning. Rather than teaching all transitions, limit your instruction to the ones in the passages. Identify the key transition words and point out their meaning. In addition, teach students some basic sentence patterns and verbs to express opinions. Model for students statement patterns such as the following:
>
> *I predict that . . .*
>
> *Based on this transition word, I conclude that . . .*

TEACH Using the *Notebooks*

Read the selection. The three versions of the *Reader's Notebook* allow you to teach the same selections to students who demonstrate differing levels of achievement. Average achieving students in your class may read the selection in the *Student Edition*. The *Reader's Notebooks* provide a range of other options as you work with struggling readers, special education students, special needs students, and English learners:

- Students reading just at or below grade level may benefit from the extra guidance provided in the *Reader's Notebook* version of the selection.

- Have your special education and special needs students and English learners read the adapted version of the selection in the *Reader's Notebook Adapted Version* or *Reader's Notebook English Learner's Version.*

- If the *Reader's Notebook* does not include the selection, have students read the text in the *Student Edition*.

Whenever possible, give your struggling readers, special education and special needs students, and English learners individualized attention by pairing them with aides, parent volunteers, or student peers.

Set purposes and limits. To keep students focused and motivated and to prevent them from becoming overwhelmed as they read a selection, clearly establish a reading purpose for students before assigning a manageable amount of text. Once you identify a focus question or a purpose, revisit the question occasionally as students read. You can do this with a brief whole-group dialogue or by encouraging students in pairs to remember the question. In addition, your effective modeling will also provide the scaffolding for students to begin internalizing these strategies for effective reading.

Model your thinking. Describe and model strategies for navigating different kinds of text. Use the questions raised in the side notes as a starting point. Then, explain how you arrive at an answer. Alternatively, ask a student to explain his or her responses to classmates.

Reinforce new vocabulary. Present key words when they occur within the context of the reading selection. Review the definition as it appears on the page. Then, make the words as concrete as possible by linking each to an object, a photo, or an idea.

Build interactivity. The side notes in the *Notebooks* are an excellent way to encourage student interactivity with the selections. To build students' ability to use these notes, model several examples with each selection. These are not busy work; they are activities that build fluency and provide the scaffolding necessary for student success.

Whenever possible, get students physically involved with the page. Many side-note questions invite students to use highlighters or colored pencils to circle, underline, or number key information. In addition, some students may find that using a small piece of cardboard or heavy construction paper helps to focus and guide their reading from one paragraph or page to the next.

Vary modes of instruction. To maintain student attention and interest, monitor and alternate the mode of instruction or activity. For example, alternate between teacher-facilitated and student-dominated reading activities. Assign brief amounts of text at a time, and alternate between oral, paired, and silent reading.

Monitor students' comprehension. As students use the side notes in the margins of the *Notebooks*, build in opportunities to ensure that students are on purpose and understanding. Consider structured brief conversations for students to share, compare, or explain their thinking. Then, use these conversations to praise the correct use of strategies or to redirect students who need further support. In addition, this is an excellent chance for you to reinforce students' use of the *Note-taking Guide* and provide models of effective study notes for students to emulate.

Reinforce the reading experience. When students read the selection for the first time, they may be working on the decoding level. If time allows, students should read the selection twice to achieve a greater fluency and comfort level.

APPLY THE SKILLS: Post-reading Activities

Invite reader response. Have students using the *Reader's Notebooks* complete the *Reader's Response* question following the selection.

Conduct a full-class discussion. When students have finished reviewing the selection—whether in the *Notebook* or in the grade-level textbook—include all students in your class in a post-reading analysis. To guide an initial discussion, use the *Respond* question in the *Critical Reading* section in the textbook. You will find that questions such as the following examples will provide strong springboards for classroom interaction:

Respond: What advice would you have given the mother and daughter? Why?

Respond: What questions would you like to ask the writer about her experience?

Respond: Do you find the boy's actions courageous, touching, or silly? Explain your response.

Encourage students to support their answers to these questions with evidence from the text or their own lives. In addition, invite students to respond appropriately to classmates' ideas. These questions will lead students from simply getting the gist of a selection to establishing a personal connection to the lesson content.

Direct student analysis with scaffolded questions. When you are ready to move students into more challenging critical thinking questions, have your average-achieving students use the instruction and questions in the grade-level textbook. Have students performing just at or one grade below reading level use the questions in the *Reader's Notebook*. Have struggling readers, special education students, special needs students, and English learners use the questions on the *After You Read* page in the *Reader's Notebook Adapted Version* and *Reader's Notebook English Learner's Version*.

- Questions in the *Notebooks*, written in simpler language and providing more explicit support, will be more accessible to students currently achieving below grade level. Students will be able to apply concepts at their own level.

- Some special education or special needs students or English learners may be prepared to answer questions in the grade-level text. The two-part questions in the *Critical Reading* section are written to build and support student analysis. For the first part, students use lower-level thinking skills to identify information or to recall important details in a selection. For the second part, students use a higher-level thinking skill based on the answer to the first part.

Look at these examples of scaffolded questions from the grade-level textbooks:

(a) Recall: Why does the boy tell his father to leave the sickroom?
(b) Infer: What does this reveal about the boy?

(a) Recall: Why does the boy think he will die?
(b) Interpret: What is the meaning of the story's title?

Reinforce literary analysis and reading skills. Have students complete the *Literary Analysis* and *Reading Skills* questions on the *After You Read* pages. Depending on the students' individual capabilities, determine whether students will use the questions in the grade-level textbook or the simplified versions in the *Notebooks.*

Model expectations. Make sure that students understand your assessment criteria in advance. Provide models of student work, whenever possible, for them to emulate, along with a non-model that fails to meet the specified assessment criteria. Do not provide exemplars that are clearly outside of their developmental range. Save student work that can later serve as a model for students with different levels of academic preparation.

Lead students to closure. To achieve closure, ask students to end the class session by writing three to five outcome statements about their experience in the day's lesson, expressing both new understandings and needs for clarification.

Encourage self-monitoring and self-assessment. Remember to provide safe opportunities for students to alert you to any learning challenges they are experiencing. Consider having students submit anonymous written questions (formulated either independently or with a partner) about confusing lesson content. Later, you can follow up on these points of confusion at the end of class or in the subsequent class session.

EXTEND Using the Student Edition

Present the unabridged selection for students who read the adapted version. Build in opportunities for students to read the full selection in the grade-level textbook. This will allow them to apply familiar concepts and vocabulary and stretch their literacy muscles.

Play an audio reading of the unabridged selection. Use the *Listening to Literature Audio CDs.* Students who read the adapted version may benefit from reading along while listening to a professional recording of the selection. Encourage students to use their fingertips to follow the words as they are read.

Revisit and reinforce strategies. Recycle pre- and post-reading tasks regularly so that students can become more familiar with the task process and improve their performance. If they are constantly facing curricular novelty, special education and special needs students never have the opportunity to refine their skills and demonstrate improved competence. For example, if you ask them to identify a personality trait of an essential character in a story and then support this observation with relevant details in an expository paragraph, it would make sense to have them write a similar paragraph in the near future about another character.

Show students how to transfer skills. Consider ways in which students can transfer knowledge and skills gleaned from one assignment/lesson to a subsequent lesson. For example, discuss with students the ways in which they can apply new vocabulary and language strategies outside of the classroom. In addition, demonstrate the applicability of new reading and writing strategies to real-world literacy tasks. Include periodic writing tasks for an authentic audience other than the teacher, such as another class, fellow classmates, local businesses, family, etc.

Offer praise and encourage growth. Praise students' efforts to experiment with new language in class, both in writing and in speaking.

Informational Texts

The *Reader's Notebook*, the *Reader's Notebook Adapted Version*, and the *Reader's Notebook English Learner's Version* present unabridged versions of all of the Informational Texts features from the student book. As with other selections, questions prompt students to interact with the text in a variety of ways, helping them gain competence in reading informational materials such as newspaper articles, business documents, and product directions and warranties.

The prereading page for each selection previews the type of informational material in the lesson and presents the reading skill that is addressed in the student edition.

The selection pages include many of the same types of side notes that appear with other selections. Additional **Informational Texts** notes focus on specific features of informational materials.

In the *Reader's Notebooks*, an **After You Read** page follows each selection. This page provides additional support for students by focusing on reading comprehension, reading skills, and timed writing activities.

The Summary Translations

Translated summaries of all selections in *Prentice Hall Literature* are provided to support students whose first language is other than English. The summaries present the main ideas and key details to help students understand each selection. The English summary is followed by summaries in Spanish, Haitian Creole, Filipino, Hmong, Chinese, Vietnamese, and Korean.

Helping Students Use the Turbo Vocabulary Pages

The Turbo Vocabulary pages are located at the end of each *Notebook*. These pages provide ways for students to work with the vocabulary in the selections and to record new vocabulary words they come across in their reading. The Turbo Vocabulary section contains the following types of worksheets.

Prefixes, Suffixes, and Word Roots

Two-page charts give roots, prefixes, and suffixes that will help students improve their vocabulary. The chart gives the meaning of the word part and an example. Space is provided in the chart for students to write in other word parts that they come across in their reading. Point out to students words that contain these word parts as you read in class.

Learning About Etymologies

Understanding word origins, or etymology, can help students understand and remember the meanings of words. These pages discuss the different ways that words have entered English. Students learn how to discover word etymologies in a dictionary.

How to Use a Dictionary

These pages teach students how to read a dictionary entry. Practice working with dictionary entries is provided. Students are encouraged to list new words in the chart and provide the pronunciation, part of speech, origin, meaning, and a sample sentence for each word.

Academic Words

The *Reader's Notebook* gives seventeen high-use academic words in a chart. It gives the pronunciation and meaning of the words. Students fill in the chart with examples of the word that they find in their reading. The *Adapted* and *English Learner's* versions list ten academic vocabulary words for students to learn and practice with.

Word Attack Skills: Phonics and Word Patterns

This section helps students to look for vowel-consonant patterns in words. Learning these patterns will enable to students to read longer words. Guide students to find the appropriate patterns to fill in the chart.

Vocabulary and the SAT®

These pages describe the SAT® and its purpose. Exercises help students learn and practice the types of vocabulary questions that are used on the SAT®.

Communication Guide: Diction and Etiquette

Students read about and practice formal and informal diction. Phrases and sentence starters for in-class discussion are given. Prompt students to use these phrases when answering or asking questions so that they become more natural.

Words in Other Subjects

This page provides students with a place to write down academic words that they come across in other subjects. Many academic words can be used across disciplines. Help students record and define important words for study in other subjects. An example sentence will help reinforce the meaning.

Vocabulary Flash Cards

The first set of these cards gives Vocabulary Builder words from Unit 1. The front of the card shows the word. The back shows the definition, the part of speech, and an example sentence. Students should use the blank cards provided to study words from other units. Students can test themselves using these cards or test each other.

Vocabulary Fold-A-List

The first list uses Vocabulary Builder words from Unit 1. Students can test themselves by filling in the definition of each word and then folding the paper over to check their definitions. The other side of the list provides definitions for which students can fill in the appropriate words. Once again, by folding the paper over, they can check their answers. Blank Vocabulary Fold-A-List pages are provided for studying words in other units.

Commonly Misspelled Words

The words listed on these pages cause problems for many people. You may wish to assign some of the words to be studied with flash cards or fold-a-lists. The pages can also serve as a reference for students to look up words before writing them. Blanks are provided on the second page for students to add words that they frequently misspell.

Personal Thesaurus

These alphabetized pages provide a place for students to record new vocabulary words in groups with other new or familiar words that have similar meanings.

ANSWERS TO UNIT 1

"The Seafarer"
Translated by Burton Raffel

"The Wanderer"
Translated by Charles W. Kennedy

"The Wife's Lament"
Translated by Ann Stanford

p. 2 Graphic Organizer
Sample response:
"The Seafarer"
Event/Idea: Although he is drawn to life at sea, the speaker still sees this kind of life as a form of exile.
Historical Context: Anglo-Saxons had a very strong sense of community. The fellowship and community of the mead-hall was important to a man. All that seemed good and that gave a man his identity was tied up with home and community.

"The Wife's Lament"
Event/Idea: The woman's husband tells her to move her home, even though she has few loved ones there.
Historical Context: Women had few rights.

p. 3 Note-taking Guide
Sample response:
The Seafarer: food (line 11); his kinsmen (line 25); passion and wine of the cities (line 28); pleasures of life on land (lines 44–45); orchards, towns, and fields (lines 48–49); wealth of the world (lines 66–67); the glory of kingdoms from long ago (line 81)
The Wanderer: his home (line 5); his comrades (line 10); his mead-hall (line 25); gifts of fine gold and treasure (lines 29, 31); Earth's delight (line 30); the days of his youth (line 31); his kinsmen (line 45)

p. 4 Note-taking Guide
Sample response:
The Wife's Lament: her home and friends (line 9); her loved ones (line 16); her previous life (line 41)

p. 5 After You Read
1. The speaker feels that her husband, her previous life, and her home are lost.
2. **Graphic Organizer**
Sample response:
Poem: "The Wanderer"
Cause of Suffering: His lord is dead. He is exiled.
Insight Gained: Life is short and hard. Look to God for strength.
Poem: "The Wife's Lament"
Cause of Suffering: She is banished by her husband.
Insight Gained: Love and life are fragile. Longing and waiting are difficult to endure.
3. Sample response: Without knowing that the husband had the right to banish his wife and that the wife had little choice in the matter, it would be difficult to understand the situation in "The Wife's Lament."

The Essential Question
Answers will vary. Sample response: The Anglo-Saxon sense of home is very much like ours. Then and now, home is a place of refuge, where family members feel connected to one another and safe from the world outside.

from Beowulf
Translated by Burton Raffel

p. 6 Graphic Organizer
Sample response:
Original: Then he saw, hanging on the wall, a heavy / Sword, hammered by giants, strong / And blessed with their magic, the best of all weapons / But so massive that no ordinary man could lift / Its carved and decorated length.
Key Details: he; saw a sword; hanging on the wall
Paraphrase: Beowulf saw a magical sword of great size and weight hanging on the wall.

p. 7 Note-taking Guide
Sample response:
Setting: Kingdom of the Danes
Problem: Grendel has been killing Hrothgar's men.

Goal: To get rid of Grendel

Event 1: Grendel attacks Hrothgar's men at Herot.

Event 2: Beowulf tears off Grendel's arm, and the monster flees.

Event 3: Beowulf slays Grendel's mother.

Event 4: Beowulf faces a fierce dragon in his final battle.

Climax: Beowulf slays the dragon with his sword but is mortally wounded himself.

Resolution: Beowulf, along with the dragon's treasure, is buried in a tower built for him by the Geats.

p. 8 Activate Prior Knowledge

Sample response:

1. glowing red eyes
2. horns growing out of his head
3. dark, shaggy hair covering his body

p. 8 Literary Analysis

Students should underline "the strongest of the Geats—greater / And stronger than anyone anywhere in this world—" and circle "harsh / And unending, violent and cruel, and evil."

p. 8 Reading Strategy

Sample response: He knew how to sail and would take them to Denmark. They set sail on their ship, which was lined with armor. Aided by the wind, they traveled rapidly. Then, right at the estimated time, they saw the high green hills of the land to which they were traveling.

p. 9 Literary Analysis

Students should circle "I've stood on these cliffs longer / Than you know, keeping our coast free / Of pirates, raiders sneaking ashore / From their ships, seeking our lives and our gold" and "you've offered no password, no sign."

p. 9 Literary Analysis

The following details suggest these values: leadership—"Men who follow Higlac"; "known far and wide / As a leader of men"; courage—"famous soldier"; fatherhood—"My father / Was a famous soldier, known far and wide / As a leader of men. His name was Edgetho. / His life lasted many winters . . ."

p. 9 Stop to Reflect

Sample response: The watcher will respond positively because Beowulf answers his questions directly and says that he comes in friendship.

p. 10 Reading Strategy

Sample response: As you know, your people are being killed by a mysterious creature that hunts at night. Perhaps I can help your king get rid of this creature. If he does not accept my offer to help, his sufferings may not end. The main idea is that the Danes' suffering will not end unless their King accepts Beowulf's help in killing the creature.

p. 10 Reading Check

Sample response: Beowulf, a Geat, has heard about Grendel's attacks on King Hrothgar's men. With a group of followers, he travels by ship to Hrothgar's kingdom in order to offer his help. When they reach the shore of Hrothgar's realm, they are challenged by a watchman. Beowulf's answer satisfies the watchman, and the man begins leading them to Hrothgar.

p. 11 Literary Analysis

Students should underline "Have watched me rise from the darkness of war, / Dripping with my enemies' blood"; "I drove / Five great giants into chains"; and "I swam / In the blackness of night, hunting monsters / Out of the ocean, and killing them one / By one."

p. 11 Reading Strategy

Sample response: Greetings, Hrothgar. I serve my cousin, King Higlac. I have heard how Grendel has attacked your great mead-hall. Wise men among the Geats advised me to travel to your kingdom and offer my aid. They know how strong I am. I have killed many enemies in war, chained up five giants, and slain monsters in the ocean. Now I am ready to take on Grendel.

p. 12 Literary Analysis

Sample response: Beowulf's offer to fight Grendel with his bare hands makes Beowulf seem even more daring and fearless.

p. 12 Literary Analysis

Students may say that it is heroic to look at the worst possible outcome, as Beowulf does, and accept it as a possibility.

p. 12 Reading Check

During the night, Grendel leaves the marsh and sneaks toward the hall, hoping to kill more men.

p. 13 Literary Analysis

Students should circle "But fate, that night, intended / Grendel to gnaw the broken bones / Of his last human supper."

p. 13 Reading Strategy

Sample response: Then, Grendel tried to grab Beowulf, who was pretending to sleep. However, Beowulf grabbed the monster, bent the monster's claws back, and began to rise.

p. 13 Stop to Reflect

Grendel is fearful and wants to run away. In contrast, Beowulf is confident, remembering his boasts to Hrothgar and gripping the monster more powerfully.

p. 14 Literary Analysis

Students should circle "the Almighty's enemy" because it indicates that Grendel is evil because he is the enemy of God. Students should circle "mighty protector of men" because it indicates that Beowulf is good because he fights to protect others.

p. 14 Reading Check

Sample response: Grendel grabs Beowulf, thinking that Beowulf is asleep. However, Beowulf seizes the monster in a powerful grip. Grendel tries to escape, and the mead-hall shakes with the struggle. Beowulf's men strike at the monster with their weapons, but magic spells prevent them from harming Grendel. The monster loses strength. His arm and shoulder snap off as he runs away to his home in the swamp.

p. 15 Literary Analysis

Some students may say that hanging Grendel's arm from the rafters is an appropriate action because it proves to the Danes that Grendel is defeated and that Beowulf has successfully completed his mission. Other students may say that it is cruel to display Grendel's arm because witnesses can tell the Danes what happened without this bloody evidence.

p. 15 Reader's Response

Students may say that the battle between Grendel and Beowulf would make a good action movie because it is filled with suspense, it includes gory details, and the hero wins in the end.

p. 15 Thinking About the Skill

Students may say that paraphrasing helped them better understand the passages that seemed difficult at first because paraphrasing forced them to pause and identify the key details in each sentence. After students identified the key details, they were able to find the main idea or essential message of difficult passages.

p. 16 After You Read

1. Sample response: Beowulf and his men are good. Grendel is evil. Grendel is attacking Hrothgar's people. He is a monster that must be killed if Hrothgar's people are to survive. Beowulf is brave and offers his help.

2. **Graphic Organizer**

Sample response:

What It Tells About the Anglo-Saxons: The Anglo-Saxons liked stories about people who were "larger than life."

Feature: good winning over evil

Why It Is Pleasing: Evil will always be defeated.

What It Tells About the Anglo-Saxons: The Anglo-Saxons honored doing good deeds over bad behavior.

3. Sample response: The Geats built the tower as requested by Beowulf. They put Beowulf's ashes inside, and they buried the dragon's treasure nearby. Then, twelve Geats rode their horses around the monument. They told stories about Beowulf. Everyone cried and praised the great king.

The Essential Question

Answers will vary. Sample response: As personified in Grendel, the Anglo-Saxons defined evil as monstrous—vicious, cruel, and relentless—striking without warning and wreaking havoc. As personified by Beowulf, the Anglo-Saxons defined good as heroic—battling evil to the death, winning honor, fame, and glory.

Informational Texts: Web Site Search Tools

p. 18 Vocabulary Builder

Students should circle "11th."

p. 18 Vocabulary Builder

Measure means "poetic rhythm."

p. 19 Vocabulary Builder

Tract means "a short piece of writing."

p. 19 Vocabulary Builder

Students should write "poetry" and "poetic."

p. 19 Comprehension Builder

A researcher could look at manuscripts of Old English poems at the British Library, the Exeter Cathedral, the Bodleian Library at Oxford, and the cathedral library in Vercelli, Italy.

p. 20 After You Read

Thinking About Web Site Search Tools

1. The Web site's search program found 12 hits for Anglo Saxon poetry.

2. I would use the Exeter Book link to learn more about Old English riddles and didactic poems.

Reading Skill

3. I would use the hit labeled "The major manuscripts" because the lines below specifically mention *Beowulf*.

4. Answers will vary. Sample response: Web sites for literary journals and magazines, Web sites devoted to poetry or British literature.

from A History of the English Church and People Bede Translated by Leo Sherley-Price

p. 21 Graphic Organizer

Sample response:

Purpose: to inform

Language: factual—"Britain . . . is an island"

Style: long, descriptive sentences

Rhetorical Strategy: comparing the unfamiliar and the familiar—"there are in Britain, in harmony with the five books of the divine law, five languages . . ."

p. 22 Note-taking Guide

Sample response:

England: 800 miles long, 200 miles wide

Ireland: wider than England, but shorter in length

Both: islands

p. 23 After You Read

1. Sample response: Factors that are important in uniting a people and giving them a common identity include a shared religion and a shared language.

2. **Graphic Organizer**

Sample response:

Necessary Background: "Ireland is broader than Britain, and its mild and healthy climate is superior."

Evidence: "Snow rarely lies longer than three days, so that there is no need to store hay in summer"; "The island abound in milk and honey, and there is no lack of vines, fish, and birds, while deer and goats are widely hunted."

Clear Organization: The organization is clear in its listing of Ireland's attributes.

3. Sample response: Bede makes bold claims about Ireland being immune from poison. Bede uses description to tell about the pleasant climate.

The Essential Question

Answers will vary. Sample response: Bede describes England as an island lying at a considerable distance from the coasts of Germany, France, and Spain. Because of its northerly location, Britain's summer nights are short and its winter nights are long.

The Prologue *from* The Canterbury Tales Geoffrey Chaucer Translated by Nevill Coghill

p. 24 Graphic Organizer

Sample response refers to lines 811–821:

When? during the journey

Who? the pilgrims

Where? on the way to Canterbury and back

What? compete to tell the best story

Why? to make the trip pass more quickly

How? give the fullest measure of good morality and general pleasure

p. 25 Note-taking Guide

Sample response:

1. **Knight:** distinguished; fought in crusades; follows codes of chivalry; a noble soldier

2. **Squire:** the Knight's son; about 20; a knight-in-training; likes to joust; likes music and poetry; sings; plays flute; likes showy clothes

3. **Yeoman:** the Knight's attendant; dresses like a forest hunter

4. **Nun:** high rank; dainty; speaks French; good manners

5. **Monk:** "manly" man; good rider; likes to hunt; loose in his religious practices

6. **Friar:** likes the company of innkeepers and barmaids; not interested in helping the poor

7. **Merchant:** seems successful; hides the fact that he is in debt

8. Oxford Cleric: has no money; loves to read, learn, and teach; idealistic; cares only about his studies and his faith; quiet

p. 26 Activate Prior Knowledge
Sample response:
1. told stories
2. listened to music
3. read a book

p. 26 Stop to Reflect
Students may circle "Whan," "Aprill," "March," "rootë," and "bathëd."

p. 26 Stop to Reflect
Sample response:
1. Whan/When ✔
2. Aprill/April ✔
3. March/March ✔
4. rootë/root ✔
5. bathëd/bathed ✔

p. 27 Reading Strategy
Who? the narrator
Where? The Tabard, an inn in Southwark
What? to go on a pilgrimage to Canterbury
Whom? twenty-nine other pilgrims on their way to Canterbury

p. 27 Literary Analysis
Students should circle two of the following examples of direct characterization: "a most distinguished man"; "had followed chivalry, / Truth, honor, generousness and courtesy"; "He had done nobly"; "ever honored for his noble graces."

p. 27 Reading Check
The speaker meets a group of twenty-nine pilgrims on their way to visit the shrine of St. Thomas à Becket at Canterbury Cathedral.

p. 28 Literary Analysis
Students should circle one of these examples of direct characterization: "He never yet a boorish thing had said / In all his life to any"; "He was a true, a perfect gentle-knight." Students should circle one of these examples of indirect characterization: "he was not gaily dressed"; "He wore a fustian tunic stained and dark / With smudges where his armor had left mark." Sample response: In the indirect characterization, either of these details of the Knight's dress reveal that he is more concerned with honor than he is with his appearance.

p. 28 Stop to Reflect
The Knight is distinguished, a seasoned soldier who is more concerned with his honor than with his appearance. By contrast, the Squire is younger and more boyish. He is also more concerned with love than with war, although he has done well in battle. Because the Squire is a lover, he is more concerned with appearance than the Knight is.

p. 29 Reading Strategy
1. her singing
2. her ability to speak French
3. her excellent table manners

p. 29 Reading Check
The first four characters that the speaker describes are the Knight, the Squire, the Yeoman, and the Nun.

p. 30 Literary Analysis
Some students may say that the Nun would get along best with the Knight because he is distinguished and courteous and she would look up to him and admire his good manners. Other students may say that the Nun would get along best with the Squire because, as a lady's man, he might be very polite to her.

p. 30 Stop to Reflect
Students may say that they would like to travel with the Knight because he is trustworthy, kind, and reliable. He may also be useful should they encounter trouble on their journey.

p. 30 Literary Analysis
Students should circle "The Rule of good St. Benet or St. Maur / As old and strict he tended to ignore; / He let go by the things of yesterday / And took the modern world's more spacious way."

p. 31 Literary Analysis
The fineness of his clothing and the expensive pin, designed as a lover's knot, seem to indicate that the Monk is more interested in material things than a member of a religious order should be.

p. 31 Reading Check

Sample response: The Nun is a very dainty woman who speaks French and prizes good manners. The Monk enjoys manly pursuits such as hunting, does not like to follow strict religious rules, likes to have fun and eat good food, and wears expensive clothing. The Friar is very jolly and associates with wealthy landowners.

p. 32 Reading Strategy

1. In return for pardons, the Friar received gifts.
2. If people gave generously, the Friar assumed that they regretted their sins.

p. 32 Literary Analysis

The Friar's scorn for lepers and needy people indicates that he is not a sincerely religious person.

p. 33 Literary Analysis

Sample response: The characters associated with religious institutions are the Nun, the Monk, and the Friar. The attitudes of the Monk and the Friar especially suggest that there was a great deal of corruption in religious life, with pardons being sold to rich people. Furthermore, the preoccupation of all three characters with their appearances suggests that church figures were profiting from charity more than they ought.

p. 33 Literary Analysis

Students should circle "He told of his opinions and pursuits / In solemn tones and how he never lost" and "none knew he was in debt." Sample response: The Merchant deceives people because he hides his true financial conditions while boasting that he never loses money.

p. 33 Reading Check

The Friar is dressed as grandly as "a Doctor or a Pope." He wears an expensive cape made of "double-worsted." The Merchant wears "motley dress," meaning clothes of various colors or clashing styles. He has a beaver hat from Flanders and buckled boots. The Oxford Cleric dresses in a shabby, threadbare way: "The thread upon his overcoat was bare."

p. 34 Stop to Reflect

Students should circle "He had not found the stone for making gold"; "Whatever money from his friends he took / He spent on

learning or another book"; and "His only care was study." Unlike the Friar, who is an expert "beggar" and places a high value on money, the Oxford Cleric does not have much money and does not care so much about it. The Oxford Cleric focuses more on his learning than material gain.

p. 34 Reading Strategy

1. The speaker is planning to repeat exactly what the other pilgrims say in their stories.
2. A problem may result if what the other pilgrims say is "rudely spoken or unfit."
3. Although his words may be crude or vulgar, the speaker will follow his plan to avoid being "untrue."

p. 35 Literary Analysis

1. **direct characterization:** Students may choose from these statements: "A very striking man"; "fit to be a marshal in a hall"; "no finer burgess in Cheapside"; "Bold in his speech, yet wise and full of tact"; "There was no manly attribute he lacked"; and "a merry-hearted man."
2. **indirect characterization:** Students may choose from these actions: He gives the pilgrims "great welcome" and he serves "the finest victuals." Both of these details indicate that the Host is generous and able.

p. 35 Reading Check

The Host welcomes the guests and prepares a fine dinner for them. Then, he tells them that he has a plan that will help them pass the time on the journey to and from Canterbury. He asks them to consent to this plan, and they do.

p. 36 Reading Strategy

1. Each pilgrim will tell two tales on the way to Canterbury and two on the way back.
2. The stories will be judged by whether they provide "good morality and general pleasure."
3. On their return from Canterbury, the winner will be given "a supper" at The Tabard, paid for by the other pilgrims.

p. 36 Reading Check

The Host says that he will be the judge of the tales and that anyone who does not obey the rules of the game will pay for the costs of the journey. Then, he has them draw straws to see who will begin.

p. 37 Reader's Response

Students may say that it would have been fun to go on the pilgrimage to Canterbury because the pilgrims seemed like a diverse and interesting group of people, and judging by the Host's description of them, they made up a lively group. Students may also say that participating in the game would have been fun and that they would have looked forward to hearing the stories.

p. 37 Thinking About the Skill

Sample response: Analyzing direct and indirect characterization would help readers better understand short stories and novels because it would give them a deeper familiarity with each character and the role that each character plays in the story. Such an analysis could reveal the virtues and faults of each character.

p. 38 After You Read

1. Sample response: The Squire's showy clothing, his love for poetry and music, and his skills in dancing and writing tell the reader that the Squire is a romantic young man who is more interested in pleasing the ladies than he is in serving his king.

2. **Graphic Organizer**
Sample response:
Character: Pardoner
Detail: sells papal pardons; claims to own several holy relics that are really fakes; makes money through flattery and avoiding the truth
Comment About Society: Corruption was out of control in the giving of pardons.
Character: Knight
Detail: truth, honor, generosity, courtesy
Comment About Society: Society promoted civility and virtuous behavior.

3. Students should refer the description of the Knight in lines 43–50.
Sample response:
Who: a Knight
What: rode to battle
Where: in his sovereign's war
How: followed chivalry and done nobly

The Essential Question

Answers will vary. Sample response: In medieval society, people dressed in ways that clearly reflected their profession and station in life. Chaucer describes a character's clothing in order to reveal that character's personality and social standing. The squire's clothes, for example, show that he is a young man who has money to spend on fine things. The yeoman, in contrast, dresses as a forest hunter, befitting his lower station as the Knight's attendant.

"The Pardoner's Tale" *from* The Canterbury Tales Geoffrey Chaucer Translated by Nevill Coghill

p. 39 Graphic Organizer

Sample response:
Passage: " . . . And all my antics are a joy to see."
Reread Earlier Passage: "I take great pains, and stretching out my neck / To east and west I crane about and peck / Just like a pigeon sitting on a barn. / My hands and tongue together spin the yarn. . . ."
Clarification: The antics are the silly acts the Pardoner performs. He stretches his neck and pecks like a pigeon.

p. 40 Note-taking Guide

Sample response:
Box 2: They meet an old man, who tells them where to find Death.
Box 3: Instead, they find a pile of gold florins.
Box 4: They scheme about how to take the gold.
Final Event: They end by killing one another. They find Death after all.

p. 41 After You Read

1. The moral example of "The Pardoner's Tale" shows that when rioters become obsessed with gold, they are willing to do anything to get it, including killing friends.

2. Their search is a test. They have pledged to undertake a quest to find and destroy death.

3. **Graphic Organizer**
Sample response:
Reread Earlier Passage: "And up they started in their drunken rage" (line 125); "Then all this money will be ours to spend" (line 253); "And that with poison he could kill his friends" (line 269)
Meaning: The excesses of the rioters could include their drinking, their greed, and their willingness to kill for money.

The Essential Question

Answers will vary. Sample response: The Pardoner's tale shows that greed destroys those who allow themselves to be ruled by it. Ironically, the Pardoner admits that he preaches only to increase his sales of fake relics and pardons—in other words, to dupe his listeners and satisfy his own greed. Through the Pardoner, Chaucer exposes one element of hypocrisy in medieval society—the corrupt clergy.

"The Wife of Bath's Tale"
from The Canterbury Tales
Geoffrey Chaucer
Translated by Nevill Coghill

p. 42 Graphic Organizer

Sample response:

Passage: "A woman wants the self-same sovereignty / Over her husband as over her lover, / And master him . . ."

Unfamiliar Word: sovereignty

Context Clue: master him

Conclusion: If a woman wants to master her husband, sovereignty must mean control or power.

p. 43 Note-taking Guide

Sample response:

Man's Action: A knight attacks a maiden.

Woman's Reaction: The maiden petitions the king.

Outcome: The knight is brought before the king and queen for justice.

Woman's Action: The queen asks the king for permission to determine the knight's fate.

Man's Reaction: The king grants permission for the queen to determine the knight's fate.

Outcome: The queen does not kill the knight. Instead, she sends him on a quest.

p. 44 After You Read

1. Sample response: The Wife of Bath is well off and attractive, whereas the old woman is impoverished and extremely unattractive. Despite their differences, the Wife of Bath and the old woman are both wise and confident.

2. **Graphic Organizer**

Sample response:

Good Morality/Lesson: The knight receives a merciful punishment. / The Knight is forced to marry the old woman. Gentility is defined as a gift from God and the exercise of good values. / Poverty is described as not shameful. / The knight is rewarded for deferring to the Wife's judgment.

General Pleasure/Entertainment Value: The Wife ridicules friars. / The Wife describes the court and the knight's journey. / The Wife includes magical characters in her story. / The Wife includes twists and turns of the plot.

Final Judgment: The Host would probably be entertained by the tale. He might disagree with the Wife's ideas.

3. Sample response: The clues include the knight's perception that he will never find the answer he needs and his decision to return to the Queen.

The Essential Question

Answers will vary. Sample response: Chaucer's story reflects social trends. By describing one woman who wants to dominate her husband, the story suggests that the social norm is for men to be dominant.

from Sir Gawain and the Green Knight
Translated by Marie Borroff

from Morte d'Arthur
Sir Thomas Malory

p. 45 Graphic Organizer

Sample response:

Passage: "Gawain by Guenevere / Toward the king doth now incline: / 'I beseech, before all here, / That this melee may be mine.'"

Summary: Gawain is beside Guenevere. He moves forward and says that he wants the task to be his.

p. 46 Note-taking Guide

Sample response:

Box 2: A huge green knight rides a green horse into the hall.

Box 3: The Green Knight challenges any of the knights to attack him.

Box 4: Gawain accepts the Green Knight's challenge and cuts off the Green Knight's head.

Box 5: Gawain befriends the lord and lady of a wondrous castle.

Box 6: Gawain breaks his promise to the lord and keeps the green girdle.

Box 7: The Green Knight makes three passes with the ax, two representing the days that Gawain kept his promise to the lord and one representing the day that Gawain failed to keep his promise.

Box 8: Gawain admits his failure to live up to his pledge, feels ashamed, and asks for forgiveness. The Green Knight forgives Gawain and welcomes Gawain back to the castle.

p. 47 Note-taking Guide
Sample response:

Box 2: Arthur meets Mordred to arrange a truce.

Box 3: They fight, and Arthur is wounded.

Box 4: Sir Lucan dies.

Box 5: Arthur sends Sir Bedivere to throw Excalibur into the water and to report back to Arthur what Sir Bedivere sees.

Box 6: Sir Bedivere fails Arthur twice when he fails to throw Excalibur into the water. When Sir Bedivere does throw the sword into the water, a hand reaches up and grabs the sword.

Box 7: Three ladies take Arthur away on a barge as he lies dying.

Box 8: Sir Bedivere meets a hermit who has received a dead body from a group of women; Sir Bedivere assumes that this body is King Arthur's.

p. 48 Activate Prior Knowledge
Sample response:
1. Guinevere was King Arthur's queen.
2. King Arthur's castle was Camelot.
3. Arthur and his knights sat at a round table.

p. 48 Reading Strategy
Sample response: In a dream, King Arthur saw himself dressed in gold and sitting in a chair fastened to a wheel. Then, the wheel turned upside down, and he fell into black waters filled with horrible creatures. They seized Arthur, and he cried for help.

p. 48 Literary Analysis
Students should circle "'ladies for whom I have foughten for when I was man living. And all these are those that I did battle for in righteous quarrels . . .'"

p. 49 Stop to Reflect
Sample response: People living in the Middle Ages took seriously the warnings they received from dreams, as Arthur's actions show by his following the dream's instructions and delaying the battle.

p. 50 Stop to Reflect
Students may say that many conflicts result from misunderstandings. To illustrate their point, students may describe an argument with a friend over a misinterpreted remark.

p. 50 Literary Analysis
Students should circle "But ever King Arthur rode throughout the battle of Sir Mordred many times and did fully nobly, as a noble king should do, and at all times he fainted never," and "And Sir Mordred did his devoir that day and put himself in great peril."

p. 50 Reading Check
A soldier draws his sword to kill a snake that has bitten him. Seeing this gesture, soldiers on both sides think that the soldier means to attack someone, and they begin fighting.

p. 51 Stop to Reflect
Some students may say that they agree with Sir Lucan's advice not to attack Mordred because they think that enough harm has been done and that King Arthur should try to preserve his own life. Others may say that they disagree with the advice because they think that King Arthur is right to avenge himself on Sir Mordred, who acted treacherously in trying to seize Arthur's kingdom.

p. 51 Reading Strategy
1. With his spear, King Arthur wounds Mordred.
2. With his sword, Mordred wounds Arthur.
3. Mordred dies of his wound.

p. 51 Literary Analysis
Students should circle "pillagers and robbers were come into the field to pill and to rob many a full noble knight of brooches and bracelets and of many a good ring and many a rich jewel."

p. 52 Stop to Reflect
Students may say that Arthur senses that he is dying and therefore wants to get rid of his magical sword. Some students may realize that the sword must be discarded because no one other than Arthur should use it.

p. 52 Reading Check
The two still alive are Arthur himself and Sir Bedivere.

p. 53 Literary Analysis
King Arthur requests that Sir Bedivere throw the sword into the lake. King Arthur knows

what will happen if Sir Bedivere does what he is asked to do. Sir Bedivere is undergoing a test of his honesty.

p. 53 Literary Analysis
Students should circle "And there came an arm and an hand above the water and took it and clutched it, and shook it thrice and brandished; and then vanished away the hand with the sword into the water."

p. 53 Literary Analysis
Students may say that the barge and the women are magical. The dress of these women, with "black hoods," their nobility, and their sudden, unexplained appearance all support the notion that they are supernatural.

p. 54 Stop to Reflect
Some students may say that Arthur will recover and will point to the magical boat and the women as evidence that Arthur's wound will be supernaturally healed. Others may say that Arthur will not recover because the women weep and shriek as though Arthur is dying.

p. 54 Reading Strategy
Sample response: In the morning, Sir Bedivere discovers a chapel and a hermitage. In the chapel, a hermit is down on all fours near a newly dug grave. This hermit is the former Bishop of Canterbury. The hermit says that at midnight, a number of women brought him a body and gave him a thousand gold coins to bury the body.

p. 54 Reading Check
Sir Bedivere sees a boat with many women in it, one of whom is a queen. The women are wearing black hoods and are weeping. Bedivere places Arthur in the boat, where Arthur is received by three of the women. Arthur put his head in one woman's lap. The queen asks Arthur why he has avoided her for so long. Then the boat is rowed away.

p. 55 Stop to Reflect
Students may say that the words on Arthur's tomb suggest that Arthur will return and bring in a new golden age of peace and harmony.

p. 55 Reader's Response
Students may say that such a code of honor does survive in today's world. They may describe instances in which people defend others who are not able to defend themselves, such as lawyers who donate their time to clients who cannot afford to pay them.

p. 55 Thinking About the Skill
Students may say that summarizing would help them better understand essays because summarizing helps readers identify the main points of a work.

p. 56 After You Read
1. Sample response: Arthur feels betrayed because Mordred is both his son and a knight. This betrayal of father and king seems to signal the breakdown of the loyalties that once sustained Camelot.

2. **Graphic Organizer**
Sample response:
Gawain's Reactions
What He Does: He gives back the girdle. He wants to gain back the Green Knight's respect.
What He Feels: He blushes and is ashamed. He is angry with himself for not keeping a promise and for being afraid.
Bedivere's Reactions
What He Says: "My lord . . . your commandment shall be done, and I shall lightly bring you word again."
What He Does: The value of the sword keeps him from throwing it in the lake. Then, he lies to King Arthur, telling him that he did throw the sword in the lake.
What He Feels: He feels reluctant to throw the sword in the lake. Then, after doing King Arthur's bidding, he feels sad that his king is leaving him.
3. Sample response: King Arthur met his son Mordred to arrange a truce between them. The truce was broken when a soldier drew his sword to kill a snake. King Arthur killed Mordred, but the king was badly wounded and knew that he was dying. He was taken to the island of Avilion by a group of beautiful women.

The Essential Question
Answers will vary. Sample response: The authors accept and uphold the code of chivalry in the tales they tell and the heroes they portray. Sir Gawain and Arthur act with honor and humility. Both personify the chivalrous knight. Their actions and decisions reveal the code.

ANSWERS TO UNIT 2

Sonnets 1, 35, 75
Edmund Spenser

Sonnets 31, 39
Sir Philip Sidney

p. 57 Graphic Organizer
Sample response:

Sonnet 1
Poet's Lines: "And happy rhymes bathed in the sacred brook / Of Helicon whence derived is, / When ye behold that angel's blessed look, / My soul's long lacked food, my heaven's bliss"
Paraphrase: My muse will inspire me to write happy words.

Sonnet 35
Poet's Lines: "My hungry eyes through greedy covetize, / Still to behold the object of their pain"
Paraphrase: I wish to see what causes me pain.

Sonnet 75
Poet's Lines: "Again I wrote it with a second hand, / But came the tide, and made my pains his prey."
Paraphrase: The poet wrote his beloved's name again, but once again the tide destroyed his work.

Sonnet 31
Poet's Lines: "With how sad steps, O Moon, thou climb'st the skies! / How silently, and with how wan a face!"
Paraphrase: You appear sick and pale tonight, moon.

Sonnet 39
Poet's Lines: "Come sleep! O sleep, the certain knot of peace, / The battling place of wit, the balm of woe"
Paraphrase: I need sleep, which is peaceful and healing. Sleep can also be a source of ideas.

p. 58 Note-taking Guide
Sample response:
Row 1: a delicate, pure lily
Row 2: hunger for food
Row 3: an eternal representation of his beloved's qualities
Row 4: a person
Row 5: peace

p. 59 After You Read
1. **Graphic Organizer**
Sample response:
Spencer, Sonnet 1
Speaker's Situation: He is amazed by his subject.
Types of Images: starry light, flashing eyes
Speaker's Conclusion: He loves and honors his subject.
Sidney, Sonnet 31
Speaker's Situation: The speaker is lovesick.
Types of Images: The image is a pale moon.
Speaker's Conclusion: The beloved is ungrateful.
2. Sonnet 31 is half Petrarchan (*abba abba*) and half Spenserian (*cdcdee*); Sonnet 39 is much like Spenserian but contains a slight variation (*abab abab cdcdee*).
3. I want to sleep; sleep offers peace, healing, and freedom. Sleep, save me from despair, and you'll be rewarded.

The Essential Question
Answer will vary, but students should support answers with details from the sonnet.

"The Passionate Shepherd to His Love"
Christopher Marlowe

"The Nymph's Reply to the Shepherd"
Sir Walter Raleigh

p. 60 Graphic Organizer
Sample response:
"The Passionate Shepherd to His Love"
Shepherd
Feelings: The shepherd feels passionate about living a simple life in a natural setting.
Goals: The shepherd wants someone to live with him in harmony with nature.
Me
Feelings: The notion sounds fine, but such situations rarely turn out as one hopes they will.
Goals: My goal would be the same as the shepherd's.
Themes: the pleasure of simple things

"The Nymph's Reply to the Shepherd"
Nymph
Feelings: The Nymph feels skeptical about the shepherd's proposal.
Goals: The Nymph wishes to say no to the shepherd.

Me

Feelings: People should look at situations honestly, avoiding unwarranted optimism.
Goals: I want to avoid disappointments.
Themes: fantasy vs. reality

p. 61 Note-taking Guide
Sample response:

What Does the Shepherd Promise? He promises her a life of bliss. He also promises her a bed of flowers, a gown of the finest wool, slippers with gold buckles, and a belt.
What Does the Nymph Respond? It would be wonderful if life were that idyllic.
Who Is More Convincing? Why? Some students may say that the shepherd is more convincing because he is positive and has a clear plan. Others may say that the nymph is more convincing because she tells a more complete story.

p. 62 After You Read
1. **Graphic Organizer**
Sample response:
Nymph's Realism: Rocks grow cold. Flocks leave the field. Rivers rage. Flowers wither and die. Gowns fade and wear thin.
2. In the first poem, the speaker sells his version of an unchanging life of bliss. In the second poem, the speaker proves more cynical and explains the shortcomings of such a situation.
3. Sample response: Yes. The shepherd wants to share all that he sees and feels.

The Essential Question
Answer will vary, but students should support opinions with details from the text.

Poetry of Shakespeare

p. 63 Graphic Organizer
Sample response:
Quatrain 2: The speaker wants to be like someone else.
Relation of 1 and 2: Change in Theme: The speaker moves from pitying himself to envying others.

p. 64 Note-taking Guide
Sample response:
Sonnet 29
Whom the speaker addresses: his beloved
Main idea of the couplet: When the speaker thinks about his beloved, he wouldn't change places with a king.

Sonnet 106
Whom the speaker addresses: the general public
Main idea of the couplet: We are able to view beauty, but lack the words or ability to praise it.
Sonnet 116
Whom the speaker addresses: the general public
Main idea of the couplet: The speaker is convinced that true love never falters. He says that if he is wrong, he never wrote, and no man ever loved.
Sonnet 130
Whom the speaker addresses: the general public
Main idea of the couplet: Despite his beloved's physical imperfections, the speaker thinks that she is beyond comparison.

p. 65 After You Read
1. Sonnet 106 is full of phrases and clauses and contains only two sentences. Sonnet 116 uses fewer complex sentences. Sonnet 116 contains six sentences.
2. **Graphic Organizer**
Sample response:
Theme: the constancy of beauty
Connection to Theme: The beloved is like those people.
Message of Quatrain 2: These writers of old tried to describe beauty like yours.
Connection to Theme: All writing about beauty describes the beloved.
Message of Quatrain 3: These writers prophesied your beauty, but they lacked skill.
Connection to Theme: Writings of the past are not sufficient to describe the beloved's beauty.
Message of Couplet: We can see your beauty but lack words to praise it.
3. Sample response: Yes, each quatrain or couplet addresses a main point.

The Essential Question
Answer will vary, but students should support answers with details from the sonnets.

from The King James Bible

p. 66 Graphic Organizer
Sample response:
Inference: The Lord watches over faithful people, protecting them from danger and leading them to the right place.

p. 67 Note-taking Guide

Sample response:

Deeds Listed in Text: He restoreth my soul: he leadeth me in the paths of righteousness for his name's sake.

How God is Comforting and Protecting: God helps me lead a good life.

p. 68 Note-taking Guide

Audience: the general public and Jesus' disciples

Purpose: to teach people to live virtuously

Advice Given: Do not worship money; do not worry about basic needs. God will provide, just as he does for birds and for plants.

p. 69 Note-taking Guide

Sample response:

Young Son

How he lives his life: wastefully

What he does at the end: He humbles himself before his father and apologizes.

Older Son

How he lives his life: He works hard at home.

How he feels at the end: He is resentful of his younger brother's treatment.

Message of the story: It is never too late to repent. Like the father in the parable, God is forgiving and glad to welcome back those who return.

p. 70 After You Read

1. Sample response: Because it offers advice to all about how to live virtuously, the sermon, an oral lesson, is effective in teaching and in reaching a wide audience.

2. **Graphic Organizer**

Sample response:

"Sermon on the Mount"

Images: Familiar/Unfamiliar: Familiar: birds, lilies

Simple/Difficult? Difficult: Solomon's glory

Memorable? Why? Yes. The sermon teaches lessons that most people understand.

"Parable of the Prodigal Son"

Images: Familiar/Unfamiliar: rebellious child, father's love

Simple/Difficult? Simple: jealous brother

Memorable? Why? Yes. Emotions are universal.

3. Sample response: It means, "I will have a place in heaven" or "I will have eternal life with God."

The Essential Question

Answer will vary, but students should support answers with details from the text.

The Tragedy of Macbeth, Act I
William Shakespeare

p. 71 Graphic Organizer

Sample response:

Detail: "Yet do I fear thy nature; / It is too full o' the milk of human kindness. . . ."

Reveals: This detail reveals Lady Macbeth's fears that her husband will fail to gain the throne if he is unwilling to kill his enemies and opponents.

Detail: "Hie thee hither, / That I may pour my spirits in thine ear, / And chastise with the valour of my tongue / All that impedes thee from the golden round. . . ."

Reveals: This detail reveals Lady Macbeth's strong will and her desire that her husband become king.

Likely Outcome: When Macbeth returns, Lady Macbeth will talk him into killing Duncan to win the throne of Scotland.

p. 72 Note-taking Guide

Sample response:

Background Information: Macbeth is returning from a battle in which he showed great bravery and skill. His fellow noblemen admire him greatly.

Witches' Prediction: The witches predict that Macbeth will be Thane of Cawdor and also king and that Banquo will father kings.

Macbeth's Plan: Macbeth decides to kill Duncan while the king spends the night in Macbeth's castle.

p. 73 After You Read

1. Sample response: The weather and the witches themselves seem ominous. Banquo's reaction also suggests the possibility of evil and death.

2. Lady Macbeth believes that the witches' prophecy will come true and plans to persuade Macbeth to fulfill his destiny.

3. **Graphic Organizer**

Sample response:

Act I, Scene vi, 3–10: picture of a castle as a backdrop; birds chirping and hautboys playing; bright lighting

The Essential Question

Answer will vary, but students should support answers with details from the play.

The Tragedy of Macbeth, Act II
William Shakespeare

p. 74 Graphic Organizer

Sample response:

Number of Lines: 7

Number of Sentences: 4

Meaning: Am I seeing a dagger, or am I imagining one?

p. 75 Note-taking Guide

Sample response:

Macbeth's vision: Macbeth sees a dagger hovering in the air in front of him; the dagger soon becomes covered with drops of blood.

Who is murdered: Duncan and his servants

How Malcolm and Donalbain react: The two princes fear that they will be assassinated next. Donalbain flees to Ireland, and Malcolm seeks safety in England.

p. 76 After You Read

1. **Graphic Organizer**

Sample response:

Iambic Feet: "Macbeth does murder sleep'"— "the" and "sleep"

Trochaic or Anapestic Feet: "innocent" (anapest)

2. The porter's speech is comic because it contrasts sharply with what has happened, both because of its prose form and because immediately following the murder, the porter interrupts to look for a tip, discussing drunkenness while drunk himself.

3. Sample response: When he hears the bell ring, Macbeth announces that he will kill the king. Macbeth refers to the bell as Duncan's death knell—so it would be better for Duncan not to hear it.

The Essential Question

Answers will vary, but students should support ideas with details from the play.

The Tragedy of Macbeth, Act III
William Shakespeare

p. 77 Graphic Organizer

Sample response:

Link to Act I, Scene iii, lines 65–69: Witches prophesy that Banquo will father kings, so Macbeth may view Fleance, Banquo's son, as a threat.

Macbeth's Lines, Act III, Scene i, line 35: Banquo is going for a ride. Macbeth asks "Goes Fleance with you?"

Link to Future Actions: Perhaps Macbeth is planning to murder Banquo and Fleance.

p. 78 Note-taking Guide

Sample response:

Cause: Macbeth fears Banquo and resents him because of the witches' prophecy.

Effect: Macbeth feels guilty and sees Banquo's ghost at a banquet.

Prediction: Macbeth's guilt will drive him mad.

Cause: Macbeth believes that his position is worthless if he must always look over his shoulder, so he vows to kill any possible enemies.

Effect: Macbeth becomes increasingly bloodthirsty, and the other Scottish noblemen begin to turn against him.

Prediction: The Scottish noblemen will unite against the brutal king.

Cause: Macduff fears that Macbeth will try to kill him. Macduff also wants to persuade Malcolm, the rightful Scottish king, to return to Scotland and fight for his crown.

Effect: Macbeth notes Macduff's absence at his banquet and begins to suspect Macduff of plotting against him.

Prediction: Macduff will have his vengeance on Macbeth. Malcolm will return to Scotland.

p. 79 After You Read

1. Sample response: The external conflict stems from the witches' prediction that Banquo, not Macbeth, will father a line of kings.

2. **Graphic Organizer**

Sample response:

Proposed Actions: Macbeth vows to visit the witches to learn more about their predictions.

3. Sample response: It seems unlikely that Macbeth is the third murderer. If he had been, he would not have been so surprised to learn of Fleance's escape.

The Essential Question

Answers will vary, but students should support ideas with details from the play.

The Tragedy of Macbeth, Act IV
William Shakespeare

p. 80 Graphic Organizer
Sample response:
Scene i, 52
Appeals to which sense? sight; touch
Scene i, 53
Images: "yesty waves"
Appeals to which sense? sight

p. 81 Note-taking Guide
Sample response:
Description of Image: armed head
Message: This apparition warns Macbeth to beware of Macduff.
Macbeth's Reaction: Macbeth accepts this message without surprise, for he suspects Macduff of plotting against him.
Description of Image: bloody child
Message: This apparition tells Macbeth that no "man of woman born" will ever be able to harm him.
Macbeth's Reaction: Macbeth receives this prediction happily, but notes that he will still kill Macduff.
Description of Image: a child wearing a crown and holding a tree
Message: This apparition indicates that Macbeth will not be defeated until Birnam forest marches to Dunsinane hill.
Macbeth's Reaction: Macbeth is overjoyed at this news, for he thinks it means that he will never be defeated.
Description of Image: a line of eight kings, the last holding a mirror, followed by Banquo
Message: These apparitions do not speak, and the witches vanish without telling Macbeth what the image means.
Macbeth's Reaction: Macbeth thinks that this vision confirms the witches' earlier prediction that Banquo would father kings. The reminder makes him angry and frustrated.

p. 82 After You Read
1. **Graphic Organizer**
Sample response:
Vivid Imagery: "groans, and shrieks that rent the air"
Emotions Expressed: anguish, frustration, sadness

2. Sample response: In Scene iii, lines 39–41, Malcolm describes Scotland: "It weeps, it bleeds, and each new day a gash is added to her wounds." In Scene iii, lines 168–170, Ross adds that Scotland sighs, groans, and shrieks, and that violence and death are common.
3. Sample response: "Bleeding" and "carrying a yoke" appeal to sight; "sinking beneath the burden" and "gashes" appeal to touch; "weeping" appeals to hearing.

The Essential Question
Answers will vary, but students should support ideas with details from the play.

The Tragedy of Macbeth, Act V
William Shakespeare

p. 83 Graphic Organizer
Sample response:
Modern Psychiatrist: A modern psychiatrist might prescribe medicine to help Lady Macbeth sleep. A modern psychiatrist might also suggest therapy or counseling to treat her troubled mind.

p. 84 Note-taking Guide
Sample response:
Macbeth
Outcome: Macbeth is slain by Macduff.
Lady Macbeth
Outcome: Lady Macbeth loses her mind and kills herself.
Macduff
Outcome: Macduff finds Macbeth and kills him in one-on-one combat.
Malcolm
Outcome: Malcolm is recognized as king when Macbeth is killed.

p. 85 Activate Prior Knowledge
Students may make the following predictions:
1. Macbeth will die.
2. Malcolm will become the new king of Scotland.

p. 85 Literary Analysis
Students may circle these words: "I have supped full with horrors. / Direness, familiar to my slanderous thoughts, / Cannot once start me."

p. 86 Stop to Reflect
1. Macbeth compares life to "a poor player"
2. He also compares life to "a tale / Told by an idiot . . ." These comparisons reveal that Macbeth sees no meaning in life. The "player,"

or actor, performs his part and disappears. The tale means "nothing."

p. 86 Reading Check
1. He learns from Seyton that Lady Macbeth is dead.
2. He learns from the messenger that the forest appears to be moving towards the castle.

p. 87 Literary Analysis
Malcolm is the son of the king that Macbeth killed, and Malcolm, rather than Macbeth, should be the king of Scotland. Macbeth killed Macduff's family, so Macduff has a personal score to settle with Macbeth.

p. 87 Reading Strategy
Macbeth's faith in the witches' prophecy suggests that many members of the audience may have believed in witchcraft and the supernatural.

p. 88 Literary Analysis
Students should circle these words: "But swords I smile at, weapons laugh to scorn, / Brandished by man that's of a woman born." Students may indicate that this belief in his invulnerability makes Macbeth seem smaller in stature. If Macbeth is invulnerable, he does not need courage to fight.

p. 88 Stop to Reflect
The passage reveals that Macduff's mission in this battle is to kill Macbeth.

p. 88 Reading Check
1. Some of Macbeth's men fight against him.
2. Some of Macbeth's men try not to injure Malcolm's men.

p. 89 Literary Analysis
Macbeth's remark refers to his killing of Macduff's family. He almost seems to express a sense of guilt or remorse for this deed, showing that he is aware of his own evil.

p. 89 Stop to Reflect
Because Macduff's mother died before he was born, Macduff was technically not "of woman born."

p. 89 Literary Analysis
Macbeth appears unheroic because he relies on a prophecy, not on his own virtues and attributes, to overcome his enemies.

p. 90 Literary Analysis
Students may circle these words: "I will not yield, / To kiss the ground before young Malcolm's feet . . ."; "Yet I will try the last. Before my body / I throw my warlike shield. Lay on, Macduff; / And damned be him that first cries 'Hold, enough!'" Most students will agree that Macbeth's defiance gives him a kind of nobility because he chooses to fight although he faces almost certain defeat.

p. 90 Reading Check
When Siward says, "So great a day as this is cheaply bought," he indicates that the forces of good have won, and have done so with little loss of life.

p. 91 Reading Strategy
Siward's reaction to his son's death suggests that military men of the time may have believed it was unmanly to display feelings of grief in public. However, Malcolm's willingness to mourn for Young Siward indicates that this attitude may not have been shared by everyone.

p. 91 Stop to Reflect
Students may choose two items from these changes; Malcolm will become king; Malcolm's thanes will become earls; those who fled Scotland will return; Malcolm will restore justice and the rule of law.

p. 92 Reading Check
Macduff says, "Hail, King!"

p. 92 Reader's Response
Some students may admire Macbeth's defiance because it shows a desperate courage. Other students may decide that Macbeth is displaying the desperation of a cornered rat and is therefore not to be admired.

p. 92 Thinking About the Skill
Many students will recognize that excerpts from literature, by demonstrating the beliefs of the past, could improve students' understanding of history.

p. 93 After You Read
1. Possible answer: The doctor hears her say, "who would have thought the old man to have so much blood in him?" He tells the attendant that she has heard too much. He says that "Foul whip'rings are abroad. Unnatural deeds do breed unnatural troubles."

2. Graphic Organizer

Sample response:

Flaw: ambition; desire for power

Events that Lead to Disaster: Macbeth prepares his castle against an attack from Malcolm and Macduff. Macbeth anxiously awaits a battle that he cannot win against an overwhelming force. Macbeth vows to fight to the death. Macbeth tells about the insignificance of life. Macbeth fights Macduff.

Lively Action: the sword fights toward the end of the act

3. Sample response: We can infer that Elizabethans understood the mind / wellness connection because the doctor realizes that Lady Macbeth's suffering is mental, not physical. Also, the doctor's appeal to God to help her reveals a belief in the connection between religion and medicine.

The Essential Question

Answers will vary, but students should support ideas with details from the play.

Informational Texts: Feature Articles

p. 97 After You Read
Thinking About the Feature Article

1. Architects and theater designers were asked to create modern versions of the Globe Theatre for the exhibit "Reinventing the Globe."

2. With certainty, historians can describe the stage, which jutted out into the audience.

Reading Skill

3. Students should cite the quote, "It doesn't have to be going to this old, stodgy building. It could be much more accessible, transient, and lighter."

4. The author includes the comment that the stage that jutted out into the crowd was one of its most impressive attributes, and he says that most of Shakespeare's famous dramas were performed there.

ANSWERS TO UNIT 3

Poetry of Donne

p. 98 Graphic Organizer
Sample response:
Situation: The speaker must leave his beloved.
Motivation: The speaker is reassuring his beloved that his reason for leaving is not that he has grown tired of her.

p. 99 Note-taking Guide
Sample response:
Song
To Whom It Is Addressed: the speaker's beloved
Main Idea: The speaker's beloved should not be sad about his temporary absence.
A Valediction
To Whom It Is Addressed: the speaker's beloved
Main Idea: The speaker will return to his beloved.
Holy Sonnet 10
To Whom It Is Addressed: death
Main Idea: Death is not to be feared, for it brings rest for the body and freedom for the soul.

p. 100 Note-taking Guide
Sample response:
Oval 1: The church is the head of humankind, and all humankind is the church's body.
Oval 2: The church is for all people, and so are the church's actions.
Oval 3: All of humankind is like a book, of which God is the author.
Oval 4: The deepest afflictions make humankind more fit for God.

p. 101 Activate Prior Knowledge
Sample response:
1. One person is a blade of grass, and humanity is a vast meadow.
2. One person is a drop of water, and humanity is a river or an ocean.

p. 101 Literary Analysis
all mankind = one volume
author of all mankind = God
death of a person = translation into a better language
age, sickness, war, and justice = translators
heaven = library where books lie open

p. 102 Reading Strategy
Students should say that the speaker uses questions to get the audience involved. The speaker wants to engage his audience, not frustrate them by pointing out what they do not know.

p. 102 Literary Analysis
Students should underline "No man is an island, entire of itself; every man is a piece of the continent, a part of the main." In his famous conceit, Donne compares a single human life to an island and all of humankind to a continent.

p. 102 Reading Check
Donne believes that humans should rely on God for security.

p. 102 Reader's Response
Some students may agree with Donne, pointing out that the successful community or "continent" relies on participation from each individual. Other students may disagree, saying that each human must remain separate from the community in order to retain his or her individuality.

p. 103 After You Read
1. Graphic Organizer
Sample response:
First Form of Treasure: affliction
Second Form of Treasure: current money
Relationship Between Forms of Treasure:
Affliction becomes "current money" when used to make one more fit for God.
2. The paradox is "unkindly kind."
3. Sample response: In "Song," the speaker is the devoted lover. The situation is the impending departure of the lover. The speaker's motivation is to reassure his beloved that he will return to her.

The Essential Question
Answers will vary. Some students may say that Donne's conceits were imaginative ways to express ideas. For example, comparing the speaker and the beloved to a compass is a unique way to describe a love's relationship. The conceits make readers think about the subject in new ways. Others students may say that Donne's conceits do not help him express his ideas because they seem forced and are too different from the ideas in the poems.

Poetry of Jonson

p. 104 Graphic Organizer
Sample response:

"On My First Son"

Inference: The speaker is a father whose son has died.

Text Evidence: The boy lived until he was seven years old and then "scaped world's, and flesh's rage."

Experience: The speaker asks his son to "Rest in soft peace," which is a term we often use as a blessing for the dead.

"Still to Be Neat"

Inference: The speaker disapproves of the lady's appearance.

Text Evidence: The speaker dislikes the lady's artifice and overdone appearance, for "they strike mine eyes, but not my heart."

Experience: A natural look can be more appealing. People who try to hard to look good are often considered vain.

"Song: To Celia"

Inference: The speaker believes that Celia's love enlarges life, including his own.

Text Evidence: The speaker sends Celia a wreath, and "it grows and smells, I swear, / Not of itself, but thee."

Experience: Love adds joy to one's life.

p. 105 Note-taking Guide
Sample response:

On My First Son

Lines: "Farewell, thou child of my right hand, and joy; / My sin was too much hope of thee, loved boy."

Main Idea: The speaker had great love and expectations for his son, but now the boy has died.

Still to Be Neat

Lines: "Such sweet neglect more taketh me / Than all th'adulteries of art."

Main Idea: The poet is attracted to simple, natural beauty more than to artful appearance.

Song: To Celia

Lines: "Or leave a kiss but in the cup, / And I'll not look for wine."

Main Idea: The speaker needs only Celia's love in order to live.

p. 106 After You Read
1. Sample response: "Still to Be Neat" captures the speaker's true feelings in his yearning for "sweet neglect" rather than "th'adulteries of art."

2. **Graphic Organizer**
Sample response:

Figurative Language: "Drink to me only with thine eyes"

Repetition: end rhymes such as *mine, wine, thine* and *cup, sup*

Imagery: "But might I of Jove's nectar sup"

3. The speaker loved his son, referring to him as the child of his right hand and his child of joy.

The Essential Question
Answers will vary. Sample response: No, Jonson's clarity results from his precise word choice. Both his word choice and balance help create his poems' emotional effect.

"To His Coy Mistress"
Andrew Marvell

"To the Virgins, to Make Much of Time"
Robert Herrick

"Song"
Sir John Suckling

p. 107 Graphic Organizer
Sample response:

Passage: "Song"

Text Evidence: "If of herself she will not love, / Nothing can make her: / The devil take her!"

Experience: It is a waste of time to pine for someone who does not care for you.

Speaker's Attitude: The speaker is impatient but kind—he is hoping his words will help the young lover move on.

p. 108 Note-taking Guide
Sample response:

To His Coy Mistress

To Whom is the Speaker talking? The speaker is talking to his mistress.

What is the Speaker's Message? Young women should not waste time by being coy, but should love while they are young.

To the Virgins, to Make Much of Time

To Whom is the Speaker talking? The speaker is talking to every young, unmarried woman.

What is the Speaker's Message? Women should marry young to avoid losing the opportunities afforded by youth.

Song

To Whom is the Speaker talking? The speaker is talking to a young man who cannot win his beloved.

What is the Speaker's Message? Do not waste your time waiting for a woman who may never return your love.

p. 109 After You Read

1. Sample response: In the beginning, the speaker seems to have plenty of time to woo his lady; the mood is expectant yet relaxed. In the end, however, the speaker realizes that he and his mistress must immediately take advantage of the moment because time is passing very quickly.

2. **Graphic Organizer**
Sample response:

To His Coy Mistress
Carpe Diem Images: "Time's winged chariot"
Qualities: Fanciful? Simple? fanciful
Humorous? Passionate? Reasonable? passionate

To the Virgins, to Make Much of Time
Carpe Diem Images: "Old time is still a-flying
Qualities: Fanciful? Simple? simple
Humorous? Passionate? Reasonable? reasonable

Song
Carpe Diem Images: "Nothing can make her: / Devil take her!"
Qualities: Fanciful? Simple? simple
Humorous? Passionate? Reasonable? humorous

3. Sample response: The speaker is mildly provoked by his mistress's flirtatious refusal to give in to him. There is gentle mockery in his description of an eternal courtship.

The Essential Question

Answers will vary. Sample response: Herrick provides a traditional treatment of the *carpe diem* theme. Marlowe provides a different interpretation of the theme by having the speaker describe how he would woo his beloved if they only had enough time. Suckling gives the theme new life by having the speaker encourage the listener to give up on the beloved rather than pursue her.

Poetry of Milton

p. 110 Graphic Organizer
Sample response:
"Sonnet VII"
Main Clause: "my semblance might deceive the truth"
Supporting Element: "That I to manhood am arrived so near"
Supporting Element: "And inward ripeness doth much less appear"
Supporting Element: "That some more timely-happy spirits endureth"
Supporting Element: N/A

"Sonnet XIX"
Main Clause: "I fondly ask"
Supporting Element: "Doth God exact labor, light denied?"
Supporting Element: "When I consider how my light is spent / Ere half my days, in this dark world and wide"
Supporting Element: "And that one talent which is death to hide, / Lodged with me useless, though my soul more bent / To serve there with my Maker"
Supporting Element: "lest he returning chide"

from **Paradise Lost**
Main Clause: "Sing Heavenly Muse"
Supporting Element: "Of man's first disobedience"
Supporting Element: "and the fruit / Of that forbidden tree"
Supporting Element: "whose mortal taste / Brought death into the world"
Supporting Element: "With loss of Eden, till one greater Man / Restore us, and regain the blissful seat"

p. 111 Note-taking Guide
Sample response:
Sonnet VII: The speaker is reflecting on his twenty-fourth birthday; he is concerned that he has not accomplished more; he is not doing enough with his talent.
Have in Common: The speaker decides to trust God to make use of him.
Sonnet XIX: The speaker is blind; his talent is now useless; he is unable to serve God with his talent.

p. 112 Note-taking Guide
Sample response:
Presentation of Subject: Adam and Eve's disobedience to God in the Garden of Eden
Invocation: Call for Help: Call to the "Heavenly Muse"
Beginning of Story in the Middle: The battle between God and his host and Satan and his followers in heaven is over; Satan and his host are cast into the lake of fire; Satan determines that he and his host will do only evil.

p. 113 Activate Prior Knowledge
Sample response:
1. Satan is a physically imposing, winged creature.
2. Satan's goal is to replace God as the ruler of the universe.

p. 113 Reading Strategy
The Heavenly Muse will assist Milton in singing about man's first disobedience. Milton will be writing about things that have not yet been described in prose or rhyme.

p. 114 Literary Analysis
Students should underline "Heaven," "Creator," "Most High," "throne and monarchy of God," and "Almighty Power." Students should circle "infernal Serpent," "envy and revenge," and "host / Of rebel angels."

p. 114 Reading Check
Students should say that Satan desired to be equal with God and that he led a war against God in the heavens.

p. 115 Literary Analysis
Sample response:
1. round dungeon
2. unending torture
3. sorrow without hope, peace, or rest

p. 115 Reading Strategy
Sample response: Satan sees his fellow rebel angels in the midst of the fire, and next to him, he sees Beelzebub.

p. 116 Stop to Reflect
Some students may say that "courage never to submit or yield" is admirable no matter who expresses it. Other students may say that such courage is not admirable when it is employed to bring about evil.

p. 116 Reading Check
Satan's goal is to renew the struggle with God by using either force or deception.

p. 117 Stop to Reflect
Satan and his host cannot die because they are of "heavenly essences."

p. 117 Literary Analysis
Sample response:
1. Beelzebub appears willing to give up because he cannot see the point in continuing the war against a mightier force.
2. Satan appears unwilling to give up the fight. He wants to continue to "do ill" and to act "contrary to [God's] will."

p. 118 Literary Analysis
Students may circle "eyes / That sparkling blazed," "other parts besides / Prone on the flood, extended long and large," "in bulk as huge / As whom the fables name of monstrous size," and "So stretched out huge in length the Archfiend lay." Sample response: Satan is lying face forward on the burning waves, with his head lifted up and his eyes flashing. He is huge, as large as a whale or some other great sea beast.

p. 118 Reading Check
Students should say that Satan proposes to move from the burning lake to a "dreary plain," where they will regroup their forces and determine how to "most offend" their enemy.

p. 119 Reading Strategy
1. The subject of the first part of the sentence is Satan.
2. Satan lifts himself from the burning lake.
3. As a result, the flames "slope" their points and leave a valley in their midst.

p. 119 Literary Analysis
Milton helps you picture the surface on which Satan lands by comparing its color to the burnt surface resulting from the eruption of a volcano.

p. 120 Stop to Reflect
Students may say that it indicates that the mind can make a bad situation seem good or a good situation seem bad simply by analyzing a situation differently. Students may agree or disagree with this idea on the basis of their personal beliefs in the power of inner realities to transform outer realities.

p. 120 Reading Check
Satan and Beelzebub are planning to call the other rebel angels from the pool so that they can plot their strategy against God.

p. 120 Reader's Response
Some students may say that they are impressed by the sheer physical bulk of the rebel angels and by Satan's continued defiance. Other students may be so offended by the evil of Satan and his host that they do not regard them as impressive in any manner. Students should provide reasons for their responses.

p. 120 Thinking About the Skill
Some students may point out that some modern films and tales are, like epics, lengthy narratives in which a hero battles against the forces of evil; therefore, analyzing the elements of Milton's narrative could help students understand these contemporary films and tales.

p. 121 After You Read
1. **Graphic Organizer**
Sample response:
Sonnet VII
Speaker's Situation: The speaker feels that he has not accomplished enough.
Effect on Ambition: His work is hindered.
Solution and How It Helps: The speaker draws on the conviction that whatever he achieves is the will of heaven.
Sonnet XIX
Speaker's Situation: The speaker is blind and believes that he can no longer serve God.
Effect on Ambition: He can no longer work.
Solution and How It Helps: The speaker is comforted by the conviction that submission to God's will is all that God requires of him.
2. Students may say that Satan is a powerful personality through his great courage in the face of failure and despair and his ability to unite his forces with a single goal.
3. Student's should identify "I fondly ask" as the main clause.

The Essential Question
Answers will vary. Sample response: In Satan's last line in from *Paradise Lost* is "Better to reign in Hell than serve in Heaven," Milton's concise word choice expresses Satan's attitude and the difference that he sees between Hell and Heaven. The contrast between doing what one wants in Hell and serving God in Heaven makes the line powerful.

from Pilgrim's Progress
John Bunyan

p. 122 Graphic Organizer
Sample response:
Specific symbols with names that signal their meaning: Pliable = someone who is easily persuaded, or someone who lacks commitment; Help = a person who is kind and helpful; Slough of Despond = a place of unhappiness and sin; Giant Despair = overwhelming despair; Vanity = a place where everyone is self-centered
Main message or lesson: The journey to salvation is difficult and encumbered by influences that will distract the traveler.

p. 123 Note-taking Guide
Sample response:
Christian: Christian falls into the Slough; He is unable to pull himself out of the mire; After Help pulls him out, he resumes his journey toward the Celestial City.
Pliable: Pliable falls into the Slough; He climbs out of the Slough but does not help Christian climb out.
Help: Help pulls Christian out of the Slough; He explains to the narrator what the Slough is and why people continue to fall into it; He tells the narrator that despite the king's efforts, the Slough cannot be repaired.

p. 124 After You Read
1. Answers will vary. Sample response:
Christian: He leaves the City of Destruction for the Celestial City. He carries a burden of sin. He is rescued by Help and continues his journey.
Pliable: He tries to get Christian to return to the City of Destruction. He eventually goes with Christian, but he abandons Christian in the swamp.
2. It represents unhappiness and sin—a place where people get trapped and have great trouble escaping.

3. **Graphic Organizer**
Sample response:
Character/Place: City of Destruction
Symbolic Role: This place represents troubled environment in which a person lives.
Character/Place: Castle of Doubt
Symbolic Role: This place represents the second-guessing that a person engages in while searching for salvation.
Character/Place: Slough of Despond
Symbolic Role: This is a place where temptations hold a person back.
Character/Place: Help
Symbolic Role: This is a friend who helps one get out of trouble.
Character/Place: Pliable
Symbolic Role: This is an easily distracted person who may or may not assist the seeker.

The Essential Question
Answers will vary. Sample response: This selection shows that in Bunyan's time, most people believed that faith was necessary to help them get through troubling times. For example, Christian's own strength was insufficient to pull him out of the Slough of Despond; Help arrives to save him. *Pilgrim's Progress* probably affirmed what people believed about the necessity of faith and encouraged them to continue to seek God despite life's difficulties.

from Eve's Apology in Defense of Women
Amelia Lanier

"To Lucasta, on Going to the Wars"
Richard Lovelace

"To Althea, from Prison"
Richard Lovelace

p. 125 Graphic Organizer
Sample response:
"Eve's Apology"
Connection: The speaker seeks to free women from full blame for the Fall, arguing that Adam was more to blame because he sinned willingly, while Eve was deceived.

"To Althea, from Prison"
Historical Context: England was controlled by radical Puritans who had little tolerance for Loyalists, Catholics, and even moderate Puritans; those who challenged Puritan rule were often imprisoned and even killed.

Connection: The speaker defends the traditions of freedom of thought and political choice.

p. 126 Note-taking Guide
Sample response:
Eve's Apology
Speaker: The speaker is a woman with a powerful pro-woman argument.
Audience: The intended audience is men and the public in general.
Main Idea/Purpose: The speaker seeks to free women from their current state of domestic bondage, which had resulted from the belief that Eve was to blame for the dismissal from the Garden of Eden.
Lucasta
Speaker: The speaker is a man going to war.
Audience: The speaker's beloved is the audience.
Main Idea/Purpose: The speaker explains that he must go to war, and that placing a higher value on honor than on his beloved enables him to love her more.
Althea
Speaker: The speaker is an imprisoned man.
Audience: Althea and the general public make up the audience.
Main Idea/Purpose: The speaker says that although his body is confined, his mind is free.

p. 127 After You Read
1. The speaker remains free because "Stone walls" and "iron bars" cannot imprison the mind and soul.
2. **Graphic Organizer**
Sample response:
Tradition Lanier Opposes: Lanier opposes the traditional belief that Eve deserved more blame for the fall of humans.
Lanier's Beliefs About Tradition: Lanier believes that Adam is more responsible for the fall of humans because of his privileged position.
3. Imprisoned for his steadfast support of the king, Lovelace defies his captors and asserts that, like a caged bird, he will sing praises to "the glories of [his] King" even more effectively.

The Essential Question
Answers will vary. Sample response: Lovelace was reflecting dominant social attitudes about women, and Lanier was trying to change

those attitudes. Lovelace's poems portray a man at the center of the action. The woman either is asked to understand his behavior or is described in terms of only her physical beauty. Lanier attempted to change dominant social attitudes that blamed Eve, and by extension, all women, for the Biblical account for humanity's fall from grace. Instead of blaming women, Lanier argues that they are responsible for giving men knowledge.

from A Journal of the Plague Year
Daniel Defoe

p. 128 Graphic Organizer
Sample response:
When? the Plague Year (1664-1665)
Who? H. F. (fictional narrator)
Where? London
What? The face of London has changed.
Why? The entire city is filled with fear, pain, and sorrow.
How? A plague has spread throughout the city leaving many dead in its wake.

p. 129 Note-taking Guide
Sample response:
What he hears: The narrator hears the "voice of mourning" in the streets.
Where he goes: The narrator goes to a mass grave in Aldgate churchyard.
What he sees: The narrator sees the buriers literally dumping plague victims into the pit; he later sees a man grieving for his wife and children at the edge of the pit.
How he feels: The narrator is at first intrigued and then truly grieved to see the man suffering the loss of his family. The narrator says that the sight is "awful" and "full of terror."

p. 130 After You Read
1. Sample response: The fact that both narrators use the pronoun *I* to relate experiences and that they limit comments to what they see and know shows that these experiences are told by first-person narrators.
2. **Graphic Organizer**
Sample response:
Questions: What event is greatly changing London?
Answers: The arrival of bubonic plague, a deadly disease, is changing London.
Questions: Why is a great pit dug in a London churchyard?

Answers: People are dying so rapidly that they had to be buried quickly.
Questions: When is the narrator's parish obliged to refill the large pit it had finished on September 4?
Answers: The parish had to refill the pit a little more than two weeks later on September 30.
3. Answers may vary. Students may say that questioning made their reading more active and focused because it helped them concentrate on the details that Defoe gives in his *Journal.*

The Essential Question
Answers will vary, but students should describe a landmark event in their own region that would make a good story. Students may recall events such as floods, tornadoes, or hurricanes.

Informational Texts: Reports

p. 134 After You Read
Thinking About Reports
1. The causes of congestion in London are many years of under-investment combined with significant rates of increase in London's population.
2. Reduced traffic delays, improved journey time reliability, reduced waiting time at bus stops, and lower fuel consumption will have economic benefits.

Reading Skill
3. Sample response: The chart shows the total traffic entering the charging zone during charging hours. It also shows the progress and effect of the congestion charging program.
4. A bulleted list highlights the key transport priorities.

from Gulliver's Travels
Jonathan Swift

"A Modest Proposal"
Jonathan Swift

p. 135 Graphic Organizer
Sample response:
What Swift Says: "One emperor lost his life, and another his crown."
What He Means: King Charles I "lost his life" and King James lost "his crown."

What Swift Says: ". . . but the books of the Big-Endians have been long forbidden, and the whole party rendered incapable by law of holding employments."

What He Means: Catholic literature was banned, and Catholics could not hold public office.

p. 136 Note-taking Guide

Sample response:

Details to Achieve This Purpose: The dispute among the Lilliputians about whether to break an egg at the large or the small end represents the dispute between Catholicism and Protestantism. The war between Lilliput and Blefuscu represents the tension between Protestant England and Catholic France.

Details to Achieve This Purpose: The king of Lilliput wants to enslave the people of Blefuscu and make them break their eggs at the small end, representing England's desire to conquer France and force the French into Protestantism.

p. 137 Activate Prior Knowledge

Sample response:
1. Athos, a giant in Greek mythology, threw an entire mountain at Zeus.
2. Godzilla was a giant ape who destroyed cities.
3. In Arthurian Legend, the Green Knight was a giant whose head grew back after it was severed.

p. 137 Literary Analysis

Swift compares the conflict between Catholics and Protestants to a dispute over whether to break eggs from the large or small end.

p. 138 Literary Analysis

Students should circle "Big-Endians," "Blefuscu," "Lustrog," and "Brundecral." Sample response: All of these names sound foolish and therefore suggest that Swift thinks the conflict itself is foolish.

p. 138 Literary Analysis

Swift is suggesting that the result of intolerance is death, bloodshed, and destruction.

p. 138 Reading Check

Lilliput is in danger because Blefuscu is about to attack.

p. 139 Reading Strategy

The word *glumgluffs* is a silly word, especially as a word for measurement. This word choice supports Swift's purpose of entertaining readers.

p. 139 Stop to Reflect

Sample response: Swift's descriptions of Gulliver's preparations are fascinating, especially because Swift is playful with regard to scale. For example, the "strongest cable" that the Lilliputians have is like "packthread" to Gulliver.

p. 140 Literary Analysis

Students should circle the phrase "These I took out and fastened as strongly as I could upon my nose and thus armed went on boldly with my work in spite of the enemy's arrows, many of which struck against the glasses of my spectacles, but without any other effect further than a little to discompose them." Sample response: Swift is satirizing bitterness, intolerance, and pride. Gulliver's calmness and refusal to retaliate are the opposites of these attitudes.

p. 140 Stop to Reflect

Sample response: Although the tiny arrows are a product of Swift's fantasy, Gulliver deals with them very realistically as he pulls them out of his hands and face and rubs ointment over the wounds. Also, although capturing the fleet is fantastic, Gulliver's waiting for the tide to fall is realistic.

p. 140 Reading Check

Sample response: Gulliver first fastens the boats together with cords and then cuts the ships' anchors. Then, Gulliver crosses the channel with the ships in tow, pulling the entire fleet into the Lilliputian port.

p. 141 Literary Analysis

Gulliver's protest that he will never help enslave a free people emphasizes how power-hungry the Emperor of Lilliput is and reveals that as soon as the Emperor has an advantage over Blefuscu, he will take total control of the country.

p. 141 Reader's Response

Students should support their answers with details from the text.

p. 141 Thinking About the Skill

Sample response: Today's satires demonstrate techniques similar to those Swift used in *Gulliver's Travels,* so analyzing and evaluating Swift's text will enable me to interpret contemporary satires.

p. 142 Note-taking Guide

Sample response:

Details to Achieve This Purpose: The king of Brobdingnag laughs at Gulliver and asks whether Gulliver is a "Whig or a Tory"; the king's laughter indicates that the dispute between England's two political parties is ridiculous in the grand scheme of things. When the king turns to his "first minister," he continues to ridicule the things of which Gulliver spoke, such as the nobility of England and the "scourge of France."

Details to Achieve This Purpose: The king's horror at Gulliver's solemn proposal of using gunpowder and cannon to destroy another city is a strong critique of England's power-hungry rulers.

p. 143 Note-taking Guide

Sample response:

Understatement: "I am not in the least pain upon that matter"; "I am not so violently bent of my own opinion"

Exaggeration: "We should see an honest emulation among the married women, which of them could bring the fattest child to the market"; "men would become as fond of their wives, during the time of their pregnancy, as they are now of their mares in foal"

Sarcasm: "this food will be somewhat dear, and therefore very proper for landlords"; "as they have already devoured most of the parents, [the landlords] seem to have the best title to the children"

p. 144 After You Read

1. **Graphic Organizer**

Sample response:

Items in Text: disagreement over egg-breaking/Lilliput/Blefuscu

Targets of Swift's Satire: foolish arguments concerning religion/England/France

2. Sample response: Swift writes of the Big-Endians and the Little-Endians, who go to war over the proper way to break an egg. This situation involves an ironic contradiction between reality and appearance, in which the egg-breaking appears to be serious, but is actually quite trivial.

3. Sample response: Details such as roads crowded with beggars and starving children in rags, and children who become thieves or indentured servants in order to survive describe the dire social conditions that Swift desires to change.

The Essential Question

Answers will vary. Sample response: Swift wanted society to change its views on religion, warfare, and politics. Swift believed that some religious conflicts were petty, and in *Gulliver's Travels,* Chapter 1, he used satire to compare these conflicts with the Lilliputians' squabbles about which end of an egg's shell to break. In *Gulliver's Travels,* Chapter 2, Swift used the King of Brobdingnag to satirize English enthusiasm for warfare and weaponry. In "A Modest Proposal," Swift used satire to present an idea to help with "the Irish problem." He knew that his proposal was repellent, but so was the current practice of excessively taxing the poor Irish peasants.

from An Essay on Man
Alexander Pope

from The Rape of the Lock
Alexander Pope

p. 145 Graphic Organizer

Sample response:

Lines: 155–160

Purpose: to satirize

What Does It Mean? It shows how silly people can react over such insignificant actions.

Lines: 79–88, Canto V

Purpose: to satirize

What Does It Mean? It shows more overreaction to the cutting of hair.

p. 146 Note-taking Guide

Sample response:

Setting: Hampton Court, where Belinda plays a game of cards with two men.

Events:

1. The baron cuts off a lock of Belinda's hair.
2. A battle to restore Belinda's lost lock ensues.

3. The lock ascends to heaven and becomes a comet.

End Result: Belinda's name is remembered forever.

p. 147 After You Read
1. Graphic Organizer
Sample response:
Lines in Poem: Canto III, 161–162
Action/Activity: Belinda's lock is cut.
Lines in Poem: Canto V, 21–34
Action/Activity: The women "battle" against the men.
Lines in Poem: Canto V, 53–56
Action/Activity: The baron defies Belinda.
2. These lines offer an elaborate comparison in the style of an epic, using the word like to begin the simile.
3. Sample response: Pope pokes fun by describing the preparation and consumption of coffee as a profound and moving ritual. He entertains by describing the effects of coffee on the baron's brain and the sylphs' frantic efforts to keep the coffee from spilling.

The Essential Question
Answers will vary. Sample response: Although Pope mocks humanity in the selection from *An Essay on Man* by describing humanity as "The glory, jest, and riddle of the world!" he invites readers to consider human nature and to view themselves seriously. Pope's main goal in "The Rape of the Lock" is to entertain readers with his mockery. Pope thinks that society's rituals are extravagant and silly, but they seem to serve a purpose. For example, comparing a card game to an epic battle indicates that courtship rituals are taken too seriously, but such rituals were necessary for people to meet, get to know each other, and marry.

from A Dictionary of the English Language
Samuel Johnson

from The Life of Samuel Johnson
James Boswell

p. 148 Graphic Organizer
Sample response:
What I Know: how to use a dictionary and what a dictionary contains
What I Want to Know: how Johnson chose the words and spellings for his dictionary

What I Learned: Johnson read other writers to see how they used words.

p. 149 Note-taking Guide
Sample response:
Johnson's Feelings About Writers of Dictionaries: Johnson believes that they are doomed to criticism.
Johnson's Feelings About the English Language: Johnson believes that English has been neglected too long and is in a state of confusion.
Johnson's Feelings About His Own Dictionary: Johnson is content with it, regardless of its flaws.
Johnson's Feelings About Himself: Johnson is proud of his accomplishment, but does not expect his effort to garner praise.

p. 150 Note-taking Guide
Sample response:
Contradictory Qualities: Johnson had an irritable temper but a kind heart.
Illness and Infirmaties: Johnson's health made him melancholy at times.
Studies and Intellectual Pursuits: Johnson had accumulated a vast body of knowledge from his diverse intellectual pursuits.
Common Conversation: Johnson expressed his thoughts in elegant language and with great force.

p. 151 After You Read
1. Sample response: In the Preface to the *Dictionary of the English Language,* "those who toil at the lower employments" is a formal way of referring to people who work with their hands rather than by their intellect. In *Life of Samuel Johnson,* "to obtain the acquaintance of that extraordinary man" is a formal way of stating that Boswell would like to meet or be introduced to someone whom he respects.
2. Graphic Organizer
Sample response:
Johnson's Dictionary: *patron* One who countenances, supports or protects. Commonly a wretch who supports with insolence, and is paid with flattery.
Modern Dictionary: *patron* 1. noun someone who supports an organization, an artist, a musical performer, etc., especially by giving money 2. the support that a patron gives to an organization, etc. 3. someone who often uses a particular store, restaurant, company, etc.

Similarities/Differences: Johnson's definition is still accurate in its commonly used sense.

3. Students should record details such as relying on the rules of general grammar, using experience and analogy to make decisions, and borrowing from works of great writers.

The Essential Question

Answers will vary. Sample response: Both Johnson and Boswell are cultural innovators because their words set a standard for later writers to follow. Johnson's dictionary helped order the English language. Boswell's biography of Johnson portrays Johnson accurately, including his flaws. Johnson is also a cultural conservative because he wanted to preserve the English language.

"Elegy Written in a Country Churchyard"
Thomas Gray

"A Nocturnal Reverie"
Anne Finch, Countess of Winchilsea

p. 152 Graphic Organizer
Sample response:
"Elegy Written in a Country Churchyard"
Original: "Now fades the glimmering landscape on the sight"
Paraphrase: Nightfall is making it difficult to see the landscape.

"A Nocturnal Reverie"
Original: "When in some river, overhung with green, / The waving moon and trembling leaves are seen"
Paraphrase: The moonlight and trees are reflected in the river.

p. 153 Note-taking Guide
Sample response:
Elegy Written in a Country Churchyard
Neoclassical
polished expression: "Awaits alike the inevitable hour. / The paths of glory lead but to the grave."
complicated vocabulary: "The boast of heraldry, the pomp of power, / And all that beauty, all that wealth e'er gave"
Romantic
nature and simple folk: "The lowing herd winds slowly o'er the lea, / "The plowman homeward plods his weary way"

deep feelings: "Full many a flower is born to blush unseen, / And waste its sweetness on the desert air."

A Nocturnal Reverie
Neoclassical
polished expression: "When freshened grass now bears itself upright"
complicated vocabulary: "Or from some tree, famed for the owl's delight, / She, hollowing clear, directs the wanderer right"
Romantic
nature and simple folk: "When nibbling sheep at large pursue their food"
deep feelings: "But silent musings urge the mind to seek / Something, too high for syllables to speak"

p. 154 After You Read
1. The speaker appears to accept the universal anonymity that awaits everyone in death, and he expects the comfort of heaven.
2. **Graphic Organizer**
Sample response:
Stated Ideas: Humans need to be remembered after death.
Feelings Expressed: wistfulness
Message About Life: Nature plays an important role in both the life and death of humans.
Stated Ideas: Nature makes the human spirit content and inspires human beings by its beauty.
Feelings Expressed: ecstasy in the face of the sublime
Message About Life: Nature gives human beings solace.
3. Sample response: When it is so peaceful, the speaker wishes to remain outside all night.

The Essential Question
Answers will vary, but students should note that the beauty, dignity, and peace that both Gray and Finch find in their outdoor settings help them draw the conclusion that these virtues are more important than ambitious pursuits.

"The Aims of *The Spectator*"
Joseph Addison

p. 155 Graphic Organizer
Sample response:
Topic: people who are able to speak only of the events of the day
Details: There are men who are "unfurnished with ideas, till the business and conversation of the day has supplied them." They have nothing to offer society, and should remain within their "chambers" until they read *The Spectator* each morning.
Inference: Author's Attitude: Addison mocks those who, in his opinion, cannot think for themselves.

p. 156 Note-taking Guide
Sample response:
Families: "well regulated"; "for their good to order this paper to be punctually served up, and to be looked upon as part of the tea equipage"
Gentlemen, My Good Brothers: "the fraternity of spectators, who live in the world without having anything to do in it"; "Have no other business with the rest of mankind but to look upon them"
The Blanks of Society: "unfurnished with ideas"; "poor souls"; "needy persons"
The Female World: "the toilet is their great sense of business, and the right adjusting of their hair the principle enjoyment of their lives"

p. 157 After You Read
1. **Graphic Organizer**
Sample response:
Analytic or Descriptive: descriptive
General or Of a Specific Era? specific era
Logical or Humorous? humorous
2. Addison encourages an attitude of "instruction" and "diversion" in regard to both learning and entertainment.
3. Addison's attitude about the "blanks of society" is mildly mocking. He considers them uninformed people who cannot think for themselves and who generally irritate the people around them.

The Essential Question
Answers will vary. Sample response: Addison believes that people are a product of what they read and how they behave. He wants his readers to engage in more wholesome and educational pursuits to "distinguish themselves from the thoughtless herd of their ignorant and unattentive brethren." Addison hopes that his paper will appeal to women who enjoy intellectual discussion. Addison seems to be both reflecting and influencing social trends. The fact that his paper's circulation was increasing ("there are already three thousand of them distributed every day. . . .") suggests a growing social trend to read periodicals. The growing popularity of Addison's journal also suggests that he was influencing that trend. For example, he writes "I must reckon about three-score thousand disciples in London and Westminster . . ."

ANSWERS TO UNIT 4

"To a Mouse"
Robert Burns

"To a Louse"
Robert Burns

"Woo'd and Married and A'"
Joanna Baillie

p. 158 Graphic Organizer
Sample response:
Sleekit: sleek
saunt an' sinner: saint and sinner
dinna: do not

p. 159 Note-taking Guide
Sample response:
"To a Mouse"
Whom/What the Speaker Addresses: a mouse
Speaker's Main Message: I apologize for accidentally destroying your house with my plow; your unexpected loss is similar to human beings' plans coming undone.
"To a Louse"
How the Speaker Finds His Topic: The speaker sees a louse on the bonnet of a well-dressed lady.
Whom/What the Speaker Addresses: a louse
Speaker's Main Message: Proud, conceited behavior is ridiculous.
"Woo'd and Married and A'"
How the Speaker Finds His Topic: The speaker is present at a wedding.
Whom/What the Speaker Addresses: the reader
Speaker's Main Message: Being married is more important than wealth or possessions, especially when the husband loves the wife.

p. 160 After You Read
1. Sample response: The speaker's language suggests that he is one of the common folk, someone who is in touch with the basics of life.
2. **Graphic Organizer**
Sample response:
Poem: "To a Mouse"
Subject: the uprooting of a mouse's nest
Message: Even the most carefully considered plans can go awry.
Poem: "To a Louse"
Subject: a louse crawling on a lady's bonnet

Message: If we could see ourselves as others do, we would act less foolishly.
Poem: "Woo'd and Married and A'"
Subject: a young bride's unhappiness over her lack of rich adornments
Message: Love can make up for the lack of riches.
3. Sample response: The footnotes provide translations for words that are written in dialect, which help you understand the meanings of difficult words in the poems.

The Essential Question
Answers will vary. Sample response: In "Woo'd and Married and A'," a young, impoverished bride laments her lack of finery and her upcoming marriage to a man with no money. Baillie's description of the bride shows true insight into the mind of a foolish, immature, and materialist girl because the girl experiences disappointment when she should be happy that anyone wants to marry her at all. Baillie further proves the girl's immaturity when her worries are finally soothed by the groom's flattery.

Poetry of Blake

p. 161 Graphic Organizer
Sample response:
Archetypal Perspective: The lamb is an archetypal image that people associate with innocence and gentleness.
Political and Historical Perspectives: The first stanza of "The Chimney Sweeper" reveals the cruel fate of poor children in Blake's time.

p. 162 Note-taking Guide
Sample response:
The Lamb
Key Words: tender, meek, mild, child
Key Ideas: The creator of the lamb and child is benevolent. Both the child and the lamb are symbols for Jesus.
The Tyger
Key Words: burning, fearful, dread, terrors
Key Ideas: Perhaps the creator of the tiger is responsible for evil as well as good.
The Chimney Sweeper
Key Words: weep, soot, coffins, Angel
Key Ideas: The chimney sweeps are living in terrible conditions and are supposed to be confronted by the prospect of heaven after they die.

Infant Sorrow

Key Words: helpless, naked, struggling, sulk

Key Ideas: The world is cruel and difficult, even for the infants just entering it.

p. 163 After You Read

1. The speaker, like the lamb and the lamb's creator, is a child and presumably "meek and mild."

2. Sample response: The symbol of the lamb represents innocence and Christ.

3. **Graphic Organizer**

Sample response:

Who Suffers? Tom Dacre and the other chimney sweeps suffer.

Why? They must work as chimney sweeps.

Is Suffering Fair? No; they are young and were forced into this work.

Suggested Solution: Do your duty, and earn heaven as a reward.

Is the Solution Fair? No; the situation of the chimney sweeps is still unjust.

The Essential Question

Answers will vary, but students should support their opinions with details from the poems.

Introduction to *Frankenstein*
Mary Wollstonecraft Shelley

p. 164 Graphic Organizer

Sample response:

Prediction: Shelley found the idea for *Frankenstein* in another story.

New Information: "'We will each write a ghost story,' said Lord Byron. . . ."

Revised Prediction: She found her idea while working on the contest that the stories inspired.

p. 165 Note-taking Guide

Sample response:

Who Is Involved: Mary Shelley, Percy Shelley, Lord Byron, and John William Polidori

When It Takes Place: It takes place while visiting Lord Byron one rainy summer.

Where It Takes Place: Switzerland

What Happens: After reading ghost stories, Lord Byron suggests the idea that each person create an original ghost story.

How It Happens: One night, after a discussion of Dr. Darwin's experiments and the possibilities of reanimating a corpse, Shelley imagines a vision of the creation of a creature that inspires her story.

p. 166 After You Read

1. The intensity of Mary Shelley's vision suggests that she finds Dr. Darwin's experiments deeply disturbing for their implications about human power over creating life.

2. **Graphic Organizer**

Sample response:

Gothic Characteristic: elements of the supernatural

Example in Shelley: Both stories feature ghosts, one of which delivers a supernatural kiss of death.

3. Students may say that because Shelley was not able to sleep that night, she was deeply affected by the conversation.

The Essential Question

Answers will vary, but students should support their ideas with details from the introduction.

Poetry of Wordsworth

p. 167 Graphic Organizer

Sample response:

Celebration of Common Folk: (*from* "The Prelude") Wordsworth hopes that the French Revolution can bring happiness to both "the meek and lofty," and he sees the world as one that belongs to "all of us," not just to the social elite.

Love of Nature: ("Lines Composed a Few Miles Above Tintern Abbey") Wordsworth finds solace in his memories of being in nature while he is "'mid the din / Of towns and cities."

Admiration for French Revolution: (*from* "The Prelude") Wordsworth describes the beginning of the French Revolution as a time "When Reason seemed the most to assert her rights . . ." and when it seemed possible to rebuild society on just and rational principles.

Loss of Faith in Reason: (*from* "The Prelude") When the French Revolution fails to do as Wordsworth had hoped, Wordsworth finds that he has been "betrayed . . . by reasonings false" and places his trust in his heart that is guided by nature.

p. 168 Note-taking Guide

Sample response:

Who: the poet Wordsworth, who addresses his sister Dorothy

When: summer

Where: the Wye River valley near Tintern Abbey

What: Wordsworth returns to Tintern Abbey, noting that his memories of his last visit were a source of comfort to him, and speculates on the evolution of his reaction to nature from spontaneous joy to a more mature acknowledgment of the unity in nature.

Why: Maturity and its deeper understanding of reason have changed his feelings about nature, although both visits elicited strong reactions, and he wishes for his sister to share his feelings for this place and remember it and him in the future.

p. 169 Activate Prior Knowledge
Sample response:

1. On the return to visit to the lake, there were more boats docked at the pier.
2. More summer homes had been built along the shore.
3. The water had become polluted.

p. 169 Literary Analysis
Students should circle "waters, rolling from their mountain springs / With a soft inland murmur"; "steep and lofty cliffs"; "wild secluded scene"; and "more deep seclusion."

p. 169 Reading Strategy
Wordsworth believes that life in cities is harmful to the human spirit. The words "in lonely rooms, and 'mid the din / Of towns and cities . . . / In hours of weariness . . ." suggest that life in cities is lonely, noisy, and wearying.

p. 170 Literary Analysis
Sample response: This is a lyric poem because it expresses Wordsworth's personal thoughts and emotions on returning to Tintern Abbey.

p. 170 Stop to Reflect
Sample response: By comparing himself to a deer leaping on "the mountains," Wordsworth suggests that he felt a spontaneous, unthinking joy on his first visit.

p. 170 Reading Check
When Wordsworth was in lonely, noisy cities and towns, memories of this landscape gave him "sensations sweet" in his "blood," "heart," and "purer mind."

p. 171 Literary Analysis
Students may circle "A presence"; "a sense sublime"; "Whose dwelling is the light of setting suns"; "A motion and a spirit, that impels / All thinking things, all objects of all thought, / And rolls through all things." The words *presence, sublime,* and *spirit* are often associated with the spiritual or otherworldly realms, and the fact that this presence dwells in "the light of setting suns" also seems to be a reference to heaven.

p. 171 Stop to Reflect
Sample response: Given his deep feeling for nature and his apparent dislike of towns and cities, Wordsworth would probably endorse the environmental movement's efforts to protect nature in its wild state.

p. 172 Literary Analysis
He talks about nature as if it were a "she" that could receive, and not betray, human love.

p. 172 Stop to Reflect
1. He is asking the moon to shine on his sister and the winds to blow on her. He also seems to ask that her memory of this visit and his words heal her if she feels pain or grief in the future. Finally, he wants her to remember that during their visit, this landscape was dearer to him for its own sake and for hers.
2. He may be directing his request to God, Nature, or both. Some students may say God because prayers are usually thought of as being directed to God. Other students may say Nature because Wordsworth has already described Nature as a kind of goddess in lines 122–133.

p. 172 Reading Check
Thoughts of Wordsworth himself, his words, and their visit to Tintern Abbey will comfort her.

p. 172 Reader's Response
Students may say that they would have liked to go on a hike with Wordsworth because he appreciates nature as much as they do. Students may say that they, too, see nature as a magical place and they would find it so much more meaningful to share the hike with someone who feels the same way about it.

p. 173 Note-taking Guide
Sample response:

from The Prelude: Although the French Revolution seemed at first to be driven by reason, the ideals became convoluted and the French became "oppressors," conquering other regions. Wordsworth tries to justify continued faith in the cause, but in the end loses his conviction, advocating instead faith in his heart guided by nature.

The World Is Too Much With Us: Wordsworth believes that people are too caught up in material concerns to appreciate the power of nature.

London, 1802: The poet says that England is lacking in "inward happiness" and is filled with selfish, mediocre people. It needs Milton's moral vision and example to help restore it to its former ways.

p. 174 After You Read

1. Sample response: Although to his original pleasure is added a "sad perplexity" on his second visit, he also experiences a new pleasure the second time knowing that his present experience will nourish him again when he remembers it later.

2. **Graphic Organizer**
Sample response:
Specific and Simple: "Therefore I am still / A lover of the meadows and the woods . . ."
Abstract but Simple: "The anchor of my purest thoughts . . ."
Abstract and Difficult: "A motion and a spirit, that impels / All thinking things . . ."
3. Sample response: These lines suggest that political idealism, youthful enthusiasm, and a desire for change were important elements of this context.

The Essential Question

Answers will vary, but students should support their ideas with details from the poems.

Informational Texts: Traffic Reports

p. 176 Vocabulary Builder

Students should circle "Northwest England," "National Park," "National Park," and "National Parks."

p. 177 Vocabulary Builder

Volumes means "total amounts."

p. 177 Vocabulary Builder

"Private" is an antonym of *public*.

p. 177 Comprehension Builder

Answers will vary. Sample response: Large volumes of traffic lead to issues such as pollution, noise, distractions from the scenery, congestion, attempts to encourage us of public transport, competition for parking, and dangers to walkers, cyclists, and horse riders.

p. 178 Comprehension Builder

Answers will vary. Sample response: The goals of traffic management in Lake District National Park are to protect the landscape, to improve the quality of residents' lives, to help visitors enjoy the park, and to use transportation that does not harm the area.

p. 178 Vocabulary Builder

The Lake District National Park *set out* its traffic management policies in the Lake District National Park Management Plan.

p. 178 Vocabulary Builder

Routes is used as a noun.

p. 179 After You Read

Thinking About the Traffic Report
1. Most tourists use private cars to reach the Lake District National Park.
2. Answers will vary. Sample response: Decision-makers must balance needs so the park is preserved, so tourists can continue to enjoy it, and so local residents will not suffer from too much traffic. If decision-makers limit travel on secondary roads to local residents, tourists may decide not to visit the area. Without tourists, the local economy will suffer.

Reading Skill

3. The labels along the side of the chart show the number of vehicles in 24 hours, and the labels along the bottom show the years.
4. The vertical bars represent the flow of vehicles; the symbol is explained in the right margin.

Poetry of Coleridge

p. 180 Graphic Organizer

Sample response:
Poetic Sound Device: Assonance
"The Rime of the Ancient Mariner": The moving Moon went up the sky
"Kubla Khan": So twice five miles of fertile ground

Effects of sounds on images in the two poems: The *o* sounds bring notice to the Moon's rising. The *i* sounds again accent the distance.

Poetic Sound Device: Slant Rhyme

"The Rime of the Ancient Mariner": And the good south wind still blew behind

"Kubla Khan": A mighty fountain momently was forced; / Amid whose swift half-intermitted burst

Effects of sounds on images in the two poems: Both slant rhymes call attention to the actions being described.

p. 181 Note-taking Guide
Sample response:

The Rime of the Ancient Mariner

Details of the Setting: The mariner's story takes place long ago, on board a ship on the ocean.

Kubla Khan

Details of the Setting: The poem takes place in Xanadu, in a pleasure dome whose grounds are "twice five miles" in size and contain gardens, creeks, incense-bearing trees, and sunny spots of greenery.

p. 182 Activate Prior Knowledge
Students may recall the same intense feelings of loneliness when they saw a film about a teenager who moved to another country and had to attend a different school in a different culture. A scene in which the teenager is eating in the cafeteria alone while the other students stare or laugh at him may have evoked the same feelings of loneliness.

p. 182 Literary Analysis
In the line "The guests are met, the feast is set . . ." students should circle "met" and "set."

p. 183 Literary Analysis
Students should circle "Red as a rose" and "merry minstrelsy."

p. 183 Literary Analysis
Examples of assonance include "Wedding," "Guest," and "breast." The internal rhyme is "Guest" and "breast."

p. 183 Literary Analysis
Possible examples of consonance are "cold" and "emerald," although *-ald* receives a secondary rather than a primary stress, and "mist" and "mast," although "mast" is not a stressed syllable in the iambic line.

p. 184 Literary Analysis
The words repeated are "The ice was . . ." This group of words is repeated four times.

p. 184 Literary Analysis
An example of consonance is "wind sprung up behind." An example of internal rhyme is "day, for food or play . . ."

p. 184 Reading Check
He "shot the Albatross."

p. 185 Stop to Reflect
Students may say that Coleridge wants this spiteful act to seem unmotivated and unexplained. Perhaps the lack of motivation or explanation emphasizes that the important thing about the deed is the way in which it separates the Mariner from Nature and from his fellow men. According to this view, the cause of evil is less important than its effect. Students may also say that the Mariner is unaware of his own motivation.

p. 185 Literary Analysis
Students should circle the two consonant sounds that are alliterated, *f* and *b*. Sample response: The noticeable *f* alliteration conveys the sense of a ship moving swiftly through the waves because it mimics the sound of the wind.

p. 185 Reading Strategy
In "The Rime of the Ancient Mariner," Coleridge uses end rhyme at the end of the second and fourth lines. The first and third lines do not rhyme. This creates an *abcb* rhyme scheme.

p. 186 Reading Strategy
The alliteration accents the Mariner's negative view of the ocean at this time.

p. 186 Literary Analysis
An example of assonance is "tongue" and "utter" in line 135. An example of internal rhyme is "cross" and "Albatross" in line 141.

p. 186 Reading Check
The sun burns bright, the men are tortured by thirst, slimy things crawl in the water, the sailors believe that the Mariner brought on this curse by killing the Albatross so they hang the bird around his neck, and something heads toward the boat from the West.

p. 187 Literary Analysis
Students should circle "utter," "dumb," "sucked," and "blood." Students may say that

because *uh* is a sound one utters when one cannot formulate a word, it is the perfect sound to convey the idea that the men cannot speak.

p. 187 Literary Analysis

The words "grace" and "grate" are an example of assonance because they have the same vowel sound in stressed syllables ending with different consonant sounds.

p. 187 Stop to Reflect

Students may say that something unfortunate will probably occur, given the ominous names of the two characters on the other ship.

p. 188 Literary Analysis

The old-fashioned form of *quote* is "Quoth," and the old-fashioned form of *climbed* is "clomb."

p. 188 Literary Analysis

Students should circle "With heavy thump, a lifeless lump . . ." By emphasizing the sound of the body falling, the internal rhyme imitates what is being described.

p. 188 Reading Check

After they meet the ship with Death and Life-in-Death, the Mariner's shipmates die and fall to the deck.

p. 189 Literary Analysis

Students should circle the word "alone" four times and the word "wide" twice. Sample response: The *o* and *i* sounds almost sound as though someone is groaning and then saying "I, I." The emotional message seems to be that the speaker is suffering.

p. 189 Literary Analysis

The phrase "wicked whisper" is an example of alliteration because the accented first syllable of each word begins with a w sound. The phrase is also an example of assonance because the accented syllable in each word contains the same vowel sound followed by a different consonant.

p. 189 Stop to Reflect

Students may say that he sees a curse because his killing of the Albatross resulted in their deaths.

p. 190 Stop to Reflect

Students may say that the Mariner's love for the water snakes reconnects him with nature and the world after the act of killing the

Albatross had separated him from nature and his fellow creatures. Feeling reconnected with the world, the Mariner is then able to pray and establish a connection with God. Because he has overcome the curse resulting from his killing the Albatross, the bird itself falls from around his neck.

p. 190 Reading Strategy

Answers will vary. The *fl* sound in "Kubla Khan" creates tension for a wild image. The *sh* and *s* sounds in the underlined passage creates calm for the image of sleep.

p. 190 Reading Check

The new feeling that the Mariner experiences is one of love for nature's creatures, even those that previously repelled him.

p. 191 Literary Analysis

Students should circle "sails," "sigh," and "sedge." Students may say that the s alliteration imitates the kind of whispering, sighing sound of the wind in the sails and in sedge.

p. 191 Stop to Reflect

Students may say that such details as dead men rising up and working "the ropes" are like those in a nightmare or horror movie. They may compare this image with those of zombies or the living dead in a scary film.

p. 192 Stop to Reflect

Students should circle the word "sounds" twice and the word "sound" once. Sample response: The more likely answer is #2 because someone as careful and thorough in his use of sound devices as Coleridge would probably take care in his placement of words. By varying the position of the words sound and sounds, Coleridge is imitating the way in which the sweet sounds repeat in different ways, "Now mixed, now one by one."

p. 192 Literary Analysis

Students should identify the s sound in "ceased," "still," and "sails."

p. 192 Reading Check

After the Mariner woke, the wind came, the ship was propelled forward, the rain fell, the dead crew rose and began to work the ropes, sweet sounds came from the spirits that animated the bodies of the crew, and the ship continued sailing, "Moved onward from beneath."

p. 193 Literary Analysis

The words "flung" and "blood" are an example of assonance, and the words "blood" and "head" are an example of consonance.

p. 193 Stop to Reflect

Sample response: The Mariner is undergoing penance, or suffering to make up for his sin of killing the Albatross. The spirit indicates that the Mariner has suffered for that evil deed and will have to suffer still more in order to win forgiveness.

p. 194 Literary Analysis

Students should circle the long *i* sound that appears twice in "fly" and twice in "high." Sample response: The emphasis of the repetition lends urgency to the demand that the voice is making.

p. 194 Literary Analysis

Students should identify the short *i* sound that appears in the words "fitter," "fixed," "in," and "glitter."

p. 194 Reading Check

These voices say that the Mariner was the one who killed the Albatross, which was loved by a particular spirit. One of them says that the Mariner has suffered and will suffer more to make up for this deed. One of them wonders why the ship sails so quickly when there is no wind. The other says that the ship will slow down as the Mariner comes out of his trance.

p. 195 Stop to Reflect

Students may say that this wind is symbolic because, "like a welcoming," it is somehow a sign that the Mariner has come through his troubles and is returning home.

p. 195 Stop to Reflect

Sample response: The lighthouse and church would be the first structures that the Mariner sees because they are the tallest ones. Coleridge might have thought that a "kirk" (or any place of worship) is like a lighthouse for the spirit because it shows people what is right and wrong, helps them avoid crashing on the "rocks" of sin, and gives them a direction for living.

p. 196 Literary Analysis

Students should circle "hand," "land," "sight," and "light."

1. Each line in this stanza rhymes with another line, so four lines rhyme.

2. This rhyme pattern is not typical. In the four-line stanzas, often only the second and fourth lines rhyme.

3. Students may say that Coleridge uses the harmony of the rhymes at this point because the "heavenly sight" being described is also harmonious.

p. 196 Reading Check

The Pilot, the Pilot's boy, and the Hermit come in a boat to welcome the Mariner.

p. 197 Literary Analysis

The words "are" and "sere" are an example of consonance in line 530. Students may say that just as consonance is less than a full rhyme, the sails are less than perfect. Therefore, consonance is suitable for describing such sails.

p. 197 Stop to Reflect

The strange, signaling light; the warped planks; the thin, dry sails; and "the fiendish look" probably cause the Pilot to react as he does.

p. 198 Stop to Reflect

The Pilot yells and falls down "in a fit"; the Hermit prays; and the Pilot's boy seems to go crazy, laughing and rolling his eyes.

p. 198 Stop to Reflect

Sample response: For the Mariner, telling the story over and over is a form of penance, because it means that the Mariner has to suffer over and over and to realize again and again the evil of what he did.

p. 198 Reading Check

He wanders around the world telling his story.

p. 199 Stop to Reflect

Students should circle "He prayeth well, who loveth well / Both man and bird and beast," or "He prayeth best, who loveth best / All things both great and small; / For the dear God who loveth us, / He made and loveth all." Sample response: Because God made and loves all things, we should imitate him by also loving all fellow creatures.

p. 199 Stop to Reflect

Sample response: The Wedding Guest may be a sadder man because he sympathizes with the Mariner's sufferings or because he realizes that he needs to gain in the ability to love. The Wedding Guest may be a wiser man because he has learned the Mariner's lesson of respect of all nature.

p. 199 Reader's Response

Students may say that this poem would make a good horror film because it has elements of the supernatural that are especially creepy, such as the slimy creatures in the water, the dead crewmates rising to sail the ship, or the scene in which the Nightmare Life-in-Death and Death both come across the water.

p. 199 Thinking About the Skill

Sample response: Sound devices usually do not play as obvious a role in prose fiction as they do in poetry. In poems such as "The Rime of the Ancient Mariner," the patterns of sound are important in supporting the meaning. However, some sound devices, such as consonance, assonance, and alliteration, do play a role in prose fiction.

p. 200 After You Read

1. Coleridge uses internal rhyme.
2. Graphic Organizer
Sample response:

"The Rime of the Ancient Mariner"
Language: "I watched the water snakes . . . they reared, the elfish light / Fell off in hoary flakes"; "The Mariner hath his will"; "To thee, thou Wedding Guest!"; "He rose the morrow morn"
Effect: The mythical serpents described and the archaic words are associated with legends of knights and so suit the theme of redemption. The old-fashioned language makes the tale seem stranger, suiting the supernatural events of the poem.

"Kubla Khan"
Language: "In Xanadu did Kubla Khan / A stately pleasure dome decree"; "A savage place! as holy and enchanted / As e'er beneath a waning moon was haunted / By woman wailing for her demon lover!"

Effect: The mention of exotic names and the archaic language help create a world of fantasy. The description of the setting as both beautiful and haunting suit the theme of mingled beauty and danger.
3. Sample response: The use of poetic devices makes the last few lines of "Kubla Khan" more musical and hypnotic, enhancing the description of the wild-eyed visionary.

The Essential Question

Answers will vary. Students may suggest that in "Kubla Khan," Coleridge creates a setting in a mythical land that is sensual, hedonistic, wild, and savage—a place where all of the senses are heightened. "The Rime of the Ancient Mariner" moves through scenes of natural upheaval and eerie beauty, where Death and Life-in-Death direct a harrowing penance. The mariner's tale is juxtaposed against the backdrop of a celebratory wedding feast.

Poetry of Byron

p. 201 Graphic Organizer

Sample response:
Passage: No more-no more-Oh! Never more, my heart, / Canst thou be my sole world, my universe! / Once all in all, but now a thing apart, / Thou canst not be my blessing or my curse: (*from* Don Juan)
Questions: 1. To whom is the speaker speaking? 2. Why can this person or thing not be the center of his life anymore?
Answers: 1. The speaker speaks to his own heart. 2. The speaker is getting older, and realizes that he is not invincible.
Passage: What are the hopes of man? Old Egypt's King / Cheops erected the first pyramid / And largest, thinking it was just the thing / To keep his memory whole, and mummy hid: / But somebody or other rummaging / Burglariously broke his coffin's lid: / Let not a monument give you or me hopes, / Since not a pinch of dust remains of Cheops. (*from* Don Juan)
Questions: 1. What happened to King Cheops? 2. Why does the speaker tell this story?
Answers: 1. King Cheops built a pyramid in his own honor and was then robbed after he died. 2. The speaker is pointing out that Cheops wasted his time by trying to aggrandize himself.

p. 202 Note-taking Guide
Sample response:
She Walks in Beauty
Subject of Poem: a woman's beauty
Description in Poem: "like the night / Of cloudless climes and starry skies"; "the name-less grace / Which waves in every raven tress"; "So soft, so calm, yet eloquent"
Speaker's Feelings: The speaker is filled with wonder at the woman's beauty and links her physical beauty with her spiritual beauty.
Apostrophe to the Ocean
Subject of Poem: the ocean
Description in Poem: "thou deep and dark blue ocean"; "Thy shores are empires"; "Dark-heaving—boundless, endless, and sublime"
Speaker's Feelings: The speaker is in awe of the immeasurable depths, power, and endurance of the ocean.
from Don Juan
Description in Poem: "I / Have squandered my whole summer while 'twas May"; "My days of love are over"; "All things that have been born were born to die"
Speaker's Feelings: The speaker is sad that he is aging and believes that his best days have passed.

p. 203 After You Read
1. Sample response: The mood of the speaker's reflections is comic, and his observations are amusing in their honesty.
2. **Graphic Organizer**
Sample response:
Simile: "She walks in beauty, like the night / Of cloudless climes and starry skies"
What Is Being Described: a beautiful woman in mourning
Associations Suggested: mystery; twilight; enchantment
Metaphor: "I / Have squandered my whole summer while 'twas May"
What Is Being Described: the speaker's youth
Associations Suggested: the changing seasons; life's temporary nature; the foolishness of youth
Personification: "thou dost arise / And shake him off from thee"
What Is Being Described: the ocean's power over man
Associations Suggested: man's vulnerability; the ocean's immense force

3. Most students will say that their questioning made their reading more focused and that they better understood what they were reading.

The Essential Question
Answers will vary, but students should support their ideas with details from the poems.

Poetry of Shelley

p. 204 Graphic Organizer
Sample response:
Center box: "All overgrown with azure moss and flowers / So sweet, the sense faints picturing them!"
Sensory "Texture": soft; fragrant
Associations: overwhelmingly pleasant, full of the beauty of nature
Center box: "Chorus Hymeneal, / Or triumphal chant"
Sensory "Texture": a heavenly sound
Associations: religious; joyous

p. 205 Note-taking Guide
Sample response:
Ozymandias
Words used to describe it: "cold command," "pedestal," "colossal"
Ode to the West Wind
Words used to describe it: "Destroyer and preserver," "tameless, swift and proud," "Scatter"
To a Skylark
Words used to describe it: "blithe spirit," "a star of heaven," "sprite"

p. 206 After You Read
1. Sample response: His expression suggests that he was a proud, condescending ruler.
2. **Graphic Organizer**
Sample response:
Image: "If I were a swift cloud to fly with thee" ("Ode to the West Wind")
How Vivid? very vivid
Associated Ideas: Clouds are breezy and free, and they travel with the wind.
Link: Nature and Spirit: The speaker yearns to be a cloud and have the same free-dom in his spirit to fly with the west wind.
Image: "Thy skill to poet were, thou scorner of the ground! / Teach me half the gladness / That thy brain must know" ("To a Skylark")
How Vivid? fairly

Associated Ideas: The bird is like a poet of the animal world.

Link: Nature and Spirit: The speaker wishes to learn how to experience the same kind of joy as the skylark.

3. Sample response: In "Ozymandias," the statue's broken face lying on the ground in a permanent frown is a striking image because it represents how temporary life is and how even the most powerful of human beings cannot escape death.

The Essential Question

Answers will vary. Sample response: Shelley's poems reflect his desire to overthrow tyrants to bring in a new age of equality and justice. For example, in "Ozymandias," the monument's size, frown, sneer, and wrinkled lip, as well as the intimidating words on the pedestal, express the attempt to control others. This attempt at dominion from beyond the grave is futile because the statue lies in broken pieces. The speaker depicts Ozymandias as intimidating and controlling and describes the tyrant's monument as a "wreck." In "To a Skylark," the speaker depicts the skylark soaring, singing, and joyous—free from the difficulties of human life. The wind in "Ode to the West Wind" embodies a powerful, restless, striving force, moving everywhere in rebellion against tyrants like Ozymandias.

Poetry of Keats

p. 207 Graphic Organizer

Sample response:

"On First Looking into Chapman's Homer"

Original Words: "Then felt I like some watcher of the skies / When a new planet swims into his ken"

Paraphrase: I felt like an astronomer who discovers a new planet.

"Ode to a Nightingale"

Original Words: "Fade far away, dissolve, and quite forget / What thou among the leaves has never known, / The weariness, the fever, and the fret"

Paraphrase: I would like to fade away with you and forget those things that you have never known, such as tiredness, illness, or stress.

"Ode on a Grecian Urn"

Original Words: "When old age shall this generation waste, / Thou shalt remain, in midst of other woe"

Paraphrase: When those men who are alive today are gone, you will still be here to see the troubles of another generation.

p. 208 Note-taking Guide

Sample response:

Speaker's Attitude: Filled with wonder and inspiration

Poem: "Fears"

Subject: The speaker's fear of dying before he has written a great deal

What the Poem Shows: The challenge of finding love and fame

Speaker's Attitude: Mournful but philosophical; thoughtful; intense

Poem: "Nightingale"

Subject: Admiration for the nightingale

What the Poem Shows: The desire to imitate the ease of the song he hears; poetic inspiration

Speaker's Attitude: Heartsick but wishful and reflective

p. 209 Note-taking Guide

Sample response:

Speaker's Observation: The urn can capture a flowery tale better than his own rhyme. His interest in the scenes and the stories they tell cause him to ask questions.

Images: Pictures of men, maidens, boughs, and grass on the urn.

Speaker's Observation: The artistic beauty of the urn is unending and true in a way that the real world can never be because the real world is transitory.

p. 210 Activate Prior Knowledge

Sample response: The Parthenon in Athens, Greece, might tell people to take better care of one another and the environment. The Parthenon was (and still is) the symbol of wisdom, harmony, and balance because of its perfect symmetry and its simple beauty. However, the Parthenon fell victim to people's destructive nature when Turkish gunpowder exploded in its center. Today, pollution is destroying what remains of the temple.

p. 210 Reading Strategy

Sample response: The two lovers beneath the tree will never kiss. However, their love will never end and the girl's beauty will never fade.

p. 210 Stop to Reflect

Keats means that, being forever depicted in pursuit, the Lover will never reach his beloved. However, because he and she are captured in a work of art, they will always remain young and he will always love her.

p. 211 Literary Analysis

Students should draw lines connecting lines 31 and 33, lines 32 and 34, lines 35 and 38, lines 36 and 39, and lines 37 and 40. Students may circle any two of the following: "Lead'st," "thou," "thy," "art," or "e'er." Students should circle "O Attic shape!" and "Thou, silent form."

p. 211 Stop to Reflect

Sample response: Item #2 is a closer approximation to the kind of "truth" the urn expresses. It cannot explain anything in a scientific or a verbal sense. However, it can capture and display forever, or at least for a long time, the liveliness of human emotions.

p. 211 Reading Check

Sample response: Keats sees men or gods pursuing young women, a young musician playing pipes, and a priest leading a young cow to the sacrifice.

p. 211 Reader's Response

Students may say that they looked as closely at a Vermeer painting they once saw in a museum. They were captivated by the young woman in the painting and felt a certain amount of awe to be able to look into the face of a person who lived over three hundred years ago.

p. 212 After You Read

1. Sample response: The speaker sees his own world as perplexed and dull, whereas that of the nightingale is full of permanent, dream-like joy.
2. Sample response: Keats honors the nightingale by praising its song of painless ecstasy and its ability not to be defeated by death. He honors the urn by marveling at its permanent beauty, which he considers an important truth.

3. Graphic Organizer

Sample response:
Poem: "Homer," lines 9–10
Paraphrase: I felt like an astronomer who sees a new planet in his telescope.
Poem: "Nightingale," lines 71–72
Paraphrase: Speaking about desolation and hopelessness is enough to kill the joy I felt by thinking about your life. It brings me back to my own sad life.
Poem: "Grecian Urn," lines 3–4
Paraphrase: Historian of the woods, who can tell an elaborate story better than our poem . . .

The Essential Question

Answers will vary, but students should support their ideas with details from the poems.

"On Making an Agreeable Marriage"
Jane Austen

from A Vindication of the Rights of Women
Mary Wollstonecraft

p. 213 Graphic Organizer

Sample response:
On Making an Agreeable Marriage
Other Clues From the Text: Austen admits to being unable to make up her mind about her niece's suitor. "It seems as if your being secure of him . . . has made you Indifferent."
Writer's Purpose: to dissuade her niece from marrying a man she does not love, despite his good qualities
How Purpose Affects Meaning: Austen's purpose illustrates the true meaning of the text, which is a social commentary on both human nature and marriage at the time of writing.

A Vindication of the Rights of Woman
Other Clues From the Text: "Vindication" in the title is a defense. She starts off saddened by the state of things and then calls for change in women's rights.
Writer's Purpose: to advocate equal rights for women
How Purpose Affects Meaning: Wollstonecraft's meaning is clear and in accord with her purpose—women should have the same rights as men.

p. 214 Note-taking Guide

Sample response:

Appeals to Logic: ". . . Your mistake has been one that thousands of women fall into. He was the *first* young Man who attached himself to you. That was the charm, & most powerful it is."

Appeals to Morality: ". . . I shall turn around & entreat you not to commit yourself further, & not to think of accepting him unless you really do like him. Anything is to be preferred or endured rather than marrying without Affection; and if his deficiencies of Manner &c &c strike you more than all his good qualities, if you continue to think strongly of them, give him up at once."

Appeals to Emotions: ". . . don't be frightened by the idea of his acting more strictly up to the precepts of the New Testament than others."

p. 215 Note-taking Guide

Sample response:

Appeals to Logic: "The conduct and manners of women, in fact, evidently prove that their minds are not in a healthy state . . ."

Appeals to Morality: ". . . their apparent inferiority with respect to bodily strength must render them in some degree dependent on men in the various relations of life; but why should it be increased by prejudices that give a sex to virtue, and confound simple truths with sensual reveries?"

Appeals to Emotions: ". . . a profound conviction that the neglected education of my fellow creatures is the grand source of misery I deplore . . ."

p. 216 Activate Prior Knowledge

Sample response:
1. equal pay for equal work
2. freedom from harassment

p. 216 Literary Analysis

Students should circle "the subject of education"; "the neglected education of my fellow creatures is the grand source of misery I deplore, and that women, in particular, are rendered weak and wretched by a variety of concurring causes"; and "One cause of this barren blooming I attribute to a false system of education gathered from the books written on this subject by men who, considering females rather as women than human creatures, have been more anxious to make them alluring . . . than affectionate wives and rational mothers . . ." The subject of this essay is the lack of education in women. This essay explains that women's education has been neglected, resulting in silly or vain women who have been brought up to be admired, rather than to be strong or useful women.

p. 216 Stop to Reflect

Sample response: The sophisticated ideas, vocabulary, and sentence structure suggest that Wollstonecraft was well educated.

p. 217 Reading Strategy

Sample response: Judging by the bracketed passage, Wollstonecraft wanted to change the education of women so that it emphasized strength of body and mind rather than beauty and attractiveness.

p. 217 Literary Analysis

Sample response:
1. Women are preoccupied with clothes and fashion, wear makeup, and think up silly names for pets.
2. Women are still very interested in clothing and makeup, as can be seen from the great number of makeover shows on television. Some women are also guilty of giving silly names to their pets and even go so far as to dress their pets.

p. 217 Reading Strategy

The words "degraded" and "mistaken" indicate that she disagrees with and wants to replace the "notions of female excellence" dominant during her time. These words show that the "notions of female excellence" are not only incorrect but are also humiliating to women and therefore must be altered. By raising this point, she claims that what society values in women does nothing to help them gain rights, respect, or equality.

p. 218 Literary Analysis

Charged language such as "contemptible infantine airs," with its negative associations, appeals to the readers' emotions.

p. 218 Reading Check

Exceptions include "Many individuals" who "have more sense than their male relatives."

p. 218 Reader's Response

Students may say that Wollstonecraft would not be surprised by the advances women have made today because she always believed that women had the potential to do as men do if given the same education as men. Students may use U.S. Secretary of State Condoleezza Rice as an example of a woman who has met her potential.

p. 218 Thinking About the Skill

Students may say that determining Wollstonecraft's purpose helped them better understand her essay because in doing so, they applied background information to understand Wollstonecraft's point of view. Furthermore, knowing why she chose to write this essay helped students identify her main points and her support for those main points.

p. 219 After You Read

1. Sample response: Because society encourages women to be weaker than men, it causes some women to act childishly and slyly.

2. **Graphic Organizer**

Sample response:

Love: "Anything is to be preferred or endured rather than marrying without Affection."

Importance: high

Suitability for Each Other: She seems to imply that it is not as important because they will become more suitable for each other if they are bound together: "I have no doubt that he will get more lively & like yourselves as he is more with you;—he will catch your ways if he belongs to you."

Importance: moderate

Money: She cites the fact that he is the eldest son of a man of fortune.

Importance: moderate

Respectability: "he is I dare say such a Scholar as your agreeable, idle Brothers would ill bear a comparison with"; she also cites his strict religious nature and her appeal to it.

Importance: high

3. Sample response: Austen's purpose is to advise her niece. Her tactful tone and modest denials of expertise indicate that she does not want to come across as telling her niece what to do. She uses emotional and moral appeals. Wollstonecraft's purpose is to persuade a more general audience by argument

on a specific issue, as indicated by her title. Wollstonecraft analyzes a social problem directly. Both works reveal the limited rights of women in the eighteenth and early nineteenth centuries, but Austen's commentary is subtle, whereas Wollstonecraft's is bold.

The Essential Question

Answers will vary, but students should include the words *independence*, *values*, and *rebellious* in their answers and support their opinions with details from the texts.

ANSWERS TO UNIT 5

Poetry of Tennyson

p. 220 Graphic Organizer

Sample response:

***from* In Memoriam, A. H. H.**

Speaker's Motivations: the early death of a friend

Speaker's Beliefs: Grief must be embraced to affirm the value of love.

Speaker's Conflicts: The speaker is overcome by despair, grief, and anger over a friend's death

Author's Assumptions and Beliefs: Death cannot destroy friendship.

"The Lady of Shalott"

Speaker's Motivations: the position of the creative artist in society

Speaker's Beliefs: Like many artists, the Lady of Shalott is removed from life, looking at it secondhand and not experiencing it for herself.

Speaker's Conflicts: The artist is distanced from life, seeing life as material for his or her depictions.

Author's Assumptions and Beliefs: Life of the imagination isolates one from reality. It is better to live in reality because our fantasies can never be realized. Once our fantasies become reality, the allure of fantasy is destroyed.

***from* The Princess: Tears, Idle Tears**

Speaker's Motivations: a longing for the past

Speaker's Beliefs: Past love and happiness cannot be truly possessed.

Speaker's Conflicts: The speaker longs for the irrecoverable past.

Author's Assumptions and Beliefs: Life is transient.

"Ulysses"

Speaker's Motivations: dissatisfaction with idle old age

Speaker's Beliefs: He feels that he still has noble work to do before he dies.

Speaker's Conflicts: He is frustrated and dissatisfied with growing old in Ithaca and longs for new adventures and challenges.

Author's Assumptions and Beliefs: It is good to courageously seek adventure; one should let go of the past and "seek a newer world."

p. 221 Note-taking Guide

Sample response:

In Memoriam: The speaker is angry that his friend has been taken from him. The difficulty of loss can be softened by memories.

Tears, Idle Tears: The speaker is in despair about having no more time with the deceased person.

Ulysses: The speaker mourns the loss of youth and desires to seek new adventures.

p. 222 Note-taking Guide

Sample response:

Column 1, Row 2: She sings.

Column 1, Row 3: She weaves and views the world through a mirror.

Column 2, Row 2: She is dissatisfied.

Column 2, Row 3: She sees others living their lives through the mirror.

Column 3, Row 2: She leaves her loom to look from the window at Sir Lancelot, and the mirror cracks; the curse is upon her.

Column 3, Row 3: She goes down to the river.

Column 4, Row 2: She climbs into the boat and sings as she floats down the river toward Camelot.

Column 4, Row 3: She dies while singing; the men and women of Camelot look at her in wonder.

p. 223 Activate Prior Knowledge

Sample response:

1. Knights wore armor.
2. Knights were governed by the code of chivalry.
3. Lords and ladies lived in castles.

p. 223 Stop to Reflect

Students should indicate that the island is in the middle of the river that flows to Camelot. On either side of the river are fields of barley and rye, and the road to Camelot runs through a field.

p. 223 Literary Analysis

Students may circle "who hath seen her wave her hand," "at the casement seen her stand," or "is she known in all the land." Students should point out that the speaker is a third-person narrator who watches and relates the events but does not participate in them.

p. 224 Literary Analysis

Students should circle "She has heard a whisper say, / A curse is on her"; "She knows not what the curse may be"; and "little other care hath she."

p. 224 Reading Strategy

Sample response:

1. Weaving a "magic web with colors gay" could describe the work of poets, painters, composers, and other artists.

2. Like the Lady of Shalott, artists may protect themselves from life. They may disengage themselves from reality, choosing to view life only as it is reflected in the "mirror" of their art.

p. 225 Stop to Reflect

Students should say that these lines reveal the Lady of Shalott's weariness of her unchanging way of life. She realizes that she is cut off from experiencing reality, which she can see only glimpses of in her mirror.

p. 225 Literary Analysis

Sample response:

1. "red-cross knight forever kneeled / To a lady in his shield."

2. "blazoned baldric."

3. "Thick-jeweled shone the saddle leather." Sample response: Because the Lady of Shalott is a visual artist, weaving pictures on her loom, these beautiful details may especially impress her.

p. 225 Reading Check

Sir Lancelot rides close to the "bower eaves."

p. 226 Literary Analysis

Sample response: Unexpectedly seeing the splendid form of Sir Lancelot may have awakened feelings of love in the Lady of Shalott.

p. 226 Literary Analysis

Sample response:

1. The reader would not have such a complete view of the world outside her island.

2. The Lady of Shalott would not have described Sir Lancelot as objectively as the speaker does.

p. 226 Literary Analysis

The speaker suggests that the Lady of Shalott is aware of the consequences of looking out her window at Sir Lancelot.

p. 227 Reading Strategy

Students should circle "Singing in her song she died." Then, students should circle item 1. Sample response: Item 2 best expresses the author's message because the author believes that artists should not isolate themselves from reality so that they can understand and describe it.

p. 227 Reading Check

Sample response: No, Lancelot does not appear to know the lady or why she is in Camelot.

p. 227 Reader's Response

Sample response: The Lady of Shalott is a sympathetic character because she is not given the choice to engage in reality. She interprets the brief images in her mirror; doing so may have given her a false view of reality.

p. 228 After You Read

1. The loss of the speaker's friend makes the scene bleak and empty.

2. The speaker's inner conflict is about his insatiable longing for adventure after he has settled down.

3. **Graphic Organizer**

Sample response:

Past

Ulysses: He remembers the past with satisfaction.

The Lady of Shalott: The past is identical with the present.

Present

Ulysses: He is restless in the present.

The Lady of Shalott: The present is unchanging.

Future

Ulysses: The future is full of opportunity.

The Lady of Shalott: The future is doomed.

5. Sample response: In *In Memoriam* the author reveals that he is deeply grieved by the death of a friend, but he believes that death cannot destroy friendship. Although his friend has died, he believes that his friend's spirit is with him. His image of the chrysalis shows that Tennyson sees death as only a transformation, as when a caterpillar turns into a butterfly. The friendship has changed, not ended. Furthermore, Tennyson believes that

he must embrace his grief to affirm the value of his love for his friend.

The Essential Question

Answers will vary, but may include the following ideas: Tennyson wanted to promote traditional values such as religion and love ("In Memoriam, A.H.H."); romance ("Lady of Shalott"); appreciation of times past or loved ones lost ("The Princess: Tears, Idle Tears"); and wisdom, hard work, honor, and strength ("Ulysses"). Students should explain their answers by including specific references to the poetry.

"My Last Duchess"
Robert Browning

"Life in a Love"
Robert Browning

"Love Among the Ruins"
Robert Browning

"Sonnet 43"
Elizabeth Barrett Browning

p. 229 Graphic Organizer

Sample response:

My Last Duchess: The speaker's love is limited, if even existent; The speaker is jealous and controlling.

Sonnet 43: The speaker's love is limitless; The speaker is adoring and passionate.

Both: address the topic of relationships; suggest a vulnerable side to the speakers

p. 230 Note-taking Guide

Sample response:

Meaning: The painting on the wall is of the Duke's late wife.

Inferences: The Duke seems to care more about owning a fine piece of art than about his wife's death.

p. 231 Activate Prior Knowledge

Sample response:

1. giving directions to servants
2. receiving callers

p. 231 Literary Analysis

Sample response:

1. The reference to "my last Duchess" in line 1 reveals that the speaker is a duke.
2. The word "you" in line 5 refers to the silent listener.

p. 231 Stop to Reflect

Sample response: "She had / A heart—how shall I say?—too soon made glad, / Too easily impressed; . . ." This passage reveals that the proud Duke was jealous of any attention that his wife gave to others.

p. 232 Reading Check

Sample response: Given that "all smiles stopped" rather abruptly and that the Duke is about to remarry, it is reasonable to infer that the Duke commanded that his wife be killed.

p. 232 Reading Check

Students should say that the Duke tells the agent that he is confident that all of his requirements for a dowry will be met and that the "fair daughter" is the first "object" that the Duke wishes to gain.

p. 232 Reading Strategy

In "Life in a Love," the speaker expresses a deep and enduring love. The speaker of "My Last Duchess," the Duke, expresses a selfish love for his late wife or does not love her.

p. 232 Reader's Response

Sample response: The Duke is a persuasive speaker, and the reader is impressed by his confidence and sheer force of will.

p. 232 Thinking About the Skill

Students should say that making inferences about characters in fiction helps readers understand characters' motives and also enables readers to grasp the deeper meanings in fiction.

p. 233 Note-taking Guide

Sample response:

"Life in a Love": Students should check **Believes in love forever.**

"Love Among the Ruins": Students should check **Believes that his love is greater than even a great civilization.**

Sonnet 43: Students should check **Believes in love forever** and **Believes in love that will continue after death.**

p. 234 Apply the Skills

1. Sample response: The listener and speaker interact when the speaker addresses the listener as "you" or "Sir" and when the speaker asks the listener a question, as in "'Will't please you rise?'"

2. Graphic Organizer

Sample response:

Line 14: natural pause at comma on **"-ly, called"**

Line 15: natural pause after **"-ess' cheek;"**

Line 16: natural pause after **"to say"**

3. Both speakers express a deep and abiding love. However, it seems that the love expressed by the speaker of "Life in a Love" is not returned. The speaker of "Sonnet 43" seems to be speaking to someone who returns her love.

The Essential Question

Answers will vary. Sample response: The speaker in Elizabeth Barrett Browning's sonnet seems more dramatic. The speaker in the sonnet uses language such as "the depth and breadth and height / My soul can reach," "the ends of Being," and "I love thee with the breath, / Smiles, tears, of all my life!"

from Hard Times
Charles Dickens

p. 235 Graphic Organizer

Sample response:

Detail: "Teach these boys and girls nothing but Facts. Facts alone are wanted in life."

Detail: "You are never to fancy."

Context: Educational theories and practices stress fact and discourage the use of imagination.

Author's Purpose: to criticize and satirize the educational practices of his time

Meaning of Work: The insistence of the educational system on eliminating imagination from the world is dangerous and counterproductive.

p. 236 Note-taking Guide

Sample response:

Details That Support Purpose: Thomas Gradgrind asks students to use only the facts to define a horse; a government official wants to keep to the facts by not decorating walls or floors; a teacher who discourages imagination is named "M'Choakumchild."

p. 237 Activate Prior Knowledge

Students should write a brief definition of a horse, including details that they regard as important.

p. 237 Literary Analysis

Students should circle "Facts" and "reasoning animals."

p. 237 Reading Strategy

Sample response:

1. Dickens makes fun of utilitarians when he compares the speaker's hair to "a plantation of firs to keep the wind from its shining surface."
2. Dickens makes fun of utilitarians when he compares the speaker's head to "the crust of a plum pie." Both details reveal a mocking tone that accomplishes Dickens' purpose of making fun of utilitarians.

p. 238 Reading Check

Students may circle "fact and calculation," "a rule and a pair of scales," and "question of figures."

p. 238 Reading Strategy

1. Dickens compares Gradgrind to a cannon.
2. This comparison emphasizes the destructive aspect of utilitarianism.
3. Dickens' comparison relates Gradgrind's destruction of the children's imaginations to "Murdering the Innocents," the title of the chapter.

p. 238 Reading Check

Gradgrind wants the students to believe that facts are all that is important in life.

p. 239 Stop to Reflect

Sample response: Because Sissy's father works with horses, it is likely that she has greater first-hand knowledge of horses than does Gradgrind.

p. 239 Reading Strategy

Sample response:

1. "cold eyes": Like his dry, dull definition of a horse, Bitzer has "cold eyes."
2. "unwholesomely deficient": Like himself, Bitzer's definition is "unwholesomely deficient" in that it leaves out such details as the beauty and strength of a horse.

p. 240 Literary Analysis

Students should point out that phrases such as "government official," "the bar of his little Public-office," and "ready to fight all England" suggest that supporters of the utilitarian philosophy were eager to spread their ideas through the country, possibly through the school system.

p. 240 Reading Strategy

Students should say that Dickens achieves this purpose by showing that the children are not interested in thinking about the content of the question but about the mechanics of getting the predetermined "right" answer. The children respond automatically to the question based on the speaker's reactions to other answers.

p. 240 Reading Check

It is not proper to decorate a room with pictures of horses because horses do not "in reality—in fact" walk up and down the walls of a room.

p. 241 Reading Strategy

Sample response: "Grad" pertains to education ("graduate") and "grind" is both slang for a person who educates in a dull, mechanical manner and a term that describes a destructive process. Together, the name "Gradgrind" seems to relate the education process to a dull and possibly destructive action.

p. 241 Stop to Reflect

The gentleman shows a lack of imagination when he cannot seem to differentiate between real flowers and images of flowers.

p. 241 Literary Analysis

By forecasting a "board of fact," which will make the people a "people of fact," the passage reflects Dickens's strong concern that utilitarianism will bring about a flat, dull society incapable of intellectual pursuits and artistic creativity.

p. 242 Reading Strategy

The name "M'Choakumchild" suggests that the teacher will choke the imagination of children and supports Dickens's purpose by suggesting that utilitarianism will likewise choke the people of England.

p. 242 Reading Strategy

Students may circle "turned at the same time, in the same factory, on the same principles, like so many pianoforte legs" and "ten chilled fingers." Sample response: Dickens uses these words and phrases to show that a person is not necessarily a great teacher just because he or she knows many facts and figures.

p. 242 Reading Check

Dickens says that Mr. M'Choakumchild would have been a better teacher if he had learned "a little less."

p. 243 Stop to Reflect

Sample response: Because Bitzer and Sissy have been contrasted early in the novel, it is likely that they will be pitted against each other at some future point.

p. 243 Reader's Response

Some students may say that they would obey Mr. Gradgrind's order and alter their description of a horse while other students may say that they would respond defiantly and refuse to change their definition.

p. 243 Thinking About the Skill

Students should say that a novel like Hard Times can convey social commentary as effectively as an essay because the novel engages readers' emotions and enhances the commentary through the use of vivid details, memorable actions, and humor.

p. 244 After You Read

1. The setting suggests that society has made the process of obtaining an education rigid and largely unpleasant.

2. **Graphic Organizer**

Sample response:

Passage: Gradgrind calls Sissy "Girl 20."

Intended Effect on Reader: Gradgrind's stubborn application of theory makes him look ridiculous.

Intended Message: Gradgrind's theories are foolish.

3. Sample response: The name "M'Choakumchild" suggests that the instructor will "choke" rather than teach children, implying that Dickens wishes to show the dangerous nature of the teacher's ideas.

The Essential Question

Answers will vary. Sample response: Dickens would think that an education system has great influence on children, and is therefore greatly responsible for the type of adults children become. His social commentary focuses on the teachers' insistence that the children not show any individuality or creativity and suggests that most children quickly conform to the wishes of school leaders.

Informational Texts: Web Sites

p. 246 Vocabulary Builder
Students should circle "novelist."

p. 246 Vocabulary Builder
Students should underline "conversational" and "curatorial."

p. 247 Vocabulary Builder
Sample response: A *virtual* tour allows people to visit a museum online rather than in person.

p. 247 Comprehension Builder
A person must have a computer with Internet access.

p. 247 Vocabulary Builder
Students should complete the sentence with one of the following: the dining room, the morning room, the back parlour, or the stairs to the first floor.

p. 248 Vocabulary Builder
Patient is used as an adjective.

p. 248 Vocabulary Builder
Jump means "change quickly from one position or idea to another."

p. 249 Vocabulary Builder
The word *this* draws attention to the word *room*.

p. 249 Vocabulary Builder
Sample response: Dickens probably *made use of* the study as a quiet place for writing.

p. 249 Comprehension Builder
Sample response: Charles Dickens had a desk that he used for writing. He probably used this desk in all the homes in which he lived from 1839 to the end of his life.

p. 250 After You Read
Thinking About the Web Site
1. You would click Opening Hours for information about the museum's hours of operation.
2. Dickens's study is on the first floor.

Reading Skill
3. The Web site will provide detailed information about the Dickens Museum and offer a virtual tour.

4. The purpose of the Andalusia brochure is to provide information about Andalusia and Flannery O'Connor's experiences while living there.

from Jane Eyre
Charlotte Brontë

p. 251 Graphic Organizer
Sample response:
Assumption: Answers will vary. The author assumes that the teacher punishes Burns for no good reason.
Analysis: Answers will vary. The author may have had or witnessed teachers in similar institutions treat girls unfairly in this manner. The author may want me to believe that the teacher is acting out of bad intentions or a mean character.

p. 252 Note-taking Guide
Sample response:
Jane Eyre
Similarities: Jane is an orphan and a student at Lowood.
Differences: Jane is brooding, has a temper, and says that she will not accept unjust treatment patiently.
Helen Burns
Similarities: Helen is a student at Lowood, and she is intelligent and thoughtful.
Differences: Helen accepts unjust treatment and even finds fault with herself.

p. 253 Activate Prior Knowledge
Sample response:
Advantages
1. With all girls or all boys, fewer distractions would be present at school.
2. Living at school could help students concentrate on schoolwork.
Disadvantages
1. There would be less opportunity to meet a variety of people.
2. Students might become homesick.

p. 253 Literary Analysis
Students may circle "I felt ready to perish with cold" and "how small my portion seemed! I wish it had been doubled." Two important problems at Lowood appear to be the lack of adequate heating and insulation and the insufficient amount and poor quality of the food.

p. 254 Reading Strategy

Students should note that the passage reveals that Miss Scatcherd is unreasonably harsh and demanding of the students.

p. 254 Stop to Reflect

Students should note that Miss Smith is kind to Jane and does not appear to be critical of the girls, as is Miss Scatcherd.

p. 254 Reading Check

Sample response: Miss Scatcherd's treatment of Helen Burns is harsh and unfairly critical.

p. 255 Literary Analysis

Students should note that Jane's "unavailing and impotent anger" reinforces the sense that Burns's beating is malicious and unwarranted, which shows that Brontë feels that corporal punishment is cruel and unfair.

p. 255 Reading Strategy

Students may circle details such as the snack at play-hour, the hour of freedom, and the warm room. Sample response:
1. The gratefulness with which the girls receive the meager snack reveals how nearly starved they are throughout the day.
2. The freedom of one hour reveals the harshness of every other hour's being devoted to school or chores.
3. The temporary warmth of the room emphasizes the prevailing coldness of the school.

p. 256 Stop to Reflect

Some students may say that they agree with Helen's idea because they believe that each person has the inner qualities needed to endure under such circumstances. Other students may disagree because they do not believe that their experiences are guided by fate.

p. 256 Reading Check

Sample response: Helen accepts the beating, arguing that while Miss Scatcherd is severe and unaccepting of Helen's faults, she is not cruel. Jane refuses to accept the beating because she believes that it is cruel and disgraceful.

p. 257 Literary Analysis

Sample response: "'Miss Temple is full of goodness'"; "'it pains her to be severe.'" These traits suggest that this is the ideal behavior of teachers, and that Miss Scatcherd is, therefore, far from ideal.

p. 257 Stop to Reflect

Students should say that the passage reveals Helen's deep love and longing for her home.

p. 257 Reading Strategy

Students should say that Helen may identify with the martyred King Charles, who was killed unjustly. Students may infer that Helen felt that she was being punished unjustly at Lowood, although she does not admit those feelings to Jane.

p. 258 Stop to Reflect

Students should evaluate Jane's thoughts through their own personal experience.

p. 258 Reading Check

Helen advises Jane to forget Mrs. Reed's cruelty toward her.

p. 259 Stop to Reflect

Students should say that Helen is unlikely to attempt to correct societal injustices because Helen believes that all such wrongs will be righted after death.

p. 259 Reading Strategy

Students should say that Helen's behavior is in keeping with her beliefs, because she does not protest the injustice of the monitor's bullying.

p. 259 Reader's Response

Students may choose to agree with either Jane or Helen. Students should support their answers with details from the text and knowledge gained from their own experience.

p. 260 After You Read

1. Helen says that Miss Scatcherd is severe as well as neat, punctual, and particular. Helen says that Miss Scatcherd punishes Helen to teach her to correct her faults. Jane says that Miss Scatcherd is simply mean-spirited, cross, and cruel.

2. **Graphic Organizer**

Sample response:

Row 1: During that time in England, it was common to send orphaned children away to schools such as Lowood.

Row 2: Most people in England were Christians, and schools generally taught Christian beliefs.

Row 3: At that time, it was not unusual for teachers to punish students physically.

3. Sample response: The author wants you to believe that girls were not treated well and they had few options, that girls must take responsibility for themselves so as not burden their families, and that an education was very important for girls from poor families.

The Essential Question
Answers will vary. Sample response: Charlotte Brontë includes many details that depict the school as a place in which students are treated unfairly. Her inclusion of these details shows that she has a negative opinion of institutions that allow or promote cruelty toward children. As a popular novel, *Jane Eyre* may have helped to change the conditions at schools like Lowood by appealing to readers' sympathies.

"Dover Beach"
Matthew Arnold

"The Widow at Windsor"
Rudyard Kipling

"Recessional"
Rudyard Kipling

p. 261 Graphic Organizer
Sample response:
"Dover Beach"
Mood: sad, melancholy
How the Mood Relates to the Historical Period: The speaker's sadness and concern relate to the conflict and responsibility that come with maintaining an empire.

"The Widow at Windsor"
Mood: bitter, angry
How the Mood Relates to the Historical Period: The speaker is bitter and angry because the empire relies on the poor to support itself.

"Recessional"
Mood: cautious, critical
How the Mood Relates to the Historical Period: The speaker is worried that the British Empire is failing because people have grown too proud and too sure of their power.

p. 262 Note-taking Guide
Sample response:
Dover Beach: "the turbid ebb and flow / Of human misery"; "The Sea of Faith / Was once, too, at the full"

The Widow at Windsor: "Walk wide o' the Widow at Windsor / For 'alf o' Creation she owns"; "We've brought 'er the same with the sword an' the flame."

p. 263 Note-taking Guide
Sample response:
Stanza 1: England is powerful, but God is in control of England.
Stanza 2: Human accomplishments fade, but God's accomplishment is eternal.
Stanza 3: The power of England is fading like that of the ancient empire.
Stanza 4: The British have grown arrogant, forgetting to revere God.
Stanza 5: England has put trust in armies rather than in God.
Main Idea of Poem: Great power should be accompanied by humility, not by pride.

p. 264 After You Read
1. The mood is cautious and critical, warning people that they have become too proud and that the empire is failing.
2. **Graphic Organizer**
Sample response:
Image: "The eternal note of sadness"
Where It Appears: line 14
Mood It Evokes: loss, sadness
Image: "turbid ebb and flow / Of human misery"
Where It Appears: lines 17–18
Mood It Evokes: confusion, sense of futility
Image: "The Sea of Faith . . . Retreating"
Where It Appears: lines 21 and 26
Mood It Evokes: irrevocable loss of religious meaning
Image: "ignorant armies clash by night"
Where It Appears: line 37
Mood It Evokes: sense of foreboding
Theme of poem: Victorian culture is unable to give meaning to life, so humans are confused and driven by conflict.
3. The mood and theme in each poem indicate that the British Empire was declining and losing power, that people believed that the British Empire had many problems and challenges, and that the empire had not benefited all people.

The Essential Question
Answers will vary, but students should support their ideas with details from the poem.

"Remembrance"
Emily Brontë

"The Darkling Thrush"
Thomas Hardy

"Ah, Are You Digging on My Grave?"
Thomas Hardy

p. 265 Graphic Organizer
Sample response:
Stanza 2: Her thoughts are turning from her beloved.
Stanza 3: She had been faithful to the memory of her beloved for fifteen years.

p. 266 Note-taking Guide
Sample response:
"Remembrance"
Sadness: "All my life's bliss from thy dear life was given— / All my life's bliss is in the grave with thee."
Stanza: 5
Hope: "Then did I learn how existence could be cherished, / Strengthened and fed without the aid of joy; . . ."
Stanza: 6
"The Darkling Thrush"
Sadness: "The ancient pulse of germ and birth / Was shrunken hard and dry. . . ."
Stanza: 2
Hope: "In a full-hearted evensong / Of joy illimited; . . ."
Stanza: 3
"Ah, Are You Digging on My Grave?"
Sadness: "No tendance of her mound can loose / Her spirit from Death's gin."
Stanza: 2
Hope: "What feeling do we ever find / To equal among human kind / A dog's fidelity!"
Stanza: 5

p. 267 After You Read
1. **Graphic Organizer**
Remembrance
Number of Lines: First Stanza: 4; **Last Stanza:** 4
Rhyme Scheme: *abab*
Meter: varies

The Darkling Thrush
Number of Lines: First Stanza: 8; **Last Stanza:** 8
Rhyme Scheme: *ababcdcd*
Meter: ballad

"Ah, Are You Digging on My Grave?"
Number of Lines: First Stanza: 6; **Last Stanza:** 6
Rhyme Scheme: *abcccb*
Meter: 4-3-4-4-4-3
2. The irony is in the deceased woman's belief that someone is mourning her passing, when in reality all have put her from their minds; even her faithful dog visited her grave only to bury a bone, forgetting that the area was her "resting-place."
3. The speaker asks whether she has forgotten to love her dead beloved. Each stanza builds toward her realization that her feelings for the past are a danger for her.

The Essential Question
Answers will vary, but students should support their ideas with details from the poem.

"God's Grandeur"
Gerard Manley Hopkins

"Spring and Fall: To a Young Child"
Gerard Manley Hopkins

"To an Athlete Dying Young"
A. E. Housman

"When I Was One-and-Twenty"
A. E. Housman

p. 268 Graphic Organizer
Sample response:
"God's Grandeur"
Biographical Details: Hopkins became a Catholic priest in the Jesuit order. He also had a love of nature.
Details in Author's Work: "The world is charged with the grandeur of God"; "Generations have trod, have trod, have trod; / And all is seared with trade; bleared, smeared with toil"; "for all this, nature is never spent"
Author's Beliefs: No matter what people do, they can never obliterate God's grandeur in nature.

"Spring and Fall: To a Young Child"
Biographical Details: Hopkins had a love of nature and a strong religious faith.
Details in Author's Work: "Leáves, like the things of man"
Author's Beliefs: Death is part of the human condition, just as it is a part of nature.

"To an Athlete Dying Young"
Biographical Details: Housman suffered grief at a young age when his mothered died. His love was unrequited while at Oxford.
Details in Author's Work: "early though the laurel grows / It withers quicker than the rose."
Author's Beliefs: Disillusionment comes with age.

"When I Was One-and-Twenty"
Biographical Details: He despaired over an unrequited love while at Oxford.
Details in Author's Work: "Give . . . not your heart a way."
Author's Beliefs: Love can hurt, but Housman's mocking tone shows that he may find the pursuit of love worth the pain.

p. 269 Note-taking Guide
Sample response:
"God's Grandeur"
Beauty: "The world is charged with the grandeur of God."
Line: 1
Mortality: "Why do men then not now reck his rod?"
Line: 4
"Spring and Fall: To a Young Child"
Beauty: "Leáves, like the things of man, you / With your fresh thoughts care for, can you?"
Line: 3–4
Mortality: "Sórrow's spríngs áre the same."
Line: 11

p. 270 Note-taking Guide
Sample response:
"To an Athlete Dying Young"
Words/Phrases: "Smart lad, to slip betimes away . . ."
Line Number: 9

"When I was One-and-Twenty"
Words/Phrases: "Tis paid with sighs a plenty . . ."
Line Number: 13

p. 271 After You Read
1. Gĕnĕrátĭŏns hăve tród, hăve tród, hăve tród. Sample response: The line uses two trochees and three iambs, and counterpoint rhythm occurs when two opposing rhythms appear together.

2. Students should say that the trochaic lines interrupt the regular rhythm, introducing a kind of silence where the missing stresses are expected.
3. Hopkins was devoted to nature. Hopkins's love of nature is reflected in his poem "God's Grandeur." For example, Hopkins explains that although the land has been "bleared, smeared with toil" by humans, "nature is never spent."

The Essential Question
Answers will vary. Students may express the following views: Reading Hopkins takes more time and is more complicated. Reading Hopkins aloud sounds nice because of the rhythm. Housman is more straightforward but not as rhythmic or descriptive.

ANSWERS TO UNIT 6

Poetry of Yeats

p. 272 Graphic Organizer
Sample response:
"When You Are Old"
Symbols: Yeats had an unrequited love for Maud Gonne.
Yeats's Philosophy: Love hides his face.

"The Lake Isle of Innisfree"
Symbols: Yeats desired a Walden-like retreat.
Yeats's Philosophy: "And a small cabin build there, . . ."

"The Wild Swans at Coole"
Symbols: Yeats was interested in the passage of time.
Yeats's Philosophy: The swans' abrupt flight suggests that time is passing very rapidly.

"The Second Coming"
Symbols: Yeats was interested in the rise and fall of civilizations.
Yeats's Philosophy: "Mere anarchy is loosed upon the world, . . ."

"Sailing to Byzantium"
Symbols: Yeats was interested in the immortality of art.
Yeats's Philosophy: "Monuments of unaging intellect."

p. 273 Note-taking Guide
Sample response:
When You Are Old: Students should check "Aging" and "Loss."
The Lake Isle of Innisfree: Students should check "Change."
The Wild Swans at Coole: Students should check "Aging," "Loss," and "Change."
The Second Coming: Students should check "Change."
Sailing to Byzantium: Students should check "Aging" and "Loss."

p. 274 After You Read
1. Students may agree that "things fall apart" because they believe that modern society is more violent. Other students may disagree and say that with modern laws and technology, the world is becoming more organized and coherent.
2. **Graphic Organizer**
Sample response:
Symbol: swans

Personal/Traditional: both
Vivid/Flat in Effect: vivid
Rich/Poor in Associations: rich
Easy/Hard to Interpret: easy
Symbol: Sphinx
Personal/Traditional: traditional
Vivid/Flat in Effect: flat
Rich/Poor in Associations: rich
Easy/Hard to Interpret: hard
3. Answers will vary. The symbol of the falcon / falconer represents a breakdown in society. The "blood-dimmed tide" is the rise of violence and war. A "rough beast" is a new era.

The Essential Question
Answers will vary, but students should support their answers with details from the poems.

Poetry of Eliot

p. 275 Graphic Organizer
Sample response:
Answers will vary depending on which poem students choose. Sample answers:
Modernist Elements: Repeated images of death, emptiness, brokenness of mind and body; "Mistah Kurtz—he dead" is from Conrad's *Heart of Darkness*; "Stuffed men" could refer to "stuffed shirts," which is often a way of referring to politicians.
Information About Historical Period: The rise of industrialization; post-World War I era and the Treaty of Versailles
Conclusion: The progress of the time, and the apparent blindness of those making the decisions (the hollow men, the stuffed men) will ultimately lead to the destruction of the world.

p. 276 Note-taking Guide
Sample response:
Segment: I
Description of Scene: a cold evening at a smoggy, industrial city block
Despair: ✔
Segment: II
Description of Scene: people awakening to old morning air and beginning their dull routines
Despair: ✔
Segment: III
Description of Scene: a miserable, dream-filled night
Despair: ✔

Segment: IV
Description of Scene: repetition of daily activities, but with a small amount of hope that the cycle will be broken
Hopefulness: ✔

p. 277 Note-taking Guide
Sample response:
Character: Magnus
Goal: to find the infant Jesus
Difficulties Encountered: weather; uncooperative camels; lack of shelter; unfriendly towns
Result: found the infant Jesus
Resolution Or Lack of Resolution: The speaker could not determine whether he had witnessed birth or death.
Years Later, Continuing Problems: Because the speaker has a new spiritual consciousness, he is uneasy with the traditional beliefs of his people.

p. 278 Activate Prior Knowledge
Students may describe a trip to see relatives or friends over the holidays, a trip to a historic location, or a trip to attend an important sports event.

p. 278 Literary Analysis
Students should circle a long line, such as "And the night-fires going out, and the lack of shelters," and a short line, such as "The very dead of winter."

p. 278 Stop to Reflect
Students may note that the speaker's attitude is surprisingly self-concerned and irate.

p. 279 Literary Analysis
Sample response: Instead of giving a detailed description of the birth he traveled so long to witness, the speaker merely says that he found "the place" and that "it was (you may say) satisfactory." This modernist "less is more" understatement forces the reader to fill in the gaps of the speaker's experience with his or her own imagination.

p. 279 Reading Strategy
Sample response: The speaker reveals despair at being caught between old traditions and new beliefs.

p. 279 Reading Check
Students may cite winter weather, uncooperative camels, lack of shelter, unfriendly towns,

lack of information, expenses, and traveling at night as hardships.

p. 279 Reader's Response
Students may describe the difficulty of moving to a new neighborhood, starting a job, or meeting new people.

p. 279 Thinking About the Skill
Answers will vary. Sample response: it is interesting to see how a writer makes candid social criticisms and observations in a written work, such as a poem. It is also helpful to see ideas introduced in a different way. It is helpful to see that some social critiques are relevant to more than one historical period.

p. 280 Note-taking Guide
Sample response:
Part I: "hollow men"; "dried voices"; "shape without form"
Part II: "death's dream kingdom"; "fading star"; "rat's coat"
Part III: "cactus land"; "supplication of a dead man's hand"; "prayers to broken stone"
Part IV: "valley of dying stars"; "hollow valley" "death's twilight kingdom"
Part V: "prickly pear"; "Falls the Shadow"; "Not with a bang but a whimper"

p. 281 After You Read
1. The cycle of time is one day, from evening through the night to morning and back to evening.
2. Students should note that the journey itself is described in detail, but the details of the birth are glossed over.
3. Sample response: Images include "burnt-out ends of smoky days"; "Of withered leaves about your feet / And newspapers from vacant lots"; and "With the other masquerades / That time resumes." All three images depict waste, decay, or futility.
4. **Graphic Organizer**
Sample response:
Passage: "And voices are / In the wind's singing / More distant and more solemn / Than a fading star."
Modernist Characteristics: fragmented
Relation to Historical Background: yes

The Essential Question
Answers will vary, but students should support opinions with details from the poems.

"In Memory of W. B. Yeats"
W. H. Auden

"Musée des Beaux Arts"
W. H. Auden

"Carrick Revisited"
Louis MacNeice

"Not Palaces"
Stephen Spender

p. 282 Graphic Organizer
Sample response:
Allegory
In Memory of W. B. Yeats: Auden uses allegory to tell that art rises above life and survives because it is, not because it changes the world.
Musée des Beaux Arts: Auden uses allegory to show that calamity or disaster for one person happens during the everyday activities of others.
Pastoral
Carrick Revisited: Through his pastoral, MacNeice presents a message that an artist's experiences are part of his or her art.
Not Palaces: This pastoral expresses hope that poetry can bring change.

p. 283 Note-taking Guide
Sample Response:
In Memory of W. B. Yeats
Topic/Inspiration: the death of W. B. Yeats
Theme: the power of poetry to teach joy in the human condition

Musée des Beaux Arts
Topic/Inspiration: the death of Icarus
Theme: It is the nature of life and of suffering that the world goes on, even while individuals suffer.

Carrick Revisited
Topic/Inspiration: the speaker's visit to his childhood home
Theme: the irrefutable influence of childhood experience on human character

Not Palaces
Topic/Inspiration: the function of poetry in modern life
Theme: the rejection of old artistic attitudes in favor of art that produces social change

p. 284 After You Read
1. Answers will vary. Sample response: Poetry has little to do with the personal lives or polit-ical beliefs of poets. Good poetry is immortal and tells of humanity and its limitations.
2. **Graphic Organizer**
Sample response:
Poem: In Memory of W. B. Yeats:
Subgenre: allegory
Example or Element of Subgenre: In a short, symbolic "story," lines 36–41 tell how art rises above life
Poem: Musée des Beaux Arts:
Subgenre: allegory
Example or Element of Subgenre:
Lines 14–21 create a specific incident that is symbolic of disaster and suffering in general. It encapsulates the theme that "people suffer, yet the world moves on."
Poem: Carrick Revisited:
Subgenre: pastoral
Example or Element of Subgenre: Lines 1–5 tell about the importance of a childhood home.
Poem: Not Palaces:
Subgenre: pastoral
Example or Element of Subgenre: The last few lines celebrate an idealized future in the same way that a pastoral celebrates idealized rural settings.
3. One poem celebrates an idealized place and the other poem celebrates an idealized future. "Carrick Revisited" celebrates the influence of a place in which the speaker lived. "Not palaces" celebrates the potential of poetry.

The Essential Question
Answers will vary, but students should sup-port answers with details from the poem.

"The Lady in the Looking Glass:
A Reflection"
Virginia Woolffrom

from **Mrs. Dalloway**
Virginia Woolf

from **A Room of One's Own:**
from **Shakespeare's Sister**
Virginia Woolf

p. 285 Graphic Organizer
Sample response:
Answers will vary, depending on further details and questions.
Detail: "Such fools we are, she thought, crossing Victoria Street."

Question: Why does she think that everyone is a fool?
Answer: "She" is Mrs. Dalloway, and "him" is Scrope Pervis, who is observing her on the street. She doesn't understand why people love living in London."

p. 286 Note-taking Guide
Sample response:
How she appears throughout the story: elegant, well-known and respected, mysterious and exciting
How she appears at the end of the story: old, empty, and friendless

p. 287 Note-taking Guide
Sample response:
Character: Clarissa Dalloway
What does she want? to buy flowers for her party
Why does she want this? so that she can throw a successful party and gain social status
What others think about her: She has "a touch of bird about her"; she is vivacious and charming.
What she thinks about herself: She is socially-conscious, but mostly concerned with her party; she loves the comfort of her life.
Character: Judith
What does she want? to act
Why does she want this? She likes theater.
What others think about her: They laugh; no woman can be an actor, she is told.
What she thinks about herself: The essay implies that she is skilled and hard-working.

p. 288 After You Read
1. The looking glass first provides a view of Isabella through her possessions; when Isabella herself appears in the mirror, it provides a real view of the emptiness of Isabella's life.
2. **Graphic Organizer**
Sample response:
Similar/Different: Both narrators have many impressions. The narrator in "The Lady in the Looking Glass: A Reflection" is limited by her associations, while the narrator in "Mrs. Dalloway" has no limitations.
Mrs. Dalloway: omniscient narrator tells story
3. Answers will vary. Possible questions: Who is Mrs. Dalloway? Who is Peter Walsh? What is Mrs. Dalloway doing?

The Essential Question
Answers will vary, but students should support answers with details from the story.

"The Lagoon"
Joseph Conrad

"Araby"
James Joyce

p. 289 Graphic Organizer
Sample response:
The Lagoon
Effect: The Rajah's men capture and kill Arsat's brother.

Araby
Cause: The narrator waits for his uncle to get home to give him money for the bazaar.

p. 290 Note-taking Guide
Sample response:
Beginning Action: Arsat falls in love with Diamelen; Arsat, his brother, and Diamelen run away from the Malaysian ruler.
Climax Action: Arsat leaves his brother to die in order to save his and Diamelen's lives.
Ending Action: Diamelen dies, and Arsat goes back to face his pursuers.

p. 291 Note-taking Guide
Sample response:
Exposition: The young narrator describes the street on which he lives and then describes his friend Mangan's older sister. The narrator daydreams about Mangan's sister and follows her to school, but he never speaks to her.
Rising Action: Mangan's sister speaks to the narrator unexpectedly; the narrator promises to bring her something from *Araby* if he goes. He continues to daydream about her so much that his schoolwork suffers. On the day of the bazaar, the narrator's uncle does not arrive home and give him money until past nine o'clock; the narrator finally arrives at the bazaar as it is closing. A young woman laughing with two young men asks whether the narrator wants to buy something; the narrator unexpectedly declines.
Climax: The narrator suddenly realizes that he has been very foolish.
Falling Action: The narrator departs from the dark and deserted hall.
Resolution: The narrator is stricken by grief and anger at his vanity and foolishness.

p. 292 Activate Prior Knowledge
Students may describe their anticipation of an important social, family, or athletic event.

p. 292 Stop to Reflect
Students should indicate that the last sentence refers to the respectability of the street rather than its wealth or poverty.

p. 293 Reading Strategy
He watches through a window to see her leave in the morning. Then, he follows her so that he can be close to her and look at her.

p. 293 Stop to Reflect
Some students may say that the narrator's daydreams are positive because of their imaginative and motivational qualities. Other students may say that the narrator's daydreams are harmful because they are unrealistic and exaggerated. Still other students may say that the daydreams are neither positive nor harmful, but that they are typical for a boy of this age.

p. 293 Stop to Reflect
The comparison reveals how deeply affected the narrator is by Mangan's sister.

p. 294 Reading Check
The narrator hears about Araby from Mangan's sister.

p. 294 Reading Strategy
He is thinking about Mangan's sister and his upcoming visit to Araby.

p. 294 Stop to Reflect
Sample response: Araby may seem special and desirable to the narrator because it sounds exotic and because it is the first thing that Mangan's sister speaks to him about.

p. 295 Reading Strategy
He is angry because his uncle is late coming home and because Mrs. Mercer may have annoyed him, too.

p. 295 Stop to Reflect
Sample response: The narrator's uncle is not fully aware of the importance the narrator places on the bazaar as he arrives home very late and forgets to give the narrator money. Both the uncle and aunt suggest that it is too late to go to the bazaar, but the aunt is more sympathetic because she urges the uncle to give the narrator money even though it may be too late.

p. 296 Literary Analysis
Sample response: If the narrator has an epiphany, it will probably be related to the disappointment he feels upon his arrival at the dark and empty hall.

p. 296 Reading Check
Sample response: The narrator finds a large, darkened hall with a gallery inside. Most of the stalls are closed. He sees a young woman laughing with two young men and two other men in front of a curtain, counting coins.

p. 296 Reading Strategy
He is shocked by what he sees. Araby seems nothing like what he had imagined. This realization probably has distracted him from his purpose.

p. 297 Literary Analysis
Sample response:
1. The narrator may think that he has been striving for foolish things because he placed much too high a value on Mangan's sister, who did not think of him at all; he may also think that his romanticizing of Mangan's sister and the bazaar gave him unrealistic expectations.
2. The narrator has feelings of anger and grief.

p. 297 Literary Analysis
Students should complete the sentence with "disguises" or another like term.

p. 297 Reader's Response
Some students may say that the narrator is not being too hard on himself because the anger and disappointment that accompanied his realization are just responses to his unrealistic expectations. Other students may say that the narrator is being too hard on himself because they believe that such romantic ideals are natural in young people.

p. 297 Thinking About the Skill
Answers will vary. Sample response: Students may say that closely following the events and their causes and effects helped them focus on the story. Students may say that closely studying causes and effects helped them better understand the narrator.

p. 298 After You Read

1. Sample response: Readers would not know the antagonism the locals felt or the mystery that surrounds Arsat.

2. Sample response: The narrator feels the vacancy of the bazaar—the mundane conversation of the stall keepers, the shoddy products being offered, and the sense that he has overpaid and expected too much from "Araby" all add to the sinking feeling that he has.

3. **Graphic Organizer**

Sample response:

Cause: Arsat's wife becomes very sick, and Tuan cannot help her.

Effect: Arsat decides to go back and face the people who captured and killed his brother.

The Essential Question

Answers will vary, but students should support answers with details from the story.

"The Rocking-Horse Winner"
D. H. Lawrence

"A Shocking Accident"
Graham Greene

p. 299 Graphic Organizer

Sample response:

The Rocking-Horse Winner

Background Knowledge: Some students may say that they feel as though they need more money. Consequently, they may find ways to get more money.

Details from Text: Many references to the need for money at the beginning of the story seem to be significant. The mother claims that the family is "poor" because the "father has no luck."

Predictions: Someone in the family will be lucky and win money.

Confirm Predictions: Paul wins money betting on horses.

A Shocking Accident

Background Knowledge: Students may say that they have been in situations that did not end as badly as they thought they might.

Details from Text: The story tells how Jerome has suffered over the years by telling this story. Sally's unpredictable response would make for a good surprise ending.

Predictions: Sally's reaction to Jerome's story will be different than other people's reactions.

Confirm Predictions: Sally reacts with shock at such a terrible event.

p. 300 Note-taking Guide

Sample response:

Box 3: Paul decides that he is lucky.

Box 4: Uncle Oscar discovers that Paul is betting on horses and winning.

Box 5: Paul secretly gives his mother five thousand pounds.

Box 6: Paul's "lucky" ability to know the winning horse begins to fade.

Box 7: Paul rides his rocking horse furiously until he knows the name of the next winner, becoming violently ill.

Box 8: Paul wins seventy thousand pounds for his mother.

Box 9: Paul dies.

p. 301 Note-taking Guide

Sample response:

1. **How does Jerome feel about his father?** Jerome loves his father deeply.

2. **How does his father die?** A pig fell on him from a balcony.

3. **How do people react to the story?** People laugh at the story.

4. **Why is he afraid to tell Sally about how his father died?** Jerome is afraid that Sally will laugh.

5. **How does she react?** Sally is horrified, and does not laugh.

6. **How does her reaction make Jerome feel?** Jerome feels joyful.

p. 302 After You Read

1. **Graphic Organizer**

Sample response:

Symbolic Meanings: Effort to satisfy a need that cannot be satisfied

Passages That Illustrate: "But even for the Lincoln he didn't 'know,' and he lost fifty pounds. He became wild-eyed and strange, as if something were going to explode in him."

Links to Overall Theme: the destructive nature of greed

Symbolic Meanings: Frightening power of desire and wishes

Passages That Illustrate: "His eyes blazed at her for one strange and senseless second, as he ceased urging his wooden horse. Then he fell with a crash to the ground . . ."

Links to Overall Theme: Expending such effort to gain money takes away the enjoyment of life.

2. Both stories reveal, through the third-person viewpoint, the thoughts and feelings of more than one character.

3. Answers will vary, but students should list the information they used to make a prediction about one of the selections. Then, they should explain whether their predictions were accurate.

The Essential Question

Answers will vary, but students should support answers with details from the story.

"The Soldier"
Rupert Brooke

"Wirers"
Siegfried Sassoon

"Anthem for Doomed Youth"
Wilfred Owen

p. 303 Graphic Organizer

Sample response:

Passage: The Soldier

Relevant Details: The soldier is "blest" by English sun and full of "English air." When the soldier dies, the English dust of his body will enrich the foreign soil.

Essential Message: Because the soldier is English, the dust of his body transforms foreign ground to English soil. The speaker's reverence for English soil sets a tone of loyalty to and love for England.

Passage: Wirers

Relevant Details: The speaker's word choice and tone are blunt and jarring. The death of "Young Hughes" is glossed over by the cynicism of the narrator.

Essential Message: The tone of the poem is angry and cynical. The narrator seems to believe that soldiers' lives are trivialized and uselessly sacrificed.

Passage: Anthem for Doomed Youth

Relevant Details: Soldiers are described as cattle, and their deaths are anonymous. They do not have the "mockeries" of church bells when they die.

Essential Message: The narrator suggests that it is inappropriate to hold elaborate funerals for fallen soldiers. The soldier were sent to war to "die as cattle"; to ceremoniously honor

and mourn their death is both futile and hypocritical.

p. 304 Note-taking Guide

Sample response:

The Soldier

Central Image/Idea: A soldier's life, or dead body, is equated with England in a foreign soil.

Wirers

Central Image/Idea: A boy's life is sacrificed to mend the fence on the war front.

Anthem for Doomed Youth

Central Image/Idea: A young soldier's life can never be mourned enough.

p. 305 After You Read

1. Sample response: "Wirers" vividly conveys the horrors of war through the eyes of a soldier, and "Anthem for Doomed Youth" conveys the horrors of war by focusing on the unceremonial deaths of the soldiers; both poems are effective in communicating the horrors of war.

2. **Graphic Organizer**

Sample response:

Passage, poem: "The Soldier"

Word Choice: gentleness, peace, heaven

Images: field, England, rich earth, flowers, rivers, sun

Tone: patriotic, touching, sentimental

3. Sample response: The "holy glimmers of good-byes," "pallor of girls' brows," "tenderness of patient minds," and "drawing-down of blinds" help underscore the message that no public acknowledgement equals the loss the death of the soldiers represents.

The Essential Question

Answers will vary, but students should support answers with details from the poem.

"The Demon Lover"
Elizabeth Bowen

p. 306 Graphic Organizer

Sample response:

Literary Work: Demon Lover

Atmosphere: mysterious

Weapons: her mind; rationalization

Tactics: find a taxi and have the driver help her

Main Goal: to avoid "the hour arranged"

End Result: She is taken away in a taxi, presumably by her ex-fiancé.

Primary Source: Wartime Speech
Atmosphere: grim
Weapons: bombers, guns, and tanks
Tactics: retaliate, strengthen the front in France, and increase industrial output
Main Goal: win the war
End Result: He urges people to prepare for upcoming conflicts.

p. 307 Note-taking Guide
Sample response:
Characters: Mrs. Drover
Setting: It is late afternoon in humid London; Mrs. Drover goes to retrieve a few things from her shut-up London home.
Problem: Mrs. Drover discovers a letter addressed to her from her presumed-dead fiancé of many years ago.
Event 1: Mrs. Drover reads the letter.
Event 2: Mrs. Drover remembers her old fiancé's promise and when they parted.
Event 3: Mrs. Drover recalls when she was given the news of her old fiancé's presumed death.
Event 4: Mrs. Drover feels as though she is being watched as she leaves the house.
Event 5: Mrs. Drover walks to the thorough-fare to get a taxi.
Event 6: Mrs. Drover discovers that the taxi driver is her old fiancé.
Conclusion: Mrs. Drover is trapped within the taxi as it drives off into the deserted streets.

p. 308 After You Read
1. Mrs. Drover is upset because it appears to be from her old fiancé, whom she thought was dead; the letter contains an eerie reminder of a past promise.
2. Sample response: The letter and the memory of the fiancé are intrusions from the past; that the letter arrived from a person thought to be dead, and without the help of the Post Office, brings a supernatural feel to the story.
3. **Graphic Organizer**
Sample response:
Ambiguity: "no human eye watched" "Dead air came out to meet her . . ."
What Does it Reveal? These passages hint at the watchful presence of the dead fiancé.

The Essential Question
Answers will vary, but students should support answers with details from the story.

"Vergissmeinicht"
Keith Douglas

"Postscript: For Gweno"
Alun Lewis

"Naming of Parts"
Henry Reed

p. 309 Graphic Organizer
Sample response:
"Vergissmeinicht"
Images of Love or Tenderness: "dishonored picture of his girl," "she would weep to see," "lover and killer are mingled";
Images of War or Violence: "nightmare ground" "frowning barrel of his gun" "entry of a demon" "burst stomach like a cave"

"Postscript: For Gweno"
Images of Love or Tenderness: "you abide, a singing riv within my dreaming side";
Images of War or Violence: "mad tormented valley," "blood and hunger rally," "Death the wild beast"

"Naming of Parts"
Images of Love or Tenderness: "Japonica glistens like coral," "blossoms are fragile and motionless," "early bees assaulting and fumbling";
Images of War or Violence: The poem contains no concrete images of war or violence; however, it describes the process of learning to use a killing tool.

p. 310 Note-taking Guide
Sample response:
"Vergissmeinicht"
Speaker: a soldier who has survived a bloody battle
What the Speaker Is Experiencing: The soldier returns to the scene of the battle and sees the corpse of an enemy soldier who had shot at him.
How the Speaker Feels: The speaker feels detached, "almost with content," but he recognizes the pain the dead soldier's lover will feel.

"Postscript: For Gweno"
Speaker: a soldier who is writing to his lover
What the Speaker Is Experiencing: The soldier is facing battle.
How the Speaker Feels: The soldier understands that he may die.

"Naming of Parts"

Speaker: a soldier in basic training

What the Speaker Is Experiencing: He is learning the various parts of his gun and how to use them.

How the Speaker Feels: The speaker is distracted by the signs of spring all around him.

p. 311 After You Read

1. Answers may vary. Students may infer that the speaker is bored, that he is not interested in learning about his gun, or that he is sensitive and enjoys nature.

2. **Graphic Organizer**

Sample response:

"Vergissmeinicht" Death and killing "dishonor" love, causing lovers "mortal hurt." War shows that a person can be both a "lover and killer."

"Postscript: For Gweno" Even through war's brutality and possible death, love will endure.

"Naming of Parts" Despite the dull training required when preparing to kill, the speaker's sensitive, tender nature still exists.

3. These experiences are universal—most people understand the consequences of warfare and have experienced love. The poets want to show that, even in the violence of war, love still exists.

The Essential Question

Answers will vary, but students should support answers with details from the poems.

"Shooting an Elephant"
George Orwell

"No Witchcraft for Sale"
Doris Lessing

p. 312 Graphic Organizer

Sample response:

Shooting an Elephant

Aspect of Theme: Cultural Conflict: The Burmese expect Orwell to kill an elephant, but Orwell does not want to do it.

Source of Conflict: The Burmese follow Orwell as he tracks the elephant so that they can watch him kill it.

Details of Conflict: The elephant went wild and killed a man. The Burmese have a law that says that a mad elephant must be killed.

Result of Conflict: Orwell kills the elephant.

No Witchcraft for Sale

Aspect of Theme: Cultural Conflict: Gideon does not want to reveal the medical secrets of his people to the Farquars.

Source of Conflict: A scientists asks the Farquars to reveal how Gideon saved their son from blindness.

Details of Conflict: A snake spits into Teddy's eyes, which could lead to blindness. Gideon uses the root of a plant to cure Teddy.

Result of Conflict: Gideon reveals which plant he used to cure Teddy.

p. 313 Note-taking Guide

Sample response:

Where it takes place: Moulmein, in Lower Burma

The problems Orwell faces: Orwell must kill an elephant that has temporarily gone wild and killed a Burmese man.

The actions he takes: Orwell kills the elephant with two thousand Burmese looking on.

His feelings and thoughts: Orwell does not want to kill the elephant because it is no longer necessary, but he has to kill the elephant in order to avoid looking like a fool to the Burmese. He also realizes that the British Imperialists are actually at the mercy of the colonized because the British can only pretend to be in control.

p. 314 Activate Prior Knowledge

Students may describe an elephant that they saw at a zoo or on television. Students should provide realistic descriptions of the elephant's physical characteristics.

p. 314 Literary Analysis

The term "important" usually indicates that a person is respected. Orwell's use of the term is ironic because his importance arose from the fact that he was hated by the Burmese.

p. 314 Reading Check

The "dirty work" Orwell refers to includes the British practices of keeping prisoners in "stinking cages of the lockups" and flogging men with bamboo.

p. 315 Reading Strategy

It shows Orwell's hatred for both the British policies and the Burmese.

p. 315 Literary Analysis

1. Orwell rightfully condemns the British for forcing their rule upon a powerless people, but instead of voicing compassion for the Burmese in his next statement as one expects, he remarks that it would be the "greatest joy" to kill a Burmese priest. It is the juxtaposition of these opposing feelings that results in irony.

2. The tone of the follow-up remark is brutal, which, contrasted with the compassion of the first statement, results in further irony.

p. 315 Stop to Reflect

Sample response: Orwell will find the elephant running mad through the rice fields, trampling the crop and trumpeting loudly.

p. 316 Reading Strategy

Students should say that Orwell appears to be exasperated by the perpetual uncooperativeness of the Burmese. His exasperation shows his impatience with what he thinks is poor communication among villagers and how difficult it is to gather information.

p. 316 Reading Check

Orwell discovers the body of a Burmese man who had just been killed by the elephant.

p. 317 Literary Analysis

Sample response:

1. Yes, one would expect people to be interested if an elephant had destroyed their homes.

2. The Burmese show interest when they think that Orwell is going to kill the elephant.

3. The response is ironic because the Burmese are placing the greatest importance on watching the elephant be shot, when in reality the more important matter is the destruction of their homes.

p. 317 Literary Analysis

Sample response: After seeing how the elephant destroyed people's huts and trampled a Burmese man to death, the image of the same elephant's peaceful behavior in the rice field is unexpected and ironic.

p. 317 Stop to Reflect

Students may suggest that the pressure of a great crowd will influence Orwell's behavior because he needs to appear as though he is in control of the situation if he is to maintain the semblance of authority.

p. 318 Literary Analysis

Sample response: Orwell looks like a "white man with is gun" leading a crowd of Burmese, but in reality he is controlled by the Burmese.

p. 318 Stop to Reflect

Sample response: Orwell realizes that although Imperialist Britain appears to be in control of the colonized countries, it is the colonizers who had lost their freedom because they had to continually act in a manner that impressed the colonized if they were to maintain the appearance of control. This resulted in the colonizers having to conform their behavior to the expectations of the colonized people.

p. 318 Reading Check

Orwell does not want to kill the elephant because its wildness appears to have worn off and because the elephant is very valuable.

p. 319 Literary Analysis

The fact that Orwell is more concerned with being laughed at than killed is ironic because in reality, death is a much more important matter than is being the object of laughter. Orwell sees no need to kill the elephant, but the villagers want him to kill it. Orwell must do something that he does not want to do in order to maintain his authority.

p. 319 Stop to Reflect

Sample response: "He looked suddenly stricken, shrunken, immensely old" conveys a very vivid emotional sense of the bullet's impact on the elephant. "An enormous senility seemed to have settled upon him" describes a sudden and rapid aging of the elephant's mind and body, conveying a strong sense of approaching death.

p. 320 Stop to Reflect

Some students may say that the essay would have been better if Orwell had not gone into such detail about the elephant's death because they find the physical details of the death distasteful. Other students may say that the essay would have been worse if the details had been omitted because they appreciate the realistic and powerful description of the elephant's physical decline.

p. 320 Literary Analysis

Sample response: Orwell sees this scene differently from the way the villagers do. The villagers are enthusiastic and see an opportunity to take what they can from the dead elephant. Orwell sees this as a failure—a failure to do the right thing for the sake of his image and for the British Empire.

p. 320 Reading Check

Sample response: Orwell shoots the elephant five times with the elephant rifle but does not succeed in killing the elephant because he did not aim correctly. Orwell continues to shoot the elephant with his smaller rifle, but eventually he leaves the elephant to die on its own.

p. 321 Literary Analysis

Sample response:
1. The reason the "younger men" provide is ironic because they value the life of an animal over the life of a human.
2. The irony reveals the arrogant and insensitive attitudes of the British colonizers toward the colonized Burmese.

p. 321 Reader's Response

Some students may say that they would not have shot the elephant because it was no longer mad and held a high value; they may also say that they would not have killed it because it would be wrong to give in to the pressure of the Burmese crowd. Other students may say that they would have killed the elephant because it may still have been dangerous; they may also say that it was necessary to maintain the appearance of control over the situation and over the Burmese.

p. 321 Thinking About the Skill

Students should say that breaking down specific examples of irony from the text helped them better understand irony as a literary device.

p. 322 Note-taking Guide

Sample response:
Event: Teddy is born.
Detail: Gideon and the servants are pleased for the Farquars.
Event: Teddy is given a scooter.
Detail: Teddy frightens Gideon's young son.
Event: A tree snake spits in Teddy's eyes.
Detail: Gideon heals Teddy with an antidote an unknown plant.
Event: The Farquars want Gideon to show a scientist the plant.
Detail: Gideon is angry and misleads them all.

Event: The relationship between the Farquars and Gideon heals.
Detail: They joke about the incident.

p. 323 Activate Prior Knowledge

Some students may agree that there are probably undiscovered plants with medicinal properties; other students may not believe that there are plants with unknown medicinal value. Students should provide evidence from recent books, articles, or documentaries to support their choice.

p. 323 Stop to Reflect

Students should circle "soft gold tufts." Sample response: Gideon may be fascinated by Teddy's blond hair because it is so unlike the black hair of Africans.

p. 323 Reading Check

Gideon and the Farquars have a close relationship; it is as though they are good friends.

p. 324 Reading Strategy

Both feature white Europeans who have authority over local people.

p. 324 Literary Analysis

Students should point out that Teddy's remark to Gideon is defiant and assumes superiority over Gideon and his son. It also indicates that Teddy is already being influenced by the values of colonial white culture, which separates him from Gideon.

p. 324 Reading Check

Teddy offers Gideon an orange.

p. 325 Literary Analysis

Students should circle "Gideon would not let his flesh touch the flesh of the white child" and "it was in the way a white man uses toward a servant, expecting to be obeyed."

p. 325 Reading check

Gideon goes to get a medicinal plant.

p. 326 Stop to Reflect

Students should say Gideon chews the root because it needed to be in dissolved form in order to be effective, and that the concoction must be directly applied to Teddy's eyes in order for it to work.

p. 326 Literary Analysis

Sample response: White Europeans seem to believe that the antidotes found in medicinal plants should be made available to everyone in the form of a modern drug. By contrast, Africans are reluctant to share their knowledge of healing and native plants with the Europeans, possibly because they believe that it is a sacred knowledge that should be passed from generation to generation among their own people rather used for mass production and profit by the Europeans.

p. 326 Reading Check
Gideon saves Teddy from blindness by chewing the root of a medicinal plant and then spitting the solution into Teddy's eyes.

p. 327 Literary Analysis
Students may circle "they were kind, simple people, who liked to think of something good coming about because of them. But when the scientist began talking of the money that might result, their manner showed discomfort." Students may also circle "Their feelings over the miracle (that was how they thought of it) were so strong and deep and religious, that is was distasteful to them to think of money. The scientist, seeing their faces, went back to his first point, which was the advancement of humanity." Both selections demonstrate a conflict within the white culture over the cure as a means of financial gain and as the means of healing for its own sake.

p. 327 Literary Analysis
Students may say that Gideon considers knowledge of the root's curative powers to be sacred and a gift, whereas the scientist and the Farquars appear to want to profit from making that knowledge available to everyone.

p. 328 Stop to Reflect
Some students may believe that Gideon is unreasonable because he is withholding valuable information. Other students may believe that Gideon is not being unreasonable because he wants only to preserve the customs and beliefs of his culture.

p. 328 Reading Check
Sample response:
1. Gideon says he cannot remember which root it is.
2. Gideon says that the root does not exist.
3. Gideon says that it was not the root but his spit that healed Teddy's eyes.

p. 329 Stop to Reflect
Some students may say that Gideon is going to lead the scientist and the Farquars to the root because he is tired of being bothered and appears to have given in. Other students may say that Gideon is not going to lead them to the root because he does not believe that the scientist and the Farquars should know of it.

p. 329 Literary Analysis
Students should say that the scientist's humor masks his disbelief in the healing power of the flowers Gideon gave him, pointing out that the scientist had little faith in such reports of healing plants. Gideon's impoliteness indicates his displeasure with the Farquars rather than his disrespect for modern science.

p. 329 Literary Analysis
Gideon is actually a better doctor; he knows what plant to use for a specific ailment, whereas the "white man's doctor" does not know.

p. 330 Literary Analysis
Some students may say that the conflict is completely resolved because the relationship between Gideon and Teddy seems to be completely healed. Other students may say that the conflict has not been resolved, pointing out that Gideon's laughter was "polite" and that he looked at Teddy with sadness.

p. 330 Reading Check
Gideon first laughs hard, but then he looks "sadly" at Teddy and says "'Ah, Little Yellow Head, how you have grown! Soon you will be grown up with a farm of your own . . .'"

p. 330 Reader's Response
Sample response: No; cultural differences like those between Gideon and the Farquars, which are based on the values of white colonialism, are too deeply rooted to be resolved so easily.

p. 330 Thinking About the Skill
Sample response: Yes; this story enables the reader to better understand such experiences by giving an in-depth look at how the conflict affects both sides.

p. 331 After You Read
1. Orwell's feeling is ironic because in reality, Orwell enforces British rule over the Burmese.

2. Graphic Organizer
Sample response:
Farquars' Values: The Farquars believe that white people are superior.
Incident: Teddy frightens Gideon's son.
Gideon's Values: Gideon is accepting of Teddy's estrangement.
Farquars' Values: The Farquars cannot control the outcome.
Incident: A snake spits in Teddy's eyes.
Gideon's Values: Gideon immediately finds the correct antidote.
Farquars' Values: The Farquars believe that the curative powers of the root should be available to everyone.
Incident: The Farquars want Gideon to find the root.
Gideon's Values: Gideon believes that the knowledge of the root is sacred.
3. Sample response: An aspect of the theme in both stories is cultural conflict. Cultural conflict in "Shooting an Elephant" arises when Orwell shoots an elephant because the Burmese expect him to do so. In "No Witchcraft for Sale," cultural conflict arises when the Farquars ask Gideon to reveal the plant he used to cure Teddy.

The Essential Question
Answers will vary, but students should support answers with details from the story.

"The Train from Rhodesia"
Nadine Gordimer

"B. Wordsworth"
V. S. Naipaul

p. 332 Graphic Organizer
Sample response:
Effects on Setting, Character, or Conflict:
2. The artist chases the train to make a sale.
3. The man treats the artist poorly.

p. 333 Note-taking Guide
Sample response:
Setting (Place): a train
Details: The train pulls into a station crowded with natives selling carved wood animals.
Characters: a young woman, a man, and a native
Details: The young woman and man are newly married; the native is trying to sell his carvings.

Problems: The young woman wants to buy a carved lion but decides that it is too expensive.
Details: The husband buys the lion at a greatly reduced price, but the young woman is unexpectedly angry with him.

p. 334 Note-taking Guide
Sample response:
What character says: B. Wordsworth says that he is writing a great poem, one line per month. He says that the boy is a poet, too.
What character does: B. Wordsworth goes to the boy's house and asks to watch the bees. He teaches the boy the constellations and appreciation of beauty.
What others say about character: The boy says that B. Wordsworth makes the world more exciting and that he speaks and acts deliberately, as if he were experiencing things for the first time.
What character thinks: B. Wordsworth is troubled by the limitations he has encountered in life, but he is happy to have met the boy.

p. 335 After You Read
1. The young woman's inner conflict is over the "void" within her that made her feel as though "the hour was not worth their grasp."
2. Graphic Organizer
Sample response:
"B. Wordsworth"
Setting: Trinidad in the 1940s, under British colonial rule
Characterization: A young boy in Trinidad and a black poet learn about each other through conversation. The young boy lives alone with his mother and at first thinks ill of the poet. The poor poet lives alone, survives on little, and considers himself a brother to William Wordsworth. The poet seems to be beaten down by society, but the boy learns from the poet that life is about appreciation and struggle.
Conflicts: The poet struggles against society to survive and realize his dreams. The boy struggles against society to know and understand the poet.
3. The conflict between man and society is shaped by the effects of colonial rule on the people of Trinidad. The black poet suffers and struggles against the restrictions placed on him because he is considered inferior by the society in which he lives. The boy struggles to

understand the effects that society has on the poet and why the poet is judged so harshly by society and fails to succeed.

The Essential Question
Answers will vary, but students should support opinions with details from personal experiences.

Poetry of Walcott

p. 336 Graphic Organizer
Sample response:
Poem: *from* Midsummer, XXIII
Allusion: "the riot police and the skinheads exchanged quips you could trace to the Sonnets"
Affect Understanding: It helps me understand that the speaker feels excluded from a culture shared by the police and the skinheads.
Poem: *from* Omeros, *from* Chapter XXVIII
Allusion: "So there went the Ashanti one way, the Mandingo another, the Ibo another, the Guinea . . ."
Affect Understanding: It helps me understand that many peoples from Africa shared the experience of being taken from their homes, enslaved, and sent away without family to new places.

p. 337 Note-taking Guide
Sample response:
Context details: "like Boer cattle under Tory whips"; "add some color to the British theater"
Conflict in poet's mind: Walcott feels disloyal to his countrymen in light of the race riots.

p. 338 Note-taking Guide
Sample response:
Detail 1: "". . . these shadows are reprinted now on the white sand . . .'"
Detail 2: "". . . our eyes showed dried fronds in their brown irises . . .'"
Detail 3: "". . . ribbed corpses floated . . .'"
Detail 4: "". . . black waiter bringing the bill.'"
Detail 5: "". . . multiply their ruin . . ."
Detail 6: "". . . each man was a nation . . ."

p. 339 After You Read
1. Each man was "a nation in himself" because he was separated from his tribe, from his family, and from his friends.
2. Walcott's political critique of his role as a West Indian poet in British society mirrors

the theme of understanding a West Indian's place in British society. Walcott questions whether he, as a poet, has ever been truly welcome and a part of British society, for West Indians as a group are generally excluded and considered separate.

3. **Graphic Organizer**
Sample response:
Allusion: *from* Omeros: "our skulls on the scorching decks"
Literary: Literary
Historical: inhuman treatment on slave ships
Allusion: *from* Midsummer XXIII: "like Boer cattle under Tory whips that drag every wagon / nearer to apartheid"
Literary: Scholarly
Historical: British racial segregation
Popular: Segregation is still present in modern life.

The Essential Question
Answers will vary, but students should support answers with details from the poems.

"Follower"
Seamus Heaney

"Two Lorries"
Seamus Heaney

"Outside History"
Eavan Boland

p. 340 Graphic Organizer
Sample response:
"Follower"
Passage: "I wanted to grow up and plow, / To close one eye, stiffen my arm. / All I ever did was follow / In his broad shadow round the farm."
Main Points: The speaker wanted to plow. He remembers following his father around the farm.
Summary: The son wanted to be a farmer, like his father.
Main Idea: The son follows his father, looks up to him, and wants to be like him.

"Two Lorries"
Passage: stanzas 1–2
Main Points: The coalman delivers good-quality coal and asks the narrator's mother on a date; the Magherafelt bus passes the house; the narrator's mother is moved by the lorry and tempted to accept.

Summary: The coalman delivers a load of good-quality coal to the narrator's house and asks the narrator's mother on a date. The mother is tempted to go because the coal is so good and the sight of the half-empty lorry moves her.

Main Idea: A coalman asks a woman for a date, and she is flattered.

"Outside History"

Passage: entire poem

Main Points: The stars are "outside history"; the stars reveal human mortality; one must choose to live either in myth or history; one cannot undo past losses.

Summary: People are not outsiders to history; they must choose between disengagement with the present and therefore the past, or engagement in the present struggle and therefore the pain of the past. The narrator chooses to participate in Ireland's painful history, knowing that her efforts cannot restore past losses or undo the pain.

Main Idea: The speaker wants to be part of her country's history even though she cannot help those in the past.

p. 341 Note-taking Guide

Sample response:

Follower

Images: father's shoulders, son, following behind the plow

Central Image: The son follows behind his father as he plows the field.

Two Lorries

Images: coal trucks, smoke and ashes, rain, mother, bomb

Central Image: the bus station bombing

Outside History

Images: stars, rivers, fields, pain of human suffering and death

Central Image: past and present struggle

p. 342 After You Read

1. Students may choose from a number of words, including "shafts," "furrow," "headrig," "hobnailed," "plod," and "yapping."

2. **Graphic Organizer**

Sample response:

Diction

Examples: "iron inklings," "mortal," "ordeal"

Conclusion: Philosophical / abstract diction

Imagery

Examples: "a landscape," "those fields," "roads clotted"

Conclusion: simple, general imagery with abstract ideas

Rhythm/Rhyme

Examples: irregular

Conclusion: conversational

Form

Examples: 3-line stanza

Conclusion: simple

3. Sample response: In the first incident, the poet's mother chats with the coal deliveryman who invites her to see a film. She declines; the coalman drives off to the city. In the second incident, a terrorist-driven truck explodes, destroying the bus station in which the poet used to meet his mother. In a vision, the poet sees his mother's ghost at the bus station, attended by the coalman as a figure of death. The poem's main idea is that the speaker does not want to lose Ireland to conflict and war.

The Essential Question

Answers will vary, but students should support answers with details from the poems.

"Come and Go"
Samuel Beckett

"That's All"
Harold Pinter

p. 343 Graphic Organizer

Sample response:

Come and Go

Characters: Three older women with covered faces. They have been friends since childhood.

Dialogue: Repetition of dialogue, except with different speakers. Some of the characters' dialogue is whispered and unknown to readers.

Situation: The women are sitting together as they did when they were schoolgirls.

That's All

Characters: Two women—only named "Mrs. A" and "Mrs. B" and a third woman who is not present.

Dialogue: Limited; with two exceptions, Mrs. B only says "Yes," or "Oh, yes." Mrs. A does most of the talking. The dialogue is repetitive.

Situation: The two women are talking about the third woman. There is no stage direction or elaboration on setting, costumes, etc.

p. 344 Note-taking Guide
Sample response:
Come and Go
Ru: wears a faded violet overcoat; like the others, her face is hidden under a hat; she tells a secret and has a secret told about her; she asks more personal and emotional questions at the end of the play.
Vi: wears a faded red overcoat; like the others, her face is hidden under a hat; she tells a secret and has a secret told about her.
Flo: wears a faded yellow overcoat; like the others, her face is hidden under a hat; she tells a secret and has a secret told about her; she is able to feel the rings that are not there.
That's All
Mrs. A.: dominates the conversation; closely monitors what others are doing (for example, knows when, where, and how often the third woman goes shopping)
Mrs. B.: says very little throughout the play; seems either to agree with Mrs. B. or be distracted and uninterested in the conversation.
Third Woman: not present, but is the subject of the conversation; has changed her normal routine and seems to be avoiding Mrs. A.

p. 345 After You Read
1. Answers will vary. Students may note that by focusing on dialogue, the playwrights have simplified the dramas. The characters' repetitive, simple dialogue indicates how poorly people communicate, although communication is central to human relationships.
2. **Graphic Organizer**
Sample response:
Come and Go
Plot and Action: Action is limited to the characters' moving on and off stage and talking to one another. There is no traditional plot—no building action, climax, or resolution.
Dialogue: The play is very brief, and dialogue is mostly limited to questions and statements repeated by each character.
Staging: The stage directions are explicit and descriptive.
That's All
Plot and Action: There is no traditional plot, and the action consists of conversation between two women.
Dialogue: The dialogue is brief, with Mrs. A. speaking more than Mrs. B.
Staging: There are no stage directions.

3. Sample response: In the first incident, the poet's mother chats with the coal deliveryman who invites her to see a film. She declines; the coalman drives off to the city. In the second incident, a terrorist-driven truck explodes, destroying the bus station in which the poet used to meet his mother. In a vision, the poet sees his mother's ghost at the bus station, attended by the coalman as a figure of death. The poem's main idea is that the speaker does not want to lose Ireland to conflict and war.

The Essential Question
Answers will vary, but students should support opinions with details from the story.

"Do Not Go Gentle into That Good Night"
Dylan Thomas

"Fern Hill"
Dylan Thomas

"The Horses"
Ted Hughes

p. 346 Graphic Organizer
Sample response:
"Do Not Go Gentle into That Good Night"
How Elements Communicate Theme: The repetitive form of the villanelle adds importance to Thomas's message; the tumbling style gives Thomas's words urgency.
How Details Communicate Theme: Thomas compares death to night, and urges that people should resist the dying of the light, showing that people have something to hold onto. Thomas many different types of men—wise men, good men, wild men, grave men—each of whom have reasons to resist death. Thomas closes with an appeal to his father, adding personal weight to his message.
Effectiveness of Elements and Details: The elements are very effective in communicating Thomas's theme clearly and in communicating the importance of his message. The details add interest and personal feeling to the theme, making it easier for the reader to relate.

p. 347 Note-taking Guide
Sample response:
Poem: "Do Not Go Gentle"
Main Idea/Writer's Message: The poet faces the approaching death of his father. He urges readers to fight death, rather than accept it.

Poem: "Fern Hill"

Main Idea/Writer's Message: The poet looks back fondly on his carefree youth and laments the loss of youth and the "chains" that the passage of time imposes.

Poem: "The Horses"

Main Idea/Writer's Message: The poet recalls an encounter with horses in nature. He celebrates the peacefulness and mystery of the experience and of nature.

p. 348 After You Read

1. **Graphic Organizer**

Sample response:

Style: Words tumble out in a rush.

Examples: "Now as I was young and easy under the apply boughs / About the lilting house and happy as the grass was green."

Style: Shows an attitude of wonder about life

Examples: "Time let me play and be / Golden in the mercy of his means."

Style: Uses complex poetic forms

Examples: Villanelle form of "Do Not Go Gentle into That Good Night"

2. Thomas's tumbling, rushing style reflects the carefree and playful nature of childhood, which is part of the poem's theme.

3. Hughes's style involves using short bursts of images. This use of imagery focuses the reader's attention on the wild and remote beauty that the speaker sees in nature.

The Essential Question

Answers will vary, but students should support answers with details from the poems.

"An Arundel Tomb"
Philip Larkin

"The Explosion"
Philip Larkin

"On the Patio"
Peter Redgrove

"Not Waving but Drowning"
Stevie Smith

p. 349 Graphic Organizer

Sample response:

Poem: "An Arundel Tomb"

Sentence: "Rigidly they / Persisted, linked, through lengths and breadths / Of time."

Meaning: They remained where they were throughout all time.

Poem: "The Explosion"

Sentence: "At noon, there came a tremor; cows / Stopped chewing for a second; sun / Scarfed as in a heat-haze, dimmed."

Meaning: A tremor came at noon, causing the cows to stop chewing and the sun to dim.

Poem: "On the Patio"

Sentence: "Suddenly I dart out into the patio, / Snatch the bright glass up and drain it, / Bang it back down on the thundery steel table for a refill."

Meaning: The narrator runs outside, empties the glass, and slams it back down on the table so that it can fill up again.

Poem: "Not Waving but Drowning"

Sentence: "Poor chap, he always loved larking / And now he's dead / It must have been too cold for him his heart gave way, / They said."

Meaning: The drowned man loved to have fun, but he is now dead. People thought it was too cold for him.

p. 350 Note-taking Guide

Sample response:

Poem: "An Arundel Tomb"

Important Symbols and Their Meanings: Symbol: The images on the tomb are unintended symbols of enduring love; Meter: Iambic tetrameter; Rhyme scheme: *abbcac*

Theme: Death and its effect on those who survive

Poem: "The Explosion"

Important Symbols and Their Meanings: Symbol: The unbroken eggs represent what is lost; Meter: Trochaic tetrameter; Rhyme scheme: unrhymed

Theme: Death and its effect on those who survive

Poem: "On the Patio"

Important Symbols and Their Meanings: Symbols: The thunderstorms represent the power and force of nature; the wineglass is a symbol of human attempts to capture and possess that force; Meter: Free verse; Rhyme scheme: unrhymed

Theme: The desire to possess the energy and life force of nature

Poem: "Not Waving but Drowning"

Important Symbols and Their Meanings:

Symbol: The water is a symbol of the dead man's isolation; Meter: Varying meter; Rhyme scheme: *abcb*

Theme: People are often misinterpreted for an entire lifetime.

p. 351 After You Read

1. The images concern both the violent descent of the rain from the clouds above and its effect on the patio below.

2. Sample response: The dead man means that for all his life he was unable to cope with the circumstances of his life.

3. **Graphic Organizer**

"An Arundel Tomb": Thĕir própĕr hábĭts vághĕly shówn / Ăs jóintĕd ármŏr, stíffenĕd pléat . . .

"The Explosion": Ít wăs sáid, ănd fór ă sécŏnd / Wíves săw mén ŏf thé ĕxplósiŏn . . .

4. Readers should pause at the end lines punctuated by a comma, a semicolon, or a colon and come to a stop at the end of lines ending with a period.

The Essential Question

Answers will vary, but students should support answers with details from the poem.

"Prayer"
Carol Duffy

"In the Kitchen"
Penelope Shuttle

p. 352 Graphic Organizer

Sample response:

Elements of Parallel Structure:

"In the Kitchen" "I am trying to love the world . . ." and the personified actions of inanimate objects ("The ironing-board thanks . . ." "The new fridge hums . . .")

"Prayer" "Some days, although we . . . Some nights, although we . . ." and the repetition of place names. The sonnet form itself imposes parallel structure.

p. 353 Note-taking Guide

Sample response:

Examples of Personification:

"In the Kitchen" "ironing-board thanks," "new fridge hums," "chair recites," "table leaves no stone unturned," "clock votes"

"Prayer" the tree sings and the train chants

p. 354 After You Read

1. Sample response: The rustling of tree leaves can sound like musical notes. The rhythmic sounds of a train on a track (and its occasional whistle or low rumbling sounds) mimic the sounds of Latin chanting.

2. Graphic Organizer

"In the Kitchen"

Speaker's Loss: her husband and companion

How the Speaker Finds Comfort: through the company of everyday objects that have taken on human qualities; through the effort of "trying to love the world / back to normal"

"Prayer"

Speaker's Loss: loss of prayer, faith

How the Speaker Finds Comfort: by listening to the musical sounds of the trees, train, piano scales, the radio; by directing others to "Pray for us now."

3. The speaker is working toward feeling love and hope again. The speaker is also trying to restore order to her life by getting the "seas back on the maps / where they belong."

The Essential Question

Answers will vary, but students should support answers with details from the poem.

"A Devoted Son"
Anita Desai

p. 355 Graphic Organizer

Sample response:

Rakesh

Action: He bows to touch his father's feet.

Cause: Rakesh wants to show respect in a traditional way.

Action: He moves back home after finishing school in the United States.

Cause: Rakesh feels obligated to his family and community.

Varma

Action: He asks his grandchildren to get sweets for him.

Cause: Rakesh has put Varma on a diet in which Varma can have few foods that he likes.

Action: He swats a bottle of tonic from Rakesh's hands.

Cause: Varma is tired of the endless medical treatments that must endure at the hands of his son.

p. 356 Note-taking Guide

Sample response:

Character: Rakesh

Dynamic: yes

Details: At the beginning of the story, Rakesh follows the traditional path of a devoted son. Rakesh's education introduces him to modern

ideas, and by the time he is established as a doctor, Rakesh ignores his father's wishes in favor of practicing new, modern medicine.
Character: Varma
Static: yes
Details: Varma remains traditional throughout the story. He does not undergo significant changes, and when his son refuses to honor his wishes regarding diet, Varma considers his son to be very disrespectful.

p. 357 After You Read
1. Sample response: Rakesh's mother and wife are static characters because neither undergoes significant change.
2. **Graphic Organizer**
Sample response:
Varma
Beginning: He is happy and proud of Rakesh's success in school.
Middle: His wife has died, and he has health problems coupled with unusual behaviors.
End: He is hostile toward his son and the medical treatments.
3. The speaker is working toward feeling love and hope again. The speaker is also trying to restore order to her life by getting the "seas back on the maps / where they belong."

The Essential Question
Answers will vary, but students should support opinions with details from the story.

"Next Term We'll Mash You"
Penelope Lively

p. 358 Graphic Organizer
Sample response:
Setting: an expensive and elite boarding school
Characters: Charles; his parents, Mr. and Mrs. Manders; Mr. and Mrs. Spokes, the headmaster and his wife; other students
Social Class: wealthy, upper class
Motivations: Charles: wants to please his parents, wants to get by; Mr. and Mrs. Manders: want to be part of the upper class, want to fit in with their wealthy friends; Mr. and Mrs. Spokes: want to run the school and maintain traditions; Other students: want to keep the social order in place, want to bully new students
Reactions: Charles: is quiet and overwhelmed; Mr. and Mrs. Manders: drop names, make

judgments about people and the surroundings; Mr. and Mrs. Spokes: act very matter-of-fact about money and connections, try to welcome Charles and his parents to the school; Other students: make threats toward Charles
What these elements reveal: Some people want to become part of the exclusive upper-class world; the boarding school setting can be a cruel place.

p. 359 Note-taking Guide
Sample response:
School Grounds: The grounds are nice, with spacious playing fields and a country setting.
Staff: There is a maid in a uniform. The headmaster and his wife are well-dressed and comfortable with their status.
Cost: The school is more expensive than others.
What Their Friends Say About the School: The school is popular among their friends from the city; their friends approve of the headmaster and his wife.

p. 360 After You Read
1. Charles's mother notices that Mrs. Spokes is wearing old but expensive clothes and good jewelry. Her attitude and voice show confidence.
2. **Graphic Organizer**
Sample response:
A word that describes Charles is shy.
Details that reveal this: He sits quietly in the car and in the headmaster's office.
A word that describes Charles's mother is shallow / phony.
Details that reveal this: She is very concerned about appearances.
3. Answers will vary. Students may suggest that there is separation between social classes in England and that places like the boarding school help reinforce such attitudes. Going to an elite boarding school may help Charles later because he might develop relationships with wealthy and well-connected people. The path to the upper class leads through elite schools.

The Essential Question
Answers will vary, but students should support answers with details from the story.

from We'll Never Conquer Space
Arthur C. Clarke

p. 361 Graphic Organizer
Sample response:
Is an opinion clearly stated?
Example: "Man will never conquer space."
Do facts support ideas?
Example: Distance creates too much of a barrier to communication.
Are there words and phrases that readers will remember?
Example: "The price of space is time."
Are there appeals to reason or emotion?
Example: (logic) Some objects in space are too far away, even if we could travel at the speed of light.
Does the author address differing opinions?
Example: Clarke says that scientists who claim that we will never cross "cosmic gulfs" are wrong.
Are unfamiliar ideas clarified?
Example: Clarke explains a simplified way of using very large numbers.

p. 362 Note-taking Guide
Sample response:
Forever Too Large: We can never abolish the space between the stars.
"Time Barrier": Nothing travels faster than light; the distance between colonies renders communication between solar systems impossible.
Independent "Colonies": Even if the speed of light is somehow surpassed, the quantity of space is too much to be conquered; colonies will be so far separated that humans will lose the bonds of "kinship and understanding."

p. 363 After You Read
1. Sample response: Do individuals believe that further space exploration is necessary?
2. **Graphic Organizer**
Sample response:
Things Compared: the spread of ant colonies and the future spread of human colonies in space
Similarities: The isolation of space colonies is like the isolation of ant colonies.
What is Explained: Human "civilization" in space would have as much unity as ant "civilization" on Earth.
3. Answers will vary. Sample response: Space is too vast; it may be covered but not con-

quered. We will be isolated in space even if we can colonize distant planets. Communication will be a problem.

The Essential Question
Answers will vary, but students should support answers with details from the essay.

Informational Texts: Case Studies

p. 367 After You Read
Thinking About the Case Study
1. Answers will vary. Sample response: Clarke wanted rocket technology to be used to develop orbiting space stations that could send and receive radio signals.
2. Answers will vary. Sample response: Clarke concluded that although the initial cost would be great, it would still be less than other methods of replacing and running communication networks.

Reading Skill
3. The rocket would become an artificial satellite that circles the world.
4. Rockets would have to be twice as fast as those already being designed, and materials would need to be ferried up by rockets to the location where the space station would be built.

"I'm Like A Bird"
from Songbook
Nick Hornby

p. 368 Graphic Organizer
Sample response:
Thesis or Main Idea: Some of today's pop music is valuable to the existing culture.
Differing Opinions: Some people think that pop music is "beneath" them. One reason that pop music lacks value is that it is not meant to last.
Emotional, Logical, Humorous Appeals:
Pop songs provide a harmless pleasure. People need more of that. Pop songs satisfy an emotional need.

p. 369 Note-taking Guide

Sample response:

Why Pop Music Is Valuable

Reason 1: Pop music provides a harmless, simple pleasure that is easy to satisfy.

Reason 2: Hornby's need to "solve" the song makes it appealing.

Reason 3: Pop music's short lifetime and limited appeal allow listeners to enjoy a variety of songs.

p. 370 After You Read

1. Hornby's view is that popular music has value, even though that value is not of the highest quality.

2. **Graphic Organizer**

Sample response:

Informal Tone: "It is, after all, a harmless need. . . ."

Opinions/Observations: The best music was written decades ago. Still, pop music can be enjoyable, and that is its value. Pop music is also disposable.

Reveals Author's Background/Personality: Hornby's references show that he is knowledgeable about music and art. Hornby enjoys a variety of music; he makes his own personal tapes of new and favorite songs.

3. Answers will vary. Students may identify with the argument that even people who are snobs about music can find new songs to enjoy.

The Essential Question

Answers will vary, but students should support answers with details from the essay.

ANSWERS TO UNIT 1

"The Seafarer"
Translated by Burton Raffel

"The Wanderer"
Translated by Charles W. Kennedy

"The Wife's Lament"
Translated by Ann Stanford

p. 2 Graphic Organizer
Sample response:
"The Seafarer"
Event/Idea: Although he is drawn to life at sea, the speaker still sees this kind of life as a form of exile.
Historical Context: Anglo-Saxons had a very strong sense of community. The fellowship and community of the mead-hall was important to a man. All that seemed good and that gave a man his identity was tied up with home and community.

"The Wife's Lament"
Event/Idea: The woman's husband tells her to move her home, even though she has few loved ones there.
Historical Context: Women had few rights.

p. 3 Vocabulary Warm-up
1. unfurl
2. billowing
3. strive
4. perched
5. whirled
6. scorch
7. smitten
8. terns

p. 4 Reading Warm-up
Sample response:
1. (map the world's oceans); *Strive* means "to exert much effort or energy."
2. The *swelling* sails on their longships also permitted voyages across the freezing Atlantic to Iceland and North America.

3. (the riches of the east); Someone *smitten* might daydream, write, or sing about the person or thing that fascinates him.
4. (on their canoes); *Perched* means "to stand, sit, or rest on an elevated place or position."
5. hot; A hot iron might *scorch* a shirt.
6. (their sails); It's common to see a flag *unfurl* as it is raised.
7. (hovered and whirled over their vessels); You might find terns near any seaport or along coastlines.
8. Something that *whirled* would spin rapidly, often changing direction.

p. 5 Note-taking Guide
Sample response:
The Seafarer: food (line 11); his kinsmen (line 25); passion and wine of the cities (line 28); pleasures of life on land (lines 44–45); orchards, towns, and fields (lines 48–49); wealth of the world (lines 66–67); the glory of kingdoms from long ago (line 81)
The Wanderer: his home (line 5); his comrades (line 10); his mead-hall (line 25); gifts of fine gold and treasure (lines 29, 31); Earth's delight (line 30); the days of his youth (line 31); his kinsmen (line 45)

p. 6 Note-taking Guide
Sample response:
The Wife's Lament: her home and friends (line 9); her loved ones (line 16); her previous life (line 41)

p. 7 After You Read
1. The speaker feels that her husband, her previous life, and her home are lost.
2. **Graphic Organizer**
Sample response:
Poem: "The Wanderer"
Cause of Suffering: His lord is dead. He is exiled.
Insight Gained: Life is short and hard. Look to God for strength.
Poem: "The Wife's Lament"
Cause of Suffering: She is banished by her husband.

Insight Gained: Love and life are fragile. Longing and waiting are difficult to endure.

3. Sample response: Without knowing that the husband had the right to banish his wife and that the wife had little choice in the matter, it would be difficult to understand the situation in "The Wife's Lament."

The Essential Question

Answers will vary. Sample response: The Anglo-Saxon sense of home is very much like ours. Then and now, home is a place of refuge, where family members feel connected to one another and safe from the world outside.

from Beowulf
Translated by Burton Raffel

p. 8 Graphic Organizer

Sample response:

Original: Then he saw, hanging on the wall, a heavy / Sword, hammered by giants, strong / And blessed with their magic, the best of all weapons / But so massive that no ordinary man could lift / Its carved and decorated length.

Key Details: he; saw a sword; hanging on the wall

Paraphrase: Beowulf saw a magical sword of great size and weight hanging on the wall.

p. 9 Vocabulary Warm-up

1. mail
2. protector
3. swayed
4. boast
5. fleeing
6. truce
7. feud
8. inherited

p. 10 Reading Warm-up

Sample response:

1. (from chain links woven together to form a metal fabric.) *Mail* offered defense because a sword could not cut through it.
2. The metal mesh allowed the warrior flexibility as lifted his weapon or shifted from side to side to avoid an enemy's blade. *Swayed* means "shifted from side to side."
3. Mail probably did serve as a *protector* from a bullet because it was not thick or strong enough to stop the bullet. A *protector* keeps people or things safe from harm.

4. (it indicated wealth and position); *Boast* means "to brag."
5. (his father); It was helpful if mail was *inherited* because mail was expensive and took a long time to make.
6. when a battle or feud ended; Sometimes a truce is reached because both sides wish to stop the killing and neither is strong enough to win.
7. (battle); A *feud* is a long, bitter quarrel. Unlike a war, it often involves two families.
8. Even when running away, they had an advantage. I have seen a rabbit *fleeing* a dog.

p. 11 Note-taking Guide

Sample response:

Setting: Kingdom of the Danes

Problem: Grendel has been killing Hrothgar's men.

Goal: To get rid of Grendel

Event 1: Grendel attacks Hrothgar's men at Herot.

Event 2: Beowulf tears off Grendel's arm, and the monster flees.

Event 3: Beowulf slays Grendel's mother.

Event 4: Beowulf faces a fierce dragon in his final battle.

Climax: Beowulf slays the dragon with his sword but is mortally wounded himself.

Resolution: Beowulf, along with the dragon's treasure, is buried in a tower built for him by the Geats.

p. 12 Stop to Reflect

Students should circle "sprawled in sleep, suspecting / Nothing, their dreams undisturbed." Students may say that Grendel will kill the warriors and eat them.

p. 12 Reading Check

Students may circle "greed" and "delighted with his night's slaughter."

p. 13 Reading Strategy

Students should circle *b*.

p. 13 Reading Check

Sample response: This man will fight Grendel. Grendel will not kill this man so easily. Grendel is in for a surprise.

p. 14 Stop to Reflect

The "shepherd of evil" and the "guardian of crime" is Grendel. Students should circle *a*.

p. 14 Reading Check

Students should circle *b.*

p. 15 Literary Analysis

Students should circle "Beowulf / Longed only for fame" and "So fame / Comes to men who mean to win it / And care about nothing else!" Students should circle *a.*

p. 15 Reading Strategy

Students may circle "magic," "no ordinary man could lift," and "drew it." Sample response: The sword was magical, and it was much too heavy for an ordinary man to lift. Nevertheless, Beowulf was able to pick it up.

p. 16 Stop to Reflect

The sword can kill Grendel's mother because it is a magic sword. Students should circle "hammered by giants, strong / And blessed with their magic" on page 15.

p. 16 Literary Analysis

Sample response:

1. He is an important person in his society. In fact, he has become its king.

2. He battles forces that threaten the peace or order of that society. In this case, he battles the fire-breathing dragon.

p. 17 Reading Check

Students should circle "The monster came quickly toward him, / Pouring out fire and smoke" and "Flames beat at the iron / Shield" and label these cause. Students should circle "then it began to melt" and label it effect.

p. 17 Literary Analysis

Students should circle "Fought with fate against him." The epic reflects values of glory, bravery, and fighting ability.

p. 17 Reading Strategy

Sample response: The dragon jumped in pain and struck Beowulf, spreading flame everywhere.

p. 18 Stop to Reflect

Students should circle "he reminds Wiglaf to claim the dragon's treasure for the Geats" on page 17. Sample response: Beowulf is such a great hero that his people honor him with riches at his burial site. The people are so grief-stricken by Beowulf's death that they do not want riches from the dragon that killed Beowulf. The people want their great king and hero to have riches on his trip to the other world, perhaps in accordance with their beliefs.

p. 18 Literary Analysis

Sample response: The early Anglo-Saxons seem to admire a leader who is courageous, unselfish, concerned, and a monarch who is "mild" or moderate (as opposed to tyrannical) and who performs great deeds.

p. 19 After You Read

1. Sample response: Beowulf and his men are good. Grendel is evil. Grendel is attacking Hrothgar's people. He is a monster that must be killed if Hrothgar's people are to survive. Beowulf is brave and offers his help.

2. **Graphic Organizer**

Sample response:

What It Tells About the Anglo-Saxons: The Anglo-Saxons liked stories about people who were "larger than life."

Feature: good winning over evil

Why It Is Pleasing: Evil will always be defeated.

What It Tells About the Anglo-Saxons: The Anglo-Saxons honored doing good deeds over bad behavior.

3. Sample response: The Geats built the tower as requested by Beowulf. They put Beowulf's ashes inside, and they buried the dragon's treasure nearby. Then, twelve Geats rode their horses around the monument. They told stories about Beowulf. Everyone cried and praised the great king.

The Essential Question

Answers will vary. Sample response: As personified in Grendel, the Anglo-Saxons defined evil as monstrous—vicious, cruel, and relentless—striking without warning and wreaking havoc. As personified by Beowulf, the Anglo-Saxons defined good as heroic—battling evil to the death, winning honor, fame, and glory.

Informational Texts: Web Site Search Tools

p. 21 Vocabulary Builder

Students should circle "11th."

p. 21 Vocabulary Builder

Measure means "poetic rhythm."

p. 22 Vocabulary Builder

Tract means "a short piece of writing."

p. 22 Vocabulary Builder

Students should write "poetry" and "poetic."

p. 22 Comprehension Builder
A researcher could look at manuscripts of Old English poems at the British Library, the Exeter Cathedral, the Bodleian Library at Oxford, and the cathedral library in Vercelli, Italy.

p. 23 After You Read
Thinking About Web Site Search Tools
1. The Web site's search program found 12 hits for Anglo Saxon poetry.
2. I would use the Exeter Book link to learn more about Old English riddles and didactic poems.

Reading Skill
3. I would use the hit labeled "The major manuscripts" because the lines below specifically mention *Beowulf*.
4. Answers will vary. Sample response: Web sites for literary journals and magazines, Web sites devoted to poetry or British literature.

from A History of the English Church and People
Bede
Translated by Leo Sherley-Price

p. 24 Graphic Organizer
Sample response:
Purpose: to inform
Language: factual—"Britain . . . is an island"
Style: long, descriptive sentences
Rhetorical Strategy: comparing the unfamiliar and the familiar—"there are in Britain, in harmony with the five books of the divine law, five languages . . ."

p. 25 Vocabulary Warm-up
1. extracted
2. amber
3. lingers
4. climate
5. breadth
6. horizon
7. twilight
8. fortified

p. 26 Reading Warm-up
Sample response:
1. (jewelry); *Amber* is a hard, yellow or orange material that comes from fossils.
2. a lot of information about Stonehenge; Jason extracted the loose tea leaves from the hot tea in the pot.

3. place, strengthened against attack; The opposite of *fortified* is unprotected and vulnerable.
4. (the sun); The *horizon* is the line where the earth and sky appear to meet.
5. dim light; *Twilight* occurs after the sun has set, during the time before dark when there is still a small amount of light in the sky.
6. (The mystery of Stonehenge); has not yet been solved
7. (seven feet); A synonym for *breadth* is width.
8. (rainy); The word 'weather' could be substituted for the word *climate* in this sentence.

p. 27 Note-taking Guide
Sample response:
England: 800 miles long, 200 miles wide
Ireland: wider than England, but shorter in length
Both: islands

p. 28 After You Read
1. Sample response: Factors that are important in uniting a people and giving them a common identity include a shared religion and a shared language.
2. **Graphic Organizer**
Sample response:
Necessary Background: "Ireland is broader than Britain, and its mild and healthy climate is superior."
Evidence: "Snow rarely lies longer than three days, so that there is no need to store hay in summer"; "The island abound in milk and honey, and there is no lack of vines, fish, and birds, while deer and goats are widely hunted."
Clear Organization: The organization is clear in its listing of Ireland's attributes.
3. Sample response: Bede makes bold claims about Ireland being immune from poison. Bede uses description to tell about the pleasant climate.

The Essential Question
Answers will vary. Sample response: Bede describes England as an island lying at a considerable distance from the coasts of Germany, France, and Spain. Because of its northerly location, Britain's summer nights are short and its winter nights are long.

The Prologue
from The Canterbury Tales
Geoffrey Chaucer
Translated by Nevill Coghill

p. 29 Graphic Organizer
Sample response refers to the Innkeeper's long sentence on p. 39:
When? during the journey
Who? the pilgrims
Where? on the way to Canterbury and back
What? compete to tell the best story
Why? to make the trip pass more quickly
How? give the fullest measure of good morality and general pleasure

p. 30 Vocabulary Warm-up
1. prudent
2. distinguished
3. adversity
4. devout
5. repented
6. pilgrimages
7. courteous
8. dispense

p. 31 Reading Warm-up
Sample response:
1. (slow, difficult); By studying hard, you can overcome the adversity that results from poverty and neglect.
2. well-known and excellent in their field; Someone who is distinguished is highly regarded in his field. For example, Thurgood Marshall was a distinguished Supreme Court justice.
3. the advice of other travelers; Pilgrimages are long journeys to an important place, such as a holy shrine.
4. treat a fellow traveler rudely; A courteous person is polite and considerate of other's needs and feelings.
5. (hoping to find protection in numbers); *Prudent* means "careful and thoughtful"— someone who is prudent would not take risks.
6. (valued performing religious acts); A *devout* person takes extra care observing and respecting religious traditions.
7. wishing to cleanse themselves of remorse; *Repented* means "felt regret and decided to reform."
8. (granting); distribute

p. 32 Note-taking Guide
Sample response:
1. **Knight:** distinguished; fought in crusades; follows codes of chivalry; a noble soldier
2. **Squire:** the Knight's son; about 20; a knight-in-training; likes to joust; likes music and poetry; sings; plays flute; likes showy clothes
3. **Yeoman:** the Knight's attendant; dresses like a forest hunter
4. **Nun:** high rank; dainty; speaks French; good manners
5. **Monk:** "manly" man; good rider; likes to hunt; loose in his religious practices
6. **Friar:** likes the company of innkeepers and barmaids; not interested in helping the poor
7. **Merchant:** seems successful; hides the fact that he is in debt
8. **Oxford Cleric:** has no money; loves to read, learn, and teach; idealistic; cares only about his studies and his faith; quiet

p. 33 Literary Analysis
1. Students may circle "a most distinguished man" and label it direct.
2. Students may circle "done nobly in his sovereign's war" and label it indirect.
3. Sample response: The characterization shows that the Knight is distinguished, honorable, brave, and loyal.

p. 33 Reading Check
The "freshest flowers, red and white" are sewn on the Squire's outfit.

p. 34 Reading Check
1. The Squire can write and recite songs and poems.
2. The Squire can joust and dance.
3. The Squire can draw.

p. 34 Stop to Reflect
Sample response:
1. The French that the Nun speaks is not very good. It is schoolgirl French, not proper French.
2. The Nun speaks French because she wants to seem sophisticated and courtly.

p. 35 Reading Strategy
Students should circle "His bridle" and label it *What?* Students should circle "when he rode" and label it *When?* Students should circle "Monk" and label it *Who?*

p. 35 Reading Check
The Monk abandons "The Rule of good
St. Benet or St. Maur."

p. 35 Literary Analysis
Students should check "scholarly," "religious,"
and "single-minded."

p. 36 Literary Analysis
Students should circle "The thought of moral
virtue filled his speech" or "he would gladly
learn, and gladly teach."

p. 36 Read Fluently
Sample response: The words are funny
because they are ironic. The Doctor is stingy,
miserly, and greedy.

p. 37 Reading Check
The Wife of Bath knows the cures for problems related to love.

p. 37 Literary Analysis
Students may circle "a holy-minded man,"
"poor," "rich in holy thought and work," or
"a learned man."

p. 38 Stop to Reflect
Students should circle *a.*

p. 38 Reading Check
The Miller plays the bagpipes on the way out
of town.

p. 39 Read Fluently
Students should circle *d.*

p. 39 Reading Strategy
1. The Innkeeper proposes that the pilgrims
tell stories.
2. The pilgrims each will tell two stories going
to Canterbury and two stories coming from
Canterbury.
3. The pilgrims should tell stories to make the
trip pass more quickly.

p. 40 After You Read
1. Sample response: The Squire's showy
clothing, his love for poetry and music, and
his skills in dancing and writing tell the
reader that the Squire is a romantic young
man who is more interested in pleasing the
ladies than he is in serving his king.
2. **Graphic Organizer**
Sample response:
Character: Pardoner
Detail: sells papal pardons; claims to own
several holy relics that are really fakes; makes
money through flattery and avoiding the truth

Comment About Society: Corruption was
out of control in the giving of pardons.
Character: Knight
Detail: truth, honor, generosity, courtesy
Comment About Society: Society promoted
civility and virtuous behavior.
3. Students should refer the description of
the Knight on p. 27.
Sample response:
Who: a Knight
What: rode to battle
Where: in his sovereign's war
How: followed chivalry and done nobly

The Essential Question
Answers will vary. Sample response: In
medieval society, people dressed in ways that
clearly reflected their profession and station
in life. Chaucer describes a character's clothing in order to reveal that character's
personality and social standing. The squire's
clothes, for example, show that he is a young
man who has money to spend on fine things.
The yeoman, in contrast, dresses as a forest
hunter, befitting his lower station as the
Knight's attendant.

"The Pardoner's Tale"
from **The Canterbury Tales**
Geoffrey Chaucer
Translated by Nevill Coghill

p. 41 Graphic Organizer
Sample response:
Passage: " . . . And all my antics are a joy to
see."
Reread Earlier Passage: "I take great pains,
and stretching out my neck / To east and
west I crane about and peck / Just like a
pigeon sitting on a barn. / My hands and
tongue together spin the yarn. . . ."
Clarification: The antics are the silly acts the
Pardoner performs. He stretches his neck and
pecks like a pigeon.

p. 42 Vocabulary Warm-up
1. pulpit
2. congregation
3. dignity
4. sermon
5. vice
6. wary
7. discourse
8. vanity

p. 43 Reading Warm-up

Sample response:

1. (self-respect); To live with *dignity,* a person should take pride in the way he or she looks, speak with respect to others, and walk away if others try to insult him or her.
2. this weekly speech; A medieval *sermon* might have been about obeying the king or about the reasons to go on a pilgrimage.
3. (at the front of the church); A *pulpit* is a raised platform that a speaker stands on or desk that a speaker stands behind.
4. every member of; Tithing was a system in which every member of the *group of worshipers* was expected to give a tithe, or one-tenth of their earnings, to support the church.
5. complaining too freely; People in the modern United States are not too *wary* about complaining about taxes, since they know they have a right to freedom of speech.
6. (virtue); A *vice* is a bad or immoral habit, such as laziness or cheating.
7. excessive pride; Checking your looks in a mirror ten times a day is a sign of *vanity.*
8. (explaining); Simple people, such as medieval farmers, probably would not have the patience or the education to follow a complicated *discourse,* but they would find a play entertaining.

p. 44 Note-taking Guide

Sample response:

Box 2: They meet an old man, who tells them where to find Death.
Box 3: Instead, they find a pile of gold florins.
Box 4: They scheme about how to take the gold.
Final Event: They end by killing one another. They find Death after all.

p. 45 After You Read

1. The moral example of "The Pardoner's Tale" shows that when rioters become obsessed with gold, they are willing to do anything to get it, including killing friends.
2. Their search is a test. They have pledged to undertake a quest to find and destroy death.
3. **Graphic Organizer**
Sample response:
Reread Earlier Passage: "And up they started in their drunken rage" (line 125); "Then all this money will be ours to spend" (line 253); "And that with poison he could kill his friends" (line 269)

Meaning: The excesses of the rioters could include their drinking, their greed, and their willingness to kill for money.

The Essential Question

Answers will vary. Sample response: The Pardoner's tale shows that greed destroys those who allow themselves to be ruled by it. Ironically, the Pardoner admits that he preaches only to increase his sales of fake relics and pardons—in other words, to dupe his listeners and satisfy his own greed. Through the Pardoner, Chaucer exposes one element of hypocrisy in medieval society—the corrupt clergy.

"The Wife of Bath's Tale"
from The Canterbury Tales
Geoffrey Chaucer
Translated by Nevill Coghill

p. 46 Graphic Organizer

Sample response:
Passage: "A woman wants the self-same sovereignty / Over her husband as over her lover, / And master him . . ."
Unfamiliar Word: sovereignty
Context Clue: master him
Conclusion: If a woman wants to master her husband, sovereignty must mean control or power.

p. 47 Vocabulary Warm-up

1. reprove
2. purged
3. void
4. bottled
5. crone
6. matrons
7. forlorn
8. extort

p. 48 Reading Warm-up

Sample response:

1. It was difficult for a woman to raise a family, manage assets, and maintain her reputation on her own; Matrons are mature women who are either married or widowed.
2. for re-marrying; *Reprove* means "to find fault with."
3. having no one to turn to; Being excluded from a party might make someone feel *forlorn.*
4. Marriages in the Middle Ages were not void of love and affection; *Empty* is a synonym for *void.*

5. Because there were no illusions about this type of arrangement; *Contained* means the same as "bottled up."

6. (an extravagant dowry); *Extort* means "to gain by intimidation."

7. To a degree, individual desires and preferences were *removed* from the minds of young girls; *Purged* means "removed or rid of something."

8. (deferred to her parents' choice); A *crone* is an ugly, old woman.

p. 49 Note-taking Guide
Sample response:

Man's Action: A knight attacks a maiden.

Woman's Reaction: The maiden petitions the king.

Outcome: The knight is brought before the king and queen for justice.

Woman's Action: The queen asks the king for permission to determine the knight's fate.

Man's Reaction: The king grants permission for the queen to determine the knight's fate.

Outcome: The queen does not kill the knight. Instead, she sends him on a quest.

p. 50 After You Read
1. Sample response: The Wife of Bath is well off and attractive, whereas the old woman is impoverished and extremely unattractive. Despite their differences, the Wife of Bath and the old woman are both wise and confident.

2. **Graphic Organizer**
Sample response:

Good Morality/Lesson: The knight receives a merciful punishment. / The Knight is forced to marry the old woman. Gentility is defined as a gift from God and the exercise of good values. / Poverty is described as not shameful. / The knight is rewarded for deferring to the Wife's judgment.

General Pleasure/Entertainment Value: The Wife ridicules friars. / The Wife describes the court and the knight's journey. / The Wife includes magical characters in her story. / The Wife includes twists and turns of the plot.

Final Judgment: The Host would probably be entertained by the tale. He might disagree with the Wife's ideas.

3. Sample response: The clues include the knight's perception that he will never find the answer he needs and his decision to return to the Queen.

The Essential Question
Answers will vary. Sample response: Chaucer's story reflects social trends. By describing one woman who wants to dominate her husband, the story suggests that the social norm is for men to be dominant.

from Sir Gawain and the Green Knight
Translated by Marie Borroff

from Morte d'Arthur
Sir Thomas Malory

p. 51 Graphic Organizer
Sample response:

Passage: "Gawain by Guenevere / Toward the king doth now incline: / 'I beseech, before all here, / That this melee may be mine.'"

Summary: Gawain is beside Guenevere. He moves forward and says that he wants the task to be his.

p. 52 Vocabulary Warm-up
1. slumbering
2. accorded
3. almighty
4. marvel
5. puny
6. swooned
7. fused
8. hermits

p. 53 Reading Warm-up
Sample response:
1. (loyalty, honor, self-sacrifice and defense of the weak); An antonym for *fused* is *separated*.
2. (when battles were fought in their name); *Swooned* means "fainted."
3. (the knight's beloved); It was also expected to make the knight's beloved be in awe at his attempts to be worthy of her.
4. (matrimonial decisions); *Accorded* means "given what is due or appropriate."
5. (the future husband and wife); *slumbering* means "sleeping or dozing."
6. (a wealthy father); A hermit might be found living in the wilderness or any area far away from civilization, society, and other people.
7. (expect her to marry); A puny sum is a little bit of money. Fifteen cents is a very *puny* sum.
8. (Money); almighty means "all powerful."

p. 54 Note-taking Guide

Sample response:

Box 2: A huge green knight rides a green horse into the hall.

Box 3: The Green Knight challenges any of the knights to attack him.

Box 4: Gawain accepts the Green Knight's challenge and cuts off the Green Knight's head.

Box 5: Gawain befriends the lord and lady of a wondrous castle.

Box 6: Gawain breaks his promise to the lord and keeps the green girdle.

Box 7: The Green Knight makes three passes with the ax, two representing the days that Gawain kept his promise to the lord and one representing the day that Gawain failed to keep his promise.

Box 8: Gawain admits his failure to live up to his pledge, feels ashamed, and asks for forgiveness. The Green Knight forgives Gawain and welcomes Gawain back to the castle.

p. 55 Note-taking Guide

Sample response:

Box 2: Arthur meets Mordred to arrange a truce.

Box 3: They fight, and Arthur is wounded.

Box 4: Sir Lucan dies.

Box 5: Arthur sends Sir Bedivere to throw Excalibur into the water and to report back to Arthur what Sir Bedivere sees.

Box 6: Sir Bedivere fails Arthur twice when he fails to throw Excalibur into the water. When Sir Bedivere does throw the sword into the water, a hand reaches up and grabs the sword.

Box 7: Three ladies take Arthur away on a barge as he lies dying.

Box 8: Sir Bedivere meets a hermit who has received a dead body from a group of women; Sir Bedivere assumes that this body is King Arthur's.

p. 56 Reading Check

Students should circle "Look ye come on fiercely and slay that traitor Sir Mordred, for I in no wise trust him."

p. 56 Stop to Reflect

Sample response:

Prediction: Fighting will break out.

Explanation: Each side is suspicious about the other side, so the meeting will be tense.

Therefore, if one person draws his sword for any reason, everyone will start fighting immediately.

p. 57 Reading Strategy

Students may circle "adder"; "stung a knight in the foot"; "he drew his sword to slay the adder"; and "when the host on both parties saw that sword drawn, then they blew beams, trumpets, horns, and shouted grimly."

Sample response: When a knight drew his sword to kill a snake that bit him, the warriors on both sides mistook it as a sign to start fighting.

p. 57 Literary Analysis

Students should circle *b*. Sample response: Mordred showed the ultimate disloyalty in trying to take away his king's throne.

p. 58 Read Fluently

Students should circle *a*.

p. 58 Reading Check

Students should write *T, F, T, F.* Students may circle "Arthur smote Sir Mordred under the shield, with a thrust of his spear," "throughout the body more than a fathom," "he smote his father King Arthur with his sword holden in both his hands," and "upon the side of the head, that the sword pierced the helmet and the casing of the brain."

p. 58 Stop to Reflect

Sample response: Sir Lucan and Sir Bedivere are loyal to their king, fight beside him, and try to save him. Lucan actually dies trying to save him. Mordred was disloyal, fought Arthur to grab power for himself, and was responsible for Arthur's death.

p. 59 Reading Check

Arthur asks Sir Bedivere to throw Arthur's sword, Excalibur, into the lake.

p. 59 Reading Check

Students should circle "It simply seems too valuable."

p. 59 Stop to Reflect

Sample response: Arthur expects something unusual to happen when Bedivere throws the sword in the lake, and when Bedivere reports nothing unusual, he knows that Bedivere could not have thrown the sword in.

p. 60 Literary Analysis

Students should circle *b*.

p. 60 Reading Strategy

Sample response: Bedivere carries Arthur to the water's edge, where he sees a barge filled with fair ladies mourning Arthur's injury and possible death. The ladies cry and shriek when they see Arthur.

p. 61 Reading Check

Sample response: Either he died and the ladies brought his body to the hermit, who buried it in the chapel, or he is not really dead and will return one day to rule England again.

p. 62 After You Read

1. Sample response: Arthur feels betrayed because Mordred is both his son and a knight. This betrayal of father and king seems to signal the breakdown of the loyalties that once sustained Camelot.

2. **Graphic Organizer**
Sample response:
Gawain's Reactions
What He Does: He gives back the girdle. He wants to gain back the Green Knight's respect.
What He Feels: He blushes and is ashamed. He is angry with himself for not keeping a promise and for being afraid.
Bedivere's Reactions
What He Says: "My lord . . . your commandment shall be done, and I shall lightly bring you word again."
What He Does: The value of the sword keeps him from throwing it in the lake. Then, he lies to King Arthur, telling him that he did throw the sword in the lake.
What He Feels: He feels reluctant to throw the sword in the lake. Then, after doing King Arthur's bidding, he feels sad that his king is leaving him.

3. Sample response: King Arthur met his son Mordred to arrange a truce between them. The truce was broken when a soldier drew his sword to kill a snake. King Arthur killed Mordred, but the king was badly wounded and knew that he was dying. He was taken to the island of Avilion by a group of beautiful women.

The Essential Question

Answers will vary. Sample response: The authors accept and uphold the code of chivalry in the tales they tell and the heroes they portray. Sir Gawain and Arthur act with honor and humility. Both personify the chivalrous knight. Their actions and decisions reveal the code.

ANSWERS TO UNIT 2

Sonnets 1, 35, 75
Edmund Spenser

Sonnets 31, 39
Sir Philip Sidney

p. 63 Graphic Organizer
Sample response:

Sonnet 1
Poet's Lines: "And happy rhymes bathed in the sacred brook / Of Helicon whence derived is, / When ye behold that angel's blessed look, / My soul's long lacked food, my heaven's bliss"
Paraphrase: My muse will inspire me to write happy words.

Sonnet 35
Poet's Lines: "My hungry eyes through greedy covetize, / Still to behold the object of their pain"
Paraphrase: I wish to see what causes me pain.

Sonnet 75
Poet's Lines: "Again I wrote it with a second hand, / But came the tide, and made my pains his prey."
Paraphrase: The poet wrote his beloved's name again, but once again the tide destroyed his work.

Sonnet 31
Poet's Lines: "With how sad steps, O Moon, thou climb'st the skies! / How silently, and with how wan a face!"
Paraphrase: You appear sick and pale tonight, moon.

Sonnet 39
Poet's Lines: "Come sleep! O sleep, the certain knot of peace, / The battling place of wit, the balm of woe"
Paraphrase: I need sleep, which is peaceful and healing. Sleep can also be a source of ideas.

p. 64 Vocabulary Warm-up
1. decay
2. garland
3. chamber
4. vain
5. virtues
6. weary
7. contentment
8. renew

p. 65 Reading Warm-up
Sample response:
1. (Rosy-cheeked and chubby); *Contentment* means a state of happiness or satisfaction.
2. allowing Cupid to reflect the popular taste of the day; The two friends decided to *renew* their promise to always keep in touch with one another.
3. (tired); A long, boring political speech made the whole crowd *weary*.
4. decorative flowers; A *garland* is used for decoration.
5. sleeping peacefully; A *chamber* is a private room, usually a bedroom.
6. (flaws); Devotion to his mother is a *virtue* that Cupid might possess.
7. (destroyed); *flourish, strengthen, thrive*
8. consumed with her own beauty; A *vain* person might have many photographs taken of himself.

p. 66 Note-taking Guide
Sample response:
Row 1: a delicate, pure lily
Row 2: hunger for food
Row 3: an eternal representation of his beloved's qualities
Row 4: a person
Row 5: peace

p. 67 After You Read
1. **Graphic Organizer**
Sample response:
Spencer, Sonnet 1
Speaker's Situation: He is amazed by his subject.
Types of Images: starry light, flashing eyes
Speaker's Conclusion: He loves and honors his subject.
Sidney, Sonnet 31
Speaker's Situation: The speaker is lovesick.
Types of Images: The image is a pale moon.
Speaker's Conclusion: The beloved is ungrateful.
2. Sonnet 31 is half Petrarchan (*abba abba*) and half Spenserian (*cdcdee*); Sonnet 39 is much like Spenserian but contains a slight variation (*abab abab cdcdee*).
3. I want to sleep; sleep offers peace, healing, and freedom. Sleep, save me from despair, and you'll be rewarded.

The Essential Question
Answer will vary, but students should support answers with details from the sonnet.

"The Passionate Shepherd to His Love"
Christopher Marlowe

"The Nymph's Reply to the Shepherd"
Sir Walter Raleigh

p. 68 Graphic Organizer
Sample response:
"The Passionate Shepherd to His Love"
Shepherd
Feelings: The shepherd feels passionate about living a simple life in a natural setting.
Goals: The shepherd wants someone to live with him in harmony with nature.
Me
Feelings: The notion sounds fine, but such situations rarely turn out as one hopes they will.
Goals: My goal would be the same as the shepherd's.
Themes: the pleasure of simple things

"The Nymph's Reply to the Shepherd"
Nymph
Feelings: The Nymph feels skeptical about the shepherd's proposal.
Goals: The Nymph wishes to say no to the shepherd.
Me
Feelings: People should look at situations honestly, avoiding unwarranted optimism.
Goals: I want to avoid disappointments.
Themes: fantasy vs. reality

p. 69 Vocabulary Warm-up
1. melodious
2. passionate
3. flocks
4. shepherd
5. groves
6. nymph
7. shallow
8. fragrant

p. 70 Reading Warm-up
Sample response:
1. (a red rose); *Passionate* means having intense emotion.
2. laurel trees; We went apple picking the *groves* at the orchard.

3. (gently grazing sheep); I have seen a *flock* of wild turkeys.
4. watching nearby; I think that a *shepherd* would live outdoors with his flocks, keep watch over them, and especially protect them from predators.
5. (playing) (tune on his pipes); A synonym for *melodious* is *harmonious*.
6. (lovely); A *nymph* was a young maiden who lived in the country and had a connection to nature. The nymphs featured in myths sometimes have magical powers.
7. sweet-smelling; My mother enjoys having *fragrant* candles burning in the living room.
8. (rather than deep); When someone you barely know acts overly friendly, that is a *shallow* display of friendliness.

p. 71 Note-taking Guide
Sample response:
What Does the Shepherd Promise? He promises her a life of bliss. He also promises her a bed of flowers, a gown of the finest wool, slippers with gold buckles, and a belt.
What Does the Nymph Respond? It would be wonderful if life were that idyllic.
Who Is More Convincing? Why? Some students may say that the shepherd is more convincing because he is positive and has a clear plan. Others may say that the nymph is more convincing because she tells a more complete story.

p. 72 After You Read
1. **Graphic Organizer**
Sample response:
Nymph's Realism: Rocks grow cold. Flocks leave the field. Rivers rage. Flowers wither and die. Gowns fade and wear thin.
2. In the first poem, the speaker sells his version of an unchanging life of bliss. In the second poem, the speaker proves more cynical and explains the shortcomings of such a situation.
3. Sample response: Yes. The shepherd wants to share all that he sees and feels.

The Essential Question
Answer will vary, but students should support opinions with details from the text.

Poetry of Shakespeare

p. 73 Graphic Organizer
Sample response:
Quatrain 2: The speaker wants to be like someone else.
Relation of 1 and 2: Change in Theme: The speaker moves from pitying himself to envying others.

p. 74 Vocabulary Warm-up
1. divining
2. prophecies
3. fortune
4. scorn
5. disgrace
6. despising
7. tempests
8. contented

p. 75 Reading Warm-up
Sample response:
1. (were almost always accurate); A *prophecy* is a prediction.
2. (he earned enough to live comfortably); People make *fortunes* as CEOs or professional athletes.
3. *Hating* the fact that viewers would be distressed by the inclement weather; Ted *despises* giving bad news about the rainy weather.
4. (who was happiest standing in front of maps and charts divining crucial information.); *Contented* means happy.
5. (maps and charts); *Divining* means knowing by knowledge and intuition.
6. (batten down the lawn furniture and heed small craft warnings); *Tempests* are violent wind and rain storms.
7. It wasn't his fault the weather was a *dishonor* to his profession; This is an exaggeration. Rainy and cold weather really wouldn't be a *disgrace* to a meteorologist.
8. ("so you can spend the day on your sailboat while I'm in the office reading pressure charts."); Ted *scorns* Katie because she seems to blame him for things that are not his fault.

p. 76 Note-taking Guide
Sample response:
Sonnet 29
Whom the speaker addresses: his beloved

Main idea of the couplet: When the speaker thinks about his beloved, he wouldn't change places with a king.
Sonnet 106
Whom the speaker addresses: the general public
Main idea of the couplet: We are able to view beauty, but lack the words or ability to praise it.
Sonnet 116
Whom the speaker addresses: the general public
Main idea of the couplet: The speaker is convinced that true love never falters. He says that if he is wrong, he never wrote, and no man ever loved.
Sonnet 130
Whom the speaker addresses: the general public
Main idea of the couplet: Despite his beloved's physical imperfections, the speaker thinks that she is beyond comparison.

p. 77 After You Read
1. Sonnet 106 is full of phrases and clauses and contains only two sentences. Sonnet 116 uses fewer complex sentences. Sonnet 116 contains six sentences.
2. **Graphic Organizer**
Sample response:
Theme: the constancy of beauty
Connection to Theme: The beloved is like those people.
Message of Quatrain 2: These writers of old tried to describe beauty like yours.
Connection to Theme: All writing about beauty describes the beloved.
Message of Quatrain 3: These writers prophesied your beauty, but they lacked skill.
Connection to Theme: Writings of the past are not sufficient to describe the beloved's beauty.
Message of Couplet: We can see your beauty but lack words to praise it.
3. Sample response: Yes, each quatrain or couplet addresses a main point.

The Essential Question
Answer will vary, but students should support answers with details from the sonnets.

from The King James Bible

p. 78 Graphic Organizer
Sample response:
Inference: The Lord watches over faithful people, protecting them from danger and leading them to the right place.

p. 79 Vocabulary Warm-up
1. famine
2. devoured
3. pastures
4. portion
5. perish
6. consider
7. presence
8. mercy

p. 80 Reading Warm-up
Sample response:
1. (found in); A television is a *presence* in most homes today.
2. chewed up; If the person *devoured* a meal, he or she must have been very hungry.
3. (individual craftsmen); *Portion* means "a share or part of something."
4. copying the text; These had to be ready for use before scribes could *think seriously about* copying the text and passing the pages to illustrators.
5. (they shared their food with the hungry); *Mercy* means "kindness."
6. food; the hungry; In a *famine,* people might fight over what little food was available. After a while, though, they would become too weak to fight or work, and activity would come to a stop.
7. (grazing animals); *Pastures* are grassy, open fields.
8. turned to dust; As a manuscript became older, it might begin to crumble. If someone did not copy over the work before the parchment it was written on turned to dust, then the work would *perish.*

p. 81 Note-taking Guide
Sample response:
Deeds Listed in Text: He restoreth my soul: he leadeth me in the paths of righteousness for his name's sake.
How God is Comforting and Protecting: God helps me lead a good life.

p. 82 Note-taking Guide
Audience: the general public and Jesus' disciples

Purpose: to teach people to live virtuously
Advice Given: Do not worship money; do not worry about basic needs. God will provide, just as he does for birds and for plants.

p. 83 Note-taking Guide
Sample response:
Young Son
How he lives his life: wastefully
What he does at the end: He humbles himself before his father and apologizes.
Older Son
How he lives his life: He works hard at home.
How he feels at the end: He is resentful of his younger brother's treatment.
Message of the story: It is never too late to repent. Like the father in the parable, God is forgiving and glad to welcome back those who return.

p. 84 After You Read
1. Sample response: Because it offers advice to all about how to live virtuously, the sermon, an oral lesson, is effective in teaching and in reaching a wide audience.
2. **Graphic Organizer**
Sample response:
"Sermon on the Mount"
Images: Familiar/Unfamiliar: Familiar: birds, lilies
Simple/Difficult? Difficult: Solomon's glory
Memorable? Why? Yes. The sermon teaches lessons that most people understand.

"Parable of the Prodigal Son"
Images: Familiar/Unfamiliar: rebellious child, father's love
Simple/Difficult? Simple: jealous brother
Memorable? Why? Yes. Emotions are universal.
3. Sample response: It means, "I will have a place in heaven" or "I will have eternal life with God."

The Essential Question
Answer will vary, but students should support answers with details from the text.

The Tragedy of Macbeth, Act I
William Shakespeare

p. 85 Graphic Organizer
Sample response:
Detail: "Yet do I fear thy nature; / It is too full o' the milk of human kindness. . . ."

Reveals: This detail reveals Lady Macbeth's fears that her husband will fail to gain the throne if he is unwilling to kill his enemies and opponents.

Detail: "Hie thee hither, / That I may pour my spirits in thine ear, / And chastise with the valour of my tongue / All that impedes thee from the golden round. . . ."

Reveals: This detail reveals Lady Macbeth's strong will and her desire that her husband become king.

Likely Outcome: When Macbeth returns, Lady Macbeth will talk him into killing Duncan to win the throne of Scotland.

p. 86 Vocabulary Warm-up

1. assault
2. swarm
3. plight
4. revolt
5. ambition
6. traitor *or* rebel
7. rebel *or* traitor
8. vanished

p. 87 Reading Warm-up

Sample response:

1. eager for power; *Ambition* means "desire to achieve something."
2. (one crime forces him to commit another); I am sorry for people who face the *plight* of homelessness.
3. challenging the king's authority; A *rebel* is someone who challenges or tries to overthrow authority.
4. (secretly scheming); Macbeth seems like a *traitor* because he betrays his king, plotting against him in secret.
5. (his kingdom was so stable); The American Revolution was a *revolt* by the American colonists against Britain.
6. (attacked); Any *attack* against Macbeth came from without, not from within.
7. Norse, Danes, Romans, English Saxons, and others; A *swarm* is a large, moving group of people.
8. (his reputation for peace and prosperity); *Disappeared* is a synonym for *vanished*.

p. 88 Note-taking Guide

Sample response:

Background Information: Macbeth is returning from a battle in which he showed great bravery and skill. His fellow noblemen admire him greatly.

Witches' Prediction: The witches predict that Macbeth will be Thane of Cawdor and also king and that Banquo will father kings.

Macbeth's Plan: Macbeth decides to kill Duncan while the king spends the night in Macbeth's castle.

p. 89 After You Read

1. Sample response: The weather and the witches themselves seem ominous. Banquo's reaction also suggests the possibility of evil and death.
2. Lady Macbeth believes that the witches' prophecy will come true and plans to persuade Macbeth to fulfill his destiny.
3. **Graphic Organizer**
Sample response:
Act I, Scene vi, 3–10: picture of a castle as a backdrop; birds chirping and hautboys playing; bright lighting

The Essential Question

Answer will vary, but students should support answers with details from the play.

The Tragedy of Macbeth, Act II
William Shakespeare

p. 90 Graphic Organizer

Sample response:
Number of Lines: 7
Number of Sentences: 4
Meaning: Am I seeing a dagger, or am I imagining one?

p. 91 Vocabulary Warm-up

1. repose
2. seize (*also accept* clutch)
3. clutch (*also accept* seize)
4. suspicion
5. contradict
6. conclusion
7. restrain
8. resembled

p. 92 Reading Warm-up

Sample response:

1. (relaxation); *Repose* is important for health because it probably reduces stress, lowers blood pressure, and gives the body time to recover from effort.
2. (eating); *Restrain* means "stop" or "hold back."

3. (That logic); The idea that you can succeed without doing hard work seems to *contradict* common sense.

4. comes to an end; At the *conclusion* of a party, the lights are turned back on, revealing leftover food, crumpled up napkins, and crushed cups everywhere.

5. (trust); It is a good idea to view something with *suspicion* when it sounds too good to be true, might affect your health, and will cost money.

6. (grabbing); *Seize* means "grab and hold."

7. (a bag of chips and a soda); I *clutch* my keys in the morning as I run out the door.

8. a feeling; the satisfaction of eating a good dinner; Both a meal of snack food and a good dinner can fill you up, but even if the feelings you had after each *resembled* each other, it does not change the fact that one meal is nutritious and the other is less healthy.

p. 93 Note-taking Guide
Sample response:
Macbeth's vision: Macbeth sees a dagger hovering in the air in front of him; the dagger soon becomes covered with drops of blood.
Who is murdered: Duncan and his servants
How Malcolm and Donalbain react: The two princes fear that they will be assassinated next. Donalbain flees to Ireland, and Malcolm seeks safety in England.

p. 94 After You Read
1. Graphic Organizer
Sample response:
Iambic Feet: "Macbeth does murder sleep'"—"the" and "sleep"
Trochaic or Anapestic Feet: "innocent" (anapest)

2. The porter's speech is comic because it contrasts sharply with what has happened, both because of its prose form and because immediately following the murder, the porter interrupts to look for a tip, discussing drunkenness while drunk himself.

3. Sample response: When he hears the bell ring, Macbeth announces that he will kill the king. Macbeth refers to the bell as Duncan's death knell—so it would be better for Duncan not to hear it.

The Essential Question
Answers will vary, but students should support ideas with details from the play.

The Tragedy of Macbeth, Act III
William Shakespeare

p. 95 Graphic Organizer
Sample response:
Link to Act I, Scene iii, lines 65–69:
Witches prophesy that Banquo will father kings, so Macbeth may view Fleance, Banquo's son, as a threat.
Macbeth's Lines, Act III, Scene i, line 35:
Banquo is going for a ride. Macbeth asks "Goes Fleance with you?"
Link to Future Actions: Perhaps Macbeth is planning to murder Banquo and Fleance.

p. 96 Vocabulary Warm-up
1. custom
2. confined
3. patience
4. affliction
5. remedy
6. eternal
7. absence
8. summons

p. 97 Reading Warm-up
Sample response:
1. (stomach problems); An ulcer is an example of an *affliction*.
2. a patient; A *summons* is a command to appear.
3. clean sheets, heat, and running water; The *absence* of clean sheets, heat, and running water would lead to problems with keeping an operation germ-free, so a patient might get an infection.
4. (By tradition and common practice); When seeing a modern doctor, people follow the *custom* of making an appointment and then waiting in the waiting room when they arrive.
5. (pain); *Remedy* means "a cure" or "medicine."
6. (his or her home); A *confined* patient was less of a risk because he or she would come into contact would fewer people, so there was less chance that the disease would spread.
7. while listening to complaints; A doctor would need *patience* to listen to complaints because some people go on and on in a boring way when describing their suffering.
8. (everlasting); The phrase *"eternal* rest" refers to death or the afterlife, which is a state that lasts forever.

p. 98 Note-taking Guide

Sample response:

Cause: Macbeth fears Banquo and resents him because of the witches' prophecy.

Effect: Macbeth feels guilty and sees Banquo's ghost at a banquet.

Prediction: Macbeth's guilt will drive him mad.

Cause: Macbeth believes that his position is worthless if he must always look over his shoulder, so he vows to kill any possible enemies.

Effect: Macbeth becomes increasingly blood-thirsty, and the other Scottish noblemen begin to turn against him.

Prediction: The Scottish noblemen will unite against the brutal king.

Cause: Macduff fears that Macbeth will try to kill him. Macduff also wants to persuade Malcolm, the rightful Scottish king, to return to Scotland and fight for his crown.

Effect: Macbeth notes Macduff's absence at his banquet and begins to suspect Macduff of plotting against him.

Prediction: Macduff will have his vengeance on Macbeth. Malcolm will return to Scotland.

p. 99 After You Read

1. Sample response: The external conflict stems from the witches' prediction that Banquo, not Macbeth, will father a line of kings.

2. **Graphic Organizer**

Sample response:

Proposed Actions: Macbeth vows to visit the witches to learn more about their predictions.

3. Sample response: It seems unlikely that Macbeth is the third murderer. If he had been, he would not have been so surprised to learn of Fleance's escape.

The Essential Question

Answers will vary, but students should support ideas with details from the play.

The Tragedy of Macbeth, Act IV
William Shakespeare

p. 100 Graphic Organizer

Sample response:

Scene i, 52

Appeals to which sense? sight; touch

Scene i, 53

Images: "yesty waves"

Appeals to which sense? sight

p. 101 Vocabulary Warm-up

1. vanquished
2. caldron
3. mortal
4. rumor
5. scruples
6. trifle
7. motives
8. boasting

p. 102 Reading Warm-up

Sample response:

1. (hung over a fire); A *caldron* is a large boiling pot and would probably be round, and made of metal; it would have a handle from which it could be hung over the fire.

2. (precious); A safety pin is a *trifle*.

3. causing widespread death; *Mortal* means "deadly."

4. (winning); It was hard to tell which army was winning and which would be *beaten*.

5. ideas of right and wrong; I have *scruples* about being rude to people, even if they are rude to me first.

6. they needed to feed and clothe their families; These *motives* lead modern people to find and hold jobs.

7. (exaggerated); People's *boasting* is usually about how good they are at a sport or about how great the things they own are.

8. (gossip); A *rumor* might be a story about a problem a movie star was having.

p. 103 Note-taking Guide

Sample response:

Description of Image: armed head

Message: This apparition warns Macbeth to beware of Macduff.

Macbeth's Reaction: Macbeth accepts this message without surprise, for he suspects Macduff of plotting against him.

Description of Image: bloody child

Message: This apparition tells Macbeth that no "man of woman born" will ever be able to harm him.

Macbeth's Reaction: Macbeth receives this prediction happily, but notes that he will still kill Macduff.

Description of Image: a child wearing a crown and holding a tree

Message: This apparition indicates that Macbeth will not be defeated until Birnam forest marches to Dunsinane hill.

Macbeth's Reaction: Macbeth is overjoyed at this news, for he thinks it means that he will never be defeated.

Description of Image: a line of eight kings, the last holding a mirror, followed by Banquo

Message: These apparitions do not speak, and the witches vanish without telling Macbeth what the image means.

Macbeth's Reaction: Macbeth thinks that this vision confirms the witches' earlier prediction that Banquo would father kings. The reminder makes him angry and frustrated.

p. 104 After You Read

1. **Graphic Organizer**
Sample response:
Vivid Imagery: "groans, and shrieks that rent the air"
Emotions Expressed: anguish, frustration, sadness

2. Sample response: In Scene iii, lines 39–41, Malcolm describes Scotland: "It weeps, it bleeds, and each new day a gash is added to her wounds." In Scene iii, lines 168–170, Ross adds that Scotland sighs, groans, and shrieks, and that violence and death are common.

3. Sample response: "Bleeding" and "carrying a yoke" appeal to sight; "sinking beneath the burden" and "gashes" appeal to touch; "weeping" appeals to hearing.

The Essential Question

Answers will vary, but students should support ideas with details from the play.

The Tragedy of Macbeth, Act V
William Shakespeare

p. 105 Graphic Organizer

Sample response:
Modern Psychiatrist: A modern psychiatrist might prescribe medicine to help Lady Macbeth sleep. A modern psychiatrist might also suggest therapy or counseling to treat her troubled mind.

p. 106 Vocabulary Warm-up

1. confirm
2. frets
3. exiled
4. murky
5. petty
6. snares
7. hew
8. perceive

p. 107 Reading Warm-up

Sample response:
1. Anyone who breaks these rules; An actor who was *exiled* from the theater would be unable to act in any plays and so would be out of work.
2. (seeing); I *perceive* the behavior as silly but also as fun, since it is part of a long tradition in the theater.
3. childish; I think a nickel is a *petty* amount of money.
4. (it is best not to violate the custom); If an actor said "Macbeth" five times a night in the theater and nothing went wrong, then that would *confirm* that it is all right to violate the custom.
5. (problems that could be brought on by a slip of the tongue); *Frets* means "worries."
6. caught; *Snares* are usually used to catch animals.
7. (dark); A dirty fish tank is *murky*, making it difficult to see the fish.
8. branches; Paul Bunyan and his loggers *hew* wood in the tall tales about them.

p. 108 Note-taking Guide

Sample response:
Macbeth
Outcome: Macbeth is slain by Macduff.
Lady Macbeth
Outcome: Lady Macbeth loses her mind and kills herself.
Macduff
Outcome: Macduff finds Macbeth and kills him in one-on-one combat.
Malcolm
Outcome: Malcolm is recognized as king when Macbeth is killed.

p. 109 Reading Check

The doctor sees her talking and moving her hands as though she were washing them.

p. 110 Reading Strategy

He thinks that her illness is mental rather than physical. He also thinks that she needs God's help to make her well. The belief of doctors that God healed people was a common belief during the period.

p. 110 Literary Analysis

He has locked himself in his castle in an effort to defend himself from advancing armies.

p. 111 Reading Check
Students should underline "the doctor says that she is not sick but troubled with imaginings."

p. 111 Reading Check
Malcolm tells them to use tree branches as camouflage.

p. 111 Reading Check
Macbeth is not worried by the attack because he thinks that he and his castle are strong enough to withstand it.

p. 112 Reading Check
Lady Macbeth has died.

p. 112 Reading Check
"All our yesterdays" have witnessed the deaths of fools. Students should underline "have lighted fools / The way to dusty death."

p. 112 Reading Strategy
Macbeth views life as empty and meaningless. His view foreshadows his own downfall by suggesting that all the evil acts he has committed out of ambition have turned out to be vain and profitless.

p. 113 Reading Check
Macbeth tells Macduff to get back because he has already been responsible for shedding the blood of members of Macduff's family.

p. 113 Stop to Reflect
Macduff means that words are not important. His sword will take the vengeance that he seeks for the death of his loved ones.

p. 114 Reading Strategy
Answers may vary. Sample response: Students may say that these lines reveal that people viewed prophecy and fortune telling as something undertaken by witches.

p. 114 Literary Analysis
Against all odds, Macbeth decides courageously to fight Macduff to the finish.

p. 114 Literary Analysis
Elements that illustrate lively action and vivid spectacle include Macduff's display of Macbeth's head and the general shout of acclamation for Malcolm as the new king.

p. 115 After You Read
1. Possible answer: The doctor hears her say, "who would have thought the old man to have so much blood in him?" He tells the attendant that she has heard too much. He says that "Foul whip'rings are abroad. Unnatural deeds do breed unnatural troubles."

2. **Graphic Organizer**
Sample response:
Flaw: ambition; desire for power
Events that Lead to Disaster: Macbeth prepares his castle against an attack from Malcolm and Macduff. Macbeth anxiously awaits a battle that he cannot win against an overwhelming force. Macbeth vows to fight to the death. Macbeth tells about the insignificance of life. Macbeth fights Macduff.
Lively Action: the sword fights toward the end of the act
3. Sample response: We can infer that Elizabethans understood the mind / wellness connection because the doctor realizes that Lady Macbeth's suffering is mental, not physical. Also, the doctor's appeal to God to help her reveals a belief in the connection between religion and medicine.

The Essential Question
Answers will vary, but students should support ideas with details from the play.

Informational Texts: Feature Articles

p. 119 After You Read
Thinking About the Feature Article
1. Architects and theater designers were asked to create modern versions of the Globe Theatre for the exhibit "Reinventing the Globe."
2. With certainty, historians can describe the stage, which jutted out into the audience.

Reading Skill
3. Students should cite the quote, "It doesn't have to be going to this old, stodgy building. It could be much more accessible, transient, and lighter."
4. The author includes the comment that the stage that jutted out into the crowd was one of its most impressive attributes, and he says that most of Shakespeare's famous dramas were performed there.

ANSWERS TO UNIT 3

Poetry of Donne

p. 120 Graphic Organizer
Sample response:
Situation: The speaker must leave his beloved.
Motivation: The speaker is reassuring his beloved that his reason for leaving is not that he has grown tired of her.

p. 121 Vocabulary Warm-up
1. defray
2. roam
3. tolls
4. dreadful
5. reckon
6. bind
7. desperate
8. jest

p. 122 Reading Warm-up
Sample response:
1. (awful); I think famine in Africa is *dreadful.*
2. (calculations); If I were shopping, I would need to *reckon* the cost of what I wanted to buy to make sure I had enough money.
3. (rings); The church bell *tolls* as the town crier goes from house to house, calling "Bring out your dead."
4. Rats can survive on ships; Wolves and fox *roam* the wild looking for food.
5. (any available fabric); People use sterile bandages made of gauze and cotton to *bind* wounds now.
6. panic; People with symptoms of the plague would grow *desperate* because they knew they would probably die soon.
7. (seriously); People make a *jest* out of something serious just so they can keep going. Otherwise, they would be terrified or depressed.
8. a poor person's medical costs

p. 123 Note-taking Guide
Sample response:
Song
To Whom It Is Addressed: the speaker's beloved
Main Idea: The speaker's beloved should not be sad about his temporary absence.

A Valediction
To Whom It Is Addressed: the speaker's beloved
Main Idea: The speaker will return to his beloved.
Holy Sonnet 10
To Whom It Is Addressed: death
Main Idea: Death is not to be feared, for it brings rest for the body and freedom for the soul.

p. 124 Note-taking Guide
Sample response:
Oval 1: The church is the head of humankind, and all humankind is the church's body.
Oval 2: The church is for all people, and so are the church's actions.
Oval 3: All of humankind is like a book, of which God is the author.
Oval 4: The deepest afflictions make humankind more fit for God.

p. 125 Literary Analysis
Students should circle *b.*

p. 125 Reading Strategy
Sample response: Donne is listening to church bells toll for another's death and realizes that the death of one person affects all of humanity. His motivation is to explain the importance of each person in the greater community.

p. 126 Read Fluently
Students should circle "Any man's death diminishes me."

p. 126 Stop to Reflect
Some students may say that troubles and suffering are never good for people, but other students may say that people can grow and mature as a result of overcoming hardships.

p. 127 After You Read
1. **Graphic Organizer**
Sample response:
First Form of Treasure: affliction
Second Form of Treasure: current money
Relationship Between Forms of Treasure:
Affliction becomes "current money" when used to make one more fit for God.
2. The paradox is "unkindly kind."
3. Sample response: In "Song," the speaker is the devoted lover. The situation is the impending departure of the lover. The speaker's

motivation is to reassure his beloved that he will return to her.

The Essential Question

Answers will vary. Some students may say that Donne's conceits were imaginative ways to express ideas. For example, comparing the speaker and the beloved to a compass is a unique way to describe a love's relationship. The conceits make readers think about the subject in new ways. Others students may say that Donne's conceits do not help him express his ideas because they seem forced and are too different from the ideas in the poems.

Poetry of Jonson

p. 128 Graphic Organizer

Sample response:

"On My First Son"

Inference: The speaker is a father whose son has died.

Text Evidence: The boy lived until he was seven years old and then "scaped world's, and flesh's rage."

Experience: The speaker asks his son to "Rest in soft peace," which is a term we often use as a blessing for the dead.

"Still to Be Neat"

Inference: The speaker disapproves of the lady's appearance.

Text Evidence: The speaker dislikes the lady's artifice and overdone appearance, for "they strike mine eyes, but not my heart."

Experience: A natural look can be more appealing. People who try to hard to look good are often considered vain.

"Song: To Celia"

Inference: The speaker believes that Celia's love enlarges life, including his own.

Text Evidence: The speaker sends Celia a wreath, and "it grows and smells, I swear, / Not of itself, but thee."

Experience: Love adds joy to one's life.

p. 129 Vocabulary Warm-up

1. pledge
2. rage
3. loosely
4. vows
5. state
6. sound
7. lament
8. envy

p. 130 Reading Warm-up

1. (political and economic conditions); I think the *state* of the world today is a complicated mix of destructive events and constructive, hopeful actions.
2. high taxes; People who are in a *rage* get red in the face and move their arms in big gestures.
3. (harmful); A person might *lament* the loss of his or her dog.
4. promise; People *pledge* themselves to a cause, such as the environment or workers' rights.
5. (solid); A decision is *sound* if it is practical and likely to get a good result.
6. promising; I think people should live up to their *vows* if they have thought them through first. They should not make vows they cannot or should not keep.
7. (tightly bound together); *Loosely* means "not tightly."
8. the government attempted to close them; People today often *envy* the expensive cars that others drive.

p. 131 Note-taking Guide

Sample response:

On My First Son

Lines: "Farewell, thou child of my right hand, and joy; / My sin was too much hope of thee, loved boy."

Main Idea: The speaker had great love and expectations for his son, but now the boy has died.

Still to Be Neat

Lines: "Such sweet neglect more taketh me / Than all th'adulteries of art."

Main Idea: The poet is attracted to simple, natural beauty more than to artful appearance.

Song: To Celia

Lines: "Or leave a kiss but in the cup, / And I'll not look for wine."

Main Idea: The speaker needs only Celia's love in order to live.

p. 132 After You Read

1. Sample response: "Still to Be Neat" captures the speaker's true feelings in his yearning for "sweet neglect" rather than "th'adulteries of art."

2. Graphic Organizer

Sample response:

Figurative Language: "Drink to me only with thine eyes"

Repetition: end rhymes such as *mine, wine, thine* and *cup, sup*

Imagery: "But might I of Jove's nectar sup"

3. The speaker loved his son, referring to him as the child of his right hand and his child of joy.

The Essential Question

Answers will vary. Sample response: No, Jonson's clarity results from his precise word choice. Both his word choice and balance help create his poems' emotional effect.

"To His Coy Mistress"
Andrew Marvell

"To the Virgins, to Make Much of Time"
Robert Herrick

"Song"
Sir John Suckling

p. 133 Graphic Organizer

Sample response:

Passage: "Song"

Text Evidence: "If of herself she will not love, / Nothing can make her: / The devil take her!"

Experience: It is a waste of time to pine for someone who does not care for you.

Speaker's Attitude: The speaker is impatient but kind—he is hoping his words will help the young lover move on.

p. 134 Vocabulary Warm-up

1. prime
2. strife
3. vast
4. echoing
5. transpires
6. vault
7. tarry
8. mute

p. 135 Reading Warm-up

Sample response:

1. (In his childhood); I think I will be in my *prime* at twenty-five because I will have a good job and a family by then.
2. great; The ocean and the sky are *vast*.

3. sent them home; *Tarry* means "linger."
4. (the French fashions that pleased her); I would be annoyed by a person *echoing* my ideas if he or she did not say that they were my ideas first.
5. (his concept of absolute rule); *Mute* means "unable or unwilling to speak."
6. quarreled; On a long car trip, there might be *strife* between the children in the backseat about who won the game or who started trouble first.
7. beneath; A *vault* might be dark and creepy inside.
8. (breath); An animal *transpires* using its lungs.

p. 136 Note-taking Guide

Sample response:

To His Coy Mistress

To Whom is the Speaker talking? The speaker is talking to his mistress.

What is the Speaker's Message? Young women should not waste time by being coy, but should love while they are young.

To the Virgins, to Make Much of Time

To Whom is the Speaker talking? The speaker is talking to every young, unmarried woman.

What is the Speaker's Message? Women should marry young to avoid losing the opportunities afforded by youth.

Song

To Whom is the Speaker talking? The speaker is talking to a young man who cannot win his beloved.

What is the Speaker's Message? Do not waste your time waiting for a woman who may never return your love.

p. 137 After You Read

1. Sample response: In the beginning, the speaker seems to have plenty of time to woo his lady; the mood is expectant yet relaxed. In the end, however, the speaker realizes that he and his mistress must immediately take advantage of the moment because time is passing very quickly.

2. Graphic Organizer

Sample response:

To His Coy Mistress

Carpe Diem Images: "Time's winged chariot"

Qualities: Fanciful? Simple? fanciful

Humorous? Passionate? Reasonable?
passionate

To the Virgins, to Make Much of Time
Carpe Diem Images: "Old time is still a-flying
Qualities: Fanciful? Simple? simple
Humorous? Passionate? Reasonable?
reasonable

Song
Carpe Diem Images: "Nothing can make her: / Devil take her!"
Qualities: Fanciful? Simple? simple
Humorous? Passionate? Reasonable?
humorous

3. Sample response: The speaker is mildly provoked by his mistress's flirtatious refusal to give in to him. There is gentle mockery in his description of an eternal courtship.

The Essential Question
Answers will vary. Sample response: Herrick provides a traditional treatment of the *carpe diem* theme. Marlowe provides a different interpretation of the theme by having the speaker describe how he would woo his beloved if they only had enough time. Suckling gives the theme new life by having the speaker encourage the listener to give up on the beloved rather than pursue her.

Poetry of Milton

p. 138 Graphic Organizer
Sample response:
"Sonnet VII"
Main Clause: "my semblance might deceive the truth"
Supporting Element: "That I to manhood am arrived so near"
Supporting Element: "And inward ripeness doth much less appear"
Supporting Element: "That some more timely-happy spirits endureth"
Supporting Element: N/A

"Sonnet XIX"
Main Clause: "I fondly ask"
Supporting Element: "Doth God exact labor, light denied?"
Supporting Element: "When I consider how my light is spent / Ere half my days, in this dark world and wide"
Supporting Element: "And that one talent which is death to hide, / Lodged with me useless, though my soul more bent / To serve there with my Maker"

Supporting Element: "lest he returning chide"

***from* Paradise Lost**
Main Clause: "Sing Heavenly Muse"
Supporting Element: "Of man's first disobedience"
Supporting Element: "and the fruit / Of that forbidden tree"
Supporting Element: "whose mortal taste / Brought death into the world"
Supporting Element: "With loss of Eden, till one greater Man / Restore us, and regain the blissful seat"

p. 139 Vocabulary Warm-up
1. bidding
2. chide
3. lodged
4. hideous
5. stench
6. torments
7. ordained
8. invoke

p. 140 Reading Warm-up
Sample response:
1. paint spattered on the walls and garbage strewn all over the floor; To make the cubicle less *hideous,* I would clean out the garbage and hang photos of my friends and family on the walls.
2. (odor); Rotting lunches and stale coffee are causing the *stench.*
3. official; The main room of the library is *ordained* as a place for studying and reading quietly.
4. (criticized); To *chide* someone, you might use the phrase "Now, what did I just tell you?" or "Don't make me lose my patience."
5. to tell me what to do; The authority to tell someone what to do is also *lodged* in a police officer.
6. (followed his instructions); I would do the *bidding* of my parents.
7. causing people pain; A computer that crashes just before you save your file *torments* you.
8. (my sacred right as an employee); When I become frustrated while doing a math problem, I *invoke* the help of my older brother, who is good at math.

p. 141 Note-taking Guide
Sample response:
Sonnet VII: The speaker is reflecting on his twenty-fourth birthday; he is concerned that he has not accomplished more; he is not doing enough with his talent.
Have in Common: The speaker decides to trust God to make use of him.
Sonnet XIX: The speaker is blind; his talent is now useless; he is unable to serve God with his talent.

p. 142 Note-taking Guide
Sample response:
Presentation of Subject: Adam and Eve's disobedience to God in the Garden of Eden
Invocation: Call for Help: Call to the "Heavenly Muse"
Beginning of Story in the Middle: The battle between God and his host and Satan and his followers in heaven is over; Satan and his host are cast into the lake of fire; Satan determines that he and his host will do only evil.

p. 143 Literary Analysis
Students should circle "Heavenly Muse."

p. 143 Literary Analysis
Sample response:
1. The speaker invokes the Muse.
2. The epic begins in the middle of the action.

p. 143 Reading Check
Adam and Eve disobeyed God's command that they should not taste "Of that forbidden tree."

p. 144 Read Fluently
Students should circle "The infernal Serpent." Students should underline "The mother of mankind."

p. 144 Reading Strategy
1. "Almighty Power" is the subject.
2. The simple predicate is "Hurled."
3. "Him" (Satan) is the direct object.

p. 144 Reading Check
Satan is speaking to Beelzebub.

p. 145 Literary Analysis
Sample response:
1. Satan is courageous.
2. Satan has great physical power.

p. 145 Literary Analysis
Milton is describing the war in heaven between God and Satan before the creation of the world, when God cast Satan and Satan's followers from heaven for all eternity.

p. 145 Reading Check
Satan plans to "wage eternal war" with God.

p. 146 Reading Strategy
Sample response: Satan's huge form lay in the fiery lake. God's will permits Satan to be left to his own evil devices.

p. 146 Reading Check
Heaven will bring "Infinite goodness, grace, and mercy" to humans.

p. 147 Reading Strategy
Sample response: Reason has made him equal, and force raised him above his equals.

p. 147 Literary Analysis
It is fitting for a hero, despite being subject to such terrible circumstances, to stand up against his punishment and assert himself courageously.

p. 147 Stop to Reflect
Satan prefers to be the most powerful being in hell rather than be under God's direct authority in heaven.

p. 148 After You Read
1. **Graphic Organizer**
Sample response:
Sonnet VII
Speaker's Situation: The speaker feels that he has not accomplished enough.
Effect on Ambition: His work is hindered.
Solution and How It Helps: The speaker draws on the conviction that whatever he achieves is the will of heaven.
Sonnet XIX
Speaker's Situation: The speaker is blind and believes that he can no longer serve God.
Effect on Ambition: He can no longer work.
Solution and How It Helps: The speaker is comforted by the conviction that submission to God's will is all that God requires of him.
2. Students may say that Satan is a powerful personality through his great courage in the face of failure and despair and his ability to unite his forces with a single goal.
3. Student's should identify "I fondly ask" as the main clause.

The Essential Question

Answers will vary. Sample response: In Satan's last line in from *Paradise Lost* is "Better to reign in Hell than serve in Heaven," Milton's concise word choice expresses Satan's attitude and the difference that he sees between Hell and Heaven. The contrast between doing what one wants in Hell and serving God in Heaven makes the line powerful.

from Pilgrim's Progress
John Bunyan

p. 149 Graphic Organizer

Sample response:

Specific symbols with names that signal their meaning: Pliable = someone who is easily persuaded, or someone who lacks commitment; Help = a person who is kind and helpful; Slough of Despond = a place of unhappiness and sin; Giant Despair = overwhelming despair; Vanity = a place where everyone is self-centered

Main message or lesson: The journey to salvation is difficult and encumbered by influences that will distract the traveler.

p. 150 Vocabulary Warm-up

1. apprehensions
2. slough
3. surveyors
4. mire
5. scum
6. filth
7. spew
8. midst

p. 151 Reading Warm-up

Sample response:

1. (evaluate and map out these areas); *Surveyors* use tools to measure land before it is developed, or to verify where boundaries lie, or to examine the characteristics of land.
2. an area of deep soggy mud; A synonym for *mire* is *bog* or *fen*.
3. (middle); Soraya left the table in the *midst* of the dinner party when the phone rang.
4. (disgusting dirt); A *synonym* for *filth* is *foul* or *garbage*.
5. (swamp); A desert has little to no water, making it very different from a *slough*.
6. thin, filmy layer, made of waste from plants and other impurities in the water; When Dakota finally got around to cleaning his fish

tank, he found that *scum* had formed on top of the water.
7. like a jet of water released suddenly through an opening in a dam; Synonyms for *spew* include: *pour forth, gush,* or *stream out*.
8. (alligators) (crocodiles); Ling had *apprehensions* about driving during a snowstorm.

p. 152 Note-taking Guide

Sample response:

Christian: Christian falls into the Slough; He is unable to pull himself out of the mire; After Help pulls him out, he resumes his journey toward the Celestial City.

Pliable: Pliable falls into the Slough; He climbs out of the Slough but does not help Christian climb out.

Help: Help pulls Christian out of the Slough; He explains to the narrator what the Slough is and why people continue to fall into it; He tells the narrator that despite the king's efforts, the Slough cannot be repaired.

p. 153 After You Read

1. Answers will vary. Sample response:

Christian: He leaves the City of Destruction for the Celestial City. He carries a burden of sin. He is rescued by Help and continues his journey.

Pliable: He tries to get Christian to return to the City of Destruction. He eventually goes with Christian, but he abandons Christian in the swamp.

2. It represents unhappiness and sin—a place where people get trapped and have great trouble escaping.

3. **Graphic Organizer**

Sample response:

Character / Place: City of Destruction

Symbolic Role: This place represents troubled environment in which a person lives.

Character / Place: Castle of Doubt

Symbolic Role: This place represents the second-guessing that a person engages in while searching for salvation.

Character / Place: Slough of Despond

Symbolic Role: This is a place where temptations hold a person back.

Character / Place: Help

Symbolic Role: This is a friend who helps one get out of trouble.

Character / Place: Pliable

Symbolic Role: This is an easily distracted person who may or may not assist the seeker.

The Essential Question

Answers will vary. Sample response: This selection shows that in Bunyan's time, most people believed that faith was necessary to help them get through troubling times. For example, Christian's own strength was insufficient to pull him out of the Slough of Despond; Help arrives to save him. *Pilgrim's Progress* probably affirmed what people believed about the necessity of faith and encouraged them to continue to seek God despite life's difficulties.

from Eve's Apology in Defense of Women
Amelia Lanier

"To Lucasta, on Going to the Wars"
Richard Lovelace

"To Althea, from Prison"
Richard Lovelace

p. 154 Graphic Organizer

Sample response:

"Eve's Apology"

Connection: The speaker seeks to free women from full blame for the Fall, arguing that Adam was more to blame because he sinned willingly, while Eve was deceived.

"To Althea, from Prison"

Historical Context: England was controlled by radical Puritans who had little tolerance for Loyalists, Catholics, and even moderate Puritans; those who challenged Puritan rule were often imprisoned and even killed.

Connection: The speaker defends the traditions of freedom of thought and political choice.

p. 155 Vocabulary Warm-up

1. knowledge
2. soar
3. frame
4. breach
5. excused
6. hover
7. tangled
8. voice

p. 156 Reading Warm-up

Sample response:

1. (shape); To *frame* a role means to create it according to certain expectations and limitations, to influence.
2. opposition to his policies; To *voice* something is to express a sentiment or an opinion verbally.
3. (agendas on both sides); *Tangled* means twisted together or caught in a knot.
4. (his execution); My parents say that if I *breach* their trust, I will lose my phone.
5. had since come to support the monarchy; A synonym for *excused* is *pardoned*.
6. A restoration of other freedoms, such as dancing and playing music in public places; A tax rate can *soar* when a government overspends.
7. (supporters); A bee might *hover* over a flower.
8. to encourage cultural growth in England; I have a great deal of *knowledge* about working on cars because my father is a mechanic.

p. 157 Note-taking Guide

Sample response:

Eve's Apology

Speaker: The speaker is a woman with a powerful pro-woman argument.

Audience: The intended audience is men and the public in general.

Main Idea / Purpose: The speaker seeks to free women from their current state of domestic bondage, which had resulted from the belief that Eve was to blame for the dismissal from the Garden of Eden.

Lucasta

Speaker: The speaker is a man going to war.

Audience: The speaker's beloved is the audience.

Main Idea / Purpose: The speaker explains that he must go to war, and that placing a higher value on honor than on his beloved enables him to love her more.

Althea

Speaker: The speaker is an imprisoned man.

Audience: Althea and the general public make up the audience.

Main Idea / Purpose: The speaker says that although his body is confined, his mind is free.

p. 158 After You Read

1. The speaker remains free because "Stone walls" and "iron bars" cannot imprison the mind and soul.

2. **Graphic Organizer**

Sample response:

Tradition Lanier Opposes: Lanier opposes the traditional belief that Eve deserved more blame for the fall of humans.

Lanier's Beliefs About Tradition: Lanier believes that Adam is more responsible for the fall of humans because of his privileged position.

3. Imprisoned for his steadfast support of the king, Lovelace defies his captors and asserts that, like a caged bird, he will sing praises to "the glories of [his] King" even more effectively.

The Essential Question

Answers will vary. Sample response: Lovelace was reflecting dominant social attitudes about women, and Lanier was trying to change those attitudes. Lovelace's poems portray a man at the center of the action. The woman either is asked to understand his behavior or is described in terms of only her physical beauty. Lanier attempted to change dominant social attitudes that blamed Eve, and by extension, all women, for the Biblical account for humanity's fall from grace. Instead of blaming women, Lanier argues that they are responsible for giving men knowledge.

from A Journal of the Plague Year
Daniel Defoe

p. 159 Graphic Organizer

Sample response:

When? the Plague Year (1664–1665)

Who? H. F. (fictional narrator)

Where? London

What? The face of London has changed.

Why? The entire city is filled with fear, pain, and sorrow.

How? A plague has spread throughout the city leaving many dead in its wake.

p. 160 Vocabulary Warm-up

1. dreadful
2. utmost
3. agony
4. hazard
5. venture
6. mourning
7. altered
8. calamity

p. 161 Reading Warm-up

Sample response:

1. (to sea); I would *venture* to London.

2. violent storms, a rescue from a sinking ship, and an attack by pirates who take him prisoner and force him into slavery; A synonym for *calamity* is *catastrophe*.

3. A dreadful storm might include strong winds, hail, and pounding rain; A synonym for *dreadful* is *horrific*.

4. the loss of his shipmates; *Mourning* is a feeling of bereavement a person may experience after the end, or the death, of something or someone.

5. building a strong shelter and a canoe, hunting wild goats, and sowing grain; A synonym for *utmost*, as it is used in this passage, is *best*.

6. (circumstances); The sad expression on his face *altered* when he saw Jenny, and he grinned.

7. It belongs to a member of a tribe of cannibals who bring prisoners to the island in order to eat them; A person might find no fresh water to drink or no wood with which to build a fire.

8. Friday must have been in both mental and physical agony since cannibals held him by force and he must have expected they would eat him; The word *agony* means "extreme physical or mental suffering."

p. 162 Note-taking Guide

Sample response:

What he hears: The narrator hears the "voice of mourning" in the streets.

Where he goes: The narrator goes to a mass grave in Aldgate churchyard.

What he sees: The narrator sees the buriers literally dumping plague victims into the pit; he later sees a man grieving for his wife and children at the edge of the pit.

How he feels: The narrator is at first intrigued and then truly grieved to see the man suffering the loss of his family. The narrator says that the sight is "awful" and "full of terror."

p. 163 After You Read

1. Sample response: The fact that both narrators use the pronoun *I* to relate experiences and that they limit comments to what they see and know shows that these experiences are told by first-person narrators.

2. **Graphic Organizer**
Sample response:
Questions: What event is greatly changing London?
Answers: The arrival of bubonic plague, a deadly disease, is changing London.
Questions: Why is a great pit dug in a London churchyard?
Answers: People are dying so rapidly that they had to be buried quickly.
Questions: When is the narrator's parish obliged to refill the large pit it had finished on September 4?
Answers: The parish had to refill the pit a little more than two weeks later on September 30.
3. Answers may vary. Students may say that questioning made their reading more active and focused because it helped them concentrate on the details that Defoe gives in his *Journal.*

The Essential Question

Answers will vary, but students should describe a landmark event in their own region that would make a good story. Students may recall events such as floods, tornadoes, or hurricanes.

Informational Texts: Reports

p. 167 After You Read
Thinking About Reports

1. The causes of congestion in London are many years of under-investment combined with significant rates of increase in London's population.
2. Reduced traffic delays, improved journey time reliability, reduced waiting time at bus stops, and lower fuel consumption will have economic benefits.

Reading Skill

3. Sample response: The chart shows the total traffic entering the charging zone during charging hours. It also shows the progress and effect of the congestion charging program.

4. A bulleted list highlights the key transport priorities.

from Gulliver's Travels
Jonathan Swift

"A Modest Proposal"
Jonathan Swift

p. 168 Graphic Organizer
Sample response:
What Swift Says: "One emperor lost his life, and another his crown."
What He Means: King Charles I "lost his life" and King James lost "his crown."
What Swift Says: ". . . but the books of the Big-Endians have been long forbidden, and the whole party rendered incapable by law of holding employments."
What He Means: Catholic literature was banned, and Catholics could not hold public office.

p. 169 Vocabulary Warm-up

1. prodigious
2. divert
3. contrive
4. laudable
5. contemptible
6. oppression
7. affirm
8. collateral

p. 170 Reading Warm-up
Sample response:
1. (enormous); An antonym for *prodigious* is *small.*
2. terrific; My teacher made a *laudable* effort to prepare his students for a challenging honors class the following year.
3. (distract); We tried to *divert* the child's attention with a lollipop.
4. (worthless); An antonym for *contemptible* is *respectable, admired,* or *worthy.* She held a *respectable* position as a teacher.
5. how they are weighted down by hardships and limited opportunities; *Oppression* happens anywhere that the human right to life, liberty, and free speech is denied.
6. (confirms); An antonym for *affirm* is *deny* or *veto.*
7. fantastic adventures for their characters; To *contrive* means to come up with a plan for doing something or to work out the details in order to make a scheme go forward.

8. (parallel); because each story has some-thing to say about life as its author knows it in his own society and time.

p. 171 Note-taking Guide
Sample response:
Details to Achieve This Purpose: The dis-pute among the Lilliputians about whether to break an egg at the large or the small end represents the dispute between Catholicism and Protestantism. The war between Lilliput and Blefuscu represents the tension between Protestant England and Catholic France.
Details to Achieve This Purpose: The king of Lilliput wants to enslave the people of Blefuscu and make them break their eggs at the small end, representing England's desire to conquer France and force the French into Protestantism.

p. 172 Reading Strategy
The footnotes explain the ironic meaning of Blefuscu and the satirical significance of the Lilliputian argument concerning egg-breaking.

p. 172 Literary Analysis
Sample response: Swift makes egg-breaking the cause of the conflict because it is trivial.

p. 173 Stop to Reflect
Sample response: No; it is very silly to die because one disagrees with another over how to break an egg.

p. 173 Reading Strategy
Students should circle "all true believers shall break their eggs at the convenient end," and "which is the convenient end, seems, in my humble opinion, to be left to every man's conscience."

p. 174 Literary Analysis
It is ironic because spectacles are generally used for such civilian and academic pursuits as reading and writing, not for protection in a military operation.

p. 174 Read Fluently
Students should underline "he seemed to think of nothing less than reducing the whole empire of Blefuscu into a province and governing it by a viceroy; of destroying the Big-Endian exiles and compelling that people to break the smaller end of their eggs, by which he would remain sole monarch of the whole world."

p. 174 Reading Check
Gulliver tells the Emperor that he would not help to bring a free and brave people into slavery.

p. 175 Note-taking Guide
Sample response:
Details to Achieve This Purpose: The king of Brobdingnag laughs at Gulliver and asks whether Gulliver is a "Whig or a Tory"; the king's laughter indicates that the dispute between England's two political parties is ridiculous in the grand scheme of things. When the king turns to his "first minister," he continues to ridicule the things of which Gulliver spoke, such as the nobility of England and the "scourge of France."
Details to Achieve This Purpose: The king's horror at Gulliver's solemn proposal of using gunpowder and cannon to destroy another city is a strong critique of England's power-hungry rulers.

p. 176 Note-taking Guide
Sample response:
Understatement: "I am not in the least pain upon that matter"; "I am not so violently bent of my own opinion"
Exaggeration: "We should see an honest emulation among the married women, which of them could bring the fattest child to the market"; "men would become as fond of their wives, during the time of their pregnancy, as they are now of their mares in foal"
Sarcasm: "this food will be somewhat dear, and therefore very proper for landlords"; "as they have already devoured most of the parents, [the landlords] seem to have the best title to the children"

p. 177 After You Read
1. **Graphic Organizer**
Sample response:
Items in Text: disagreement over egg-breaking / Lilliput / Blefuscu
Targets of Swift's Satire: foolish arguments concerning religion / England / France
2. Sample response: Swift writes of the Big-Endians and the Little-Endians, who go to war over the proper way to break an egg. This situation involves an ironic contradiction between reality and appearance, in which the egg-breaking appears to be serious, but is actually quite trivial.

3. Sample response: Details such as roads crowded with beggars and starving children in rags, and children who become thieves or indentured servants in order to survive describe the dire social conditions that Swift desires to change.

The Essential Question
Answers will vary. Sample response: Swift wanted society to change its views on religion, warfare, and politics. Swift believed that some religious conflicts were petty, and in *Gulliver's Travels*, Chapter 1, he used satire to compare these conflicts with the Lilliputians' squabbles about which end of an egg's shell to break. In *Gulliver's Travels*, Chapter 2, Swift used the King of Brobdingnag to satirize English enthusiasm for warfare and weaponry. In "A Modest Proposal," Swift used satire to present an idea to help with "the Irish problem." He knew that his proposal was repellent, but so was the current practice of excessively taxing the poor Irish peasants.

from An Essay on Man
Alexander Pope

from The Rape of the Lock
Alexander Pope

p. 178 Graphic Organizer
Sample response:
Lines: 155–160
Purpose: to satirize
What Does It Mean? It shows how silly people can react over such insignificant actions.
Lines: 79–88, Canto V
Purpose: to satirize
What Does It Mean? It shows more overreaction to the cutting of hair.

p. 179 Vocabulary Warm-up
1. excursion
2. vernal
3. autumnal
4. transient
5. tediousness
6. intrusion
7. languish
8. prevails

p. 180 Reading Warm-up
Sample response:
1. (weary . . . the same elements in each picture); perfect perspective, calculated composition, still postures, smooth brushstrokes

2. (relaxed and comfortable); *relax*
3. a temporary moment; *permanent*
4. travel to a garden; Our family went on an *excursion* to the art museum.
5. (spring); Robins and rain showers are *vernal.*
6. (fall); Apple picking and falling leaves are *autumnal.*
7. interrupted his work; Doing homework is an *intrusion* on my time.
8. (appear most commonly); The owl is a nocturnal bird that *prevails* at night.

p. 181 Note-taking Guide
Sample response:
Setting: Hampton Court, where Belinda plays a game of cards with two men.
Events
1. The baron cuts off a lock of Belinda's hair.
2. A battle to restore Belinda's lost lock ensues.
3. The lock ascends to heaven and becomes a comet.
End Result: Belinda's name is remembered forever.

p. 182 After You Read
1. **Graphic Organizer**
Sample response:
Lines in Poem: Canto III, 161–162
Action / Activity: Belinda's lock is cut.
Lines in Poem: Canto V, 21–34
Action / Activity: The women "battle" against the men.
Lines in Poem: Canto V, 53–56
Action / Activity: The baron defies Belinda.
2. These lines offer an elaborate comparison in the style of an epic, using the word like to begin the simile.
3. Sample response: Pope pokes fun by describing the preparation and consumption of coffee as a profound and moving ritual. He entertains by describing the effects of coffee on the baron's brain and the sylphs' frantic efforts to keep the coffee from spilling.

The Essential Question
Answers will vary. Sample response: Although Pope mocks humanity in the selection from *An Essay on Man* by describing humanity as "The glory, jest, and riddle of the world!" he invites readers to consider human nature and to view themselves seriously. Pope's main goal in "The Rape of the Lock" is to entertain readers with his mockery. Pope thinks that society's rituals

are extravagant and silly, but they seem to serve a purpose. For example, comparing a card game to an epic battle indicates that courtship rituals are taken too seriously, but such rituals were necessary for people to meet, get to know each other, and marry.

from A Dictionary of the English Language
Samuel Johnson

from The Life of Samuel Johnson
James Boswell

p. 183 Graphic Organizer
Sample response:
What I Know: how to use a dictionary and what a dictionary contains
What I Want to Know: how Johnson chose the words and spellings for his dictionary
What I Learned: Johnson read other writers to see how they used words.

p. 184 Vocabulary Warm-up
1. exuberance
2. omitted
3. accumulated
4. harmonious
5. console
6. tranquility
7. convulsive
8. longevity

p. 185 Reading Warm-up
Sample response:
1. (lively); *joyful enthusiasm*
2. (for many years); Redwood trees have *longevity*.
3. An ancient Persian myth describes the origin of chess as a son's attempt to *comfort* his mother after his brother died in battle. You might *console* someone after they have experienced a loss or misfortune.
4. shook her entire body; *Convulsive* means "having involuntary muscle spasms."
5. (chaos); *peace, calmness, serenity*
6. soft . . . sounds; A barbershop quartet is known for its *harmonious* sounds.
7. (gathering); A sports fan may have *accumulated* ticket stubs or sports memorabilia.
8. to speed up the game; Richard accidentally *omitted* the eggs, causing the cake to become inedible.

p. 186 Note-taking Guide
Sample response:
Johnson's Feelings About Writers of Dictionaries: Johnson believes that they are doomed to criticism.
Johnson's Feelings About the English Language: Johnson believes that English has been neglected too long and is in a state of confusion.
Johnson's Feelings About His Own Dictionary: Johnson is content with it, regardless of its flaws.
Johnson's Feelings About Himself: Johnson is proud of his accomplishment, but does not expect his effort to garner praise.

p. 187 Note-taking Guide
Sample response:
Contradictory Qualities: Johnson had an irritable temper but a kind heart.
Illness and Infirmaties: Johnson's health made him melancholy at times.
Studies and Intellectual Pursuits: Johnson had accumulated a vast body of knowledge from his diverse intellectual pursuits.
Common Conversation: Johnson expressed his thoughts in elegant language and with great force.

p. 188 After You Read
1. Sample response: In the Preface to the *Dictionary of the English Language*, "those who toil at the lower employments" is a formal way of referring to people who work with their hands rather than by their intellect. In *Life of Samuel Johnson*, "to obtain the acquaintance of that extraordinary man" is a formal way of stating that Boswell would like to meet or be introduced to someone whom he respects.
2. **Graphic Organizer**
Sample response:
**Johnson's *Dictionary:* ** *patron* One who countenances, supports or protects. Commonly a wretch who supports with insolence, and is paid with flattery.
Modern Dictionary: *patron* 1. noun someone who supports an organization, an artist, a musical performer, etc., especially by giving money 2. the support that a patron gives to an organization, etc. 3. someone who often uses a particular store, restaurant, company, etc.
Similarities / Differences: Johnson's definition is still accurate in its commonly used sense.

3. Students should record details such as relying on the rules of general grammar, using experience and analogy to make decisions, and borrowing from works of great writers.

The Essential Question

Answers will vary. Sample response: Both Johnson and Boswell are cultural innovators because their words set a standard for later writers to follow. Johnson's dictionary helped order the English language. Boswell's biography of Johnson portrays Johnson accurately, including his flaws. Johnson is also a cultural conservative because he wanted to preserve the English language.

"Elegy Written in a Country Churchyard"
Thomas Gray

"A Nocturnal Reverie"
Anne Finch, Countess of Winchilsea

p. 189 Graphic Organizer

Sample response:

"Elegy Written in a Country Churchyard"
Original: "Now fades the glimmering landscape on the sight"
Paraphrase: Nightfall is making it difficult to see the landscape.

"A Nocturnal Reverie"
Original: "When in some river, overhung with green, / The waving moon and trembling leaves are seen"
Paraphrase: The moonlight and trees are reflected in the river.

p. 190 Vocabulary Warm-up

1. celestial
2. curfew
3. drowsy
4. glimmering
5. rouse
6. lull
7. annals
8. anthem

p. 191 Reading Warm-up

Sample response:

1. (ten year camp history); *Annals* refers to recorded history.
2. commitment to enjoying and conserving nature; A country usually has its own *anthem.*

3. (nine o'clock sharp); Most of my friends have an eleven o'clock *curfew* on weekends.
4. I nudged him with my elbow to wake him, so he could rush up to the stage and happily claim his award; Despite trying several times, I could not *rouse* my sister from her deep sleep.
5. the shiny trophy; Coals in a dying fire can be described as *glimmering.*
6. (I closed my eyes); A *drowsy* person usually nods off or falls asleep.
7. a shooting star; an extraordinary meteor shower; The sun, planets, comets, and stars all are *celestial* elements.
8. (father whistling the camp anthem; the pleasant sound); A synonym for *lull* is *soothe.*

p. 192 Note-taking Guide

Sample response:
Elegy Written in a Country Churchyard
Neoclassical
polished expression: "Awaits alike the inevitable hour. / The paths of glory lead but to the grave."
complicated vocabulary: "The boast of heraldry, the pomp of power, / And all that beauty, all that wealth e'er gave"
Romantic
nature and simple folk: "The lowing herd winds slowly o'er the lea, / "The plowman homeward plods his weary way"
deep feelings: "Full many a flower is born to blush unseen, / And waste its sweetness on the desert air."
A Nocturnal Reverie
Neoclassical
polished expression: "When freshened grass now bears itself upright"
complicated vocabulary: "Or from some tree, famed for the owl's delight, / She, hollowing clear, directs the wanderer right"
Romantic
nature and simple folk: "When nibbling sheep at large pursue their food"
deep feelings: "But silent musings urge the mind to seek / Something, too high for syllables to speak"

p. 193 After You Read

1. The speaker appears to accept the universal anonymity that awaits everyone in death, and he expects the comfort of heaven.

2. Graphic Organizer
Sample response:
Stated Ideas: Humans need to be remembered after death.
Feelings Expressed: wistfulness
Message About Life: Nature plays an important role in both the life and death of humans.
Stated Ideas: Nature makes the human spirit content and inspires human beings by its beauty.
Feelings Expressed: ecstasy in the face of the sublime
Message About Life: Nature gives human beings solace.
3. Sample response: When it is so peaceful, the speaker wishes to remain outside all night.

The Essential Question
Answers will vary, but students should note that the beauty, dignity, and peace that both Gray and Finch find in their outdoor settings help them draw the conclusion that these virtues are more important than ambitious pursuits.

"The Aims of *The Spectator*" Joseph Addison

p. 194 Graphic Organizer
Sample response:
Topic: people who are able to speak only of the events of the day
Details: There are men who are "unfurnished with ideas, till the business and conversation of the day has supplied them." They have nothing to offer society, and should remain within their "chambers" until they read *The Spectator* each morning.
Inference: Author's Attitude: Addison mocks those who, in his opinion, cannot think for themselves.

p. 195 Vocabulary Warm-up
1. punctually
2. blemishes
3. contrived
4. folly
5. comprehended
6. multitudes
7. endeavor
8. commiseration

p. 196 Reading Warm-up
Sample response:
1. In order to share his viewpoints and earn a reputation as a writer; money, friends, and so on.
2. (delivered); Reading the newspaper *punctually* at 7 A.M. every morning was the routine.
3. To ensure that people were informed and to influence society; by being able to summarize various points and accurately respond to questions about it.
4. He often wrote about them; silliness
5. carefully crafted his essays from his own beliefs; it implies scheming or falsifying
6. people who avoided or criticized his messages / writing; pimples, scars, and so on.
7. he dismissed them; at the loss of someone or something of value
8. earned him great fame; My *endeavor* shall be to make high grades in English class this year.

p. 197 Note-taking Guide
Sample response:
Families: "well regulated"; "for their good to order this paper to be punctually served up, and to be looked upon as part of the tea equipage"
Gentlemen, My Good Brothers: "the fraternity of spectators, who live in the world without having anything to do in it"; "Have no other business with the rest of mankind but to look upon them"
The Blanks of Society: "unfurnished with ideas"; "poor souls"; "needy persons"
The Female World: "the toilet is their great sense of business, and the right adjusting of their hair the principle enjoyment of their lives"

p. 198 After You Read
1. Graphic Organizer
Sample response:
Analytic or Descriptive: descriptive
General or Of a Specific Era? specific era
Logical or Humorous? humorous
2. Addison encourages an attitude of "instruction" and "diversion" in regard to both learning and entertainment.

3. Addison's attitude about the "blanks of society" is mildly mocking. He considers them uninformed people who cannot think for themselves and who generally irritate the people around them.

The Essential Question

Answers will vary. Sample response: Addison believes that people are a product of what they read and how they behave. He wants his readers to engage in more wholesome and educational pursuits to "distinguish themselves from the thoughtless herd of their ignorant and unattentive brethren." Addison hopes that his paper will appeal to women who enjoy intellectual discussion. Addison seems to be both reflecting and influencing social trends. The fact that his paper's circulation was increasing ("there are already three thousand of them distributed every day. . . .") suggests a growing social trend to read periodicals. The growing popularity of Addison's journal also suggests that he was influencing that trend. For example, he writes "I must reckon about three-score thousand disciples in London and Westminster . . ."

ANSWERS TO UNIT 4

"To a Mouse"
Robert Burns

"To a Louse"
Robert Burns

"Woo'd and Married and A'"
Joanna Baillie

p. 199 Graphic Organizer
Sample response:
Sleekit: sleek
saunt an' sinner: saint and sinner
dinna: do not

p. 200 Vocabulary Warm-up
1. notion
2. compared
3. companion
4. trouble
5. impudence
6. social
7. schemes
8. union

p. 201 Reading Warm-up
Sample response:
1. It was a movement that lasted a long time;
A *notion* is an idea formed on an impulse or a whim.
2. (ideas of order, calm, and balance, and rejection of nature); A young man with a boring *social* life might go out to movies with a group of friends.
3. the Romantics held very specific views about nature and the individual; *Compared* means "examined to note similarities."
4. (people with nature); Students might form a *union* to try to get the dress code changed.
5. did not have respect for; The child was sent to his room for showing *impudence* to his parents.
6. (problem); One kind of *trouble* some modern societies have is racism.
7. many problems would disappear; One career that involves coming up with *schemes* is marketing.
8. (peer); My traveling *companion* is my sister.

p. 202 Note-taking Guide
Sample response:
"To a Mouse"
Whom/What the Speaker Addresses: a mouse
Speaker's Main Message: I apologize for accidentally destroying your house with my plow; your unexpected loss is similar to human beings' plans coming undone.
"To a Louse"
How the Speaker Finds His Topic: The speaker sees a louse on the bonnet of a well-dressed lady.
Whom/What the Speaker Addresses: a louse
Speaker's Main Message: Proud, conceited behavior is ridiculous.
"Woo'd and Married and A'"
How the Speaker Finds His Topic: The speaker is present at a wedding.
Whom/What the Speaker Addresses: the reader
Speaker's Main Message: Being married is more important than wealth or possessions, especially when the husband loves the wife.

p. 203 After You Read
1. Sample response: The speaker's language suggests that he is one of the common folk, someone who is in touch with the basics of life.
2. **Graphic Organizer**
Sample response:
Poem: "To a Mouse"
Subject: the uprooting of a mouse's nest
Message: Even the most carefully considered plans can go awry.
Poem: "To a Louse"
Subject: a louse crawling on a lady's bonnet
Message: If we could see ourselves as others do, we would act less foolishly.
Poem: "Woo'd and Married and A'"
Subject: a young bride's unhappiness over her lack of rich adornments
Message: Love can make up for the lack of riches.
3. Sample response: The footnotes provide translations for words that are written in dialect, which help you understand the meanings of difficult words in the poems.

The Essential Question

Answers will vary. Sample response: In "Woo'd and Married and A'," a young, impoverished bride laments her lack of finery and her upcoming marriage to a man with no money. Baillie's description of the bride shows true insight into the mind of a foolish, immature, and materialist girl because the girl experiences disappointment when she should be happy that anyone wants to marry her at all. Baillie further proves the girl's immaturity when her worries are finally soothed by the groom's flattery.

The Poetry of Blake

p. 204 Graphic Organizer

Sample response:

Archetypal Perspective: The lamb is an archetypal image that people associate with innocence and gentleness.

Political and Historical Perspectives: The first stanza of "The Chimney Sweeper" reveals the cruel fate of poor children in Blake's time.

p. 205 Vocabulary Warm-up

1. mild
2. mead
3. struggling
4. bound
5. seize
6. wept
7. rejoice
8. aspire

p. 206 Reading Warm-up

Sample response:

1. opportunities to explore their potential; A word that means the same as *seize* is *grab.*
2. to achieve their creative goals; I *aspire* to own a construction company one day.
3. (with difficulty); The salmon were *struggling* to swim upstream against the river's current.
4. (tears); My mother *wept* for joy at my sister's wedding.
5. (joy); Someone might *rejoice* about getting a great new job.
6. a peaceful meadow; Children might play tag or fly a kite in a *mead.*
7. (gentle); A word that means the opposite of *mild* is *harsh.*
8. by heavy chains; *Bound* means "tied" or "held tightly together."

p. 207 Note-taking Guide

Sample response:

The Lamb

Key Words: tender, meek, mild, child

Key Ideas: The creator of the lamb and child is benevolent. Both the child and the lamb are symbols for Jesus.

The Tyger

Key Words: burning, fearful, dread, terrors

Key Ideas: Perhaps the creator of the tiger is responsible for evil as well as good.

The Chimney Sweeper

Key Words: weep, soot, coffins, Angel

Key Ideas: The chimney sweeps are living in terrible conditions and are supposed to be confronted by the prospect of heaven after they die.

Infant Sorrow

Key Words: helpless, naked, struggling, sulk

Key Ideas: The world is cruel and difficult, even for the infants just entering it.

p. 208 After You Read

1. The speaker, like the lamb and the lamb's creator, is a child and presumably "meek and mild."
2. Sample response: The symbol of the lamb represents innocence and Christ.
3. **Graphic Organizer**

Sample response:

Who Suffers? Tom Dacre and the other chimney sweeps suffer.

Why? They must work as chimney sweeps.

Is Suffering Fair? No; they are young and were forced into this work.

Suggested Solution: Do your duty, and earn heaven as a reward.

Is the Solution Fair? No; the situation of the chimney sweeps is still unjust.

The Essential Question

Answers will vary, but students should support their opinions with details from the poems.

Introduction to *Frankenstein*
Mary Wollstonecraft Shelley

p. 209 Graphic Organizer

Sample response:

Prediction: Shelley found the idea for *Frankenstein* in another story.

New Information: "'We will each write a ghost story,' said Lord Byron . . . ."

Revised Prediction: She found her idea while working on the contest that the stories inspired.

p. 210 Vocabulary Warm-up

1. devout
2. furnish
3. acceded
4. endeavor
5. successively
6. contrive
7. adorns
8. incitement

p. 211 Reading Warm-up

Sample response:

1. (sincere); Gail is a *devout* fan of Japanese animation.
2. the belief that she would realize the great potential that her father believed she had; A synonym for *furnish* is *provide*.
3. (encouragement); *Incitement* means "encouragement" or "urging."
4. (task); An *endeavor* I might like to try some day is learning to play the piano.
5. Percy suggested that they should each *contrive* to write a horror story; *Contrive* means "plan."
6. a great work; The teacher *acceded*, so he agreed to give the students more time.
7. in a series of steps; People rehearse the scenes of plays *successively*.
8. admire it as an exceptional example of Gothic literature; Something that often *adorns* the hair of little girls is a hairclip or a bow.

p. 212 Note-taking Guide

Sample response:

Who Is Involved: Mary Shelley, Percy Shelley, Lord Byron, and John William Polidori

When It Takes Place: It takes place while visiting Lord Byron one rainy summer.

Where It Takes Place: Switzerland

What Happens: After reading ghost stories, Lord Byron suggests the idea that each person create an original ghost story.

How It Happens: One night, after a discussion of Dr. Darwin's experiments and the possibilities of reanimating a corpse, Shelley imagines a vision of the creation of a creature that inspires her story.

p. 213 After You Read

1. The intensity of Mary Shelley's vision suggests that she finds Dr. Darwin's experiments deeply disturbing for their implications about human power over creating life.

2. **Graphic Organizer**

Sample response:

Gothic Characteristic: elements of the supernatural

Example in Shelley: Both stories feature ghosts, one of which delivers a supernatural kiss of death.

3. Students may say that because Shelley was not able to sleep that night, she was deeply affected by the conversation.

The Essential Question

Answers will vary, but students should support their ideas with details from the introduction.

Poetry of Wordsworth

p. 214 Graphic Organizer

Sample response:

Celebration of Common Folk: (*from* "The Prelude") Wordsworth hopes that the French Revolution can bring happiness to both "the meek and lofty," and he sees the world as one that belongs to "all of us," not just to the social elite.

Love of Nature: ("Lines Composed a Few Miles Above Tintern Abbey") Wordsworth finds solace in his memories of being in nature while he is "'mid the din / Of towns and cities."

Admiration for French Revolution: (*from* "The Prelude") Wordsworth describes the beginning of the French Revolution as a time "When Reason seemed the most to assert her rights . . ." and when it seemed possible to rebuild society on just and rational principles.

Loss of Faith in Reason: (*from* "The Prelude") When the French Revolution fails to do as Wordsworth had hoped, Wordsworth finds that he has been "betrayed . . . by reasonings false" and places his trust in his heart that is guided by nature.

p. 215 Vocabulary Warm-up

1. region
2. uncertain
3. assist
4. orchard
5. glimpses

6. gentle
7. inward
8. duties

p. 216 Reading Warm-up
Sample response:
1. (apple); *Orchard* means "land used for growing fruit or nut trees."
2. (area); The southern *region* of the country usually has hot weather during the summer.
3. kept us cool in the summer sun; *Gentle* means "mild."
4. supervising a large staff and reporting important issues directly to the company's president; *Duties* means "obligations."
5. not sure; Sally was unfamiliar with this city, and she was *uncertain* about how to find the hotel.
6. (helped); I will *assist* the elderly woman in crossing the street.
7. faraway cities; *Glimpses* means "quick, incomplete views or looks."
8. a small lake populated by many varieties of birds; *Inward* means "located inside."

p. 217 Note-taking Guide
Sample response:
Who: the poet Wordsworth, who addresses his sister Dorothy
When: summer
Where: the Wye River valley near Tintern Abbey
What: Wordsworth returns to Tintern Abbey, noting that his memories of his last visit were a source of comfort to him, and speculates on the evolution of his reaction to nature from spontaneous joy to a more mature acknowledgment of the unity in nature.
Why: Maturity and its deeper understanding of reason have changed his feelings about nature, although both visits elicited strong reactions, and he wishes for his sister to share his feelings for this place and remember it and him in the future.

p. 218 Reading Check
Students should circle "again I hear / These waters" and "I behold these steep and lofty cliffs."

p. 218 Stop to Reflect
1. Students should underline "in lonely rooms, and 'mid the din / Of towns and cities."

2. Students should underline "in the blood, and felt along the heart."

p. 219 Read Fluently
The speaker explains that the pleasure he feels now will also be a pleasant memory for him in the future.

p. 219 Reading Check
The speaker looks differently at nature because he has matured and his point of view has changed.

p. 220 Literary Analysis
Nature inspires a feeling of connectedness and unity.

p. 220 Reading Strategy
Wordsworth now looks to nature as a guide. He will take his cues from his senses.

p. 221 Reading Check
Reason 1: The woods and cliffs become "more dear" for their own sake.
Reason 2: They are also important for his sister's sake, for the pleasure they will later provide for her.

p. 222 Note-taking Guide
Sample response:
from **The Prelude:** Although the French Revolution seemed at first to be driven by reason, the ideals became convoluted and the French became "oppressors," conquering other regions. Wordsworth tries to justify continued faith in the cause, but in the end loses his conviction, advocating instead faith in his heart guided by nature.
The World Is Too Much With Us: Wordsworth believes that people are too caught up in material concerns to appreciate the power of nature.
London, 1802: The poet says that England is lacking in "inward happiness" and is filled with selfish, mediocre people. It needs Milton's moral vision and example to help restore it to its former ways.

p. 223 After You Read
1. Sample response: Although to his original pleasure is added a "sad perplexity" on his second visit, he also experiences a new pleasure the second time knowing that his present experience will nourish him again when he remembers it later.

2. Graphic Organizer

Sample response:

Specific and Simple: "Therefore I am still / A lover of the meadows and the woods . . ."

Abstract but Simple: "The anchor of my purest thoughts . . ."

Abstract and Difficult: "A motion and a spirit, that impels / All thinking things . . ."

3. Sample response: These lines suggest that political idealism, youthful enthusiasm, and a desire for change were important elements of this context.

The Essential Question

Answers will vary, but students should support their ideas with details from the poems.

Informational Texts: Traffic Reports

p. 225 Vocabulary Builder

Students should circle "Northwest England," "National Park," "National Park," and "National Parks."

p. 226 Vocabulary Builder

Volumes means "total amounts."

p. 226 Vocabulary Builder

"Private" is an antonym of "public."

p. 226 Comprehension Builder

Answers will vary. Sample response: Large volumes of traffic lead to issues such as pollution, noise, distractions from the scenery, congestion, attempts to encourage us of public transport, competition for parking, and dangers to walkers, cyclists, and horse riders.

p. 227 Comprehension Builder

Answers will vary. Sample response: The goals of traffic management in Lake District National Park are to protect the landscape, to improve the quality of residents' lives, to help visitors enjoy the park, and to use transportation that does not harm the area.

p. 227 Vocabulary Builder

The Lake District National Park *set out* its traffic management policies in the Lake District National Park Management Plan.

p. 227 Vocabulary Builder

Routes is used as a noun.

p. 228 After You Read
Thinking About the Traffic Report

1. Most tourists use private cars to reach the Lake District National Park.

2. Answers will vary. Sample response: Decision-makers must balance needs so the park is preserved, so tourists can continue to enjoy it, and so local residents will not suffer from too much traffic. If decision-makers limit travel on secondary roads to local residents, tourists may decide not to visit the area. Without tourists, the local economy will suffer.

Reading Skill

3. The labels along the side of the chart show the number of vehicles in 24 hours, and the labels along the bottom show the years.

4. The vertical bars represent the flow of vehicles; the symbol is explained in the right margin.

Poetry of Coleridge

p. 229 Graphic Organizer

Sample response:

Poetic Sound Device: Assonance

"The Rime of the Ancient Mariner": The moving Moon went up the sky

"Kubla Khan": So twice five miles of fertile ground

Effects of sounds on images in the two poems: The *o* sounds bring notice to the Moon's rising. The *i* sounds again accent the distance.

Poetic Sound Device: Slant Rhyme

"The Rime of the Ancient Mariner": And the good south wind still blew behind

"Kubla Khan": A mighty fountain momently was forced; / Amid whose swift half-intermitted burst

Effects of sounds on images in the two poems: Both slant rhymes call attention to the actions being described.

p. 230 Vocabulary Warm-up

1. ancient
2. harbor
3. glorious
4. sheen
5. pleasure
6. blossomed
7. merry
8. burst

p. 231 Reading Warm-up

Sample response:

1. (beauty); The tailor created the *glorious* evening gown for the queen.
2. crystal blue water; cruise ships that were anchored there; The ship sailed into the *harbor* to escape the storm at sea.
3. fragrance filling the air; *Blossomed* means "bloomed."
4. have existed for hundreds of years; *Ancient* means "very old."
5. poverty in which many of the island's residents lived; *Sheen* means "sparkling brightness."
6. (enjoyment); Watching an opera gives me great *pleasure*.
7. the suffering that was really there; *Merry* means "jolly."
8. her views about the island; *Burst* means "came about suddenly."

p. 232 Note-taking Guide

Sample response:

The Rime of the Ancient Mariner
Details of the Setting: The mariner's story takes place long ago, on board a ship on the ocean.

Kubla Khan
Details of the Setting: The poem takes place in Xanadu, in a pleasure dome whose grounds are "twice five miles" in size and contain gardens, creeks, incense-bearing trees, and sunny spots of greenery.

p. 233 Reading Check

Students should circle two of the following: "an ancient Mariner," "long gray beard," or "glittering eye."

p. 233 Stop to Reflect

Students should mark "He holds him with his glittering eye—."

p. 233 Literary Analysis

Lines 1–16 introduce characters, reveal a setting, and show a dialogue.

p. 234 Stop to Reflect

Sample response: The ice splitting and the good south wind arising are connected to the presence of the Albatross.

p. 234 Literary Analysis

In lines 38 and 40, students should circle "thus" and "Albatross."

p. 234 Reading Check

First speaker: The Wedding Guest speaks lines 37–39.
Second speaker: The Mariner resumes where the Wedding Guest leaves off at line 39 and finishes at line 40.

p. 235 Reading Check

The crew hung the Albatross around the Mariner's neck.

p. 235 Reading Strategy

In "Kubla Khan," the words *dome* and *decree*, and in "The Rime of the Ancient Mariner," the words *lifeless* and *lump* and *dropped* and *down* create alliteration.

p. 235 Stop to Reflect

The mariner reminds readers of the Albatross by comparing the escape of the dead crewmen's souls to the sound of his crossbow when he shot the bird.

p. 236 Literary Analysis

1. The words *black*, *swam*, *track*, and *flash* illustrate assonance.
2. The words *glossy* and *green* illustrate alliteration.

p. 236 Read Fluently

Sample response: The Albatross's dropping symbolizes that the curse is finally lifted from the Mariner.

p. 237 Reading Check

Students should circle "He prayeth well, who loveth well / Both man and bird and beast" and "He prayeth best, who loveth best / All things both great and small."

p. 237 Stop to Reflect

Sample response:

1. The Wedding Guest is sadder because he feels bad for the mariner.
2. The Wedding Guest is wiser because he has learned the mariner's lesson of respect of all nature.

p. 237 Literary Analysis

Sample response: He uses words, such as *eftsoons*, *vespers*, *elfish*, *hoary*, and *star-dogged moon*.

p. 238 After You Read

1. Coleridge uses internal rhyme.

2. Graphic Organizer

Sample response:

"The Rime of the Ancient Mariner"

Language: "I watched the water snakes . . . they reared, the elfish light / Fell off in hoary flakes"; "The Mariner hath his will"; "To thee, thou Wedding Guest!"; "He rose the morrow morn"

Effect: The mythical serpents described and the archaic words are associated with legends of knights and so suit the theme of redemption. The old-fashioned language makes the tale seem stranger, suiting the supernatural events of the poem.

"Kubla Khan"

Language: "In Xanadu did Kubla Khan / A stately pleasure dome decree"; "A savage place! as holy and enchanted / As e'er beneath a waning moon was haunted / By woman wailing for her demon lover!"

Effect: The mention of exotic names and the archaic language help create a world of fantasy. The description of the setting as both beautiful and haunting suit the theme of mingled beauty and danger.

3. Sample response: The use of poetic devices makes the last few lines of "Kubla Khan" more musical and hypnotic, enhancing the description of the wild-eyed visionary.

The Essential Question

Answers will vary. Students may suggest that in "Kubla Khan," Coleridge creates a setting in a mythical land that is sensual, hedonistic, wild, and savage—a place where all of the senses are heightened. "The Rime of the Ancient Mariner" moves through scenes of natural upheaval and eerie beauty, where Death and Life-in-Death direct a harrowing penance. The mariner's tale is juxtaposed against the backdrop of a celebratory wedding feast.

Poetry of Byron

p. 239 Graphic Organizer

Sample response:

Passage: No more-no more-Oh! Never more, my heart, / Canst thou be my sole world, my universe! / Once all in all, but now a thing apart, / Thou canst not be my blessing or my curse: (*from* Don Juan)

Questions: 1. To whom is the speaker speaking? 2. Why can this person or thing not be the center of his life anymore?

Answers: 1. The speaker speaks to his own heart. 2. The speaker is getting older, and realizes that he is not invincible.

Passage: What are the hopes of man? Old Egypt's King / Cheops erected the first pyramid / And largest, thinking it was just the thing / To keep his memory whole, and mummy hid: / But somebody or other rummaging / Burglariously broke his coffin's lid: / Let not a monument give you or me hopes, / Since not a pinch of dust remains of Cheops. (*from* Don Juan)

Questions: 1. What happened to King Cheops? 2. Why does the speaker tell this story?

Answers: 1. King Cheops built a pyramid in his own honor and was then robbed after he died. 2. The speaker is pointing out that Cheops wasted his time by trying to aggrandize himself.

p. 240 Vocabulary Warm-up

1. ambition
2. treasure
3. express
4. squandered
5. impaired
6. conceal
7. innocent
8. praise

p. 241 Reading Warm-up

Sample response:

1. struggled to make ends meet; *Innocent* means "blameless."
2. young Byron grew up in poverty; *Squandered* means "wasted."
3. it received almost universally bad reviews; *Praise* means "expression of approval."
4. (communicate); It is important to learn how to *express* yourself in writing.
5. as many people there disagreed with his views; *Impaired* means "diminished in strength or quality."
6. Byron left England permanently and settled in Switzerland and later Italy; *Conceal* means "hide."
7. (*Don Juan*); *Treasure* means "valuable" or "precious possessions."

8. (objective); My *ambition* is to sail around the world.

p. 242 Note-taking Guide
Sample response:
She Walks in Beauty
Subject of Poem: a woman's beauty
Description in Poem: "like the night / Of cloudless climes and starry skies"; "the nameless grace / Which waves in every raven tress"; "So soft, so calm, yet eloquent"
Speaker's Feelings: The speaker is filled with wonder at the woman's beauty and links her physical beauty with her spiritual beauty.
Apostrophe to the Ocean
Subject of Poem: the ocean
Description in Poem: "thou deep and dark blue ocean"; "Thy shores are empires"; "Dark-heaving—boundless, endless, and sublime"
Speaker's Feelings: The speaker is in awe of the immeasurable depths, power, and endurance of the ocean.
from Don Juan
Description in Poem: "I / Have squandered my whole summer while 'twas May"; "My days of love are over"; "All things that have been born were born to die"
Speaker's Feelings: The speaker is sad that he is aging and believes that his best days have passed.

p. 243 After You Read
1. Sample response: The mood of the speaker's reflections is comic, and his observations are amusing in their honesty.
2. **Graphic Organizer**
Sample response:
Simile: "She walks in beauty, like the night / Of cloudless climes and starry skies"
What Is Being Described: a beautiful woman in mourning
Associations Suggested: mystery; twilight; enchantment
Metaphor: "I / Have squandered my whole summer while 'twas May"
What Is Being Described: the speaker's youth
Associations Suggested: the changing seasons; life's temporary nature; the foolishness of youth
Personification: "thou dost arise / And shake him off from thee"

What Is Being Described: the ocean's power over man
Associations Suggested: man's vulnerability; the ocean's immense force
3. Most students will say that their questioning made their reading more focused and that they better understood what they were reading.

The Essential Question
Answers will vary, but students should support their ideas with details from the poems.

Poetry of Shelley

p. 244 Graphic Organizer
Sample response:
Center box: "All overgrown with azure moss and flowers / So sweet, the sense faints picturing them!"
Sensory "Texture": soft; fragrant
Associations: overwhelmingly pleasant, full of the beauty of nature
Center box: "Chorus Hymeneal, / Or triumphal chant"
Sensory "Texture": a heavenly sound
Associations: religious; joyous

p. 245 Vocabulary Warm-up
1. antique
2. hues
3. solid
4. keen
5. scattering
6. decay
7. surpass
8. prophecy

p. 246 Reading Warm-up
Sample response:
1. politically conservative climate of the England in which he was raised; My mother loves to search flea markets for *antique* toys.
2. Shelley would develop a strong dislike of tyranny; My *prophecy* for Shelley, if he hadn't died so young, would be that he would become a member of the House of Commons, as well as a poet.
3. in his writing; *Keen* means "sharp."
4. Shelley met influential politicians and read about important issues; Someone without a *solid* political foundation might act as though the workings of the government didn't affect him or her at all.

5. throughout England and Ireland: Yes. At election time, my mailbox and front step are covered with political pamphlets, which shows that politicians still are in the habit of *scattering* their literature to potential voters.

6. (deterioration); The *decay* of the wood was caused by the moisture.

7. should be permitted to participate in political life—In other words, everyone should have a voice . . .; *Hues* means "colors."

8. many of his writer contemporaries for its beauty, style, and content; A runner wants to always *surpass* his best sprinting time.

p. 247 Note-taking Guide
Sample response:
Ozymandias
Words used to describe it: "cold command," "pedestal," "colossal"
Ode to the West Wind
Words used to describe it: "Destroyer and preserver," "tameless, swift and proud," "Scatter"
To a Skylark
Words used to describe it: "blithe spirit," "a star of heaven," "sprite"

p. 248 After You Read
1. Sample response: His expression suggests that he was a proud, condescending ruler.
2. **Graphic Organizer**
Sample response:
Image: "If I were a swift cloud to fly with thee" ("Ode to the West Wind")
How Vivid? very vivid
Associated Ideas: Clouds are breezy and free, and they travel with the wind.
Link: Nature and Spirit: The speaker yearns to be a cloud and have the same freedom in his spirit to fly with the west wind.
Image: "Thy skill to poet were, thou scorner of the ground! / Teach me half the gladness / That thy brain must know" ("To a Skylark")
How Vivid? fairly
Associated Ideas: The bird is like a poet of the animal world.
Link: Nature and Spirit: The speaker wishes to learn how to experience the same kind of joy as the skylark.
3. Sample response: In "Ozymandias," the statue's broken face lying on the ground in a permanent frown is a striking image because it represents how temporary life is and how

even the most powerful of human beings cannot escape death.

The Essential Question
Answers will vary. Sample response: Shelley's poems reflect his desire to overthrow tyrants to bring in a new age of equality and justice. For example, in "Ozymandias," the monument's size, frown, sneer, and wrinkled lip, as well as the intimidating words on the pedestal, express the attempt to control others. This attempt at dominion from beyond the grave is futile because the statue lies in broken pieces. The speaker depicts Ozymandias as intimidating and controlling and describes the tyrant's monument as a "wreck." In "To a Skylark," the speaker depicts the skylark soaring, singing, and joyous—free from the difficulties of human life. The wind in "Ode to the West Wind" embodies a powerful, restless, striving force, moving everywhere in rebellion against tyrants like Ozymandias.

Poetry of Keats

p. 249 Graphic Organizer
Sample response:
"On First Looking into Chapman's Homer"
Original Words: "Then felt I like some watcher of the skies / When a new planet swims into his ken"
Paraphrase: I felt like an astronomer who discovers a new planet.

"Ode to a Nightingale"
Original Words: "Fade far away, dissolve, and quite forget / What thou among the leaves has never known, / The weariness, the fever, and the fret"
Paraphrase: I would like to fade away with you and forget those things that you have never known, such as tiredness, illness, or stress.

"Ode on a Grecian Urn"
Original Words: "When old age shall this generation waste, / Thou shalt remain, in midst of other woe"
Paraphrase: When those men who are alive today are gone, you will still be here to see the troubles of another generation.

p. 250 Vocabulary Warm-up
1. rhyme
2. pursuit
3. realms

4. dissolve
5. brim
6. passion
7. fame
8. immortal

p. 251 Reading Warm-up
Sample response:
1. after his death; *renown*
2. He engaged in this lifelong pursuit in the face of these difficulties; *Passion* means "zeal."
3. in the face of these difficulties; *Pursuit* means "activity."
4. he decided to train to become a surgeon; *Realms* means "areas."
5. he read widely while he was in school, and he wrote his first poem, "Lines in Imitation of Spenser," in 1814; *disintegrate*
6. he was ill with the same disease that killed his brother, Tom; *Immortal* means "not subject to death."
7. with beautiful images; *Brim* means "edge."
8. gave him the renown he never had while he was alive; *Rhyme* means "the correspondence of sounds at the ends of words."

p. 252 Note-taking Guide
Sample response:
Speaker's Attitude: Filled with wonder and inspiration
Poem: "Fears"
Subject: The speaker's fear of dying before he has written a great deal
What the Poem Shows: The challenge of finding love and fame
Speaker's Attitude: Mournful but philosophical; thoughtful; intense
Poem: "Nightingale"
Subject: Admiration for the nightingale
What the Poem Shows: The desire to imitate the ease of the song he hears; poetic inspiration
Speaker's Attitude: Heartsick but wishful and reflective

p. 253 Note-taking Guide
Sample response:
Speaker's Observations: The urn can capture a flowery tale better than his own rhyme. His interest in the scenes and the stories they tell cause him to ask questions.
Images: Pictures of men, maidens, boughs, and grass on the urn.

Speaker's Observation: The artistic beauty of the urn is unending and true in a way that the real world can never be because the real world is transitory.

p. 254 Stop to Reflect
Students should circle "Thou still unravished bride," "Thou foster child," and "Sylvan historian."

p. 254 Reading Check
1. The scene on the urn takes place in Greece.
2. The scene occurs in ancient times.

p. 255 Reading Strategy
Sample response: Oh Greek vase, simple and graceful! Decorated with your pattern of men and women, tree branches and trampled weeds. You, an unspeaking object, make us think like eternity does. You, unchanging rural scene!

p. 255 Literary Analysis
Sample response: The urn is called a "friend to man" because it will be around for eternity, always portraying its message of truth and beauty.

p. 256 After You Read
1. Sample response: The speaker sees his own world as perplexed and dull, whereas that of the nightingale is full of permanent, dream-like joy.
2. Sample response: Keats honors the nightingale by praising its song of painless ecstasy and its ability not to be defeated by death. He honors the urn by marveling at its permanent beauty, which he considers an important truth.
3. **Graphic Organizer**
Sample response:
Poem: "Homer," lines 9–10
Paraphrase: I felt like an astronomer who sees a new planet in his telescope.
Poem: "Nightingale," lines 71–72
Paraphrase: Speaking about desolation and hopelessness is enough to kill the joy I felt by thinking about your life. It brings me back to my own sad life.
Poem: "Grecian Urn," lines 3–4
Paraphrase: Historian of the woods, who can tell an elaborate story better than our poem . . .

The Essential Question

Answers will vary, but students should support their ideas with details from the poems.

"On Making an Agreeable Marriage"
Jane Austen

from A Vindication of the Rights of Women
Mary Wollstonecraft

p. 257 Graphic Organizer

Sample response:

On Making an Agreeable Marriage

Other Clues From the Text: Austen admits to being unable to make up her mind about her niece's suitor. "It seems as if your being secure of him . . . has made you Indifferent."

Writer's Purpose: to dissuade her niece from marrying a man she does not love, despite his good qualities

How Purpose Affects Meaning: Austen's purpose illustrates the true meaning of the text, which is a social commentary on both human nature and marriage at the time of writing.

A Vindication of the Rights of Woman

Other Clues From the Text: "Vindication" in the title is a defense. She starts off saddened by the state of things and then calls for change in women's rights.

Writer's Purpose: to advocate equal rights for women

How Purpose Affects Meaning:
Wollstonecraft's meaning is clear and in accord with her purpose—women should have the same rights as men.

p. 258 Vocabulary Warm-up

1. conviction
2. conscientiously
3. amiable
4. uniformly
5. partial
6. deficiencies
7. comprehension
8. attribute

p. 259 Reading Warm-up

Sample response:

1. to her parents' support of her efforts; *Attribute* means "relate to a particular cause or source."

2. that she could do anything if she put her mind to it; *Conviction* means "unshakable belief."
3. carefully; *carelessly, thoughtlessly*
4. read outside of class; I have a poor *comprehension* of Spanish because I speak very little of it outside the classroom.
5. (Preferring); I love acting and am *partial* to the drama club.
6. she seldom attended the school dances because of her intense study schedule; The product was not sold to the public because it contained many dangerous *deficiencies*.
7. (consistently); *differently, unevenly*
8. (friendly); The *amiable* dog wagged its tail as we pet it.

p. 260 Note-taking Guide

Sample response:

Appeals to Logic: ". . . Your mistake has been one that thousands of women fall into. He was the *first* young Man who attached himself to you. That was the charm, & most powerful it is."

Appeals to Morality: ". . . I shall turn around & entreat you not to commit yourself further, & not to think of accepting him unless you really do like him. Anything is to be preferred or endured rather than marrying without Affection; and if his deficiencies of Manner &c &c strike you more than all his good qualities, if you continue to think strongly of them, give him up at once."

Appeals to Emotions: ". . . don't be frightened by the idea of his acting more strictly up to the precepts of the New Testament than others."

p. 261 Note-taking Guide

Sample response:

Appeals to Logic: "The conduct and manners of women, in fact, evidently prove that their minds are not in a healthy state . . ."

Appeals to Morality: ". . . their apparent inferiority with respect to bodily strength must render them in some degree dependent on men in the various relations of life; but why should it be increased by prejudices that give a sex to virtue, and confound simple truths with sensual reveries?"

Appeals to Emotions: ". . . a profound conviction that the neglected education of my fellow creatures is the grand source of misery I deplore . . ."

p. 262 Reading Strategy

Sample response: By calling women's inferior education a "misery" that she "deplore[s]," Wollstonecraft is revealing that her purpose is to inform the public about a large and important problem in society.

p. 262 Read Fluently

Like the flowers, being beautiful seems to be women's only purpose in society, which causes them to try nothing more than to please men and consequently never to reach their full potential.

p. 263 Literary Analysis

Students should circle "neglected education"; "minds are not in a healthy state"; "sacrificed to beauty"; and "prejudices."

p. 264 After You Read

1. Sample response: Because society encourages women to be weaker than men, it causes some women to act childishly and slyly.

2. **Graphic Organizer**

Sample response:

Love: "Anything is to be preferred or endured rather than marrying without Affection."

Importance: high

Suitability for Each Other: She seems to imply that it is not as important because they will become more suitable for each other if they are bound together: "I have no doubt that he will get more lively & like yourselves as he is more with you;—he will catch your ways if he belongs to you."

Importance: moderate

Money: She cites the fact that he is the eldest son of a man of fortune.

Importance: moderate

Respectability: "he is I dare say such a Scholar as your agreeable, idle Brothers would ill bear a comparison with"; she also cites his strict religious nature and her appeal to it.

Importance: high

3. Sample response: Austen's purpose is to advise her niece. Her tactful tone and modest denials of expertise indicate that she does not want to come across as telling her niece what to do. She uses emotional and moral appeals.

Wollstonecraft's purpose is to persuade a more general audience by argument on a specific issue, as indicated by her title. Wollstonecraft analyzes a social problem directly. Both works reveal the limited rights of women in the eighteenth and early nineteenth centuries, but Austen's commentary is subtle, whereas Wollstonecraft's is bold.

The Essential Question

Answers will vary, but students should include the words *independence, values,* and *rebellious* in their answers and support their opinions with details from the texts.

ANSWERS TO UNIT 5

Poetry of Tennyson

p. 265 Graphic Organizer
Sample response:

from In Memoriam, A. H. H.
Speaker's Motivations: the early death of a friend
Speaker's Beliefs: Grief must be embraced to affirm the value of love.
Speaker's Conflicts: The speaker is overcome by despair, grief, and anger over a friend's death
Author's Assumptions and Beliefs: Death cannot destroy friendship.

"The Lady of Shalott"
Speaker's Motivations: the position of the creative artist in society
Speaker's Beliefs: Like many artists, the Lady of Shalott is removed from life, looking at it secondhand and not experiencing it for herself.
Speaker's Conflicts: The artist is distanced from life, seeing life as material for his or her depictions.
Author's Assumptions and Beliefs: Life of the imagination isolates one from reality. It is better to live in reality because our fantasies can never be realized. Once our fantasies become reality, the allure of fantasy is destroyed.

from The Princess: Tears, Idle Tears
Speaker's Motivations: a longing for the past
Speaker's Beliefs: Past love and happiness cannot be truly possessed.
Speaker's Conflicts: The speaker longs for the irrecoverable past.
Author's Assumptions and Beliefs: Life is transient.

"Ulysses"
Speaker's Motivations: dissatisfaction with idle old age
Speaker's Beliefs: He feels that he still has noble work to do before he dies.
Speaker's Conflicts: He is frustrated and dissatisfied with growing old in Ithaca and longs for new adventures and challenges.

Author's Assumptions and Beliefs: It is good to courageously seek adventure; one should let go of the past and "seek a newer world."

p. 266 Vocabulary Warm-up
1. wanes
2. idle
3. smite
4. feigned
5. vexed
6. wrought
7. discerning
8. remote

p. 267 Reading Warm-up
Sample response:
1. faraway; The campsite is in a remote area of the forest.
2. (hard blow); *Smite* means "to strike or hit very hard."
3. doing nothing but resting; *busy*
4. (annoyed); I was vexed when my friend Susan kept pestering me to lend her my new necklace.
5. (pretended); Sam feigned interest in Beth's dog because he wanted to get to know her.
6. growing weaker; *strengthens*
7. (beautifully fashioned); A finely wrought item I own is an antique violin that was given to me by my Aunt Jane.
8. recognized what was happening; A piece of art that a discerning person might enjoy is a hand-blown glass vase.

p. 268 Note-taking Guide
Sample response:
In Memoriam: The speaker is angry that his friend has been taken from him. The difficulty of loss can be softened by memories.
Tears, Idle Tears: The speaker is in despair about having no more time with the deceased person.
Ulysses: The speaker mourns the loss of youth and desires to seek new adventures.

p. 269 Note-taking Guide
Sample response:
Column 1, Row 2: She sings.
Column 1, Row 3: She weaves and views the world through a mirror.
Column 2, Row 2: She is dissatisfied.

Column 2, Row 3: She sees others living their lives through the mirror.
Column 3, Row 2: She leaves her loom to look from the window at Sir Lancelot, and the mirror cracks; the curse is upon her.
Column 3, Row 3: She goes down to the river.
Column 4, Row 2: She climbs into the boat and sings as she floats down the river toward Camelot.
Column 4, Row 3: She dies while singing; the men and women of Camelot look at her in wonder.

p. 270 Literary Analysis
1. Students should circle *a*.
2. Students may circle "long fields," "clothe the wold," "meet the sky," "many-towered Camelot," "lilies blow," and "Round an island."
3. Students should note that the sound and rhythm of the words contribute to a dreamy and attractive impression.

p. 270 Reading Check
1. Students should circle "she weaves" and label it *What?*
2. Students should circle "A curse is on her if she stay / To look down to Camelot" and label it *Why?*

p. 271 Literary Analysis
Students should complete the sentence with "through the mirror." Students should circle "through a mirror clear" and "Shadows of the world appear."

p. 271 Literary Analysis
Students should choose *b*. Students may circle "broad clear brow in sunlight glowed," "coal-black curls," and "'Tirra lirra,' by the river / Sang Sir Lancelot."

p. 272 Reading Strategy
Sample response:
1. The Lady of Shalott is weary of her unchanging life and desires to experience reality. She is also attracted to Sir Lancelot.
2. The poet's message may be that people should experience reality at all costs.
3. Yes; people should live in reality, but they should also behave responsibly.

p. 272 Literary Analysis
Students should say that the speaker is not a character in the story. Students should note that the speaker is a third-person narrator who observes and relates the events of the story but does not participate in the action.

p. 273 Reading Check
The Lady of Shalott leaves the island on a boat and drifts toward Camelot, dying upon her arrival.

p. 273 Literary Analysis
Students should circle *c*.

p. 274 After You Read
1. The loss of the speaker's friend makes the scene bleak and empty.
2. The speaker's inner conflict is about his insatiable longing for adventure after he has settled down.
3. **Graphic Organizer**
Sample response:
Past
Ulysses: He remembers the past with satisfaction.
The Lady of Shalott: The past is identical with the present.
Present
Ulysses: He is restless in the present.
The Lady of Shalott: The present is unchanging.
Future
Ulysses: The future is full of opportunity.
The Lady of Shalott: The future is doomed.
5. Sample response: In *In Memoriam* the author reveals that he is deeply grieved by the death of a friend, but he believes that death cannot destroy friendship. Although his friend has died, he believes that his friend's spirit is with him. His image of the chrysalis shows that Tennyson sees death as only a transformation, as when a caterpillar turns into a butterfly. The friendship has changed, not ended. Furthermore, Tennyson believes that he must embrace his grief to affirm the value of his love for his friend.

The Essential Question
Answers will vary, but may include the following ideas: Tennyson wanted to promote traditional values such as religion and love ("In Memoriam, A.H.H."); romance ("Lady of

Shalott"); appreciation of times past or loved ones lost ("The Princess: Tears, Idle Tears"); and wisdom, hard work, honor, and strength ("Ulysses"). Students should explain their answers by including specific references to the poetry.

"My Last Duchess"
Robert Browning

"Life in a Love"
Robert Browning

"Love Among the Ruins"
Robert Browning

"Sonnet 43"
Elizabeth Barrett Browning

p. 275 Graphic Organizer
Sample response:

My Last Duchess: The speaker's love is limited, if even existent; The speaker is jealous and controlling.

Sonnet 43: The speaker's love is limitless; The speaker is adoring and passionate.

Both: address the topic of relationships; suggest a vulnerable side to the speakers

p. 276 Vocabulary Warm-up
1. sullen
2. baffled
3. ideal
4. ample
5. rarity
6. prevail
7. exceed
8. earnest

p. 277 Reading Warm-up
Sample response:

1. (confusing), (frustrating); I was *baffled* by the directions the policeman had given me.
2. their ability to understand; Another word for *exceed* is *surpass*.
3. (best); to express emotions, to bring a thought to life
4. insincere; A word that means the same as *earnest* is *sincere*.
5. time and thought; In comic books, good usually will *prevail* over evil.
6. to find a poem that evokes a response; A phrase that means the same as *rarity* is *very unusual*.
7. (negative); (happily)

8. poets whose work impresses or inspires them; A phrase that means the opposite of *ample* is *not enough*.

p. 278 Note-taking Guide
Sample response:

Meaning: The painting on the wall is of the Duke's late wife.

Inferences: The Duke seems to care more about owning a fine piece of art than about his wife's death.

p. 279 Literary Analysis
1. The Duke of Ferrara is the speaker.
2. A man representing a Count is the man that is spoken to.
3. The Duke wishes to marry the Count's daughter, and the man representing the Count is there to settle the details.

p. 279 Reading Check
The Duchess did not treat the Duke any more respectfully than she treated anyone else.

p. 280 Stop to Reflect
Sample response: Yes. It appears that the Duke resented his wife's smiling on others and commanded that she be killed.

p. 280 Reading Strategy
Unlike the speaker of "Life in a Love," the Duke expresses a selfish love for his last duchess, or he may not have loved her at all.

p. 281 Note-taking Guide
Sample response:

"Life in a Love": Students should check **Believes in love forever.**

"Love Among the Ruins": Students should check **Believes that his love is greater than even a great civilization.**

Sonnet 43: Students should check **Believes in love forever** and **Believes in love that will continue after death.**

p. 282 Apply the Skills
1. Sample response: The listener and speaker interact when the speaker addresses the listener as "you" or "Sir" and when the speaker asks the listener a question, as in "'Will't please you rise?'"
2. **Graphic Organizer**
Sample response:

Line 14: natural pause at comma on **"-ly, called"**

Line 15: natural pause after **"-ess' cheek;"**

Line 16: natural pause after **"to say"**

3. Both speakers express a deep and abiding love. However, it seems that the love expressed by the speaker of "Life in a Love" is not returned. The speaker of "Sonnet 43" seems to be speaking to someone who returns her love.

The Essential Question

Answers will vary. Sample response: The speaker in Elizabeth Barrett Browning's sonnet seems more dramatic. The speaker in the sonnet uses language such as "the depth and breadth and height / My soul can reach," "the ends of Being," and "I love thee with the breath, / Smiles, tears, of all my life!"

from Hard Times
Charles Dickens

p. 283 Graphic Organizer

Sample response:

Detail: "Teach these boys and girls nothing but Facts. Facts alone are wanted in life."

Detail: "You are never to fancy."

Context: Educational theories and practices stress fact and discourage the use of imagination.

Author's Purpose: to criticize and satirize the educational practices of his time

Meaning of Work: The insistence of the educational system on eliminating imagination from the world is dangerous and counterproductive.

p. 284 Vocabulary Warm-up

1. reign
2. contradiction
3. discard
4. established
5. immense
6. dismal
7. feeble
8. maim

p. 285 Reading Warm-up

Sample response:

1. (Queen Victoria); *Reign* usually implies royalty, while *term* means the period of time that an elected leader is in office.
2. (bleak); An antonym for *dismal* is *cheerful*.
3. what were known as the three Rs: reading, writing, and arithmetic; Karl's parents always *emphasized* good manners at the table.

4. (disagreed); Another word for *contradiction* is *opposition*.
5. beaten hard; *Injure* is a synonym for *maim*.
6. (expense); *Immense* clouds of smoke rose from the burning cornfield.
7. their assignments; An antonym for *discard* is *retain*.
8. (girls); *Weak* is a synonym for *feeble*.

p. 286 Note-taking Guide

Sample response:

Details That Support Purpose: Thomas Gradgrind asks students to use only the facts to define a horse; a government official wants to keep to the facts by not decorating walls or floors; a teacher who discourages imagination is named "M'Choakumchild."

p. 287 Literary Analysis

1. Students should circle "polluted" and "ugly."
2. Students should list social concerns relevant to the time period, such as education, poor sanitation, overcrowded housing, pollution, dangerous or unhealthy working conditions, or inadequate pay.

p. 287 Reading Check

Students should circle "Facts."

p. 287 Reading Strategy

Students should circle *d*.

p. 288 Read Fluently

Sample response: Sissy probably felt embarrassed and confused.

p. 288 Reading Strategy

Students should check "to introduce the character of Bitzer to readers," "to poke fun at the facts-only method of teaching," and "to poke fun at Mr. Gradgrind."

p. 289 Stop to Reflect

Students should circle *d*.

p. 289 Reading Check

Sample response: Sissy wants a carpet with pictures of flowers because she loves flowers.

p. 290 Literary Analysis

Sample response:

1. The teacher's name suggests that his facts-only approach to teaching chokes the creativity and imagination of children.
2. Dickens uses Mr. M'Choakumchild's character to evaluate the way that children are taught in Victorian schools.

p. 290 Reading Check

Sample response: If Mr. M'Choakumchild only knew fewer facts to drum into the students' heads, he would be a far better teacher, guiding the children to use their imaginations and to think for themselves.

p. 291 After You Read

1. The setting suggests that society has made the process of obtaining an education rigid and largely unpleasant.

2. **Graphic Organizer**
Sample response:
Passage: Gradgrind calls Sissy "Girl 20."
Intended Effect on Reader: Gradgrind's stubborn application of theory makes him look ridiculous.
Intended Message: Gradgrind's theories are foolish.

3. Sample response: The name "M'Choakumchild" suggests that the instructor will "choke" rather than teach children, implying that Dickens wishes to show the dangerous nature of the teacher's ideas.

The Essential Question

Answers will vary. Sample response: Dickens would think that an education system has great influence on children, and is therefore greatly responsible for the type of adults children become. His social commentary focuses on the teachers' insistence that the children not show any individuality or creativity and suggests that most children quickly conform to the wishes of school leaders.

Informational Texts: Web Sites

p. 293 Vocabulary Builder

Students should circle "novelist."

p. 293 Vocabulary Builder

Students should underline "conversational" and "curatorial."

p. 294 Vocabulary Builder

Sample response: A *virtual* tour allows people to visit a museum online rather than in person.

p. 294 Comprehension Builder

A person must have a computer with Internet access.

p. 294 Vocabulary Builder

Students should complete the sentence with one of the following: the dining room, the morning room, the back parlour, or the stairs to the first floor.

p. 295 Vocabulary Builder

Patient is used as an adjective.

p. 295 Vocabulary Builder

Jump means "change quickly from one position or idea to another."

p. 296 Vocabulary Builder

The word *this* draws attention to the word *room*.

p. 296 Vocabulary Builder

Sample response: Dickens probably *made use of* the study as a quiet place for writing.

p. 296 Comprehension Builder

Sample response: Charles Dickens had a desk that he used for writing. He probably used this desk in all the homes in which he lived from 1839 to the end of his life.

p. 297 After You Read
Thinking About the Web Site

1. You would click Opening Hours for information about the museum's hours of operation.
2. Dickens's study is on the first floor.

Reading Skill

3. The Web site will provide detailed information about the Dickens Museum and offer a virtual tour.
4. The purpose of the Andalusia brochure is to provide information about Andalusia and Flannery O'Connor's experiences while living there.

from Jane Eyre
Charlotte Brontë

p. 298 Graphic Organizer

Sample response:
Assumption: Answers will vary. The author assumes that the teacher punishes Burns for no good reason.
Analysis: Answers will vary. The author may have had or witnessed teachers in similar institutions treat girls unfairly in this manner. The author may want me to believe that the teacher is acting out of bad intentions or a mean character.

p. 299 Vocabulary Warm-up

1. gleeful
2. punctual
3. merit
4. commendations
5. crevices
6. retained
7. ominous
8. abyss

p. 300 Reading Warm-up

Sample response:
1. (vast)(empty); When there are few options, the future can seem like an *abyss*.
2. high point; An antonym for *gleeful* is *miserable*.
3. the attic's unfinished walls; Another word for *crevices* is cracks.
4. (disapprove); An action that might receive *commendations* is rescuing someone from a fire.
5. needlework or piano practice; *Value* is a synonym for *merit*.
6. (creaking); Jack's face wore an *ominous* expression before he broke the news.
7. her composure; An antonym for *retained* is *released*.
8. (time); *Late* is an antonym for *punctual*.

p. 301 Note-taking Guide

Sample response:
Jane Eyre
Similarities: Jane is an orphan and a student at Lowood.
Differences: Jane is brooding, has a temper, and says that she will not accept unjust treatment patiently.
Helen Burns
Similarities: Helen is a student at Lowood, and she is intelligent and thoughtful.
Differences: Helen accepts unjust treatment and even finds fault with herself.

p. 302 Literary Analysis

Students should circle the first three details. Students may circle "rushlight," "water in the pitchers was frozen," "perish with cold," and "How small my portion seemed!"

p. 302 Reading Check

The girls cannot wash because the water in the pitchers is frozen.

p. 303 Reading Strategy

The author wants you to believe that Burns is a smart and attentive student who deserves praise, and that Miss Scatcherd is a cruel and unjust teacher who treats Burns unfairly.

p. 303 Reading Check

Students should write "Helen Burns." Students should circle "every little difficulty was solved instantly when it reached Burns" and "she was ready with answers on every point,"

p. 303 Read Fluently

Sample response: Miss Scatcherd may be jealous of Helen's intelligence.

p. 304 Stop to Reflect

Students should circle *a*. Students may circle "she quietly, and without being told, unloosed her pinafore," "not a feature of her pensive face altered," and "Burns obeyed." Sample response: Burns believes that she should not disobey her teachers.

p. 304 Reading Strategy

The author assumes that the teacher's mean treatment was not common enough that a child such as Jane would accept it as normal and acceptable.

p. 305 Reading Strategy

Students should check "Poor girls often put up with bad treatment to get an education," and "The girls were not treated with the religious ideals they were taught."

p. 305 Reading Check

1. "I am . . . slatternly"
2. "I seldom put, and never keep, things in order"
3. "I am careless"
4. "I forget rules"
5. "I read when I should learn my lessons"
6. "I have no method"
7. ". . . sometimes I say, like you, I cannot bear to be subjected to systematic arrangements."

p. 306 Literary Analysis

Sample response:
1. She is mean because Miss Scatcherd is harshly critical of Helen, and the monitor knows that she can get away with it.

2. Her behavior supports the assumption that in schools students may imitate the poor behavior of their teachers.

p. 307 After You Read

1. Helen says that Miss Scatcherd is severe as well as neat, punctual, and particular. Helen says that Miss Scatcherd punishes Helen to teach her to correct her faults. Jane says that Miss Scatcherd is simply mean-spirited, cross, and cruel.

2. **Graphic Organizer**
Sample response:
Row 1: During that time in England, it was common to send orphaned children away to schools such as Lowood.
Row 2: Most people in England were Christians, and schools generally taught Christian beliefs.
Row 3: At that time, it was not unusual for teachers to punish students physically.

3. Sample response: The author wants you to believe that girls were not treated well and they had few options, that girls must take responsibility for themselves so as not burden their families, and that an education was very important for girls from poor families.

The Essential Question

Answers will vary. Sample response: Charlotte Brontë includes many details that depict the school as a place in which students are treated unfairly. Her inclusion of these details shows that she has a negative opinion of institutions that allow or promote cruelty toward children. As a popular novel, *Jane Eyre* may have helped to change the conditions at schools like Lowood by appealing to readers' sympathies.

"Dover Beach"
Matthew Arnold

"The Widow at Windsor"
Rudyard Kipling

"Recessional"
Rudyard Kipling

p. 308 Graphic Organizer

Sample response:
"Dover Beach"
Mood: sad, melancholy

How the Mood Relates to the Historical Period: The speaker's sadness and concern relate to the conflict and responsibility that come with maintaining an empire.

"The Widow at Windsor"
Mood: bitter, angry
How the Mood Relates to the Historical Period: The speaker is bitter and angry because the empire relies on the poor to support itself.

"Recessional"
Mood: cautious, critical
How the Mood Relates to the Historical Period: The speaker is worried that the British Empire is failing because people have grown too proud and too sure of their power.

p. 309 Vocabulary Warm-up

1. widow
2. vast
3. furled
4. tide
5. fling
6. valiant
7. ebb
8. retreating

p. 310 Reading Warm-up

Sample response:
1. often sailing for several days across the great ocean; A synonym for *vast* is "large."
2. tightly; to prevent them from blowing away; *Furled* means "rolled up tightly."
3. as an angry child would throw a toy; Please don't *fling* your dirty clothes on the floor.
4. mourned a husband who had died on the job; A *widow* is a woman whose husband has died.
5. (brave); An antonym for *valiant* is *cowardly*.
6. powerful incoming . . . which could knock them down and even turn over the lifeboats; *Tide* refers to the rise and fall of ocean waters each day.
7. safety further inland; The defeated army was *retreating* to safety.
8. ocean waters after the storm had passed; *Ebb* means "lessening or decline."

p. 311 Note-taking Guide

Sample response:
Dover Beach: "the turbid ebb and flow / Of human misery"; "The Sea of Faith / Was once, too, at the full"

The Widow at Windsor: "Walk wide o' the Widow at Windsor / For 'alf o' Creation she owns"; "We'ave brought 'er the same with the sword an' the flame."

p. 312 Note-taking Guide

Sample response:

Stanza 1: England is powerful, but God is in control of England.

Stanza 2: Human accomplishments fade, but God's accomplishment is eternal.

Stanza 3: The power of England is fading like that of the ancient empire.

Stanza 4: The British have grown arrogant, forgetting to revere God.

Stanza 5: England has put trust in armies rather than in God.

Main Idea of Poem: Great power should be accompanied by humility, not by pride.

p. 313 After You Read

1. The mood is cautious and critical, warning people that they have become too proud and that the empire is failing.

2. **Graphic Organizer**

Sample response:

Image: "The eternal note of sadness"

Where It Appears: line 14

Mood It Evokes: loss, sadness

Image: "turbid ebb and flow / Of human misery"

Where It Appears: lines 17–18

Mood It Evokes: confusion, sense of futility

Image: "The Sea of Faith . . . Retreating"

Where It Appears: lines 21 and 26

Mood It Evokes: irrevocable loss of religious meaning

Image: "ignorant armies clash by night"

Where It Appears: line 37

Mood It Evokes: sense of foreboding

Theme of poem: Victorian culture is unable to give meaning to life, so humans are confused and driven by conflict.

3. The mood and theme in each poem indicate that the British Empire was declining and losing power, that people believed that the British Empire had many problems and challenges, and that the empire had not benefited all people.

The Essential Question

Answers will vary, but students should support their ideas with details from the poem.

"Remembrance"
Emily Brontë

"The Darkling Thrush"
Thomas Hardy

"Ah, Are You Digging on My Grave?"
Thomas Hardy

p. 314 Graphic Organizer

Sample response:

Stanza 2: Her thoughts are turning from her beloved.

Stanza 3: She had been faithful to the memory of her beloved for fifteen years.

p. 315 Vocabulary Warm-up

1. pulse
2. dreary
3. existence
4. bleak
5. canopy
6. shone
7. check
8. sternly

p. 316 Reading Warm-up

Sample response:

1. (rhythmically hitting her window); *Pulse* means "regular beating," or "throbbing."

2. (incessant beeping from the clock); *Check* means "to stop something."

3. As Carrie stepped out the door and into the dismal, rainy day, she had a smile on her face; Many people consider paperwork *dreary*.

4. (of clouds); A different kind of *canopy* would be one over a four-poster bed.

5. She started along her usual route, dodging puddles, dog walkers, and other determined runners who were firmly refusing to let the bad weather interfere with their daily exercise; A parent who is correcting a disobedient child may need to act *sternly*.

6. (This rainy atmosphere); A landscape without trees or grass can feel *bleak*.

7. (she was filled with tranquility); *Existence* means "life."

8. By the time she headed home, a weak sun glowed through the clouds; A gold ring *shone* through the window of the jewelry store.

p. 317 Note-taking Guide
Sample response:
"Remembrance"
Sadness: "All my life's bliss from thy dear life was given— / All my life's bliss is in the grave with thee."
Stanza: 5
Hope: "Then did I learn how existence could be cherished, / Strengthened and fed without the aid of joy; . . ."
Stanza: 6
"The Darkling Thrush"
Sadness: "The ancient pulse of germ and birth / Was shrunken hard and dry. . . ."
Stanza: 2
Hope: "In a full-hearted evensong / Of joy illimited; . . ."
Stanza: 3
"Ah, Are You Digging on My Grave?"
Sadness: "No tendance of her mound can loose / Her spirit from Death's gin."
Stanza: 2
Hope: "What feeling do we ever find / To equal among human kind / A dog's fidelity!"
Stanza: 5

p. 318 After You Read
1. **Graphic Organizer**
Remembrance
Number of Lines: First Stanza: 4; **Last Stanza:** 4
Rhyme Scheme: *abab*
Meter: varies

The Darkling Thrush
Number of Lines: First Stanza: 8; **Last Stanza:** 8
Rhyme Scheme: *ababcdcd*
Meter: ballad

"Ah, Are You Digging on My Grave?"
Number of Lines: First Stanza: 6; **Last Stanza:** 6
Rhyme Scheme: *abcccb*
Meter: 4-3-4-4-4-3
2. The irony is in the deceased woman's belief that someone is mourning her passing, when in reality all have put her from their minds; even her faithful dog visited her grave only to bury a bone, forgetting that the area was her "resting-place."
3. The speaker asks whether she has forgotten to love her dead beloved. Each stanza builds toward her realization that her feelings for the past are a danger for her.

The Essential Question
Answers will vary, but students should support their ideas with details from the poem.

"God's Grandeur"
Gerard Manley Hopkins

"Spring and Fall: To a Young Child"
Gerard Manley Hopkins

"To an Athlete Dying Young"
A. E. Housman

"When I Was One-and-Twenty"
A. E. Housman

p. 319 Graphic Organizer
Sample response:
"God's Grandeur"
Biographical Details: Hopkins became a Catholic priest in the Jesuit order. He also had a love of nature.
Details in Author's Work: "The world is charged with the grandeur of God"; "Generations have trod, have trod, have trod; / And all is seared with trade; bleared, smeared with toil"; "for all this, nature is never spent"
Author's Beliefs: No matter what people do, they can never obliterate God's grandeur in nature.

"Spring and Fall: To a Young Child"
Biographical Details: Hopkins had a love of nature and a strong religious faith.
Details in Author's Work: "Leáves, like the things of man"
Author's Beliefs: Death is part of the human condition, just as it is a part of nature.

"To an Athlete Dying Young"
Biographical Details: Housman suffered grief at a young age when his mothered died. His love was unrequited while at Oxford.
Details in Author's Work: "early though the laurel grows / It withers quicker than the rose."
Author's Beliefs: Disillusionment comes with age.

"When I Was One-and-Twenty"
Biographical Details: He despaired over an unrequited love while at Oxford.

Details in Author's Work: "Give . . . not your heart a way."

Author's Beliefs: Love can hurt, but Housman's mocking tone shows that he may find the pursuit of love worth the pain.

p. 320 Vocabulary Warm-up

1. seared
2. flame
3. smudge
4. shod
5. trod
6. smeared
7. toil
8. fleet

p. 321 Reading Warm-up

Sample response:

1. (thickly coated); You might see tar being *smeared* on a driveway.
2. (a large flame); *Seared* means "burned on the surface."
3. (burning the feet); *Shod* means "to be wearing shoes."
4. (on foot); You might *trod* through an open field or a marsh.
5. (dirty smoke); A *smudge* can often be found near a door handle or on a window sill.
6. (when lighted); I've seen a bonfire *flame*.
7. (extracting the wax from the bayberries was a tedious process); Digging a trench for a pipe requires a lot of *toil*.
8. (quickly went out of fashion); *Fleet* means "rapid."

p. 322 Note-taking Guide

Sample response:

"God's Grandeur"

Beauty: "The world is charged with the grandeur of God."

Line: 1

Mortality: "Why do men then not now reck his rod?"

Line: 4

"Spring and Fall: To a Young Child"

Beauty: "Leáves, like the things of man, you / With your fresh thoughts care for, can you?"

Line: 3–4

Mortality: "Sórrow's spríngs áre the same."

Line: 11

p. 323 Note-taking Guide

Sample response:

"To an Athlete Dying Young"

Words/Phrases: "Smart lad, to slip betimes away . . ."

Line Number: 9

"When I was One-and-Twenty"

Words/Phrases: "'Tis paid with sighs a plenty . . ."

Line Number: 13

p. 324 After You Read

1. Génĕrátĭŏns hăve tród, hăve tród, hăve tród. Sample response: The line uses two trochees and three iambs, and counterpoint rhythm occurs when two opposing rhythms appear together.
2. Students should say that the trochaic lines interrupt the regular rhythm, introducing a kind of silence where the missing stresses are expected.
3. Hopkins was devoted to nature. Hopkins's love of nature is reflected in his poem "God's Grandeur." For example, Hopkins explains that although the land has been "bleared, smeared with toil" by humans, "nature is never spent."

The Essential Question

Answers will vary. Students may express the following views: Reading Hopkins takes more time and is more complicated. Reading Hopkins aloud sounds nice because of the rhythm. Housman is more straightforward but not as rhythmic or descriptive.

ANSWERS TO UNIT 6

Poetry of Yeats

p. 325 Graphic Organizer
Sample response:
"When You Are Old"
Symbols: Yeats had an unrequited love for Maud Gonne.
Yeats's Philosophy: Love hides his face.

"The Lake Isle of Innisfree"
Symbols: Yeats desired a Walden-like retreat.
Yeats's Philosophy: "And a small cabin build there, . . ."

"The Wild Swans at Coole"
Symbols: Yeats was interested in the passage of time.
Yeats's Philosophy: The swans' abrupt flight suggests that time is passing very rapidly.

"The Second Coming"
Symbols: Yeats was interested in the rise and fall of civilizations.
Yeats's Philosophy: "Mere anarchy is loosed upon the world, . . ."

"Sailing to Byzantium"
Symbols: Yeats was interested in the immortality of art.
Yeats's Philosophy: "Monuments of unaging intellect."

p. 326 Vocabulary Warm-up
1. twilight
2. glade
3. sensual
4. consume
5. core
6. innocence
7. amid
8. murmur

p. 327 Reading Warm-up
Sample response:
1. graceful; lovely; long, bendable necks; *Sensual* means "having to do with the body or the senses."
2. (center); In the *core* of an apple, I would find seeds.
3. the tall trees; The grasshopper was hiding *amid* the tall blades of grass.
4. (forest); You might see forest animals resting in a *glade*.

5. low sounds; If I were to *murmur* something to my best friend, it might be, "Let's go get a snack."
6. (covered in white feathers); I consider a baby lamb a symbol of *innocence*.
7. sunset; When it is *twilight*, I am usually helping my mom and dad fix dinner.
8. (a diet of aquatic insects and mollusks); I normally *consume* a sandwich, a piece of fruit, and a glass of milk at lunchtime.

p. 328 Note-taking Guide
Sample response:
When You Are Old: Students should check "Aging" and "Loss."
The Lake Isle of Innisfree: Students should check "Change."
The Wild Swans at Coole: Students should check "Aging," "Loss," and "Change."
The Second Coming: Students should check "Change."
Sailing to Byzantium: Students should check "Aging" and "Loss."

p. 329 After You Read
1. Students may agree that "things fall apart" because they believe that modern society is more violent. Other students may disagree and say that with modern laws and technology, the world is becoming more organized and coherent.
2. **Graphic Organizer**
Sample response:
Symbol: swans
Personal/Traditional: both
Vivid/Flat in Effect: vivid
Rich/Poor in Associations: rich
Easy/Hard to Interpret: easy
Symbol: Sphinx
Personal/Traditional: traditional
Vivid/Flat in Effect: flat
Rich/Poor in Associations: rich
Easy/Hard to Interpret: hard
3. Answers will vary. The symbol of the falcon / falconer represents a breakdown in society. The "blood-dimmed tide" is the rise of violence and war. A "rough beast" is a new era.

The Essential Question
Answers will vary, but students should support their answers with details from the poems.

Poetry of Eliot

p. 330 Graphic Organizer
Sample response:
Answers will vary depending on which poem students choose. Sample answers:
Modernist Elements: Repeated images of death, emptiness, brokenness of mind and body; "Mistah Kurtz—he dead" is from Conrad's *Heart of Darkness*; "Stuffed men" could refer to "stuffed shirts," which is often a way of referring to politicians.
Information About Historical Period: The rise of industrialization; post-World War I era and the Treaty of Versailles
Conclusion: The progress of the time, and the apparent blindness of those making the decisions (the hollow men, the stuffed men) will ultimately lead to the destruction of the world.

p. 331 Vocabulary Warm-up
1. deliberate
2. consciousness
3. grimy
4. constituted
5. gesture
6. regretted
7. temperate
8. satisfactory

p. 332 Reading Warm-up
Sample response:
1. 1,000 to 1,200 miles and three to twelve months by camel; *Constituted* means "made up of."
2. cold; One city that enjoys *temperate* weather is Los Angeles.
3. (their decision to make the trip); In *Star Wars*, Luke Skywalker later *regretted* confronting Darth Vader too soon.
4. (dirty); If I were *grimy*, the first thing I would do would be to take a bath.
5. to keep going; *Deliberate* means "thought about or intended."
6. awareness; When I come to *consciousness* in the morning, the first thing I think about is getting up in time to get ready for school.
7. (took turns kneeling); A shrug is a *gesture* that can indicate confusion.
8. acceptable; I would receive a passing grade.

p. 333 Note-taking Guide
Sample response:
Segment: I
Description of Scene: a cold evening at a smoggy, industrial city block
Despair: ✔
Segment: II
Description of Scene: people awakening to old morning air and beginning their dull routines
Despair: ✔
Segment: III
Description of Scene: a miserable, dream-filled night
Despair: ✔
Segment: IV
Description of Scene: repetition of daily activities, but with a small amount of hope that the cycle will be broken
Hopefulness: ✔

p. 334 Note-taking Guide
Sample response:
Character: Magnus
Goal: to find the infant Jesus
Difficulties Encountered: weather; uncooperative camels; lack of shelter; unfriendly towns
Result: found the infant Jesus
Resolution Or Lack of Resolution: The speaker could not determine whether he had witnessed birth or death.
Years Later, Continuing Problems: Because the speaker has a new spiritual consciousness, he is uneasy with the traditional beliefs of his people.

p. 335 Reading Check
Students may circle two of the following: "cold coming we had"; "The ways deep"; "Such a long journey"; "The weather sharp"; "The very dead of winter."

p. 335 Read Fluently
Students should describe the tone as sad, weary, or irate.

p. 336 Literary Analysis
Students should circle *d*.

p. 336 Stop to Reflect

Some students may say that the speaker's journey is positive because he witnessed a historical and miraculous event and because he gains spiritual insight. Other students may say that the speaker's journey is negative because the speaker feels alienated from his former way of life and from his people after the journey.

p. 337 Note-taking Guide

Sample response:

Part I: "hollow men"; "dried voices"; "shape without form"

Part II: "death's dream kingdom"; "fading star"; "rat's coat"

Part III: "cactus land"; "supplication of a dead man's hand"; "prayers to broken stone"

Part IV: "valley of dying stars"; "hollow valley" "death's twilight kingdom"

Part V: "prickly pear"; "Falls the Shadow"; "Not with a bang but a whimper"

p. 338 After You Read

1. The cycle of time is one day, from evening through the night to morning and back to evening.

2. Students should note that the journey itself is described in detail, but the details of the birth are glossed over.

3. Sample response: Images include "burnt-out ends of smoky days"; "Of withered leaves about your feet / And newspapers from vacant lots"; and "With the other masquer-ades / That time resumes." All three images depict waste, decay, or futility.

4. **Graphic Organizer**

Sample response:

Passage: "And voices are / In the wind's singing / More distant and more solemn / Than a fading star."

Modernist Characteristics: fragmented

Relation to Historical Background: yes

The Essential Question

Answers will vary, but students should support opinions with details from the poems.

"In Memory of W. B. Yeats"
W. H. Auden

"Musée des Beaux Arts"
W. H. Auden

"Carrick Revisited"
Louis MacNeice

"Not Palaces"
Stephen Spender

p. 339 Graphic Organizer

Sample response:

Allegory

In Memory of W. B. Yeats: Auden uses allegory to tell that art rises above life and survives because it is, not because it changes the world.

Musée des Beaux Arts: Auden uses allegory to show that calamity or disaster for one person happens during the everyday activities of others.

Pastoral

Carrick Revisited: Through his pastoral, MacNeice presents a message that an artist's experiences are part of his or her art.

Not Palaces: This pastoral expresses hope that poetry can bring change.

p. 340 Vocabulary Warm-up

1. intolerant
2. isolation
3. leisurely
4. rapture
5. miraculous
6. emphasis
7. concealment
8. interlude

p. 341 Reading Warm-up

Sample response:

1. (he simply would not allow it); He banished Daedalus and Icarus to the Labyrinth.

2. (being alone all the time); A time I found myself in *isolation* was when I had the measles and had to be kept away from my brother and sister.

3. Labyrinth; If I wanted to be sure of the *concealment* of a small treasure, I would put it in a box under my bed.

4. (stressing); One safety rule that I think deserves great *emphasis* is to always wear a seatbelt in a moving car.

5. (seemingly impossible); In ancient times, a solar eclipse was seen as a *miraculous* event.

6. slowly; One activity that I do *leisurely* is take a bath.

7. delight; After dreaming all his life about skydiving, the *rapture* Jamal felt when he leaped from the plane was unbelievable.

8. (he flew higher and higher); An *interlude* I would enjoy would be a drive out to the beach for a picnic.

p. 342 Note-taking Guide
Sample Response:
In Memory of W. B. Yeats
Topic/Inspiration: the death of W. B. Yeats
Theme: the power of poetry to teach joy in the human condition
Musée des Beaux Arts
Topic/Inspiration: the death of Icarus
Theme: It is the nature of life and of suffering that the world goes on, even while individuals suffer.
Carrick Revisited
Topic/Inspiration: the speaker's visit to his childhood home
Theme: the irrefutable influence of childhood experience on human character
Not Palaces
Topic/Inspiration: the function of poetry in modern life
Theme: the rejection of old artistic attitudes in favor of art that produces social change

p. 343 After You Read
1. Answers will vary. Sample response: Poetry has little to do with the personal lives or political beliefs of poets. Good poetry is immortal and tells of humanity and its limitations.

2. **Graphic Organizer**
Sample response:
Poem: In Memory of W. B. Yeats:
Subgenre: allegory
Example or Element of Subgenre: In a short, symbolic "story," lines 36–41 tell how art rises above life
Poem: Musée des Beaux Arts:
Subgenre: allegory

Example or Element of Subgenre:
Lines 14–21 create a specific incident that is symbolic of disaster and suffering in general. It encapsulates the theme that "people suffer, yet the world moves on."
Poem: Carrick Revisited:
Subgenre: pastoral
Example or Element of Subgenre: Lines 1–5 tell about the importance of a childhood home.
Poem: Not Palaces:
Subgenre: pastoral
Example or Element of Subgenre: The last few lines celebrate an idealized future in the same way that a pastoral celebrates idealized rural settings.
3. One poem celebrates an idealized place and the other poem celebrates an idealized future. "Carrick Revisited" celebrates the influence of a place in which the speaker lived. "Not palaces" celebrates the potential of poetry.

The Essential Question
Answers will vary, but students should support answers with details from the poem.

"The Lady in the Looking Glass: A Reflection"
Virginia Woolf

from Mrs. Dalloway
Virginia Woolf

from A Room of One's Own: *from* Shakespeare's Sister
Virginia Woolf

p. 344 Graphic Organizer
Sample response:
Answers will vary, depending on further details and questions.
Detail: "Such fools we are, she thought, crossing Victoria Street."
Question: Why does she think that everyone is a fool?
Answer: "She" is Mrs. Dalloway, and "him" is Scrope Pervis, who is observing her on the street. She doesn't understand why people love living in London."

p. 345 Vocabulary Warm-up
1. heiress
2. abundantly

3. distinguished
4. perpetual
5. profound
6. dislodge
7. futility
8. substantial

p. 346 Reading Warm-up
Sample response:

1. novels and stories; A synonym for *abundantly* might be *lavishly* or *plentifully*.
2. near-impossibility; *Futility* means "a sense that nothing will come of it; it is useless."
3. (inheriting wealth); A woman becomes an heiress when a wealthy person upon death leaves the woman his or her money.
4. *Important* could substitute for *substantial* in the sentence; The passage says that Woolf was "abundantly praised," so this indicates that she was a *substantial* writer.
5. shake loose; In playing pick-up sticks, you must be careful not to *dislodge* other sticks.
6. important; An antonym for *profound* is *trivial*.
7. The words "of great talent" give a clue to *distinguished*; A person who looks *distinguished* is usually wellgroomed and neatly dressed and carries himself or herself proudly.
8. throughout her life, unending; A synonym for *perpetual* is *long-lasting*.

p. 347 Note-taking Guide
Sample response:

How she appears throughout the story: elegant, well-known and respected, mysterious and exciting
How she appears at the end of the story: old, empty, and friendless

p. 348 Note-taking Guide
Sample response:

Character: Clarissa Dalloway
What does she want? to buy flowers for her party
Why does she want this? so that she can throw a successful party and gain social status
What others think about her: She has "a touch of bird about her"; she is vivacious and charming.
What she thinks about herself: She is socially-conscious, but mostly concerned with her party; she loves the comfort of her life.

Character: Judith
What does she want? to act
Why does she want this? She likes theater.
What others think about her: They laugh; no woman can be an actor, she is told.
What she thinks about herself: The essay implies that she is skilled and hard-working.

p. 349 After You Read
1. The looking glass first provides a view of Isabella through her possessions; when Isabella herself appears in the mirror, it provides a real view of the emptiness of Isabella's life.
2. **Graphic Organizer**
Sample response:
Similar/Different: Both narrators have many impressions. The narrator in "The Lady in the Looking Glass: A Reflection" is limited by her associations, while the narrator in "Mrs. Dalloway" has no limitations.
Mrs. Dalloway: omniscient narrator tells story
3. Answers will vary. Possible questions: Who is Mrs. Dalloway? Who is Peter Walsh? What is Mrs. Dalloway doing?

The Essential Question
Answers will vary, but students should support answers with details from the story.

"The Lagoon"
Joseph Conrad

"Araby"
James Joyce

p. 350 Graphic Organizer
Sample response:
The Lagoon
Effect: The Rajah's men capture and kill Arsat's brother.

Araby
Cause: The narrator waits for his uncle to get home to give him money for the bazaar.

p. 351 Vocabulary Warm-up
1. fascination
2. discreetly
3. noiselessly
4. offensive
5. somber
6. fringing
7. withstand
8. enchantment

p. 352 Reading Warm-up

Sample response:

1. interest; One thing that holds great *fascination* for me is astronomy.
2. (daze); A story in which *enchantment* plays a part is *Cinderella.*
3. strung beads
4. (dark); I would wear a *somber* outfit to a funeral.
5. (if Polly dropped it on a hard tile floor); The worst kind of weather my town has had to *withstand* is a hailstorm.
6. that she would tell such an obvious lie to make a sale; They become angry and might speak out against whatever was so *offensive.*
7. silently; It would be important to move *noiselessly* in a library.
8. (tactfully); A time I had to act *discreetly* was when I had to tell my friend she had spinach on her teeth.

p. 353 Note-taking Guide

Sample response:

Beginning Action: Arsat falls in love with Diamelen; Arsat, his brother, and Diamelen run away from the Malaysian ruler.

Climax Action: Arsat leaves his brother to die in order to save his and Diamelen's lives.

Ending Action: Diamelen dies, and Arsat goes back to face his pursuers.

p. 354 Note-taking Guide

Sample response:

Exposition: The young narrator describes the street on which he lives and then describes his friend Mangan's older sister. The narrator daydreams about Mangan's sister and follows her to school, but he never speaks to her.

Rising Action: Mangan's sister speaks to the narrator unexpectedly; the narrator promises to bring her something from *Araby* if he goes. He continues to daydream about her so much that his schoolwork suffers. On the day of the bazaar, the narrator's uncle does not arrive home and give him money until past nine o'clock; the narrator finally arrives at the bazaar as it is closing. A young woman laughing with two young men asks whether the narrator wants to buy something; the narrator unexpectedly declines.

Climax: The narrator suddenly realizes that he has been very foolish.

Falling Action: The narrator departs from the dark and deserted hall.

Resolution: The narrator is stricken by grief and anger at his vanity and foolishness.

p. 355 Background

Sample response:

1. the River Liffey
2. Phoenix Park
3. the northeast part of Dublin

p. 355 Reading Strategy

Students should underline "The narrator has a serious crush on Mangan's sister."

p. 356 Reading Strategy

The narrator must wait because he needs money from his uncle.

p. 356 Reading Check

Students may circle "talking to himself," "hallstand rocking when it had received the weight of his overcoat," and "midway through his dinner."

p. 357 Read Fluently

Sample response:

1. forgetful
2. apologetic
3. generous

p. 357 Stop to Reflect

Some students may say that the description of the bazaar fits their expectations. Other students may be disappointed that the bazaar is not more elaborate.

p. 358 Stop to Reflect

Some students may say that the narrator's trip to the bazaar is a success because through it he realizes the foolishness of his infatuation. Other students may say that the narrator's trip is not successful because his dreams are ruined and he does not buy a gift for Mangan's sister.

p. 358 Literary Analysis

Sample response: The narrator realizes that his infatuation with Mangan's sister is foolish, and that he had wasted much time and energy on what was only a dream.

p. 359 After You Read

1. Sample response: Readers would not know the antagonism the locals felt or the mystery that surrounds Arsat.

2. Sample response: The narrator feels the vacancy of the bazaar—the mundane conversation of the stall keepers, the shoddy products being offered, and the sense that he has overpaid and expected too much from "Araby" all add to the sinking feeling that he has.

3. **Graphic Organizer**
Sample response:
Cause: Arsat's wife becomes very sick, and Tuan cannot help her.
Effect: Arsat decides to go back and face the people who captured and killed his brother.

The Essential Question
Answers will vary, but students should support answers with details from the story.

"The Rocking-Horse Winner"
D. H. Lawrence

"A Shocking Accident"
Graham Greene

p. 360 Graphic Organizer
Sample response:
The Rocking-Horse Winner
Background Knowledge: Some students may say that they feel as though they need more money. Consequently, they may find ways to get more money.
Details from Text: Many references to the need for money at the beginning of the story seem to be significant. The mother claims that the family is "poor" because the "father has no luck."
Predictions: Someone in the family will be lucky and win money.
Confirm Predictions: Paul wins money betting on horses.

A Shocking Accident
Background Knowledge: Students may say that they have been in situations that did not end as badly as they thought they might.
Details from Text: The story tells how Jerome has suffered over the years by telling this story. Sally's unpredictable response would make for a good surprise ending.
Predictions: Sally's reaction to Jerome's story will be different than other people's reactions.
Confirm Predictions: Sally reacts with shock at such a terrible event.

p. 361 Vocabulary Warm-up
1. furnishings
2. noiselessly
3. moderately
4. inevitably
5. colleagues
6. distinguished
7. extraordinarily
8. commiseration

p. 362 Reading Warm-up
Sample response:
1. ("big boy" bed) (dresser); *Furnishings* means "furniture or appliances, as for a room."
2. well-groomed; The *distinguished* gentleman gave a rousing speech.
3. (only the best); An animal that jumps *extraordinarily* high is a kangaroo.
4. appeared to be having a meeting in the center of the floor
5. (All) (Every one); One thing that will *inevitably* happen today is that the sun will set.
6. as if an actual horse had been badly recorded; I go to a local department store to buy *moderately* priced clothing.
7. the difficulty of finding a traditional horse; When my great-grandmother died, *commiseration* with a friend comforted me.
8. (snort) (neigh); *Noiselessly*, I tiptoed into my baby brother's room to check on him.

p. 363 Note-taking Guide
Sample response:
Box 3: Paul decides that he is lucky.
Box 4: Uncle Oscar discovers that Paul is betting on horses and winning.
Box 5: Paul secretly gives his mother five thousand pounds.
Box 6: Paul's "lucky" ability to know the winning horse begins to fade.
Box 7: Paul rides his rocking horse furiously until he knows the name of the next winner, becoming violently ill.
Box 8: Paul wins seventy thousand pounds for his mother.
Box 9: Paul dies.

p. 364 Note-taking Guide
Sample response:
1. How does Jerome feel about his father? Jerome loves his father deeply.
2. How does his father die? A pig fell on him from a balcony.

3. How do people react to the story?
People laugh at the story.

4. Why is he afraid to tell Sally about how his father died? Jerome is afraid that Sally will laugh.

5. How does she react? Sally is horrified, and does not laugh.

6. How does her reaction make Jerome feel? Jerome feels joyful.

p. 365 After You Read
1. Graphic Organizer
Sample response:
Symbolic Meanings: Effort to satisfy a need that cannot be satisfied
Passages That Illustrate: "But even for the Lincoln he didn't 'know,' and he lost fifty pounds. He became wild-eyed and strange, as if something were going to explode in him."
Links to Overall Theme: the destructive nature of greed
Symbolic Meanings: Frightening power of desire and wishes
Passages That Illustrate: "His eyes blazed at her for one strange and senseless second, as he ceased urging his wooden horse. Then he fell with a crash to the ground . . ."
Links to Overall Theme: Expending such effort to gain money takes away the enjoyment of life.
2. Both stories reveal, through the third-person viewpoint, the thoughts and feelings of more than one character.
3. Answers will vary, but students should list the information they used to make a prediction about one of the selections. Then, they should explain whether their predictions were accurate.

The Essential Question
Answers will vary, but students should support answers with details from the story.

"The Soldier"
Rupert Brooke

"Wirers"
Siegfried Sassoon

"Anthem for Doomed Youth"
Wilfred Owen

p. 366 Graphic Organizer
Sample response:
Passage: The Soldier

Relevant Details: The soldier is "blest" by English sun and full of "English air." When the soldier dies, the English dust of his body will enrich the foreign soil.
Essential Message: Because the soldier is English, the dust of his body transforms foreign ground to English soil. The speaker's reverence for English soil sets a tone of loyalty to and love for England.
Passage: Wirers
Relevant Details: The speaker's word choice and tone are blunt and jarring. The death of "Young Hughes" is glossed over by the cynicism of the narrator.
Essential Message: The tone of the poem is angry and cynical. The narrator seems to believe that soldiers' lives are trivialized and uselessly sacrificed.
Passage: Anthem for Doomed Youth
Relevant Details: Soldiers are described as cattle, and their deaths are anonymous. They do not have the "mockeries" of church bells when they die.
Essential Message: The narrator suggests that it is inappropriate to hold elaborate funerals for fallen soldiers. The soldier were sent to war to "die as cattle"; to ceremoniously honor and mourn their death is both futile and hypocritical.

p. 367 Vocabulary Warm-up
1. shrill
2. muffled
3. concealed
4. toil
5. eternal
6. mended
7. stride
8. bore

p. 368 Reading Warm-up
Sample response:
1. (faint); If a noise is coming from the other side of a closed door, it might sound *muffled*.
2. (cries); Some people found her voice beautiful, but to me it was *shrill*.
3. digging the trenches; *Work* is a synonym for *toil*.
4. (endless); A phrase that means the opposite of *eternal* is *short-lived*.
5. this part of the war; *Hid* is a synonym for *concealed*.

6. *March* could substitute for *stride* in the sentence; When we finally win a game, we will *stride* down the field with pride.

7. (mind); An synonym for *bore* is *produced*.

8. my socks; Darla *mended* the broken cup with just a drop of glue.

p. 369 Note-taking Guide

Sample response:

The Soldier

Central Image/Idea: A soldier's life, or dead body, is equated with England in a foreign soil.

Wirers

Central Image/Idea: A boy's life is sacrificed to mend the fence on the war front.

Anthem for Doomed Youth

Central Image/Idea: A young soldier's life can never be mourned enough.

p. 370 After You Read

1. Sample response: "Wirers" vividly conveys the horrors of war through the eyes of a soldier, and "Anthem for Doomed Youth" conveys the horrors of war by focusing on the unceremonial deaths of the soldiers; both poems are effective in communicating the horrors of war.

2. **Graphic Organizer**

Sample response:

Passage, poem: "The Soldier"

Word Choice: gentleness, peace, heaven

Images: field, England, rich earth, flowers, rivers, sun

Tone: patriotic, touching, sentimental

3. Sample response: The "holy glimmers of good-byes," "pallor of girls' brows," "tenderness of patient minds," and "drawing-down of blinds" help underscore the message that no public acknowledgement equals the loss the death of the soldiers represents.

The Essential Question

Answers will vary, but students should support answers with details from the poem.

"The Demon Lover"
Elizabeth Bowen

p. 371 Graphic Organizer

Sample response:

Literary Work: Demon Lover

Atmosphere: mysterious

Weapons: her mind; rationalization

Tactics: find a taxi and have the driver help her

Main Goal: to avoid "the hour arranged"

End Result: She is taken away in a taxi, presumably by her ex-fiancé.

Primary Source: Wartime Speech

Atmosphere: grim

Weapons: bombers, guns, and tanks

Tactics: retaliate, strengthen the front in France, and increase industrial output

Main Goal: win the war

End Result: He urges people to prepare for upcoming conflicts.

p. 372 Vocabulary Warm-up

1. alight
2. caretaker
3. dependability
4. perplexed
5. knowledgeably
6. apprehension
7. heightening
8. assent

p. 373 Reading Warm-up

Sample response:

1. confused, wondering; I once felt perplexed when I couldn't figure out how to play the violin.

2. (supervises and takes care of property that someone else occupies); Something I would want a caretaker to do at my home would be to clean out the garage.

3. worry; One thing that gives me some apprehension is the thought of sharks in the water when I go surfing.

4. (good answer); Clay's experience with motors enabled him to answer knowledgeably Aaron's question about why the car died.

5. reliability; One aspect of my life in which I demonstrate dependability is keeping up with my homework.

6. (increasing); I usually react to heightening demands on my time and patience by making a list of what I have to do and crossing items off as I do them.

7. (common areas); Alight means "lighted."

8. agreement; I would eagerly give my assent to a job offer as a ballerina.

p. 374 Note-taking Guide

Sample response:

Characters: Mrs. Drover

Setting: It is late afternoon in humid London; Mrs. Drover goes to retrieve a few things from her shut-up London home.

Problem: Mrs. Drover discovers a letter addressed to her from her presumed-dead fiancé of many years ago.
Event 1: Mrs. Drover reads the letter.
Event 2: Mrs. Drover remembers her old fiancé's promise and when they parted.
Event 3: Mrs. Drover recalls when she was given the news of her old fiancé's presumed death.
Event 4: Mrs. Drover feels as though she is being watched as she leaves the house.
Event 5: Mrs. Drover walks to the thoroughfare to get a taxi.
Event 6: Mrs. Drover discovers that the taxi driver is her old fiancé.
Conclusion: Mrs. Drover is trapped within the taxi as it drives off into the deserted streets.

p. 375 After You Read
1. Mrs. Drover is upset because it appears to be from her old fiancé, whom she thought was dead; the letter contains an eerie reminder of a past promise.
2. Sample response: The letter and the memory of the fiancé are intrusions from the past; that the letter arrived from a person thought to be dead, and without the help of the Post Office, brings a supernatural feel to the story.
3. **Graphic Organizer**
Sample response:
Ambiguity: "no human eye watched" "Dead air came out to meet her . . ."
What Does it Reveal? These passages hint at the watchful presence of the dead fiancé.

The Essential Question
Answers will vary, but students should support answers with details from the story.

"Vergissmeinicht"
Keith Douglas

"Postscript: For Gweno"
Alun Lewis

"Naming of Parts"
Henry Reed

p. 376 Graphic Organizer
Sample response:
"Vergissmeinicht"
Images of Love or Tenderness: "dishonored picture of his girl," "she would weep to see," "lover and killer are mingled";

Images of War or Violence: "nightmare ground" "frowning barrel of his gun" "entry of a demon" "burst stomach like a cave"

"Postscript: For Gweno"
Images of Love or Tenderness: "you abide, a singing riv within my dreaming side";
Images of War or Violence: "mad tormented valley," "blood and hunger rally," "Death the wild beast"

"Naming of Parts"
Images of Love or Tenderness: "Japonica glistens like coral," "blossoms are fragile and motionless," "early bees assaulting and fumbling";
Images of War or Violence: The poem contains no concrete images of war or violence; however, it describes the process of learning to use a killing tool.

p. 377 Vocabulary Warm-up
1. beloved
2. gestures
3. mingled
4. gothic
5. fumbling
6. decayed
7. mocked
8. tormented

p. 378 Reading Warm-up
Sample response:
1. (her husband); A person who is your *beloved* is one who you love most dearly.
2. (anguished); by the thought of having left behind her comrades, her daughter had needed an operation
3. among the blooming cacti; A synonym for *mingled* is *mixed* or *melded*.
4. (of welcome); Tree branches waving in a storm might make angry *gestures* to protest the strong winds.
5. by dying while she was gone; A synonym for *mocked* is *scorned* or *jeered*.
6. (the aloe plant); After Jerry's tooth *decayed*, the dentist fixed it by placing a crown on top.
7. a document; He might have been fumbling because he was so excited and nervous about seeing his wife or because he was in a hurry to show her the document and return to Isabel.

8. fancy, angular lettering; You might find *gothic* script in books printed as far back as the twelfth century, or you might find it in letters engraved on buildings or written on school diplomas.

p. 379 Note-taking Guide
Sample response:

"Vergissmeinicht"
Speaker: a soldier who has survived a bloody battle
What the Speaker Is Experiencing: The soldier returns to the scene of the battle and sees the corpse of an enemy soldier who had shot at him.
How the Speaker Feels: The speaker feels detached, "almost with content," but he recognizes the pain the dead soldier's lover will feel.

"Postscript: For Gweno"
Speaker: a soldier who is writing to his lover
What the Speaker Is Experiencing: The soldier is facing battle.
How the Speaker Feels: The soldier understands that he may die.

"Naming of Parts"
Speaker: a soldier in basic training
What the Speaker Is Experiencing: He is learning the various parts of his gun and how to use them.
How the Speaker Feels: The speaker is distracted by the signs of spring all around him.

p. 380 After You Read
1. Answers may vary. Students may infer that the speaker is bored, that he is not interested in learning about his gun, or that he is sensitive and enjoys nature.
2. **Graphic Organizer**
Sample response:

"Vergissmeinicht" Death and killing "dishonor" love, causing lovers "mortal hurt." War shows that a person can be both a "lover and killer."

"Postscript: For Gweno" Even through war's brutality and possible death, love will endure.

"Naming of Parts" Despite the dull training required when preparing to kill, the speaker's sensitive, tender nature still exists.

3. These experiences are universal—most people understand the consequences of warfare and have experienced love. The poets want to show that, even in the violence of war, love still exists.

The Essential Question
Answers will vary, but students should support answers with details from the poems.

"Shooting an Elephant"
George Orwell

"No Witchcraft for Sale"
Doris Lessing

p. 381 Graphic Organizer
Sample response:
Shooting an Elephant
Aspect of Theme: Cultural Conflict: The Burmese expect Orwell to kill an elephant, but Orwell does not want to do it.
Source of Conflict: The Burmese follow Orwell as he tracks the elephant so that they can watch him kill it.
Details of Conflict: The elephant went wild and killed a man. The Burmese have a law that says that a mad elephant must be killed.
Result of Conflict: Orwell kills the elephant.

No Witchcraft for Sale
Aspect of Theme: Cultural Conflict: Gideon does not want to reveal the medical secrets of his people to the Farquars.
Source of Conflict: A scientists asks the Farquars to reveal how Gideon saved their son from blindness.
Details of Conflict: A snake spits into Teddy's eyes, which could lead to blindness. Gideon uses the root of a plant to cure Teddy.
Result of Conflict: Gideon reveals which plant he used to cure Teddy.

p. 382 Vocabulary Warm-up
1. scorching
2. writhing
3. invariably
4. inevitable
5. comparable
6. tyranny
7. inflicted
8. petty

p. 383 Reading Warm-up
Sample response:
1. (none comes close to matching); *Newsweek* magazine is *comparable* to *Time*.
2. of course; *Inevitable* means "something that is bound to happen."
3. (constantly); A word that means the opposite of *invariably* is *rarely*.

4. English rule; Another example of a *tyranny* would be Cambodia under Pol Pot.

5. (mean-spirited); Pulling a dog's tail is a *petty* action.

6. (painful); After falling on the court, Merry was clutching her knee and *writhing* in pain.

7. destruction; Gaby's new shoes were too tight, and *inflicted* pain on both feet.

8. fires; hot, burning

p. 384 Note-taking Guide
Sample response:
Where it takes place: Moulmein, in Lower Burma
The problems Orwell faces: Orwell must kill an elephant that has temporarily gone wild and killed a Burmese man.
The actions he takes: Orwell kills the elephant with two thousand Burmese looking on.
His feelings and thoughts: Orwell does not want to kill the elephant because it is no longer necessary, but he has to kill the elephant in order to avoid looking like a fool to the Burmese. He also realizes that the British Imperialists are actually at the mercy of the colonized because the British can only pretend to be in control.

p. 385 Reading Strategy
Sample response: Orwell is a British police officer in Burma. The Burmese are anti-European because Burma is a colony of Great Britain.

p. 385 Reading Check
Students should say that the Burmese appear to hate the British because they laugh, sneer, and shout insults at them.

p. 386 Reading Check
The subinspector calls Orwell about an elephant running wild in the town.

p. 386 Stop to Reflect
Orwell takes the rifle because he thinks the noise might be useful.

p. 387 Literary Analysis
Students should circle *b.*

p. 387 Reading Check
Students should say that Orwell does not think that the elephant is dangerous because the elephant's wildness appeared to have worn off.

p. 388 Reading Check
Students should say that Orwell knows he must shoot the elephant when he sees the large crowd of natives watching him.

p. 388 Literary Analysis
The Burmese expect Orwell to kill the elephant even though Orwell believes that the elephant is no longer a threat.

p. 388 Literary Analysis
Students should say that this is a form of situational irony.

p. 389 Reading Check
Students may circle "thousands of years old," "climbed with desperate slowness," "stood weakly," "legs sagging," "head drooping," "jolt his whole body," and "knock the last remnant of strength from his legs."

p. 389 Reading Check
The elephant "slobbers and falls," immediately seeming to "deteriorate."

p. 390 Reading Check
1. Orwell cannot bear to watch the elephant's agonizing death.
2. It takes the elephant half an hour to die.

p. 390 Stop to Reflect
Orwell's real reason for shooting the elephant is to demonstrate to the Burmese onlookers that he is in control of the situation and of them. He does not want to appear foolish to the Burmese.

p. 391 Note-taking Guide
Sample response:
Event: Teddy is born.
Detail: Gideon and the servants are pleased for the Farquars.
Event: Teddy is given a scooter.
Detail: Teddy frightens Gideon's young son.
Event: A tree snake spits in Teddy's eyes.
Detail: Gideon heals Teddy with an antidote an unknown plant.
Event: The Farquars want Gideon to show a scientist the plant.
Detail: Gideon is angry and misleads them all.
Event: The relationship between the Farquars and Gideon heals.
Detail: They joke about the incident.

p. 392 Reading Check

Students should say that the Farquars are particularly happy because they had been childless for a long time.

p. 392 Reading Check

Students may choose from the following: "Gideon plays with the little boy and helps him learn how to walk"; "Mrs. Farquar recognizes Gideon's love for her son"; "God's will"; "religious."

p. 393 Stop to Reflect

Students should note that Gideon's son is a native African and that Teddy is the son of a white colonizer.

p. 393 Reading Strategy

Answers will vary. Sample response: One theme of "Shooting an Elephant" is the cultural conflict that comes from Europeans having authority over the local inhabitants of a region. This selection has a similar theme as evidenced by Teddy's behavior toward Gideon and Gideon's youngest son.

p. 393 Reading Check

Teddy is hurt when a snake spits poison into his eyes.

p. 394 Literary Analysis

Students may choose from the following: "He ran off into the bush"; "lifted the child into the house"; "bathed his eyes"; "her remedies had no effect"; "efficacy of native herbs."

p. 394 Reading Check

Mrs. Farquar remembers seeing natives blinded by the snake poison.

p. 395 Literary Analysis

Students should circle *b*.

p. 395 Reading Check

1. Teddy's eyes are healed.
2. The Farquars give Gideon gifts and a raise in pay.

p. 396 Reading Check

Sample response:
1. flustered
2. flattered
3. discomfort

p. 396 Reading Check

Students should say that Gideon is surprised, angry, and hurt.

p. 397 Literary Analysis

Gideon picks a handful of flowers for the scientist and goes home. It is an example of situational irony because Gideon surprises the Farquars and the scientists by identifying a plant that the group has seen all along their journey.

p. 397 Stop to Reflect

The Farquars discover that Gideon is a well-known medicine man.

p. 398 Literary Analysis

Some students may say that the cultural conflict is resolved because the Gideon and the Farquars eventually resume their friendly relationship. Other students may say that the cultural conflict is not resolved because Gideon is sad when he looks at and jokes with Teddy.

p. 398 Stop to Reflect

Sample response: Gideon's last words mean that the event did not truly change the circumstances. Teddy will still grow up to be a master over the Africans.

p. 399 After You Read

1. Orwell's feeling is ironic because in reality, Orwell enforces British rule over the Burmese.
2. **Graphic Organizer**
Sample response:
Farquars' Values: The Farquars believe that white people are superior.
Incident: Teddy frightens Gideon's son.
Gideon's Values: Gideon is accepting of Teddy's estrangement.
Farquars' Values: The Farquars cannot control the outcome.
Incident: A snake spits in Teddy's eyes.
Gideon's Values: Gideon immediately finds the correct antidote.
Farquars' Values: The Farquars believe that the curative powers of the root should be available to everyone.
Incident: The Farquars want Gideon to find the root.
Gideon's Values: Gideon believes that the knowledge of the root is sacred.
3. Sample response: An aspect of the theme in both stories is cultural conflict. Cultural conflict in "Shooting an Elephant" arises when Orwell shoots an elephant because

the Burmese expect him to do so. In "No Witchcraft for Sale," cultural conflict arises when the Farquars ask Gideon to reveal the plant he used to cure Teddy.

The Essential Question
Answers will vary, but students should support answers with details from the story.

"The Train from Rhodesia"
Nadine Gordimer

"B. Wordsworth"
V. S. Naipaul

p. 400 Graphic Organizer
Sample response:
Effects on Setting, Character, or Conflict:
2. The artist chases the train to make a sale.
3. The man treats the artist poorly.

p. 401 Vocabulary Warm-up
1. rite
2. majestic
3. encouragingly
4. uninvited
5. wryly
6. vendors
7. untidy
8. compartments

p. 402 Reading Warm-up
Sample response:
1. T; Leaders have to engage in discussions and give-and-take with others.
2. T; If the ball is bouncing at top speed, it would be difficult to hit.
3. F; *Hospitable* people tend to enjoy extending themselves to others.
4. T; A tall tale is hard to believe, so listeners might be *incredulous*.
5. F; If it will *recur*, that means it is likely to happen again.
6. T; Naps usually make people less tired.
7. F; A tugged rope becomes more taut; it does not *slacken*.
8. T; The word *rippled* implies little waves.

p. 403 Note-taking Guide
Sample response:
Setting (Place): a train
Details: The train pulls into a station crowded with natives selling carved wood animals.
Characters: a young woman, a man, and a native

Details: The young woman and man are newly married; the native is trying to sell his carvings.
Problems: The young woman wants to buy a carved lion but decides that it is too expensive.
Details: The husband buys the lion at a greatly reduced price, but the young woman is unexpectedly angry with him.

p. 404 Note-taking Guide
Sample response:
What character says: B. Wordsworth says that he is writing a great poem, one line per month. He says that the boy is a poet, too.
What character does: B. Wordsworth goes to the boy's house and asks to watch the bees. He teaches the boy the constellations and appreciation of beauty.
What others say about character: The boy says that B. Wordsworth makes the world more exciting and that he speaks and acts deliberately, as if he were experiencing things for the first time.
What character thinks: B. Wordsworth is troubled by the limitations he has encountered in life, but he is happy to have met the boy.

p. 405 After You Read
1. The young woman's inner conflict is over the "void" within her that made her feel as though "the hour was not worth their grasp."
2. **Graphic Organizer**
Sample response:
"B. Wordsworth"
Setting: Trinidad in the 1940s, under British colonial rule
Characterization: A young boy in Trinidad and a black poet learn about each other through conversation. The young boy lives alone with his mother and at first thinks ill of the poet. The poor poet lives alone, survives on little, and considers himself a brother to William Wordsworth. The poet seems to be beaten down by society, but the boy learns from the poet that life is about appreciation and struggle.
Conflicts: The poet struggles against society to survive and realize his dreams. The boy struggles against society to know and understand the poet.

3. The conflict between man and society is shaped by the effects of colonial rule on the people of Trinidad. The black poet suffers and struggles against the restrictions placed on him because he is considered inferior by the society in which he lives. The boy struggles to understand the effects that society has on the poet and why the poet is judged so harshly by society and fails to succeed.

The Essential Question
Answers will vary, but students should support opinions with details from personal experiences.

Poetry of Walcott

p. 406 Graphic Organizer
Sample response:
Poem: *from* Midsummer, XXIII
Allusion: "the riot police and the skinheads exchanged quips you could trace to the Sonnets"
Affect Understanding: It helps me understand that the speaker feels excluded from a culture shared by the police and the skinheads.
Poem: *from* Omeros, *from* Chapter XXVIII
Allusion: "So there went the Ashanti one way, the Mandingo another, the Ibo another, the Guinea . . ."
Affect Understanding: It helps me understand that many peoples from Africa shared the experience of being taken from their homes, enslaved, and sent away without family to new places.

p. 407 Vocabulary Warm-up
1. horizon
2. thatched
3. fronds
4. withered
5. triangular
6. scurry
7. quips
8. ashen

p. 408 Reading Warm-up
Sample response:
1. Inez was drawn to the *splendor* of the epic oil painting. The *splendor* of the feast set before him was astonishing to William.
2. Ravi wants to *perpetuate* the idea that electric cars are the answer to our energy problems. Toni is working on inventing a *perpetual* motion machine.
3. The *reverberation* of the bell could be heard a block away. The sound of the crashing glass *reverberated* throughout the house.
4. The cause of the dinosaurs' *extinction* is a mystery. The dodo is an *extinct* bird.
5. "Beware the ides of March," was a *prophetic* warning given to Julius Caesar. The man claimed to be a *prophet*, but nothing he said ever came true.
6. The children *seethe* with excitement when they go to the amusement park. Stay away from Michael—he's *seething* with anger.
7. The sun *radiated* in all directions, heating the atmosphere of the nearby planets. The bride looked *radiant*, joy beaming from her face.

p. 409 Note-taking Guide
Sample response:
Context details: "like Boer cattle under Tory whips"; "add some color to the British theater"
Conflict in poet's mind: Walcott feels disloyal to his countrymen in light of the race riots.

p. 410 Note-taking Guide
Sample response:
Detail 1: "'. . . these shadows are reprinted now on the white sand . . .'"
Detail 2: "'. . . our eyes showed dried fronds in their brown irises . . .'"
Detail 3: "'. . . ribbed corpses floated . . .'"
Detail 4: "'. . . black waiter bringing the bill.'"
Detail 5: ". . . multiply their ruin . . ."
Detail 6: "'. . . each man was a nation . . .'"

p. 411 After You Read
1. Each man was "a nation in himself" because he was separated from his tribe, from his family, and from his friends.
2. Walcott's political critique of his role as a West Indian poet in British society mirrors the theme of understanding a West Indian's place in British society. Walcott questions whether he, as a poet, has ever been truly welcome and a part of British society, for West Indians as a group are generally excluded and considered separate.

3. Graphic Organizer
Sample response:

Allusion: *from* Omeros: "our skulls on the scorching decks"
Literary: Literary
Historical: inhuman treatment on slave ships
Allusion: *from* Midsummer XXIII: "like Boer cattle under Tory whips that drag every wagon / nearer to apartheid"
Literary: Scholarly
Historical: British racial segregation
Popular: Segregation is still present in modern life.

The Essential Question
Answers will vary, but students should support answers with details from the poems.

"Follower"
Seamus Heaney

"Two Lorries"
Seamus Heaney

"Outside History"
Eavan Boland

p. 412 Graphic Organizer
Sample response:

"Follower"
Passage: "I wanted to grow up and plow, / To close one eye, stiffen my arm. / All I ever did was follow / In his broad shadow round the farm."
Main Points: The speaker wanted to plow. He remembers following his father around the farm.
Summary: The son wanted to be a farmer, like his father.
Main Idea: The son follows his father, looks up to him, and wants to be like him.

"Two Lorries"
Passage: stanzas 1–2
Main Points: The coalman delivers good-quality coal and asks the narrator's mother on a date; the Magherafelt bus passes the house; the narrator's mother is moved by the lorry and tempted to accept.
Summary: The coalman delivers a load of good-quality coal to the narrator's house and asks the narrator's mother on a date. The mother is tempted to go because the coal is so good and the sight of the half-empty lorry moves her.

Main Idea: A coalman asks a woman for a date, and she is flattered.

"Outside History"
Passage: entire poem
Main Points: The stars are "outside history"; the stars reveal human mortality; one must choose to live either in myth or history; one cannot undo past losses.
Summary: People are not outsiders to history; they must choose between disengagement with the present and therefore the past, or engagement in the present struggle and therefore the pain of the past. The narrator chooses to participate in Ireland's painful history, knowing that her efforts cannot restore past losses or undo the pain.
Main Idea: The speaker wants to be part of her country's history even though she cannot help those in the past.

p. 413 Vocabulary Warm-up
1. expert
2. conceit
3. reins
4. ordeal
5. pluck
6. strained
7. heft
8. angled

p. 414 Reading Warm-up
Sample response:
1. a person who knows; I would like to become an *expert* in the field of sports medicine.
2. (skill); Helen's *conceit* about her beauty is a bit silly.
3. if a horse gets sores; *Ordeal* means "a very difficult or trying experience."
4. (pull them off easily); A rider might give a *pluck* to a horse's reins to have the horse change direction.
5. (slanted); One reason a person might have *angled* a car while driving is to fit into a parking space.
6. to control the horse; If a rider lost the *reins* while riding, the horse might go the wrong way.
7. Lift; It took two cheerleaders to *heft* the third one up into the air.
8. (take too much effort); Once I *strained* myself when carrying a box of books up the stairs.

p. 415 Note-taking Guide
Sample response:
Follower
Images: father's shoulders, son, following
behind the plow
Central Image: The son follows behind his
father as he plows the field.
Two Lorries
Images: coal trucks, smoke and ashes, rain,
mother, bomb
Central Image: the bus station bombing
Outside History
Images: stars, rivers, fields, pain of human
suffering and death
Central Image: past and present struggle

p. 416 After You Read
1. Students may choose from a number of
words, including "shafts," "furrow," "headrig,"
"hobnailed," "plod," and "yapping."
2. **Graphic Organizer**
Sample response:
Diction
Examples: "iron inklings," "mortal," "ordeal"
Conclusion: Philosophical / abstract diction
Imagery
Examples: "a landscape," "those fields,"
"roads clotted"
Conclusion: simple, general imagery with
abstract ideas
Rhythm/Rhyme
Examples: irregular
Conclusion: conversational
Form
Examples: 3-line stanza
Conclusion: simple
3. Sample response: In the first incident, the
poet's mother chats with the coal deliveryman
who invites her to see a film. She declines;
the coalman drives off to the city. In the
second incident, a terrorist-driven truck
explodes, destroying the bus station in which
the poet used to meet his mother. In a vision,
the poet sees his mother's ghost at the bus
station, attended by the coalman as a figure
of death. The poem's main idea is that the
speaker does not want to lose Ireland to
conflict and war.

The Essential Question
Answers will vary, but students should support answers with details from the poems.

"Come and Go"
Samuel Beckett

"That's All"
Harold Pinter

p. 417 Graphic Organizer
Sample response:
Come and Go
Characters: Three older women with covered
faces. They have been friends since childhood.
Dialogue: Repetition of dialogue, except with
different speakers. Some of the characters'
dialogue is whispered and unknown to
readers.
Situation: The women are sitting together as
they did when they were schoolgirls.
That's All
Characters: Two women—only named "Mrs. A"
and "Mrs. B" and a third woman who is not
present.
Dialogue: Limited; with two exceptions, Mrs. B
only says "Yes," or "Oh, yes." Mrs. A does most
of the talking. The dialogue is repetitive.
Situation: The two women are talking about
the third woman. There is no stage direction
or elaboration on setting, costumes, etc.

p. 418 Vocabulary Warm-up
1. nondescript
2. appalled
3. pose
4. erect
5. realize
6. clasped

p. 419 Reading Warm-up
Sample response:
1. (stood, like a man about to give a formal
speech); A person might want to stand *erect*
when he is being singled out on a stage to
receive an award.
2. this may sound odd and slightly pompous;
We *realize* that today is the last day to pur-
chase tickets.
3. (dismayed); After he felt appalled that people really did think he sounded pompous,
Jonathan tried to act humbly.
4. He sat with slumped shoulders at the edge
of the stage, his legs dangling over the side.
He put his clasped hands in his lap; A person
in an angry *pose* might be standing with
clenched fists raised in the air, bared teeth
and a frown on his face.

5. (hands); You might see *clasped* necklaces, *clasped* handcuffs, or *clasped* arms.

6. *dull, undefined*; A synonym for nondescript is characterless, or ordinary.

p. 420 Note-taking Guide
Sample response:

Come and Go

Ru: wears a faded violet overcoat; like the others, her face is hidden under a hat; she tells a secret and has a secret told about her; she asks more personal and emotional questions at the end of the play.

Vi: wears a faded red overcoat; like the others, her face is hidden under a hat; she tells a secret and has a secret told about her.

Flo: wears a faded yellow overcoat; like the others, her face is hidden under a hat; she tells a secret and has a secret told about her; she is able to feel the rings that are not there.

That's All

Mrs. A.: dominates the conversation; closely monitors what others are doing (for example, knows when, where, and how often the third woman goes shopping)

Mrs. B.: says very little throughout the play; seems either to agree with Mrs. B. or be distracted and uninterested in the conversation.

Third Woman: not present, but is the subject of the conversation; has changed her normal routine and seems to be avoiding Mrs. A.

p. 421 After You Read
1. Answers will vary. Students may note that by focusing on dialogue, the playwrights have simplified the dramas. The characters' repetitive, simple dialogue indicates how poorly people communicate, although communication is central to human relationships.

2. **Graphic Organizer**
Sample response:

Come and Go

Plot and Action: Action is limited to the characters' moving on and off stage and talking to one another. There is no traditional plot—no building action, climax, or resolution.

Dialogue: The play is very brief, and dialogue is mostly limited to questions and statements repeated by each character.

Staging: The stage directions are explicit and descriptive.

That's All

Plot and Action: There is no traditional plot, and the action consists of conversation between two women.

Dialogue: The dialogue is brief, with Mrs. A. speaking more than Mrs. B.

Staging: There are no stage directions.

3. Sample response: In the first incident, the poet's mother chats with the coal deliveryman who invites her to see a film. She declines; the coalman drives off to the city. In the second incident, a terrorist-driven truck explodes, destroying the bus station in which the poet used to meet his mother. In a vision, the poet sees his mother's ghost at the bus station, attended by the coalman as a figure of death. The poem's main idea is that the speaker does not want to lose Ireland to conflict and war.

The Essential Question
Answers will vary, but students should support opinions with details from the story.

"Do Not Go Gentle into That Good Night"
Dylan Thomas

"Fern Hill"
Dylan Thomas

"The Horses"
Ted Hughes

p. 422 Graphic Organizer
Sample response:

"Do Not Go Gentle into That Good Night"
How Elements Communicate Theme: The repetitive form of the villanelle adds importance to Thomas's message; the tumbling style gives Thomas's words urgency.

How Details Communicate Theme: Thomas compares death to night, and urges that people should resist the dying of the light, showing that people have something to hold onto. Thomas many different types of men—wise men, good men, wild men, grave men—each of whom have reasons to resist death. Thomas closes with an appeal to his father, adding personal weight to his message.

Effectiveness of Elements and Details: The elements are very effective in communicating Thomas's theme clearly and in communicating the importance of his message. The details add interest and personal feeling to the theme, making it easier for the reader to relate.

p. 423 Vocabulary Warm-up
1. flung
2. stillness
3. carefree
4. deeds
5. bearing
6. frail
7. lilting
8. cast

p. 424 Reading Warm-up
Sample response:

1. (calm); An antonym for *stillness* is *movement* or *disruptiveness*.
2. (untroubled); *Carefree* means "having few or no worries."
3. over her shoulder; A word that could substitute for *flung* is *tossed*.
4. horse as it trots gracefully; Her laughter had a *lilting* sound that was almost like music.
5. in bronze as part of a statue; A bell could also be *cast* in bronze.
6. a rider on its back; A synonym for *bearing* is *carrying*.
7. (endeavors); The Boy Scouts are required to do good *deeds*.
8. (strength); A person who has been sick could be described as *frail*.

p. 425 Note-taking Guide
Sample response:
Poem: "Do Not Go Gentle"
Main Idea/Writer's Message: The poet faces the approaching death of his father. He urges readers to fight death, rather than accept it.
Poem: "Fern Hill"
Main Idea/Writer's Message: The poet looks back fondly on his carefree youth and laments the loss of youth and the "chains" that the passage of time imposes.
Poem: "The Horses"
Main Idea/Writer's Message: The poet recalls an encounter with horses in nature. He celebrates the peacefulness and mystery of the experience and of nature.

p. 426 After You Read
1. **Graphic Organizer**
Sample response:
Style: Words tumble out in a rush.

Examples: "Now as I was young and easy under the apply boughs / About the lilting house and happy as the grass was green."
Style: Shows an attitude of wonder about life
Examples: "Time let me play and be / Golden in the mercy of his means."
Style: Uses complex poetic forms
Examples: Villanelle form of "Do Not Go Gentle into That Good Night"
2. Thomas's tumbling, rushing style reflects the carefree and playful nature of childhood, which is part of the poem's theme.
3. Hughes's style involves using short bursts of images. This use of imagery focuses the reader's attention on the wild and remote beauty that the speaker sees in nature.

The Essential Question
Answers will vary, but students should support answers with details from the poems.

"An Arundel Tomb"
Philip Larkin

"The Explosion"
Philip Larkin

"On the Patio"
Peter Redgrove

"Not Waving but Drowning"
Stevie Smith

p. 427 Graphic Organizer
Sample response:
Poem: "An Arundel Tomb"
Sentence: "Rigidly they / Persisted, linked, through lengths and breadths / Of time."
Meaning: They remained where they were throughout all time.
Poem: "The Explosion"
Sentence: "At noon, there came a tremor; cows / Stopped chewing for a second; sun / Scarfed as in a heat-haze, dimmed."
Meaning: A tremor came at noon, causing the cows to stop chewing and the sun to dim.
Poem: "On the Patio"
Sentence: "Suddenly I dart out into the patio, / Snatch the bright glass up and drain it, / Bang it back down on the thundery steel table for a refill."
Meaning: The narrator runs outside, empties the glass, and slams it back down on the table so that it can fill up again.

Poem: "Not Waving but Drowning"
Sentence: "Poor chap, he always loved larking / And now he's dead / It must have been too cold for him his heart gave way, / They said."
Meaning: The drowned man loved to have fun, but he is now dead. People thought it was too cold for him.

p. 428 Vocabulary Warm-up

1. trough
2. moaning
3. comfort
4. blurred
5. vaguely
6. persisted
7. lodged
8. prolong

p. 429 Reading Warm-up

Sample response:

1. refusing to give it up; One activity in which I have *persisted* is gymnastics.
2. (the ditch beside the road); A *trough* is a long, narrow depression, such as a ditch or a wheel rut.
3. large farm equipment operating in the fields; *Moaning* is a long, low sound like the one people make when they are in pain or very sad.
4. (pebbles); Marisol lodged a rock under the door to keep it from closing and locking behind her.
5. the passing miles; A word that means about the same as *vaguely* would be *unclearly*.
6. (her ride); People usually want to *prolong* anything that is enjoyable, such as a celebration.
7. age and weather; Jiggling the camera when taking a picture might cause a photograph to be *blurred*.
8. she had a cellphone in her pocket and could call for help if she needed to; A lost person might take *comfort* in having a map or seeing people nearby who might be able to help.

p. 430 Note-taking Guide

Sample response:
Poem: "An Arundel Tomb"
Important Symbols and Their Meanings:
Symbol: The images on the tomb are unin-

tended symbols of enduring love; Meter: Iambic tetrameter; Rhyme scheme: *abbcac*
Theme: Death and its effect on those who survive
Poem: "The Explosion"
Important Symbols and Their Meanings:
Symbol: The unbroken eggs represent what is lost; Meter: Trochaic tetrameter; Rhyme scheme: unrhymed
Theme: Death and its effect on those who survive
Poem: "On the Patio"
Important Symbols and Their Meanings:
Symbols: The thunderstorms represent the power and force of nature; the wineglass is a symbol of human attempts to capture and possess that force; Meter: Free verse; Rhyme scheme: unrhymed
Theme: The desire to possess the energy and life force of nature
Poem: "Not Waving but Drowning"
Important Symbols and Their Meanings:
Symbol: The water is a symbol of the dead man's isolation; Meter: Varying meter; Rhyme scheme: *abcb*
Theme: People are often misinterpreted for an entire lifetime.

p. 431 After You Read

1. The images concern both the violent descent of the rain from the clouds above and its effect on the patio below.
2. Sample response: The dead man means that for all his life he was unable to cope with the circumstances of his life.
3. **Graphic Organizer**
"An Arundel Tomb": Thĕir prŏpĕr hábĭts váguĕly shówn / Ăs jóintĕd ármŏr, stíffenĕd pléat . . .
"The Explosion": Ĭt wăs sáid, aňd fór ă sécoňd / Wíves săw mén ŏf thé ĕxplósiŏn . . .
4. Readers should pause at the end lines punctuated by a comma, a semicolon, or a colon and come to a stop at the end of lines ending with a period.

The Essential Question

Answers will vary, but students should support answers with details from the poem.

"Prayer"
Carol Duffy

"In the Kitchen"
Penelope Shuttle

p. 432 Graphic Organizer
Sample response:
Elements of Parallel Structure:
"In the Kitchen" "I am trying to love the world . . ." and the personified actions of inanimate objects ("The ironing-board thanks . . ." "The new fridge hums . . .")
"Prayer" "Some days, although we . . . Some nights, although we . . ." and the repetition of place names. The sonnet form itself imposes parallel structure.

p. 433 Vocabulary Warm-up
1. steadfastly
2. forgetfulness
3. recites
4. identifiable
5. secured
6. normal

p. 434 Reading Warm-up
Sample response:
1. (pattern to its line lengths or rhymes); An *identifiable* element of a traditional sonnet is its length, which is always 14 lines.
2. out loud; Keisha *recites* the words to her favorite songs in order to pass the time while waiting for the school bus.
3. (unchanging); a desire to make sense of the world, a search for meaning in that world, and a need to understand and communicate the range of human actions and emotions
4. the ordinary, closely observed, everyday objects and sounds, like an ironing board, a kettle, or a train whistle in the night; A synonym for *normal* is *typical*, or *usual*.
5. every poem is a record of something in words. In that way, poetry helps to keep alive memories of events, moments, ideas, and people. A person could combat *forgetfulness* by making a scrapbook to preserve memories of important family events.
6. poetry has secured itself permanently into the repertoire of human expression; Janice secured the boat by knotting one of its ropes to a metal ring in the side of the dock.

p. 435 Note-taking Guide
Sample response:
Examples of Personification:
"In the Kitchen" "ironing-board thanks," "new fridge hums," "chair recites," "table leaves no stone unturned," "clock votes"
"Prayer" the tree sings and the train chants

p. 436 After You Read
1. Sample response: The rustling of tree leaves can sound like musical notes. The rhythmic sounds of a train on a track (and its occasional whistle or low rumbling sounds) mimic the sounds of Latin chanting.
2. **Graphic Organizer**
"In the Kitchen"
Speaker's Loss: her husband and companion.
How the Speaker Finds Comfort: through the company of everyday objects that have taken on human qualities; through the effort of "trying to love the world / back to normal"

"Prayer"
Speaker's Loss: loss of prayer, faith
How the Speaker Finds Comfort: by listening to the musical sounds of the trees, train, piano scales, the radio; by directing others to "Pray for us now."
3. The speaker is working toward feeling love and hope again. The speaker is also trying to restore order to her life by getting the "seas back on the maps / where they belong."

The Essential Question
Answers will vary, but students should support answers with details from the poem.

"A Devoted Son"
Anita Desai

p. 437 Graphic Organizer
Sample response:
Rakesh
Action: He bows to touch his father's feet.
Cause: Rakesh wants to show respect in a traditional way.
Action: He moves back home after finishing school in the United States.
Cause: Rakesh feels obligated to his family and community.
Varma
Action: He asks his grandchildren to get sweets for him.

Cause: Rakesh has put Varma on a diet in which Varma can have few foods that he likes. Action: He swats a bottle of tonic from Rakesh's hands.

Cause: Varma is tired of the endless medical treatments that must endure at the hands of his son.

p. 438 Vocabulary Warm-up

1. humiliating
2. verandah
3. thereafter
4. amongst
5. panicky
6. distraught
7. miraculously
8. colleagues

p. 439 Reading Warm-up

Sample response:

1. in turmoil, extremely upset; A situation that might make a person feel *distraught* would be a serious illness.
2. her beloved family; A more common word for *amongst* is *among*.
3. (in front of their home); Lizzy always wanted a house with a *verandah*.
4. (failure); *Humiliating* means "extremely embarrassing."
5. (frightened); I might get a *panicky* feeling if I had to do an impromptu performance in front of thousands of people.
6. she had lived up to that promise to herself; After Roger made that mistake once, he never made it again *thereafter*.
7. (she was on her way to college); One thing I wish would *miraculously* happen in my life is that certain family members would learn to get along.
8. (co-workers); In the future, I would like to work with *colleagues* who are dedicated to the idea of working with disadvantaged children.

p. 440 Note-taking Guide

Sample response:

Character: Rakesh

Dynamic: yes

Details: At the beginning of the story, Rakesh follows the traditional path of a devoted son. Rakesh's education introduces him to modern ideas, and by the time he is established as a doctor, Rakesh ignores his father's wishes in favor of practicing new, modern medicine.

Character: Varma

Static: yes

Details: Varma remains traditional throughout the story. He does not undergo significant changes, and when his son refuses to honor his wishes regarding diet, Varma considers his son to be very disrespectful.

p. 441 After You Read

1. Sample response: Rakesh's mother and wife are static characters because neither undergoes significant change.

2. **Graphic Organizer**

Sample response:

Varma

Beginning: He is happy and proud of Rakesh's success in school.

Middle: His wife has died, and he has health problems coupled with unusual behaviors.

End: He is hostile toward his son and the medical treatments.

3. The speaker is working toward feeling love and hope again. The speaker is also trying to restore order to her life by getting the "seas back on the maps / where they belong."

The Essential Question

Answers will vary, but students should support opinions with details from the story.

"Next Term We'll Mash You" Penelope Lively

p. 442 Graphic Organizer

Sample response:

Setting: an expensive and elite boarding school

Characters: Charles; his parents, Mr. and Mrs. Manders; Mr. and Mrs. Spokes, the headmaster and his wife; other students

Social Class: wealthy, upper class

Motivations: Charles: wants to please his parents, wants to get by; Mr. and Mrs. Manders: want to be part of the upper class, want to fit in with their wealthy friends; Mr. and Mrs. Spokes: want to run the school and maintain traditions; Other students: want to keep the social order in place, want to bully new students

Reactions: Charles: is quiet and overwhelmed; Mr. and Mrs. Manders: drop names, make judgments about people and the surroundings; Mr. and Mrs. Spokes: act very matter-of-fact about money and connections, try to welcome Charles and his parents to the school; Other students: make threats toward Charles

What these elements reveal: Some people want to become part of the exclusive upper-class world; the boarding school setting can be a cruel place.

p. 443 Vocabulary Warm-up

1. headmaster
2. economist
3. untainted
4. amiable
5. inaccessible
6. relentless
7. unpredictable
8. prospectuses

p. 444 Reading Warm-up

Sample response:

1. extra cost, expensive tuition; A synonym for *inaccessible* is *unreachable*; another is *unattainable*.
2. principal, the person in charge of a private school; The *headmaster* established a new rule saying that school would end thirty minutes early every Wednesday to give students extra time to prepare classrooms for the science fair.
3. (friendly, outgoing personality); *Surly* is an antonym for *amiable*.
4. The need for fundraising is *relentless* because private schools need ongoing funds to maintain their facilities; The sun beat down with *relentless* heat and intensity.
5. These documents appear on Web sites or are printed as booklets. They explain the school's mission and describe its programs to prospective students and parents; My school offers 15 different varsity athletic teams and a wide range of academic classes.
6. (specializing in finance); An *economist* is a person who specializes in studying some aspect of finances, whether that has to do with work and productivity, how banks and businesses operate, or how changes in our climate might determine what crops can be grown and sold in the future.
7. reputation, excellence; *corrupted, stained*
8. (educational outcomes); He completed all the homework, did well on some quizzes, but forgot to study for the exam, so he felt his final grade was *unpredictable*.

p. 445 Note-taking Guide

Sample response:

School Grounds: The grounds are nice, with spacious playing fields and a country setting.
Staff: There is a maid in a uniform. The headmaster and his wife are well-dressed and comfortable with their status.
Cost: The school is more expensive than others.
What Their Friends Say About the School: The school is popular among their friends from the city; their friends approve of the headmaster and his wife.

p. 446 After You Read

1. Charles's mother notices that Mrs. Spokes is wearing old but expensive clothes and good jewelry. Her attitude and voice show confidence.
2. **Graphic Organizer**
Sample response:
A word that describes Charles is shy.
Details that reveal this: He sits quietly in the car and in the headmaster's office. A word that describes Charles's mother is shallow / phony.
Details that reveal this: She is very concerned about appearances.
3. Answers will vary. Students may suggest that there is separation between social classes in England and that places like the boarding school help reinforce such attitudes. Going to an elite boarding school may help Charles later because he might develop relationships with wealthy and well-connected people. The path to the upper class leads through elite schools.

The Essential Question

Answers will vary, but students should support answers with details from the story.

from We'll Never Conquer Space
Arthur C. Clarke

p. 447 Graphic Organizer

Sample response:
Is an opinion clearly stated?
Example: "Man will never conquer space."
Do facts support ideas?
Example: Distance creates too much of a barrier to communication.

Are there words and phrases that readers will remember?
Example: "The price of space is time."
Are there appeals to reason or emotion?
Example: (logic) Some objects in space are too far away, even if we could travel at the speed of light.
Does the author address differing opinions?
Example: Clarke says that scientists who claim that we will never cross "cosmic gulfs" are wrong.
Are unfamiliar ideas clarified?
Example: Clarke explains a simplified way of using very large numbers.

p. 448 Vocabulary Warm-up

1. virtual
2. vertically
3. ultimate
4. voyaging
5. analogy
6. separation
7. conservative
8. psychological

p. 449 Reading Warm-up

Sample response:
1. space, the last frontier; Time is a thief that robs us of our youth.
2. the wide, wild ocean; The *ultimate* goal of a sporting event is to have fun.
3. (cautious); *Conservative* means "moderate; cautious."
4. (mental); A great *psychological* victory for a typical teenager might be resisting peer pressure.
5. ocean trip; If I had time and money for *voyaging*, I would like to go to Alaska.
6. (up); It is amazing how some professional basketball players can leap so high *vertically* to dunk the ball in the basket.
7. (from home); Another word that is similar to *separation* is *detachment*.
8. that those six months changed the world; A *virtual* certainty in my life is that my mother will bake a cake for my birthday.

p. 450 Note-taking Guide

Sample response:
Forever Too Large: We can never abolish the space between the stars.
"Time Barrier": Nothing travels faster than light; the distance between colonies renders communication between solar systems impossible.

Independent "Colonies": Even if the speed of light is somehow surpassed, the quantity of space is too much to be conquered; colonies will be so far separated that humans will lose the bonds of "kinship and understanding."

p. 451 After You Read

1. Sample response: Do individuals believe that further space exploration is necessary?
2. **Graphic Organizer**
Sample response:
Things Compared: the spread of ant colonies and the future spread of human colonies in space
Similarities: The isolation of space colonies is like the isolation of ant colonies.
What is Explained: Human "civilization" in space would have as much unity as ant "civilization" on Earth.
3. Answers will vary. Sample response: Space is too vast; it may be covered but not conquered. We will be isolated in space even if we can colonize distant planets. Communication will be a problem.

The Essential Question

Answers will vary, but students should support answers with details from the essay.

Informational Texts: Case Studies

p. 455 After You Read
Thinking About the Case Study

1. Answers will vary. Sample response: Clarke wanted rocket technology to be used to develop orbiting space stations that could send and receive radio signals.
2. Answers will vary. Sample response: Clarke concluded that although the initial cost would be great, it would still be less than other methods of replacing and running communication networks.

Reading Skill

3. The rocket would become an artificial satellite that circles the world.
4. Rockets would have to be twice as fast as those already being designed, and materials would need to be ferried up by rockets to the location where the space station would be built.

"I'm Like A Bird"
from Songbook
Nick Hornby

p. 456 Graphic Organizer
Sample response:

Thesis or Main Idea: Some of today's pop music is valuable to the existing culture.

Differing Opinions: Some people think that pop music is "beneath" them. One reason that pop music lacks value is that it is not meant to last.

Emotional, Logical, Humorous Appeals: Pop songs provide a harmless pleasure. People need more of that. Pop songs satisfy an emotional need.

p. 457 Vocabulary Warm-up
1. mastering
2. inane
3. repetitive
4. forgo
5. denoting
6. cynically
7. encompass
8. akin

p. 458 Reading Warm-up
Sample response:

1. the full range; My new novel will *encompass* the entire history of this region.
2. similar to; A phrase that means the opposite of *akin* is *different from*.
3. (becoming skilled); *Mastering* a skill usually require practice and persistence.
4. The words "marks" and "different tempos and notes" indicate that those marks stand for something; I could not understand the symbols on the tag *denoting* how the shirt should be cleaned.
5. over and over; Some early-reading books could be described as *repetitive*.
6. (ridiculous); An antonym for *inane* is *sensible*.
7. the study of music; A word that means the same as *forgo* is *skip*.
8. The phrases "try to sell" and "instant success" and the word "pessimists" give clues to the meaning of *cynically*; *Cynically* has a negative tone, because it implies that someone has a selfish attitude.

p. 459 Note-taking Guide
Sample response:

Why Pop Music Is Valuable

Reason 1: Pop music provides a harmless, simple pleasure that is easy to satisfy.

Reason 2: Hornby's need to "solve" the song makes it appealing.

Reason 3: Pop music's short lifetime and limited appeal allow listeners to enjoy a variety of songs.

p. 460 After You Read
1. Hornby's view is that popular music has value, even though that value is not of the highest quality.
2. **Graphic Organizer**
Sample response:

Informal Tone: "It is, after all, a harmless need. . . ."

Opinions/Observations: The best music was written decades ago. Still, pop music can be enjoyable, and that is its value. Pop music is also disposable.

Reveals Author's Background/Personality: Hornby's references show that he is knowledgeable about music and art. Hornby enjoys a variety of music; he makes his own personal tapes of new and favorite songs.

3. Answers will vary. Students may identify with the argument that even people who are snobs about music can find new songs to enjoy.

The Essential Question
Answers will vary, but students should support answers with details from the essay.

ANSWERS TO UNIT 1

"The Seafarer"
Translated by Burton Raffel

"The Wanderer"
Translated by Charles W. Kennedy

"The Wife's Lament"
Translated by Ann Stanford

p. 1 Before You Read
Vocabulary Practice
Sample response: 1. a. lecture b. for failing to clean his room 2. a. strong b. need to be an honor student 3. a. sympathetic b. feelings for animals

p. 2 Note-taking Guide
Sample response:
The Seafarer: food (line 11); his kinsmen (line 25); passion and wine of the cities (line 28); pleasures of life on land (lines 44–45); orchards, towns, and fields (lines 48–49); wealth of the world (lines 66–67); the glory of kingdoms from long ago (line 81)
The Wanderer: his home (line 5); his comrades (line 10); his mead-hall (line 25); gifts of fine gold and treasure (lines 29, 31); Earth's delight (line 30); the days of his youth (line 31); his kinsmen (line 45)

p. 3 Before You Read
Vocabulary Practice
Sample response: 1. a. miserably b. The angry student treated the other students 2. a. careless b. other people's problems 3. a. dull b. lecture put me to sleep

p. 4 Note-taking Guide
Sample response:
The Wife's Lament: her home and friends (line 9); her loved ones (line 16); her previous life (line 41)

p. 5 After You Read
Thinking About the Selection
1. **Graphic Organizer**
Sample response:
Words he uses to describe the sea
The Seafarer: ice-cold sea, whales' home
The Wanderer: wintry
Words he uses to describe himself
The Seafarer: sea-weary, wretched, sorrowful, alone, wandering
The Wanderer: homeless, hapless, sorrowful
How he feels about life
The Seafarer: Sample response: lacking in pleasure and uncertain
The Wanderer: Sample response: uncertain and fleeting
2. Sample response: Both the seafarer and the wanderer are pessimistic about life because the world is a lonely and sad place in which pleasures are fleeting.

Talk About It
Answers will vary. Sample response: I agree that the sea affected the life of the speaker just as strongly because her husband's long journeys at sea allowed his family to plot against her and eventually ruin her marriage and bring her misery.

The Essential Question
Answers will vary. Sample response: The Anglo-Saxon sense of home is very much like ours. Then and now, home is a place of refuge, where family members feel connected to one another and safe from the world outside.

p. 6 Vocabulary Skill Review
Now You Do It
Sample response:
1. Summer vacation is a joyful time of year.
2. The sudden thunderstorm made our picnic joyless.
3. The choir sang with joyous voices.
4. I enjoy playing baseball.
5. The funny movie was enjoyable.

Talk About It

Answers will vary. Sample response: *Joyful* and *joyous* express a high degree of happiness or enthusiasm. *Joyless* conveys a sense of gloom or sorrow. *Enjoy* and *enjoyable* convey pleasure and satisfaction.

Write About It

Answers will vary. Sample response: Don't let your life be joyless! Come to Joyland, where you'll enjoy an enjoyable array of products to ensure a joyous holiday. Our joyful sales representatives will enjoy helping you.

from Beowulf
Translated by Burton Raffel

p. 7 Before You Read
Vocabulary Practice
Sample response: 1. a. friends b. are also his cousins 2. a. powerful b. destroyed trees and downed power lines 3. a. stated that is was not true b. she ate the candy before dinner

p. 8 Note-taking Guide
Sample response:
Setting: Kingdom of the Danes
Problem: Grendel has been killing Hrothgar's men.
Goal: To get rid of Grendel
Event 1: Grendel attacks Hrothgar's men at Herot.
Event 2: Beowulf tears off Grendel's arm, and the monster flees.
Event 3: Beowulf slays Grendel's mother.
Event 4: Beowulf faces a fierce dragon in his final battle.
Climax: Beowulf slays the dragon with his sword but is mortally wounded himself.
Resolution: Beowulf, along with the dragon's treasure, is buried in a tower built for him by the Geats.

p. 9 Vocabulary Builder
Grendel wants to put an end to the Danes.

p. 9 Vocabulary Builder
Students should circle "their," which appears twice in the bracketed lines.
there: in that place
homophone: *their*
meaning: owned by them

p. 10 Comprehension Builder
Students should underline "Hoping to win more, he sails to the land of the Danes to help Hrothgar and his people."

p. 10 Vocabulary Builder
blade with a steel edge: steel-edged blade
dragon who breathes fire: fire-breathing dragon

p. 11 Vocabulary Builder
Rose means "increased."

p. 11 Vocabulary Builder
Students should circle "Grendel's," "son's," and "Hrothgar's." Students should underline "mother," "death," and "friend." The nouns mean "the mother of Grendel," "the death of her son," and "the friend of Hrothgar."

p. 11 Vocabulary Builder
Students should circle "swung."

p. 12 Comprehension Builder
1. His sword cannot slice her skin.
2. His helmet does not protect him.

p. 12 Vocabulary Builder
Students should underline "fame."

p. 12 Vocabulary Builder
Students should circle "drew" and "broke."

p. 13 Vocabulary Builder
Rules means "has the official power to control a country and the people who live there."

p. 13 Vocabulary Builder
Students should circle "from" in the line that begins "Then a Geat man steals. . . ."; "from a treasure" shows the origin of the drinking cup.

p. 14 Vocabulary Builder
Students should list four of the following: "prepared," "protected," "planned," "Denied," or "raised."

p. 14 Vocabulary Builder
Iron means "a common hard metal used to make steel."

p. 14 Comprehension Builder
Answers will vary, but students should indicate that the dragon leaped up in pain, thrashing around as he breathed fire and lashed out at Beowulf.

p. 15 Vocabulary Builder
Open means "available."

p. 16 After You Read
Thinking About the Selection
1. **Graphic Organizer**
Sample response:
Grendel: cuts a Geat's body to bits with his powerful jaws; snaps short the lives of his victims with his great teeth; clutches at Beowulf with his claws
2. Beowulf offers to help the Danes kill Grendel because he wants to win more fame and glory.

Talk About It
Answers will vary. Sample response: I think it is unimportant to receive recognition or rewards for doing a good deed because people should help others without expecting anything in return.

The Essential Question
Answers will vary. Sample response: As personified in Grendel, the Anglo-Saxons defined evil as monstrous—vicious, cruel, and relentless—striking without warning and wreaking havoc. As personified by Beowulf, the Anglo-Saxons defined good as heroic—battling evil to the death, winning honor, fame, and glory.

p. 17 Vocabulary Skill Review
Now You Do It
Sample response:
Sentence 1: a short period of rain
Sentence 2: a party
Sentence 3: a piece of jewelry that you wear on your finger
Sentence 4: a group of people or things arranged in a circle
Sentence 5: a bath in which water is sprayed on the bather
Sentence 6: a small square area in which athletes box or wrestle

Talk About It
Answers will vary, but students should create sentences that include the words from this lesson in different ways.

Write About It
Answers will vary. Students should use various meanings of the words on this page.

Informational Texts: Web Site Search Tools

p. 19 Vocabulary Builder
Students should circle "11th."

p. 19 Vocabulary Builder
Measure means "poetic rhythm."

p. 20 Vocabulary Builder
Tract means "a short piece of writing."

p. 20 Vocabulary Builder
Students should write "poetry" and "poetic."

p. 20 Comprehension Builder
A researcher could look at manuscripts of Old English poems at the British Library, the Exeter Cathedral, the Bodleian Library at Oxford, and the cathedral library in Vercelli, Italy.

p. 21 After You Read
Thinking About Web Site Search Tools
1. The Web site's search program found 12 hits for Anglo Saxon poetry.
2. I would use the Exeter Book link to learn more about Old English riddles and didactic poems.

Reading Skill
3. I would use the hit labeled "The major manuscripts" because the lines below specifically mention *Beowulf.*
4. Answers will vary. Sample response: Web sites for literary journals and magazines, Web sites devoted to poetry or British literature.

from A History of the English Church and People
Bede
Translated by Leo Sherley-Price

p. 22 Before You Read
Vocabulary Practice
Sample response: 1. a. grew b. flowers in the schoolyard 2. a. very many b. cells in the plant leaf 3. a. moved b. from Africa to make a better life

p. 23 Note-taking Guide
Sample response:
England: 800 miles long, 200 miles wide
Both: islands
Ireland: wider than England, but shorter in length

p. 24 After You Read

Sample response:

Thinking About the Selection

1. **Graphic Organizer**

Statement: Mussels found in Britain produce colored pearls.

Evidence from Selection: The pearls are red, purple, violet, green, and white.

Statement: Britain has four nations.

Evidence from Selection: English, British, Scots, and Picts

Statement: Britain is united by a fifth language.

Evidence from Selection: Latin

2. Answers will vary, but should indicate that Britain is located in northern Europe.

Talk About It

Answers will vary. Sample response: I would be attracted to Britain by Bede's work because Bede describes Britain as a land of abundance, where different peoples live together.

The Essential Question

Answers will vary. Sample response: Bede describes England as an island lying at a considerable distance from the coasts of Germany, France, and Spain. Because of its northerly location, Britain's summer nights are short and its winter nights are long.

p. 25 Vocabulary Skill Review

Now You Do It

Sample response:

1. After winning the election for class president, Justin is in the driver's seat.

2. To arrive home before dark, we need to hit the road now.

3. Having overcome the problem, we should have smooth sailing from here on.

4. Finding clues and solving mysteries is right up your alley.

5. Because she wanted to travel light, Carrie crammed all of her things into a small backpack.

Talk About It

Answers will vary. Students should write a clue for each idiom on the page.

Write About It

Answers will vary, but students should use the idioms appropriately in the dialogue.

The Prologue
from The Canterbury Tales
Geoffrey Chaucer
Translated by Nevill Coghill

p. 26 Before You Read

Vocabulary Practice

Sample response: 1. a. delicately b. while an artist sketched her 2. a. integrity b. was known throughout the country 3. a. deceit b. escape responsibility for the problem

p. 27 Note-taking Guide

Sample response:

1. **Knight:** distinguished; fought in crusades; follows codes of chivalry; a noble soldier

2. **Squire:** the Knight's son; about 20; a knight-in-training; likes to joust; likes music and poetry; sings; plays flute; likes showy clothes

3. **Yeoman:** the Knight's attendant; dresses like a forest hunter

4. **Nun:** high rank; dainty; speaks French; good manners

5. **Monk:** "manly" man; good rider; likes to hunt; loose in his religious practices

6. **Friar:** likes the company of innkeepers and barmaids; not interested in helping the poor

7. **Merchant:** seems successful; hides the fact that he is in debt

8. **Oxford Cleric:** has no money; loves to read, learn, and teach; idealistic; cares only about his studies and his faith; quiet

p. 28 Vocabulary Builder

Students should circle "Canterbury," "Archbishop," "Thomas," "Becket," "April," "Tabard Inn," "London," "Chaucer," and "Knight."

p. 28 Vocabulary Builder

Students should circle "Knight," "fought," "knight," and "fight."

p. 29 Comprehension Builder

Students' answers should include three of the following: sitting and riding a horse, making songs and poems and reciting, jousting, dancing, drawing, and writing.

p. 29 Vocabulary Builder

Trace means "a very small amount of something."

p. 30 Vocabulary Builder
Sample response: He had many a dainty horse in his stable.

p. 30 Vocabulary Builder
Students should circle "barmaids." The words *bar* and *maids* create the word *barmaids*.

p. 30 Comprehension Builder
Answers will vary, but students should mention some of these characteristics: The Oxford Cleric spends most of his time studying and praying. He seldom speaks, but is very formal and respectful when he does speak.

p. 31 Vocabulary Builder
Filled means "made something full."

p. 31 Vocabulary Builder
Students should circle "measure" and "pleasure" and underline "read."

p. 32 Vocabulary Builder
Spurred means "with a small, pointed object attached."

p. 32 Vocabulary Builder
Students should write three of the following: "hard-working" describes "brother," "honest" describes "Miller," "jolly" describes "fellow," "red" describes "beard," and "his" describes "nose."

p. 32 Comprehension Builder
The Wife of Bath knows remedies or cures for the pains and ailments of love.

p. 33 Comprehension Builder
Answers will vary. Sample response: The Miller is an unpleasant person. He often argues, is not serious, and steals.

p. 33 Vocabulary Builder
Court means "a place in which legal judgments are made."

p. 33 Vocabulary Builder
He walked on water.

p. 34 Vocabulary Builder
The Pardoner *made monkeys of* the priest and his congregation by flattering them and lying to them.

p. 34 Vocabulary Builder
Plain means "easy to understand."

p. 34 Vocabulary Builder
Students should circle "I'll," "I'll," and "won't."

p. 35 After You Read
Thinking About the Selection
1. **Graphic Organizer**
Parson: has a good reputation; is educated as a clerk; thinks holy thoughts and does holy works; devoutly preaches and teaches the Gospel; is poor
Doctor: wears red and blue garments lined with taffeta; rarely reads the Bible; eats healthful food; is greedy for gold
Miller: has wide, black nostrils; wears a sword and buckler and a blue hood and white coat; is argumentative and tells dirty stories; plays bagpipes; steals grain
2. Answers will vary. Sample response: If not for the pilgrimage, many of these people would not be together because they are very different and lead lives that would not ordinarily bring them together.

Talk About It
Answers will vary. Sample response: I would prefer to travel with the Wife of Bath because she would be a pleasant and amusing traveling companion.

The Essential Question
Answers will vary. Sample response: In medieval society, people dressed in ways that clearly reflected their profession and station in life. Chaucer describes a character's clothing in order to reveal that character's personality and social standing. The squire's clothes, for example, show that he is a young man who has money to spend on fine things. The yeoman, in contrast, dresses as a forest hunter, befitting his lower station as the Knight's attendant.

p. 36 Vocabulary Skill Review
Now You Do It
tie: untie
We can tie a ribbon around the box.
Untie your shoe before you slip it off.
educated: uneducated
The manager was an educated man.
She was uneducated because she had not attended school.
lock: unlock
Don't forget to lock the door when you leave.
We could not unlock the car door.
guarded: unguarded
The bank entrance was guarded well.
The young private fell asleep and left his prisoners unguarded.

Talk About It

Answers will vary. Sample response: I think baseball games are exciting, but soccer games are unexciting.

Write About It

Answers will vary. Paragraphs should describe a student's experience and include three words containing the prefix -un.

"The Pardoner's Tale"
from The Canterbury Tales
Geoffrey Chaucer
Translated by Nevill Coghill

p. 37 Before You Read
Vocabulary Practice

Sample response: 1. a. be slow b. after the ball game 2. a. skillfully b. completed the play 3. a. walked proudly b. through the crowd with his trophy

p. 38 Note-taking Guide

Sample response:

Box 2: They meet an old man, who tells them where to find Death.

Box 3: Instead, they find a pile of gold florins.

Box 4: They scheme about how to take the gold.

Final Event: They end by killing one another. They find Death after all.

p. 39 After You Read
Thinking About the Selection
1. **Graphic Organizer**
The Pardoner

job description: He tells stories and then sells pardons and fake relics.

amount of truth in stories: His stories are all lies.

effect of stories on listeners: People feel guilty, so they pay even more for his pardons and fake relics.

similarity to the three rioters: All four are greedy.

2. The rioters cannot be trusted because each plans to kill the others to have a larger portion of gold.

Talk About It

Answers will vary. Sample response: I do think the rioters found Death under the tree because finding the gold there brought out their greed, which eventually caused the death of all three.

The Essential Question

Answers will vary. Sample response: The Pardoner's tale shows that greed destroys those who allow themselves to be ruled by it. Ironically, the Pardoner admits that he preaches only to increase his sales of fake relics and pardons—in other words, to dupe his listeners and satisfy his own greed. Through the Pardoner, Chaucer exposes one element of hypocrisy in medieval society—the corrupt clergy.

p. 40 Vocabulary Skill Review
Now You Do It

drinkable: able to drink
playable: able to be played
watchable: able to be watched
washable: able to be washed
breakable: able to be broken

Talk About It

Answers will vary, but students should be descriptive and clear in their explanations.

Write About It

Answers will vary. Students should use each -*able* word from the lesson.

"The Wife of Bath's Tale"
from The Canterbury Tales
Geoffrey Chaucer
Translated by Nevill Coghill

p. 41 Before You Read
Vocabulary Practice

Sample response: 1. a. begged b. everyone to be generous to people who need help 2. a. give b. money to organizations that will use it to help people 3. a. great skill b. at basketball helped his team win the championship

p. 42 Note-taking Guide

Sample response:

Man's Action: A knight attacks a maiden.

Woman's Reaction: The maiden petitions the king.

Outcome: The knight is brought before the king and queen for justice.

Woman's Action: The queen asks the king for permission to determine the knight's fate.

Man's Reaction: The king grants permission for the queen to determine the knight's fate.

Outcome: The queen does not kill the knight. Instead, she sends him on a quest.

p. 43 After You Read
Thinking About the Selection
1. **Graphic Organizer**
   1. To save his life, the knight must tell the queen what women most desire.
   2. To find the answer, the knight begins a journey of a year and a day.
   3. An old woman gives the knight an answer, but she wants a favor from him.
   4. The knight marries the old woman.
   5. The knight tells his wife that he can't love her because she's old, unattractive, and poor.
   6. The knight allows his wife to choose the best option for them both.
   7. The knight and his wife live happily ever after.

2. In order to live happily with his wife, the knight had to accept her and allow her to control their relationship.

Talk About It
The knight left the choice to his wife because he had learned what women most desire—to have control over their husbands.

The Essential Question
Answers will vary. Sample response: Chaucer's story reflects social trends. By describing one woman who wants to dominate her husband, the story suggests that the social norm is for men to be dominant.

p. 44 Vocabulary Skill Review
Now You Do It
gave: GAYV
tent: TENT
sprint: SPRINT
stone: STOHN
duck: DUHK
blue: BLOO

Talk About It
Partners should take turns discussing an activity and listing descriptive words. Partners should discuss whether each descriptive word is pronounced with a long or a short vowel sound.

Write About It
Answers will vary, but should include most of the words in the list above.

from **Sir Gawain and the Green Knight**
Translated by Marie Borroff
from **Morte d'Arthur**
Sir Thomas Malory

p. 45 Before You Read
Vocabulary Practice
Sample response: 1. a. persuade b. the citizens to vote on election day 2. a. skillfully b. and never fell 3. a. generosity b. came as a surprise to many

p. 46 Note-taking Guide
Sample response:
Box 2: A huge green knight rides a green horse into the hall.
Box 3: The Green Knight challenges any of the knights to attack him.
Box 4: Gawain accepts the Green Knight's challenge and cuts off the Green Knight's head.
Box 5: Gawain befriends the lord and lady of a wondrous castle.
Box 6: Gawain breaks his promise to the lord and keeps the green girdle.
Box 7: The Green Knight makes three passes with the ax, two representing the days that Gawain kept his promise to the lord and one representing the day that Gawain failed to keep his promise.
Box 8: Gawain admits his failure to live up to his pledge, feels ashamed, and asks for forgiveness. The Green Knight forgives Gawain and welcomes Gawain back to the castle.

p. 47 Before You Read
Vocabulary Practice
Sample response: 1. a. energetically b. and they were exhausted afterward 2. a. shocked b. couple cried when they saw the destroyed buildings and uprooted trees 3. a. buried b. in a place of honor near the battlefield

p. 48 Note-taking Guide
Sample response:
Box 2: Arthur meets Mordred to arrange a truce.
Box 3: They fight, and Arthur is wounded.
Box 4: Sir Lucan dies.
Box 5: Arthur sends Sir Bedivere to throw Excalibur into the water and to report back to Arthur what Sir Bedivere sees.

Box 6: Sir Bedivere fails Arthur twice when he fails to throw Excalibur into the water. When Sir Bedivere does throw the sword into the water, a hand reaches up and grabs the sword.

Box 7: Three ladies take Arthur away on a barge as he lies dying.

Box 8: Sir Bedivere meets a hermit who has received a dead body from a group of women; Sir Bedivere assumes that this body is King Arthur's.

p. 49 Vocabulary Builder
If the armies of Arthur and Mordred fight and *take huge losses*, many knights will die.

p. 49 Vocabulary Builder
Drawn means "taken out or removed from its container."

p. 50 Vocabulary Builder
Party means "a group of people involved in a argument."

p. 50 Comprehension Builder
A knight draws a sword to kill an adder, and the other knights mistake his drawn sword for a signal to fight.

p. 50 Vocabulary Builder
Students should circle "leaning" and "heap," draw a box around "great," underline "dead" once, and underline "spear" twice.

p. 51 Comprehension Builder
Answers will vary. Sample response: Arthur will be killed, as predicted in his dream.

p. 51 Vocabulary Builder
Wound means "an injury."

p. 52 Vocabulary Builder
When King Arthur was wounded, he asked Sir Bedivere to stop mourning and throw Excalibur into the lake.

p. 52 Vocabulary Builder
Spare means "to prevent someone from doing something difficult or unpleasant."

p. 52 Cultural Understanding
Sample response: Warriors gave names to their swords because they valued their swords or to make the sword seem more powerful or comfortable.

p. 53 Vocabulary Builder
Lying means "telling an untruth."

p. 53 Vocabulary Builder
Students should underline "took," "clutched," "shook," "brandished," and "vanished."

p. 53 Comprehension Builder
They say a boat holding many ladies and a queen, all wearing black hoods. The women began to cry and shriek when they saw Arthur.

p. 54 Comprehension Builder
Answers will vary. Sample response: Arthur's fate is unknown. Some people think he died, but because his body was never found, others believe that he will appear again.

p. 54 Vocabulary Builder
Some have said that King Arthur shall come again to rule his people.

p. 55 After You Read
Thinking About the Selection
1. **Graphic Organizer**
Before the First Challenge: At first, The Green Knight looks contemptuously at Arthur and his knights, including Gawain, because he thinks that no one is brave enough to accept his challenge.
Gawain at the Green Chapel: The Green Knight is impressed because Gawain has kept his word.
The Green Knight's First Blow to Gawain: The Green Knight feels contempt because Gawain flinches as the ax comes toward his neck.
The End: Yes, his opinion has changed once again. The Green Knight has had the chance to test and observe Gawain and at that point thinks that Gawain is a superior knight.
2. Gawain hides his wearing of the green girdle from the Green Knight. The Green Knight is not angry because Gawain was trying to save his own life.

Talk About It
Answers will vary. Sample response: I do believe the need for revenge led to King Arthur's death because he had won the battle and lost his life only because he tried to kill the traitor, Mordred.

The Essential Question
Answers will vary. Sample response: The authors accept and uphold the code of chivalry in the tales they tell and the heroes they portray. Sir Gawain and Arthur act with honor and humility. Both personify the chivalrous knight. Their actions and decisions reveal the code.

p. 56 Vocabulary Skill Review
Now You Do It
I became angry when my little brother used my baseball mitt without my permission.
I broke the pencil lead by pushing too hard on the paper.
She shook the carton of chocolate milk.
James had found the keys before we missed them.
Jessica has broken the class record for highest score.
Lily and I have written our third book together.

Talk About It
Partners should take turns creating sentences that contain the past and past participle forms of each verb in the chart.

Write About It
Answers will vary, but students should use as many of the verb tenses listed above as possible.

pp. 57–58 Unit Vocabulary Review
A. **Matching**
a. When there is a **controversy,** there is a serious argument about something.
b. Your **role** in something is the way you are involved in it.
c. The other people in your **tribe** are of the same race and have the same beliefs, customs, and language.
d. If you are an **exile,** you are forced to leave your country and live in another country.
e. During an **invasion,** an army of one country enters another country by force.
f. If things are **traditional,** they are part of the heritage or customs of a country or group of people.
g. **Geography** is the study of countries, oceans, rivers, mountains, and cities of the world.
h. To **form** something is to establish it.
i. An **inheritance** is money or property that a person receives from someone who has died.

B. **Word Sorting**
Noun: controversy, exile, form, geography, inheritance, invasion, role, tribe
Verb: form, exile
Adjective: traditional

Talk About It
Answers will vary, but students should use words from the word bank correctly.

Write About It
Answers will vary, but should demonstrate correct use of words from the bank.

ANSWERS TO UNIT 2

Sonnets 1, 35, 75
Edmund Spenser

Sonnets 31, 39
Sir Philip Sidney

p. 59 Before You Read
Vocabulary Practice
Sample response: 1. a. invent b. an excuse that always worked 2. a. haggard b. I knew she was sick 3. a. stagnated b. without constant stimulation

p. 60 Note-taking Guide
Sample response:
Row 1: a delicate, pure lily
Row 2: hunger for food
Row 3: an eternal representation of his beloved's qualities
Row 4: a person
Row 5: peace

p. 61 After You Read
Thinking About the Selection
1. **Graphic Organizer**
Sample response:
Moon: sad, silent, pale, weak
Sleep: refreshing, soothing, deaf to noise, blind to light
2. In the three sonnets by Spenser (1, 35, 75), the poet's subject is a person he loves.

Talk About It
Answers will vary. Sample response: I think that the feelings expressed by the poets are sincere and deeply felt.

The Essential Question
Answer will vary, but students should support answers with details from the sonnet.

p. 62 Vocabulary Skill Review
Now You Do It
Sample response:
1. Potted orchids graced the living room with their beauty.
2. The ice skaters circle the ice rink gracefully.
3. The cheating scandal was a disgrace to the school.
4. The children were rude, and their behavior was disgraceful.
5. Abby made a graceful response to her brother's criticism.

Talk About It
Answers will vary. Students should list graceful people or animals and explain why their behavior or style is graceful.

Write About It
Answers will vary, but descriptions should include several words in the *grace* word family.

"The Passionate Shepherd to His Love"
Christopher Marlowe

"The Nymph's Reply to the Shepherd"
Sir Walter Raleigh

p. 63 Before You Read
Vocabulary Practice
Sample response: 1. a. harmonious b. tunes cheered me up 2. a. calculation b. the frozen chicken will thaw in eight hours 3. a. spitefulness b. insult me

p. 64 Note-taking Guide
Sample response:
What Does the Shepherd Promise? He promises her a life of bliss. He also promises her a bed of flowers, a gown of the finest wool, slippers with gold buckles, and a belt.
What Does the Nymph Respond? It would be wonderful if life were that idyllic.
Who Is More Convincing? Why? Some students may say that the shepherd is more convincing because he is positive and has a clear plan. Others may say that the nymph is more convincing because she tells a more complete story.

p. 65 After You Read
Thinking About the Selections
1. **Graphic Organizer**
Sample response:
Nymph's View of Nature
Box 1: Answers will vary but should convey the idea that this natural beauty fades and dies with winter.
Box 2: Answers will vary but should convey the idea that with time, the animals grow old and die.
2. Answers will vary. Sample response: The views of the shepherd and the nymph are opposites.

Talk About It

Answers will vary. Sample response: It is difficult for people who disagree to be friends because they see the world differently.

The Essential Question

Answer will vary, but students should support opinions with details from the text.

p. 66 Vocabulary Skill Review

Now You Do It

Sample response:

1. **at sea:** Algebra is so difficult for me that I feel completely at sea.

2. **on cloud nine:** When I saw my high grades, I was on cloud nine.

3. **move mountains:** Because the competitors are so well prepared, we will need to move mountains to win the contest.

4. **up a river without a paddle:** Without a spare tire to change the flat, I felt up a river without a paddle.

5. **cliffhanger:** I love to read mystery stories in which each chapter ends in a cliffhanger.

Talk About It

Answers will vary, but students should make connections between the words forming the idiom and the idiom's meaning.

Write About It

Answers will vary. Students should use all of the idioms in this lesson to write a summary of a short story plot with a cliffhanger.

Poetry of Shakespeare

p. 67 Before You Read

Vocabulary Practice

Sample response: 1. a. history b. of their community's history 2. a. obstacles b. made it difficult for us to complete the project 3. a. changes b. his behavior when he thinks he is going to get a snack

p. 68 Note-taking Guide

Sample response:

Sonnet 29

Whom the speaker addresses: his beloved

Main idea of the couplet: When the speaker thinks about his beloved, he wouldn't change places with a king.

Sonnet 106

Whom the speaker addresses: the general public

Main idea of the couplet: We are able to view beauty, but lack the words or ability to praise it.

Sonnet 116

Whom the speaker addresses: the general public

Main idea of the couplet: The speaker is convinced that true love never falters. He says that if he is wrong, he never wrote, and no man ever loved.

Sonnet 130

Whom the speaker addresses: the general public

Main idea of the couplet: Despite his beloved's physical imperfections, the speaker thinks that she is beyond comparison.

p. 69 After You Read

Thinking About the Selection

1. **Graphic Organizer**

Sonnet 29: Answers may vary but should convey this general idea: When I feel worthless and life seems harsh, thinking of you lifts my spirits and makes me feel wonderful.

Sonnet 106: Answers will vary but should convey this general idea: Many poets have written of beautiful women, but none of their descriptions does justice to your beauty.

Sonnet 116: Answers will vary but should convey this general idea: True love is forever and withstands all obstacles and trials.

Sonnet 130: Answers will vary but should convey this general idea: I won't make false comparisons of my beloved's looks to beautiful flowers or her voice to music. She is not a goddess, but to me she is still beautiful.

2. Answers will vary but should convey the idea that in Sonnet 130, Shakespeare has a realistic view of his beloved.

Talk About It

Answers will vary. Sample response: The view of love in Sonnet 116 is unrealistic because love between two people doesn't always last forever.

The Essential Question

Answer will vary, but students should support answers with details from the sonnets.

p. 70 Vocabulary Skill Review
Now You Do It
Sample response:
read: reread
I will read the book this weekend.
I plan to reread my favorite book.
play: replay
The lawyer will play a recording of the emergency call.
I will replay the song until I understand all of the words.
heat: reheat
The fireplace can heat the whole room.
I will reheat dinner because it's now cold.
build: rebuild
They will build their new house this spring.
The city will rebuild the tunnel that collapsed.

Talk About It
Answers will vary. Sample response: I would be most likely to reread a book about space because I am interested in planets.

Write About It
Answers will vary. Students' news stories should notify readers about fictional upcoming events and include all of the words from the lesson.

from The King James Bible

p. 71 Before You Read
Vocabulary Practice
Sample response: 1. a. morality b. earned him the respect of his friends 2. a. benefit b. uniting the community 3. a. attendance b. always helps me relax

p. 72 Note-taking Guide
Sample response:
Deeds Listed in Text: He restoreth my soul: he leadeth me in the paths of righteousness for his name's sake.
How God is Comforting and Protecting: God helps me lead a good life.

p. 73 Before You Read
Vocabulary Practice
Sample response: 1. a. have a low opinion of b. the way his coach treated his friends on the team 2. a. status b. helped her receive support from most people in the community 3. a. hard work b. he finally planted the entire field

p. 74 Note-taking Guide
Sample response:
Audience: the general public and Jesus' disciples
Purpose: to teach people to live virtuously
Advice Given: Do not worship money; do not worry about basic needs. God will provide, just as he does for birds and for plants.

p. 75 Before You Read
Vocabulary Practice
Sample response: 1. a. wasteful b. had no money because of his extravagance
2. a. begged b. their mother to loan them money 3. a. violated b. the boundaries of polite society

p. 76 Note-taking Guide
Sample response:
Young Son
How he lives his life: wastefully
What he does at the end: He humbles himself before his father and apologizes.
Older Son
How he lives his life: He works hard at home.
How he feels at the end: He is resentful of his younger brother's treatment.
Message of the story: It is never too late to repent. Like the father in the parable, God is forgiving and glad to welcome back those who return.

p. 77 After You Read
Thinking About the Selection
1. **Graphic Organizer**
Text of Psalm 23: ". . . he leadeth me in the paths of righteousness . . ."
What God Provides the Writer: God leads me to live a good and moral life.
Text of Psalm 23: ". . . though I walk through the valley of the shadow of death, I will fear no evil: for thou art with me . . ."
What God Provides the Writer: God is always with me, so I have nothing to fear, not even death.
Text of Psalm 23: "Surely goodness and mercy shall follow me all the days of my life . . ."
What God Provides the Writer: My life will be good because God watches over me.
Text of Psalm 23: ". . . and I will dwell in the house of the Lord forever."

What God Provides the Writer: I will be with God in heaven.

2. In the Sermon on the Mount, Jesus suggests that people should not worry about earthly things such as food and clothing because if people serve God, God will provide for them.

Talk About It
Answers will vary but should include lessons such as avoiding squandering money and valuing family relationships and explanations of how the father and son may have learned the lessons from the mistakes they made.

The Essential Question
Answer will vary, but students should support answers with details from the text.

p. 78 Vocabulary Skill Review
Now You Do It
dark: darkness
the quality of being dark
quick: quickness
the quality of being quick
soft: softness
the quality of being soft
shy: shyness
the quality of being shy
great: greatness
the quality of being great

Talk About It
Answers will vary. Sample response: I think Abraham Lincoln was great because he kept the country together during critical times.

Write About It
Answers will vary. Students should use at least three words from the lesson in their poems.

The Tragedy of Macbeth, Act I
William Shakespeare

p. 79 Before You Read
Vocabulary Practice
Sample response: 1. a. crimes b. that endangered the lives of the soldiers 2. a. majestic b. carriage was pulled by white horses 3. a. supreme b. power for twenty years

p. 80 Note-taking Guide
Sample response:
Background Information: Macbeth is returning from a battle in which he showed great bravery and skill. His fellow noblemen admire him greatly.
Witches' Prediction: The witches predict that Macbeth will be Thane of Cawdor and also king and that Banquo will father kings.
Macbeth's Plan: Macbeth decides to kill Duncan while the king spends the night in Macbeth's castle.

p. 81 After You Read
Thinking About the Selection
1. **Graphic Organizer**
Before the Witches' Predictions: Macbeth is a victorious and noble warrior; he earns the king's favor.
Immediately After the Witches' Predictions: Macbeth begins to consider murdering the king so that he can become king.
At the End of Act I: Macbeth decides to murder the king.
2. Duncan's life is in danger as the result of the witches' prediction and Macbeth's decision to kill the king.

Talk About It
Answers will vary. Sample response: I think Macbeth's plans will not succeed because someone will discover the plan before Macbeth kills the king.

The Essential Question
Answer will vary, but students should support answers with details from the play.

p. 82 Vocabulary Skill Review
Now You Do It
Sample response:
1. He spoke for an hour before finally making his point.
2. The point of joining the club is to meet people.
3. They reached the point at which they needed to end the quarrel.
4. He picked it up with the point of the stick.
5. Our team scored just one point in the first half.
6. The star looked like a tiny point of light in the sky.

Talk About It

Answers will vary, but students should take turns using *point* in sentences and guessing the intended meaning.

Write About It

Answers will vary. Students should write a paragraph supporting an opinion, using as many meanings of *point* as possible.

The Tragedy of Macbeth, Act II
William Shakespeare

p. 83 Before You Read
Vocabulary Practice

Sample response: 1. a. quiet b. squirrel robbed the bird's nest 2. a. avoid answering b. changing the subject 3. a. influence b. influenced the politics in his state

p. 84 Note-taking Guide

Sample response:

Macbeth's vision: Macbeth sees a dagger hovering in the air in front of him; the dagger soon becomes covered with drops of blood.
Who is murdered: Duncan and his servants
How Malcolm and Donalbain react: The two princes fear that they will be assassinated next. Donalbain flees to Ireland, and Malcolm seeks safety in England.

p. 85 After You Read
Thinking About the Selection

1. **Graphic Organizer**
Duncan's sons, Malcolm and Donalbain, flee Scotland in fear: 4
Lady Macbeth grabs the daggers and tells Macbeth that she will smear the knives of the kings' servants with the king's blood: 2
Macbeth becomes king of Scotland: 5
Macduff discovers Duncan's bloody body: 3
Macbeth murders Duncan, the king: 1
2. Lady Macbeth smeared the blood on the servants' knives herself because Macbeth felt guilty and confused after the murder and refused to do it.

Talk About It

Answers will vary. Sample response: Lady Macbeth's greatest role in the murder was to push Macbeth to change his mind when he had decided not to do it.

The Essential Question

Answers will vary, but students should support ideas with details from the play.

p. 86 Vocabulary Skill Review
Now You Do It

Sample response:
1. The counter was stuck on 1500.
2. He is counting the days until his birthday.
3. There are countless stars in the night sky.
4. I got a great discount on a pair of pants.
5. The losing candidate demanded that election officials recount the votes.

Talk About It

Answers will vary. Sample response: stars in the sky, grains of sand on a beach, drops of water in the ocean

Write About It

Answers will vary, but poems should use at least two words with the base word *count*.

The Tragedy of Macbeth, Act III
William Shakespeare

p. 87 Before You Read
Vocabulary Practice

Sample response: 1. a. enduring b. has weathered many storms 2. a. bold b. fought the rough waters to save the woman 3. a. hostility b. The fighting boys

p. 88 Note-taking Guide

Sample response:
Cause: Macbeth fears Banquo and resents him because of the witches' prophecy.
Effect: Macbeth feels guilty and sees Banquo's ghost at a banquet.
Prediction: Macbeth's guilt will drive him mad.
Cause: Macbeth believes that his position is worthless if he must always look over his shoulder, so he vows to kill any possible enemies.
Effect: Macbeth becomes increasingly blood-thirsty, and the other Scottish noblemen begin to turn against him.
Prediction: The Scottish noblemen will unite against the brutal king.
Cause: Macduff fears that Macbeth will try to kill him. Macduff also wants to persuade Malcolm, the rightful Scottish king, to return to Scotland and fight for his crown.
Effect: Macbeth notes Macduff's absence at his banquet and begins to suspect Macduff of plotting against him.
Prediction: Macduff will have his vengeance on Macbeth. Malcolm will return to Scotland.

p. 89 After You Read
Thinking About the Selection
1. **Graphic Organizer**
Box 1: Banquo is murdered.
Box 2: Macbeth is troubled when he sees the ghost of Banquo at the banquet table.
Box 3: Macbeth plans to visit the witches again.
2. Macbeth's lords and former friends turn against him when they suspect that Macbeth murdered King Duncan.

Talk About It
Answers will vary, but students should identify a mistake that Macbeth has made, such as murdering Duncan or having Banquo murdered, and use a logical argument to explain why that action has been Macbeth's greatest mistake.

The Essential Question
Answers will vary, but students should support ideas with details from the play.

p. 90 Vocabulary Skill Review
Now You Do It
1. He will plant a garden next month.
2. Marta smiles as she walks to school.
3. I walked to the market last Saturday.
4. He planted several kinds of flowers yesterday.
5. Sue and Fatima will walk together on the beach tomorrow.
6. Dad planted that garden last year.

Talk About It
Answers will vary, but students must form sentences with the correct tense and verb.

Write About It
Answers will vary, but short stories should include *walk* in the past, present, and future tenses.

The Tragedy of Macbeth, Act IV
William Shakespeare

p. 91 Before You Read
Vocabulary Practice
Sample response: 1. a. assorted b. so each camper could have a different food 2. a. lack of control b. caused the referee to call a foul 3. a. gullible b. Hugo tells ridiculous stories to

p. 92 Note-taking Guide
Sample response:
Description of Image: armed head
Message: This apparition warns Macbeth to beware of Macduff.
Macbeth's Reaction: Macbeth accepts this message without surprise, for he suspects Macduff of plotting against him.
Description of Image: bloody child
Message: This apparition tells Macbeth that no "man of woman born" will ever be able to harm him.
Macbeth's Reaction: Macbeth receives this prediction happily, but notes that he will still kill Macduff.
Description of Image: a child wearing a crown and holding a tree
Message: This apparition indicates that Macbeth will not be defeated until Birnam forest marches to Dunsinane hill.
Macbeth's Reaction: Macbeth is overjoyed at this news, for he thinks it means that he will never be defeated.
Description of Image: a line of eight kings, the last holding a mirror, followed by Banquo
Message: These apparitions do not speak, and the witches vanish without telling Macbeth what the image means.
Macbeth's Reaction: Macbeth thinks that this vision confirms the witches' earlier prediction that Banquo would father kings. The reminder makes him angry and frustrated.

p. 93 After You Read
Thinking About the Selection
1. **Graphic Organizer**
Malcolm and Macduff make plans to seek help from the English king to overthrow Macbeth: 5
Malcolm tests Macduff's commitment to overthrow Macbeth: 3
Macbeth visits the witches and receives four messages: 1
Macbeth has Macduff's wife and children murdered: 2
Malcolm and Macduff learn that Macduff's entire family has been murdered: 4
2. In England, Macduff learns that his family members have been killed. Malcolm suggests that Macduff should respond by turning his grief into anger and seeking revenge on the murderer.

Talk About It

Answers will vary. Sample response: Macbeth allows the image of the eight kings to disturb him because the prediction that he would become king was true, so now he believes that other predictions could come true as well.

The Essential Question

Answers will vary, but students should support ideas with details from the play.

p. 94 Vocabulary Skill Review
Now You Do It

stop: short
spice: long
flung: short
lute: long
slate: long
champ: short
left: short
Pete: long
big: short

Talk About It

Students should work together to read each word correctly.

Write About It

Answers will vary. Students should list five items from their backpacks, circle words with short vowel sounds, underline words with long vowel sounds, and correctly read the names of the items to a partner.

The Tragedy of Macbeth, Act V
William Shakespeare

p. 95 Before You Read
Vocabulary Practice

Sample response: 1. a. remedy b. was stronger than the poison, so he survived 2. a. dangerous b. drive through the war zone 3. a. easy to attack b. because it was surrounded by desert

p. 96 Note-taking Guide

Sample response:

Macbeth
Outcome: Macbeth is slain by Macduff.
Lady Macbeth
Outcome: Lady Macbeth loses her mind and kills herself.
Macduff
Outcome: Macduff finds Macbeth and kills him in one-on-one combat.

Malcolm
Outcome: Malcolm is recognized as king when Macbeth is killed.

p. 97 Vocabulary Builder

Students should circle "Lady Macbeth's attendants"; this noun means "the attendants of Lady Macbeth."

p. 97 Vocabulary Builder

Unnatural means "different from what you would normally expect."

p. 98 Vocabulary Builder

The doctor tries to look after Lady Macbeth, but he cannot help her.

p. 98 Vocabulary Builder

Students should circle "countryside." The words *country* and *side* comprise the word *countryside.*

p. 98 Vocabulary Builder

Students should circle "Birnam Wood," "Dunsinane," "Malcolm," "Macbeth," and "English."

p. 99 Comprehension Builder

Students should underline "The doctor says that she is not sick but troubled with imaginings."

p. 99 Vocabulary Builder

Patient means "someone who is getting medical treatment."

p. 99 Vocabulary Builder

Students should circle "will die."

p. 100 Vocabulary Builder

Students should circle "outward walls."

p. 100 Comprehension Builder

She is dead.

p. 100 Vocabulary Builder

Students should circle "troops" and "trumpets" and underline "branches."

p. 101 Vocabulary Builder

Students should circle "hateful" and "fearful." *Hateful* means "full of hate," and *fearful* means "full of fear."

p. 101 Vocabulary Builder

Students should underline "time," circle "Un-," and draw a box around "-ly."

p. 102 Comprehension Builder
Students should underline "Here you may see the tyrant."

p. 102 Vocabulary Builder
Hail means "an old-fashioned interjection used to greet someone."

p. 103 After You Read
Thinking About the Selection
1. **Graphic Organizer**
Words or Action: Lady Macbeth wrings her hands as if washing them.
Emotion Expressed: guilt
Words or Action: Macbeth discusses his death that is supposed to occur by a man not born of woman.
Emotion Expressed: fearlessness; arrogance
Words or Action: Macbeth's reply to the doctor's description of Lady Macbeth's illness: "Throw physic [medicine] to the dogs, I'll none of it."
Emotion Expressed: anger
Words or Action: Macduff's words to Malcolm: "Hail, King! For so thou art."
Emotion Expressed: joy
2. Macduff says that he was ripped from his mother's womb.

Talk About It
Answers will vary. Sample response: I think Macbeth's and Lady Macbeth's deaths resulted from greed and ambition because their greed and ambition led them to commit evil actions that doomed them both.

The Essential Question
Answers will vary, but students should support ideas with details from the play.

p. 104 Vocabulary Skill Review
Now You Do It
1. He couldn't unlock the door because he'd lost his key.
2. She knows that hard work is the key to the project's success.
3. The song is written in the key of C major.
4. According to the map's key, this is a main highway.
5. The park is on a key near Florida.

Talk About It
Sentences will vary. Sample response: In this sentence, *key* means "a list that explains the symbols on a map."

Write About It
Answers will vary, but students should write a short story that centers around the concept of a key and should use as many meanings of *key* from the chart above as they can.

Informational Texts: Feature Articles

p. 108 After You Read
Thinking About the Feature Article
1. Architects and theater designers were asked to create modern versions of the Globe Theatre for the exhibit "Reinventing the Globe."
2. With certainty, historians can describe the stage, which jutted out into the audience.

Reading Skill
3. Students should cite the quote, "It doesn't have to be going to this old, stodgy building. It could be much more accessible, transient, and lighter."
4. The author includes the comment that the stage that jutted out into the crowd was one of its most impressive attributes, and he says that most of Shakespeare's famous dramas were performed there.

pp. 109–110 Unit Vocabulary Review
A. **Sentence Completion**
1. A belief is something that you think is true but is not something that you think is a lie.
2. Classics are books or plays that people have admired for a long time but are not plays or books that are new.
3. To colonize is to send people to live in a place but not to visit and then quickly leave.
4. An illusion is a thought that is unreal but is not a thought that is true.
5. Kingdoms are countries that a king or queen rules but are not countries with a leader who is elected.
6. Loyalties are feelings of support for a person or a country but are not feelings of betrayal.
7. Something that is pastoral is typical of life in the country but is not connected with life in the city.
8. The Reformation was a time period that involved changes in the 1500s which led to the beginning of Protestant churches but was not a time period in modern times.

9. The Renaissance was a period in Europe long ago when art and science became more important but was not a time when people had little curiosity about the world around them.

B. **Word Sorting**

Noun: beliefs, classics, illusion, kingdoms, loyalties, Reformation, Renaissance
Verb: colonize
Adjective: pastoral

Talk About It
Sentences will vary. Sample response: In kingdoms, people's loyalties must be to the king or queen.

Write About It
Answers will vary but should correctly use words from the word bank.

ANSWERS TO UNIT 3
Poetry of Donne

p. 111 Before You Read
Vocabulary Practice
Sample response: 1. a. disrespectful b. to write on the sacred stones at the site
2. a. church members b. eagerly awaited the evening service 3. a. anxiety b. to the auditorium to speak to the crowd

p. 112 Note-taking Guide
Sample response:
Song
To Whom it is Addressed: the speaker's beloved
Main Idea: The speaker's beloved should not be sad about his temporary absence.
A Valediction
To Whom it is Addressed: the speaker's beloved
Main Idea: The speaker will return to his beloved.
Holy Sonnet 10
To Whom it is Addressed: death
Main Idea: Death is not to be feared, for it brings rest for the body and freedom for the soul.

p. 113 Before You Read
Vocabulary Practice
Sample response: 1. a. long, narrow piece of land b. as the hurricane approached
2. a. house of the estate b. was made entirely of stone 3. a. lessens b. her ability to manage others

p. 114 Note-taking Guide
Sample response:
Oval 1: The church is the head of humankind, and all humankind is the church's body.
Oval 2: The church is for all people, and so are the church's actions.
Oval 3: All humankind is like a book, of which God is the author.
Oval 4: The deepest afflictions make humankind more fit for God.

p. 115 Vocabulary Builder
Students should underline "quotation" and "translation."

p. 115 Vocabulary Builder
State means "a condition of mind or being."

p. 116 Vocabulary Builder
Students should underline "man's." It shows that *death* belongs to *any man*.

p. 116 Comprehension Builder
Answers will vary but should convey the idea that all people are connected to one another as a part of humanity. Thus, the death of any one person affects every person.

p. 117 After You Read
Thinking About the Selections
1. **Graphic Organizer**
Sample response:
First, Donne compares people to: a volume of a book
Then, Donne compares people to: a piece of land from a continent
2. Both "Song" and "Valediction" are about the speaker's departure and absence from a loved one.

Talk About It
Answers will vary, but students may suggest that the speaker does not fear death because the speaker believes in eternal life after death.

The Essential Question
Answers will vary. Some students may say that Donne's conceits were imaginative ways to express ideas. For example, comparing the speaker and the beloved to a compass is a unique way to describe a love's relationship. The conceits make readers think about the subject in new ways. Others students may say that Donne's conceits do not help him express his ideas because they seem forced and are too different from the ideas in the poems.

p. 118 Vocabulary Skill Review
Now You Do It
Sample response:
1. The piano player knew my favorite songs.
2. The CD was scratched and no longer playable.
3. She can replay her favorite parts of the movie on DVD.
4. My puppy is almost always in a playful mood.
5. Mario tried to downplay his mistake.

Talk About It

Answers will vary. Students may say that they enjoy jumping rope or playing baseball because such activities are fun and give them the chance to spend time outside with their friends.

Write About It

Answers will vary, but the dialogue should include the words from the chart.

Poetry of Jonson

p. 119 Before You Read
Vocabulary Practice

Sample response: 1. a. in good condition b. enough to move into 2. a. holy b. assistance 3. a. circle made b. was decorated with a ribbon

p. 120 Note-taking Guide

Sample response:

On My First Son
Lines: "Farewell, thou child of my right hand, and joy; / My sin was too much hope of thee, loved boy."
Main Idea: The speaker had great love and expectations for his son, but now the boy has died.

Still to Be Neat
Lines: "Such sweet neglect more taketh me / Than all th'adulteries of art."
Main Idea: The poet is attracted to simple, natural beauty more than to artful appearance.

Song: To Celia
Lines: "Or leave a kiss but in the cup, / And I'll not look for wine."
Main Idea: The speaker needs only Celia's love in order to live.

p. 121 After You Read
Thinking About the Selections
1. **Graphic Organizer**
Sample response:

Still to Be Neat
What description of how women dress does the speaker give in the first stanza? The speaker describes women looking neat, as though going to a feast, powdered, and perfumed.
What sort of appearance does the speaker prefer? The speaker prefers an appearance that is that is simple, with loosely flowing robes and hair.

Song: To Celia
How does the speaker feel about the beloved? The speaker is in love with the beloved.
What does the speaker claim makes the wreath grow? The beloved's having breathed on the wreath makes it grow.
2. Sample response: The speaker in each of these poems addresses a woman, or his beloved.

Talk About It

Answers will vary. Some students may suggest that the vow to never love someone so much again is helpful because it allows a person to protect himself or herself from feeling the same type of sorrow again. Other students may suggest that the vow is harmful because it prevents a person from ever feeling a deep, powerful love.

The Essential Question

Answers will vary. Sample response: No, Jonson's clarity results from his precise word choice. Both his word choice and balance help create his poems' emotional effect.

p. 122 Vocabulary Skill Review
Now You Do It

Sample response:

behave: misbehave; The children behave well when they play together. If the children misbehave, they will be punished.
quote: misquote; I will quote from several sources in my report on climate change. Reporters sometimes misquote the people whom they interview.
inform: misinform; Businesses use brochures to inform their customers. Inaccurate reporting on a topic can misinform readers.

Talk About It

Answers will vary. Some students may suggest that many people are misinformed about new scientific discoveries because information is not widely available.

Write About It

Answers will vary, but students should include in their writing several words with the prefix mis-.

"To His Coy Mistress"
Andrew Marvell

"To the Virgins, to Make Much of Time"
Robert Herrick

"Song"
Sir John Suckling

p. 123 Before You Read
Vocabulary Practice
Sample response: 1. a. shyness b. made her a mystery to the young men around her
2. a. youth b. climbed Mount Everest
3. a. lovesick b. soldier wrote to his girlfriend every day

p. 124 Note-taking Guide
Sample response:

To His Coy Mistress
To Whom is the Speaker Talking? The speaker is talking to his mistress.
What is the Speaker's Message? Young women should not waste time by being coy, but should love while they are young.

To the Virgins, to Make Much of Time
To Whom is the Speaker Talking? The speaker is talking to every young, unmarried woman.
What is the Speaker's Message? Women should marry young to avoid losing the opportunities afforded by youth.

Song
To Whom is the Speaker Talking? The speaker is talking to a young man who cannot win his beloved.
What is the Speaker's Message? Do not waste your time waiting for a woman who may never return your love.

p. 125 After You Read
Thinking About the Selection
1. **Graphic Organizer**
First Stanza: a flower
Second Stanza: the sun
2. The speaker and his beloved in "To His Coy Mistress" do not do the many activities that the speaker imagines in the first part of the poem because he says that there is not enough time to do them.

Talk About It
Answers will vary, but students may suggest that the advice given in "Song" is helpful

because being miserable as a result of the woman's rejection will not make her change her mind.

The Essential Question
Answers will vary. Sample response: Herrick provides a traditional treatment of the *carpe diem* theme. Marlowe provides a different interpretation of the theme by having the speaker describe how he would woo his beloved if they only had enough time. Suckling gives the theme new life by having the speaker encourage the listener to give up on the beloved rather than pursue her.

p. 126 Vocabulary Skill Review
Now You Do It
Sample response:
fear: fearless; without fear
color: colorless; without color
blame: blameless; without blame
power: powerless; without power

Talk About It
Answers will vary. Students may say that they would love to be fearless because they often miss out on things because they are afraid to try them. Students may suggest that being fearless can be a problem because it is easy to get involved in dangerous things that one should not do when one is fearless.

Write About It
Poems will vary but should include three or more words from the lesson.

Poetry of Milton

p. 127 Before You Read
Vocabulary Practice
Sample response: 1. a. appearance b. of relief on her face that the season was over
2. a. not easily noticeable b. we detected the change 3. a. whisper b. went through the courtroom when the judge arrived

p. 128 Note-taking Guide
Sample response:
Sonnet VII: The speaker is reflecting on his twenty-fourth birthday; he is concerned that he has not accomplished more; he is not doing enough with his talent.
Sonnet XIX: The speaker is blind; his talent is now useless; he is unable to serve God with his talent.

Have in Common: The speaker decides to trust God to make use of him.

p. 129 Before You Read
Vocabulary Practice
Sample response: 1. a. shed light on b. the entire neighborhood 2. a. give an acceptable explanation for b. spending my entire allowance on a new dress 3. a. dishonesty b. was his most unattractive quality

p. 130 Note-taking Guide
Sample response:

Presentation of Subject: Adam and Eve's disobedience to God in the Garden of Eden
Invocation: Call for Help: Call to the "Heavenly Muse"
Beginning of Story in the Middle: The battle between God and his host and Satan and his followers in heaven is over; Satan and his host are cast into the lake of fire; Satan determines that he and his host will do only evil.

p. 131 Vocabulary Builder
Students should circle "Brought."

p. 131 Vocabulary Builder
Students should underline *spirat, spirit, spirit, spirat, spirit,* and *spir.*

p. 131 Comprehension Builder
Adam and Eve disobeyed God's command that they should not taste "Of that forbidden tree."

p. 132 Vocabulary Builder
The fallen angels and their leader have waged a war against God.

p. 132 Vocabulary Builder
Darkness means "the state of being dark."
Brightness means "the state of being bright."
Goodness means "the state of being good."

p. 133 Vocabulary Builder
Students should circle "yield." Sample response: The fallen angels did not want to yield to God.

p. 133 Vocabulary Builder
Satan assumes that "eternal punishment" is in store for all of them.

p. 133 Comprehension Builder
Satan plans to "wage eternal war" with God.

p. 134 Vocabulary Builder
Satan speaks to his followers, and then *goes on to say* that their activities will cause problems for God.

p. 134 Comprehension Builder
Heaven will bring "Infinite goodness, grace and mercy" to humans.

p. 134 Vocabulary Builder
Students should circle the phrase "the fiery pool."

p. 135 Comprehension Builder
Answers will vary. Sample response: The fallen angels now live in Hell, a place where it is always hot and dark.

p. 135 Vocabulary Builder
Students should underline "what they might regain in Heaven, or what they might lose in Hell."

p. 136 After You Read
Thinking About the Selection
1. **Graphic Organizer**
Forces of Good Led by: God
Struggle for Control of: Heaven and Earth
Forces of Evil Led by: Satan
Result of the Struggle: God defeats Satan; Satan and his followers are cast out of Heaven and down into Hell.
2. In "Sonnet XIX," Patience tells the speaker that God does not need either man's work or his gifts.

Talk About It
Answers will vary, but some students may suggest that career or accomplishments are not the best measure of a person's life. They may explain that there are other, more important aspects of a person's life that determine the kind of person he or she is, such as how that person treats other people or that person's honesty or generosity.

The Essential Question
Answers will vary. Sample response: In Satan's last line in from *Paradise Lost* is "Better to reign in Hell than serve in Heaven," Milton's concise word choice expresses Satan's attitude and the difference that he sees between Hell and Heaven. The contrast between doing what one wants in Hell and serving God in Heaven makes the line powerful.

p. 137 Vocabulary Skill Review
Now You Do It
1. Rosa looks as though she has something on her mind.
2. After Jimmy insulted him, Chen was hot under the collar.
3. He is always smiling, but Tony is really a wolf in sheep's clothing.
4. You turn a blind eye to Josh's mistakes because you like him.
5. We'll have to shake a leg if we want to get there on time.

Talk About It
Answers will vary, but students may describe getting angry when someone lied to them or when a friend promised to go somewhere with them but decided not to go at the last minute.

Write About It
Dialogues will vary but should include as many idioms from the chart as possible.

from Pilgrim's Progress
John Bunyan

p. 138 Before You Read
Vocabulary Practice
Sample response: 1. a. indulged b. in self-pity when she was not invited to the party
2. a. responsibility b. to the avid skateboarder
3. a. downward movement b. to the airport

p. 139 Note-taking Guide
Sample response:
Christian: Christian falls into the Slough; He is unable to pull himself out of the mire; After Help pulls him out, he resumes his journey toward the Celestial City.
Pliable: Pliable falls into the Slough; He climbs out of the Slough but does not help Christian climb out.
Help: Help pulls Christian out of the Slough; He explains to the narrator what the Slough is and why people continue to fall into it; He tells the narrator that despite the king's efforts, the Slough cannot be repaired.

p. 140 After You Read
Thinking About the Selection
1. **Graphic Organizer**
Box 1: bog
Box 2: very miry

Box 3: a place that cannot be mended
Box 4: the descent whither the scum and filth . . . doth continually run
2. In *Pilgrim's Progress*, Christian journeys from the City of Destruction to the Celestial City.

Talk About It
Answers will vary, but students may suggest that Bunyan is saying that human nature does not change. Fears, doubts, and discouragements will always be a part of being human.

The Essential Question
Answers will vary. Sample response: This selection shows that in Bunyan's time, most people believed that faith was necessary to help them get through troubling times. For example, Christian's own strength was insufficient to pull him out of the Slough of Despond; Help arrives to save him. *Pilgrim's Progress* probably affirmed what people believed about the necessity of faith and encouraged them to continue to seek God despite life's difficulties.

p. 141 Vocabulary Skill Review
Now You Do It
Sample response:
1. The post office has a huge column on each side of the entrance.
2. He writes a weekly column about sports for the newspaper.
3. The document had two columns per page.
4. A thin column of smoke rose from the dying campfire.
5. A long column of soldiers marched down the avenue.

Talk About It
Answers will vary. Students should write one sentence for each meaning of the word *column* and include context clues in their sentences.

Write About It
Answers will vary, but students should find three ways to use the word *column* in their writing.

from Eve's Apology in Defense of Women
Amelia Lanier

"To Lucasta, on Going to the Wars"
Richard Lovelace

"To Althea, from Prison"
Richard Lovelace

p. 142 Before You Read
Vocabulary Practice
Sample response: 1. a. judgment b. and said little to reveal her feelings 2. a. criticize b. her for being noisy during the presentation 3. a. unfaithfulness b. because her friends told her about it

p. 143 Note-taking Guide
Sample response:
Poem: "Eve's Apology"
Speaker: The speaker is a woman with a powerful pro-woman argument.
Audience: The intended audience is men and the public in general.
Main Idea/Purpose: The speaker seeks to free women from their current state of domestic bondage, which had resulted from the belief that Eve was to blame for the dismissal from the Garden of Eden.
Poem: "Lucasta"
Speaker: The speaker is a man going to war.
Audience: The speaker's beloved is the audience.
Main Idea/Purpose: The speaker explains that he must go to war, and that placing a higher value on honor than on his beloved enabled him to love her more.
Poem: "Althea"
Speaker: The speaker is an imprisoned man.
Audience: Althea and the general public make up the audience.
Main Idea/Purpose: The speaker says that although his body is confined, his mind is free.

p. 144 After You Read
Thinking About the Selection
1. **Graphic Organizer**
Where is the narrator going? to war
Who is his new mistress? the foe on the battlefield

What does he love more than Lucasta? honor
2. In "Eve's Apology," the speaker argues that the person most to blame for mankind's fall from grace was Adam.

Talk About It
Answers will vary. Sample response: I would not feel as the poet does in his position because I would be upset about losing my freedom and would not be as calm.

The Essential Question
Answers will vary. Sample response: Lovelace was reflecting dominant social attitudes about women, and Lanier was trying to change those attitudes. Lovelace's poems portray a man at the center of the action. The woman either is asked to understand his behavior or is described in terms of only her physical beauty. Lanier attempted to change dominant social attitudes that blamed Eve, and by extension, all women, for the Biblical account for humanity's fall from grace. Instead of blaming women, Lanier argues that they are responsible for giving men knowledge.

p. 145 Vocabulary Skill Review
Now You Do It
Sample response:
1. The lawyer advised them about their legal rights.
2. We were surprised by the lawless behavior in town.
3. Joe argued that it was lawful to defend himself against his attacker.
4. Jesse James was an outlaw who robbed banks.
5. When I marry, my brother will be my wife's in-law.

Talk About It
Students should use words from the chart in a discussion about television programs or movies about lawyers.

Write About It
Students should use all of the words in the chart in the skit's dialogue.

from A Journal of the Plague Year
Daniel Defoe

p. 146 Before You Read
Vocabulary Practice
Sample response: 1. a. infectious disease b. all
the students were vaccinated 2. a. anxious and
excited and talked continuously b. the doctor
gave her medication 3. a. pleading with b. the
teacher to give her an extra credit assignment

p. 147 Note-taking Guide
Sample response:
What he hears: The narrator hears the "voice
of mourning" in the streets.
Where he goes: The narrator goes to a mass
grave in Aldgate churchyard.
What he sees: The narrator sees the buriers
literally dumping plague victims into the pit;
he later sees a man grieving for his wife and
children at the edge of the pit.
How he feels: The narrator is at first
intrigued and then truly grieved to see the
man suffering the loss of his family. The narrator says that the sight is "awful" and "full of
terror."

p. 148 After You Read
Thinking About the Selection
1. **Graphic Organizer**
What event was greatly changing London?
The arrival of bubonic plague, a deadly disease, was changing London.
**Why was a great pit dug in a London
churchyard?** People were dying so rapidly
that they had to be buried quickly.
Why does the narrator go to the pit? His
curiosity drives him to see it for himself.
**What does the sexton tell the narrator
about the pit?** The pit has a voice and is
saying that all should repent.
**Why does the narrator call the pit "The
common graveyard of mankind"?** So many
people were dying that there were not enough
coffins to bury them, whether they were rich
or poor.
2. At the side of the great pit, the narrator
meets a mourner whose wife and children are
to be buried.

Talk About It
Answers will vary. Sample response: I believe
the narrator went too far because getting the
story is not worth the risk of death.

The Essential Question
Answers will vary, but students should
describe a landmark event in their own region
that would make a good story. Students may
recall events such as floods, tornadoes, or
hurricanes.

p. 149 Vocabulary Skill Review
Now You Do It
bat: short
lice: long
thumb: short
mute: long
space: long
trot: short
quick: short
chrome: long
left: short

Talk About It
Students should list another short and long
vowel word for each letter. Sample responses
include *scat, take, let, leaf, slip, splice, flock,
soap, strum,* and *fume.*

Write About It
Students' writing should include several
words for long and short vowel sounds.
Sounds should be circled and underlined correctly.

Informational Texts:
Reports

p. 153 After You Read
Thinking About Reports
1. The causes of congestion in London are
many years of under-investment combined
with significant rates of increase in London's
population.
2. Reduced traffic delays, improved journey
time reliability, reduced waiting time at bus
stops, and lower fuel consumption will have
economic benefits.

Reading Skill
3. Sample response: The chart shows the total
traffic entering the charging zone during
charging hours. It also shows the progress
and effect of the congestion charging
program.
4. A bulleted list highlights the key transport
priorities.

from Gulliver's Travels
Jonathan Swift

"A Modest Proposal"
Jonathan Swift

p. 154 Before You Read
Vocabulary Practice

Sample response: 1. a. simple b. many of the conveniences of modern life 2. a. serious arguments b. Debates about raising taxes 3. a. useful b. Flying

p. 155 Note-taking Guide

Sample response:

Details to Achieve This Purpose: The dispute among the Lilliputians about whether to break an egg at the large or the small end represents the dispute between Catholicism and Protestantism. The war between Lilliput and Blefuscu represents the tension between Protestant England and Catholic France.

Details to Achieve This Purpose: The king of Lilliput wants to enslave the people of Blefuscu and make them break their eggs at the small end, representing England's desire to conquer France and force the French into Protestantism.

p. 156 Vocabulary Builder

Students should circle "wakes," "with," and "war," and label them each with a *v.*

p. 156 Vocabulary Builder

Gulliver *drifts off to sleep* after he survives the shipwreck and swims to shore.

p. 156 Comprehension Builder

Students should underline ". . . the Emperor, his father, published an edict, commanding all his subjects, upon great penalties, to break the smaller end of their eggs. The people so highly resented this law that our histories tell us there have been six rebellions . . ."

p. 157 Vocabulary Builder

Lilliputian means "one who is from Lilliput."

p. 157 Vocabulary Builder

Students may circle "mere" and underline "strain," circle "true" and underline "believers," circle "their" and underline "eggs," circle "humble" and underline "opinion," circle "man's" and underline "conscience," or circle "chief" and underline "magistrate."

p. 158 Vocabulary Builder

Glasses means "two pieces of specially cut glass or plastic in a frame, which help people see more clearly."

p. 158 Comprehension Builder

Gulliver tells the Emperor that he would not help bring a free and brave people into slavery.

p. 159 Before You Read
Vocabulary Practice

Sample response: 1. a. anxiety b. as I waited for my job interview 2. a. notorious b. enough to be fired from her job 3. a. honesty b. made the thought of lying unacceptable

p. 160 Note-taking Guide

Sample response:

Details to Achieve This Purpose: The king of Brobdingnag laughs at Gulliver and asks whether Gulliver is a "Whig or a Tory"; the king's laughter indicates that the dispute between England's two political parties is ridiculous in the grand scheme of things. When the king turns to his "first minister," he continues to ridicule the things of which Gulliver spoke, such as the nobility of England and the "scourge of France."

Details to Achieve This Purpose: The king's horror at Gulliver's solemn proposal of using gunpowder and cannon to destroy another city is a strong critique of England's power-hungry rulers.

p. 161 Before You Read
Vocabulary Practice

Sample response: 1. a. food b. in berry bushes along the trail 2. a. product b. exported to other states 3. a. respected b. was well known on campus

p. 162 Note-taking Guide

Sample response:

Understatement: "I am not in the least pain upon that matter"; "I am not so violently bent of my own opinion"

Exaggeration: "We should see an honest emulation among the married women, which of them could bring the fattest child to the market"; "men would become as fond of their wives, during the time of their pregnancy, as they are now of their mares in foal"

Sarcasm: "this food will be somewhat dear, and therefore very proper for landlords"; "as they have already devoured most of the parents, [the landlords] seem to have the best title to the children"

p. 163 After You Read
Thinking About the Selection
1. Graphic Organizer
Gulliver's Travels, **Chapter 1**
Box 1: Gulliver lands in Lilliput.
Box 2: The people there are six inches tall.
Box 3: The cause of the rebellion is that some people reject the law that requires everyone to crack eggs at the small end.
Box 4: Gulliver helps the Secretary and his people by tying the enemy's ships together with cables and capturing the ships.
Gulliver's Travels, **Chapter 2**
Box 1: Gulliver lands in Brobdingnag.
Box 2: The people there are twelve times larger than Gulliver's size.
Box 3: Gulliver describes England to the king.
Box 4: Gulliver angers the king greatly by offering to make gunpowder for the king.
2. Swift thinks that his "modest proposal" will help draw attention to the problem of the large number of poor families with many children who are reduced to begging in Ireland.

Talk About It
Answers will vary. Sample response: I do not find the "proposal" offensive because it is satire and meant to be funny.

The Essential Question
Answers will vary. Sample response: Swift wanted society to change its views on religion, warfare, and politics. Swift believed that some religious conflicts were petty, and in *Gulliver's Travels*, Chapter 1, he used satire to compare these conflicts with the Lilliputians' squabbles about which end of an egg's shell to break. In *Gulliver's Travels*, Chapter 2, Swift used the King of Brobdingnag to satirize English enthusiasm for warfare and weaponry. In "A Modest Proposal," Swift used satire to present an idea to help with "the Irish problem." He knew that his proposal was repellent, but so was the current practice of excessively taxing the poor Irish peasants.

p. 164 Vocabulary Skill Review
Now You Do It
Sample response:
1. I think this car could use a wash.
2. He hung the wash out on the clothesline.
3. She splashes a refreshing wash on her skin.
4. We'll cover that wall with a light blue wash.
5. They walked out on the wash at low tide.
6. The wash fills with water at times of heavy rainfall.

Talk About It
Answers will vary. Sample response: In this sentence, *wash* means "a dry riverbed in a desert area."

Write About It
Answers will vary, but students' stories should use the word *wash* at least twice, with different meanings.

from An Essay on Man
Alexander Pope

from The Rape of the Lock
Alexander Pope

p. 165 Before You Read
Vocabulary Practice
Sample response: 1. a. person who never showed emotions b. she did her chores without complaint 2. a. indirectly b. showed that he agreed with her 3. a. pedestrian b. instead he played polo

p. 166 Note-taking Guide
Sample response:
Setting: Hampton Court, where Belinda plays a game of cards with two men.
Events
1. The baron cuts off a lock of Belinda's hair.
2. A battle to restore Belinda's lost lock ensues.
3. The lock ascends to heaven and becomes a comet.
End Result: Belinda's name is remembered forever.

p. 167 After You Read
Thinking About the Selection
1. Graphic Organizer
Who wins the card game? Belinda
Who cuts the lock of hair? the Baron
Whose hair is cut? Belinda's

What happens to the lock of hair at the end of the poem? It disappears; the Muse claims that it flies to the heavens as a comet. 2. The speaker describes the struggle over the lock of hair in *The Rape of the Lock* as a battle.

Talk About It

Answers will vary. Sample response: People can take care of their minds by studying, reading, and limiting television and video games. People can take care of their bodies by eating healthful foods and exercising. I believe that people can balance taking care of their minds and bodies because I usually take care of both mind and body.

The Essential Question

Answers will vary. Sample response: Although Pope mocks humanity in the selection from *An Essay on Man* by describing humanity as "The glory, jest, and riddle of the world!" he invites readers to consider human nature and to view themselves seriously. Pope's main goal in "The Rape of the Lock" is to entertain readers with his mockery. Pope thinks that society's rituals are extravagant and silly, but they seem to serve a purpose. For example, comparing a card game to an epic battle indicates that courtship rituals are taken too seriously, but such rituals were necessary for people to meet, get to know each other, and marry.

p. 168 Vocabulary Skill Review
Now You Do It

Sample response:
1. Instead of admitting his fault, Salim tried to pass the buck and blame his brother.
2. Mom will raise Cain when she learns that we broke the teacups.
3. After ten minutes of listening to Juanita's story, I told her to cut to the chase.
4. We need to finish the housework before we run out of steam.
5. We'll have to pull the plug on this project if we can't make it work.
6. As we ran out the door, Dad shouted, "Hold your horses!"

Talk About It

Answers will vary. Students should write a story that includes the idioms in the chart.

Write About It

Stories should contain all of the idioms in the chart.

from A Dictionary of the English Language
Samuel Johnson
from The Life of Samuel Johnson
James Boswell

p. 169 Before You Read
Vocabulary Practice

Sample response: 1. a. sudden behavioral changes b. we decided to make our own plans 2. a. inferior ingredients b. in packaged meats 3. a. laughable b. they made no sense at all

p. 170 Note-taking Guide

Sample response:

Johnson's Feelings About Writers of Dictionaries: Johnson believes that they are doomed to criticism.

Johnson's Feelings About the English Language: Johnson believes that English has been neglected too long and is in a state of confusion.

Johnson's Feelings About His Own Dictionary: Johnson is content with it, regardless of its flaws.

Johnson's Feelings About Himself: Johnson is proud of his accomplishment, but does not expect his effort to garner praise.

p. 171 Before You Read
Vocabulary Practice

Sample response: 1. a. hatred b. everyone in the group that tormented him 2. a. shame b. her boss told her that she might lose her job 3. a. distrust of people different from himself b. has learned to live peacefully with others

p. 172 Note-taking Guide

Sample response:

Contradictory Qualities: Johnson had an irritable temper but a kind heart.

Illness and Infirmaties: Johnson's health made him melancholy at times.

Studies and Intellectual Pursuits: Johnson had accumulated a vast body of knowledge from his diverse intellectual pursuits.

Common Conversation: Johnson expressed his thoughts in elegant language and with great force.

p. 173 After You Read
Thinking About the Selection
1. **Graphic Organizer**
What Boswell said to Johnson at their first meeting: "I come from Scotland, but I cannot help it."
Johnson's response: "That, Sir, is what a very great many of your countrymen cannot help."
How Boswell felt afterward: stunned and embarrassed
2. Samuel Johnson said that he wrote his dictionary to help others succeed.

Talk About It
Boswell described Johnson as imperfect—he had his prejudices, but he was not mean-spirited. Johnson had a good sense of humor but was easily offended. He had a good heart and was a great thinker.

The Essential Question
Answers will vary. Sample response: Both Johnson and Boswell are cultural innovators because their words set a standard for later writers to follow. Johnson's dictionary helped order the English language. Boswell's biography of Johnson portrays Johnson accurately, including his flaws. Johnson is also a cultural conservative because he wanted to preserve the English language.

p. 174 Vocabulary Skill Review
Now You Do It
Sample response:
polite: impolite
We were taught to be polite to older people.
Her children were rude and impolite.
precise: imprecise
The precise amount of money stolen was not known.
The driving directions were imprecise, and we became lost.
movable: immovable
The cabinet was heavy but movable.
The cabinet is immovable because it is bolted to the floor.
mature: immature
Janice is mature for her age.
Herman's prank shows that he is thoughtless and immature.

perfect: imperfect
Martha makes an apple pie that is perfect.
They knew that the plan was imperfect, but they needed to take action.

Talk About It
Answers will vary. Sample response: measurable/immeasurable, mobile/immobile, modest/immodest, moral/immoral, mortal/immortal, partial/impartial, passable/impassable, personal/impersonal, plausible/implausible, practical/impractical, probable/improbable, proper/improper, pure/impure

Write About It
Answers will vary, but summaries should use several words with the *im-* prefix.

"Elegy Written in a Country Churchyard"
Thomas Gray

"A Nocturnal Reverie"
Anne Finch, Countess of Winchilsea

p. 175 Before You Read
Vocabulary Practice
Sample response: 1. a. limited b. the group's funds 2. a. inexperienced and honest b. would pick up hitchhikers while driving alone on the highway 3. a. nighttime b. in the elm tree last night and saw their scratch marks the following morning

p. 176 Note-taking Guide
Sample response:
Elegy Written in a Country Churchyard
Neoclassical
polished expression: "Awaits alike the inevitable hour. / The paths of glory lead but to the grave."
complicated vocabulary: "The boast of heraldry, the pomp of power, / And all that beauty, all that wealth e'er gave"
Romantic
nature and simple folk: "The lowing herd winds slowly o'er the lea, / The plowman homeward plods his weary way"
deep feelings: "Full many a flower is born to blush unseen, / And waste its sweetness on the desert air."
A Nocturnal Reverie
Neoclassical
polished expression: "When freshened grass now bears itself upright"

complicated vocabulary: "Or from some tree, famed for the owl's delight, / She, hollowing clear, directs the wanderer right"
Romantic
nature and simple folk: "When nibbling sheep at large pursue their food"
deep feelings: "But silent musings urge the mind to seek / Something, too high for syllables to speak"

p. 177 After You Read
Thinking About the Selection
1. **Graphic Organizer**
Elegy
Time of Day: night
Setting: churchyard
Speaker's Actions: walks through churchyard
Main Idea: affirms the value of the lives of ordinary people
Nocturnal Reverie
Time of Day: night
Setting: somewhere in the country
Speaker's Actions: reviews what one would see walking through the countryside at twilight
Main Idea: celebrates the beauty of nature by moonlight
2. Answers will vary, but students should say the speaker finds these hours to be peaceful in contrast to the confusion of the day.

Talk About It
Answers will vary. Sample response: The sunlight fades over the land, and the air is quiet and still.

The Essential Question
Answers will vary, but students should note that the beauty, dignity, and peace that both Gray and Finch find in their outdoor settings help them draw the conclusion that these virtues are more important than ambitious pursuits.

p. 178 Vocabulary Skill Review
Now You Do It
Sample response:
careful: I am always careful to set my alarm clock before going to sleep.
colorful: In autumn the trees in the schoolyard are colorful.
hateful: Only someone hateful could have destroyed the garden.

useful: My dictionary is my most useful reference tool.
healthful: I try to eat healthful snacks instead of candy.

Talk About It
Answers will vary. Students should use the words from the papers drawn from the box in sentences.

Write About It
Answers will vary, but messages should include several words that end in the suffix -ful.

"The Aims of *The Spectator*" Joseph Addison

p. 179 Before You Read
Vocabulary Practice
Sample response: 1. a. disagreeable b. received a warning from the judge 2. a. unimportant things b. to pacify the frightened children 3. a. ornamentations b. that it resembled a museum more than a home

p. 180 Note-taking Guide
Sample response:
Families: "well regulated"; "for their good to order this paper to be punctually served up, and to be looked upon as part of the tea equipage"
Gentlemen, My Good Brothers: "the fraternity of spectators, who live in the world without having anything to do in it"; "Have no other business with the rest of mankind but to look upon them"
The Blanks of Society: "unfurnished with ideas"; "poor souls"; "needy persons"
The Female World: "the toilet is their great sense of business, and the right adjusting of their hair the principle enjoyment of their lives"

p. 181 After You Read
Thinking About the Selection
1. **Graphic Organizer**
Groups of Readers
Box 1: families
Box 2: wealthy, idle gentlemen
Box 3: "the blanks of society"
Box 4: women in general
Why They Should Read
Box 1: "for their good" while they eat breakfast

Box 2: in order to form "a right judgment" of other people

Box 3: to let them know what is happening in the world and give them something to talk about

Box 4: to improve their minds and divert them from the "trifles" that usually occupy them

2. Addison has the lowest opinion of "the blanks of society" and women.

Talk About It
Answers will vary. Sample response: An editor would not print such comments today because many people would be offended and his newspaper would probably lose business.

The Essential Question
Answers will vary. Sample response: Addison believes that people are a product of what they read and how they behave. He wants his readers to engage in more wholesome and educational pursuits to "distinguish themselves from the thoughtless herd of their ignorant and unattentive brethren." Addison hopes that his paper will appeal to women who enjoy intellectual discussion. Addison seems to be both reflecting and influencing social trends. The fact that his paper's circulation was increasing ("there are already three thousand of them distributed every day. . . .") suggests a growing social trend to read periodicals. The growing popularity of Addison's journal also suggests that he was influencing that trend. For example, he writes "I must reckon about three-score thousand disciples in London and Westminster . . ."

p. 182 Vocabulary Skill Review
Now You Do It
Sample response:
1. He has walked to school many times.
2. I work the late shift at the bakery.
3. They have marched at every football game.
4. She talks enthusiastically about her vacation.
5. He has worked on his bike for days.
6. Mom has talked to me before about studying.

Talk About It
Answers will vary, but students should form a sentence by correctly using the called-out tense and verb.

Write About It
Answers will vary, but e-mails must correctly use verbs in the present and present perfect tenses.

pp. 183–184 Unit Vocabulary Review
A. Sentence Completion
An **epic** is a long narrative poem that tells the story of a hero and reflects the values of a culture, **but** it is not a collection of tales told by different speakers to entertain and amuse.

A **prophet** is someone who says what will happen in the future **but** is not someone who sings of ancient legends and heroes.

Deism is the belief that God made the world but does not influence people or events **but** it is not the belief that many gods and goddesses rule the universe and intervene in human affairs routinely.

A **country** is a nation or state with its lands and people **but** it is not an uncharted wilderness without borders or boundaries.

A **theme** is the subject or main idea of a composition **but** it is not a collection of facts and details.

To be **rational** is to make decisions based on reason **but** it is not to make decisions based on emotions and intuition.

A **city** is a large, important town **but** it is not a small group of houses.

A person's **behavior** is the way he or she does things **but** it is not the beliefs that he or she has.

B. Word Sorting
Noun: behavior, city, country, deism, epic, mobility, prophet, theme
Verb:
Adjective: rational

Talk About It
Students should use Unit Vocabulary words to create sentences for the story.

Write About It
Answers will vary, but letters should correctly use words from the Word Bank.

ANSWERS TO UNIT 4

"To a Mouse"
Robert Burns

"To a Louse"
Robert Burns

"Woo'd and Married and A'"
Joanna Baillie

p. 185 Before You Read
Vocabulary Practice
Sample response: 1. a. authority b. these lands and people 2. a. disrespect b. ignoring his boss's suggestions 3. a. pleasant b. she made friends easily

p. 186 Note-taking Guide
Sample response:
"To a Mouse"
Whom/What the Speaker Addresses: a mouse
Speaker's Main Message: I apologize for accidentally destroying your house with my plow; your unexpected loss is similar to human beings' plans coming undone.
"To a Louse"
How the Speaker Finds His Topic: The speaker sees a louse on the bonnet of a well-dressed lady.
Whom/What the Speaker Addresses: a louse
Speaker's Main Message: Proud, conceited behavior is ridiculous.
"Woo'd and Married and A'"
How the Speaker Finds His Topic: The speaker is present at a wedding.
Whom/What the Speaker Addresses: the reader
Speaker's Main Message: Being married is more important than wealth or possessions, especially when the husband loves the wife.

p. 187 After You Read
Thinking About the Selections
1. **Graphic Organizer**
Sample response:
To a Louse
Subject: a louse on a woman's hat
Main Idea: We would be free from foolish pretense if we could see ourselves as others do.
Woo'd and Married and A'
Subject: a young bride on her wedding day

Main Idea: It is foolish to worry about money and possessions; the bride finally realizes that she is lucky to have a man who loves her.
2. Sample response: In "To a Mouse," the speaker says that the mouse, although homeless, is blessed because the mouse lives only in the present, without the past or the future to worry about.

Talk About It
Answers will vary. Sample response: I believe that writing in dialect is important because an author can show pride in the culture of a region or locale.

The Essential Question
Answers will vary. Sample response: In "Woo'd and Married and A'," a young, impoverished bride laments her lack of finery and her upcoming marriage to a man with no money. Baillie's description of the bride shows true insight into the mind of a foolish, immature, and materialist girl because the girl experiences disappointment when she should be happy that anyone wants to marry her at all. Baillie further proves the girl's immaturity when her worries are finally soothed by the groom's flattery.

p. 188 Vocabulary Skill Review
Now You Do It
Sample response:
1. He has a job as a taster at the ice cream factory.
2. That is a really tasty chocolate cake!
3. The canned asparagus was mushy and tasteless.
4. My sister's distaste for licorice left all the more for me!

Talk About It
Answers will vary. Students should discuss foods that they find tasty, including the ingredients, spices, or cooking methods that appeal to them.

Write About It
Answers will vary. Students should describe a favorite food in a short magazine article.

Poetry of Blake

p. 189 Before You Read
Vocabulary Practice
Sample response: 1. a. valleys b. made popular picnic spots near the foothills of the

mountains 2. a. eternal b. sometimes became involved in the lives of humans 3. a. brood b. her parents wouldn't let her go out with her friends

p. 190 Note-taking Guide
Sample response:
The Lamb
Key Words: tender, meek, mild, child
Key Ideas: The creator of the lamb and child is benevolent. Both the child and the lamb are symbols for Jesus.
The Tyger
Key Words: burning, fearful, dread, terrors
Key Ideas: Perhaps the creator of the tiger is responsible for evil as well as good.
The Chimney Sweeper
Key Words: weep, soot, coffins, Angel
Key Ideas: The chimney sweeps are living in terrible conditions and are supposed to be confronted by the prospect of heaven after they die.
Infant Sorrow
Key Words: helpless, naked, struggling, sulk
Key Ideas: The world is cruel and difficult, even for the infants just entering it.

p. 191 After You Read
Thinking About the Selections
1. Graphic Organizer
Sample response:
Mother's action: She groans.
Father's actions: He weeps; he holds the infant in his hands.
Infant's actions: The infant cries loudly and struggles in the father's hands and against the cloth in which the infant is wrapped.
2. In "The Lamb" and "The Tyger," the question that the speaker seeks an answer to is that of "who is the creator of the lamb and the tiger?"

Talk About It
Answers will vary. Students should share experiences that involve performing a good service or meeting a responsibility.

The Essential Question
Answers will vary, but students should support their opinions with details from the poems.

p. 192 Vocabulary Skill Review
Now You Do It
Sample response:
1. He had a bad fall down the stairs.
2. The shopkeeper expects a fall in sales in January.
3. Fall is my favorite season of the year.
4. That was his second fall of the match.
5. The fall of Rome came gradually.

Talk About It
The leaves are colorful during fall. In this sentence, *fall* means "the season between summer and winter." Students' sentences will vary.

Write About It
Answers will vary, but students' stories should use the word *fall* as many times as possible.

Introduction to *Frankenstein*
Mary Wollstonecraft Shelley

p. 193 Before You Read
Vocabulary Practice
Sample response: 1. a. dismal b. temperatures that were much lower than normal
2. a. agreed b. Mother's curfew rule
3. a. cliché b. to which no one responded

p. 194 Note-taking Guide
Sample response:
Who Is Involved: Mary Shelley, Percy Shelley, Lord Byron, and John William Polidori
When It Takes Place: It takes place while visiting Lord Byron one rainy summer.
Where It Takes Place: Switzerland
What Happens: After reading ghost stories, Lord Byron suggests the idea that each person create an original ghost story.
How It Happens: One night, after a discussion of Dr. Darwin's experiments and the possibilities of reanimating a corpse, Shelley imagines a vision of the creation of a creature that inspires her story.

p. 195 After You Read
Thinking About the Selection
1. Graphic Organizer
Three ways that Mary Shelley wanted her ghost story to "awaken thrilling horror" in readers: She wanted to "make the reader dread to look round, to curdle the blood, and quicken the beatings of the heart"

What she imagined "with shut eyes but acute mental vision": She imagined the terrifying sight of a man kneeling before a creature who comes to life.

What happened to make her story into a novel: She had planned only to write something short, but her husband encouraged her to write more. The result was a novel.

2. After a sleepless night Mary Shelley tried to forget her imaginings, but they haunted her, and she knew she wanted to write the story.

Talk About It

Answers will vary. Students should discuss things that they find most frightening.

The Essential Question

Answers will vary, but students should support their ideas with details from the introduction.

p. 196 Vocabulary Skill Review
Now You Do It

Sample response:

1. While he had the flu, Anthony looked as though he were at death's door.
2. Bridgett slept so deeply that she was dead to the world around her.
3. After being down forty points, we didn't have a ghost of a chance of winning.
4. The old dog, being feeble and weak, was ready to give up the ghost.

Talk About It

Answers will vary. Students should use some of the idioms in this lesson in their discussions.

Write About It

Stories will vary but should include the idioms from the lesson.

Poetry of Wordsworth

p. 197 Before You Read
Vocabulary Practice

Sample response: 1. a. isolated b. we camped overnight 2. a. confusion b. when she looked at the street map 3. a. irritating b. Chalk scraping across a blackboard

p. 198 Note-taking Guide

Sample response:

Who: the poet Wordsworth, who addresses his sister Dorothy

When: summer

Where: the Wye River valley near Tintern Abbey

What: Wordsworth returns to Tintern Abbey, noting that his memories of his last visit were a source of comfort to him, and speculates on the evolution of his reaction to nature from spontaneous joy to a more mature acknowledgment of the unity in nature.

Why: Maturity and its deeper understanding of reason have changed his feelings about nature, although both visits elicited strong reactions, and he wishes for his sister to share his feelings for this place and remember it and him in the future.

p. 199 Comprehension Builder

Students should circle "again I hear / These waters" and "I behold these steep and lofty cliffs."

p. 199 Vocabulary Builder

Seclusion means "the state of being isolated or hidden away."

p. 199 Vocabulary Builder

Students should write "sweet sensations."

p. 200 Fluency Builder

Students should circle all internal punctuation and the closing period.

p. 200 Vocabulary Builder

In the line beginning "With many recognitions . . ." *faint* is a(n) adjective.

p. 200 Comprehension Builder

Students should underline "Now he is more mature and reflective."

p. 201 Vocabulary Builder

Students should circle "living" and "thinking" and underline "air" and "things."

p. 201 Comprehension Builder

Students should underline "in nature and the language of the sense."

p. 202 Comprehension Builder

Another archaic word in line 53 is "hither."

p. 202 Comprehension Builder

Reason 1: The woods and cliffs become "more dear" for their own sake.

Reason 2: They are also important for his sister's sake for the pleasure they will later provide for her.

p. 203 Before You Read
Vocabulary Practice
Sample response: 1. a. stirred b. the girl every morning before school 2. a. shameful b. that linked the politician to the gangsters 3. a. unchanged b. and the outlook was uncertain

p. 204 Note-taking Guide
Sample response:
from **The Prelude:** Although the French Revolution seemed at first to be driven by reason, the ideals became convoluted and the French became "oppressors," conquering other regions. Wordsworth tries to justify continued faith in the cause, but in the end loses his conviction, advocating instead faith in his heart guided by nature.
The World Is Too Much With Us:
Wordsworth believes that people are too caught up in material concerns to appreciate the power of nature.
London, 1802: The poet says that England is lacking in "inward happiness" and is filled with selfish, mediocre people. It needs Milton's moral vision and example to help restore it to its former ways.

p. 205 After You Read
Thinking About the Selection
1. **Graphic Organizer**
Sample response:
Tintern Abbey: Nature is inspiring and can be powerful when people recall its beauty.
The World Is Too Much With Us: People are out of touch with nature because they are concerned with "getting and spending."
2. In "London, 1802," the speaker compares England to marshy land filled with stagnant water and Milton to a star, the sea, and the heavens.

Talk About It
Answers will vary. Sample response: At first, the speaker is thrilled that the Revolution values reason. However, when Napolean begins to conquer other lands, the speaker's opinion about the Revolution starts to change.

The Essential Question
Answers will vary, but students should support their ideas with details from the poems.

p. 206 Vocabulary Skill Review
Now You Do It
Sample response:
contaminate: decontaminate
The oil spill will contaminate the waters of the bay.
Chemical substances may decontaminate polluted water.
activate: deactivate
When we activate the timer, the lights will shut off at midnight.
We must deactivate the alarm before we can work on it.
mystify: demystify
The magician would mystify his audience with his magic tricks.
Can anyone demystify these poems for me?

Talk About It
Stories will vary, but partners should include some form of the words *activate, contaminate,* and *mystify.*

Write About It
Answers will vary, but students should include at least one other word with the prefix *de-* in their reports.

Informational Texts: Traffic Reports

p. 208 Vocabulary Builder
Students should circle "Northwest England," "National Park," "National Park," and "National Parks."

p. 209 Vocabulary Builder
Volumes means "total amounts."

p. 209 Vocabulary Builder
Private is an antonym of *public.*

p. 209 Comprehension Builder
Answers will vary. Sample response: Large volumes of traffic lead to issues such as pollution, noise, distractions from the scenery, congestion, attempts to encourage us of public transport, competition for parking, and dangers to walkers, cyclists, and horse riders.

p. 210 Comprehension Builder
Answers will vary. Sample response: The goals of traffic management in Lake District National Park are to protect the landscape, to improve the quality of residents' lives, to help visitors enjoy the park, and to use transportation that does not harm the area.

p. 210 Vocabulary Builder
The Lake District National Park *set out* its traffic management policies in the Lake District National Park Management Plan.

p. 210 Vocabulary Builder
Routes is used as a noun.

p. 211 After You Read
Thinking About the Traffic Report
1. Most tourists use private cars to reach the Lake District National Park.
2. Answers will vary. Sample response: Decision-makers must balance needs so the park is preserved, so tourists can continue to enjoy it, and so local residents will not suffer from too much traffic. If decision-makers limit travel on secondary roads to local residents, tourists may decide not to visit the area. Without tourists, the local economy will suffer.

Reading Skill
3. The labels along the side of the chart show the number of vehicles in 24 hours, and the labels along the bottom show the years.
4. The vertical bars represent the flow of vehicles; the symbol is explained in the right margin.

Poetry of Coleridge
p. 212 Before You Read
Vocabulary Practice
Sample response: 1. a. terrible b. she used salt instead of sugar in the cake batter
2. a. great joy b. Two weeks of vacation in the mountains was 3. a. clothing b. Some schools have dress codes that require students to

p. 213 Note-taking Guide
Sample response:
The Rime of the Ancient Mariner
Details of the Setting: The mariner's story takes place long ago, on board a ship on the ocean.
Kubla Khan
Details of the Setting: The poem takes place in Xanadu, in a pleasure dome whose grounds are "twice five miles" in size and contain gardens, creeks, incense-bearing trees, and sunny spots of greenery.

p. 214 Vocabulary Builder
The idiom *next of kin* means "nearest or closest relative."

p. 214 Comprehension Builder
Students should underline "He holds him with his glittering eye—."

p. 214 Vocabulary Builder
Students should circle "cracked," "growled," "roared," and "howled."

p. 215 Fluency Builder
Students should underline "cloud," "shroud," "night," and "white."

p. 215 Vocabulary Builder
Students should circle "thunder-fit."

p. 215 Vocabulary Builder
The crew of the ship *runs out of* water.

p. 216 Vocabulary Builder
Students should underline "bliss" and "woe."

p. 216 Vocabulary Builder
Students should circle "whiz," which mimics the sound or "whiz" of the crossbow.

p. 216 Vocabulary Builder
Students should circle "realizes," "suffers," and "tries."

p. 217 Vocabulary Builder
Reared means "rose up on back legs or on the back part of the body."

p. 217 Vocabulary Builder
Students should circle "fell" and "sank."

p. 217 Comprehension Builder
Answers will vary. Sample response: The mariner unconsciously blesses the water snakes and finds that he is then able again to pray. His suffering and prayers break the spell of the curse.

p. 218 Comprehension Builder
He prays best, who loves best / All things both great and small: / For the dear God who loves us, / He made and loves all.

p. 218 Comprehension Builder
Students should underline "A sadder and a wiser man, / He rose the morrow morn."

p. 219 After You Read
Thinking About the Selection
1. **Graphic Organizer**
Sample response:
Rime of the Ancient Mariner
Main Event: The speaker kills an albatross, bringing ill fortune on himself and his shipmates.

Important Idea: The speaker's crime against nature must be atoned for in order to make amends.

Kubla Khan

Main Event: The speaker imagines the exotic lands of Xanadu.

Important Idea: The speaker describes two faces of nature: sunny and orderly within the dome, wild and savage outside it.

2. Answers will vary. Sample response: In "Kubla Kahn," the speaker visits an imaginary land of Xanadu.

Talk About It

Answers will vary. Sample response: I think that a person can be his or her own worst enemy because a person's thoughts or bad habits can keep him or her from attaining goals.

The Essential Question

Answers will vary. Students may suggest that in "Kubla Khan," Coleridge creates a setting in a mythical land that is sensual, hedonistic, wild, and savage—a place where all of the senses are heightened. "The Rime of the Ancient Mariner" moves through scenes of natural upheaval and eerie beauty, where Death and Life-in-Death direct a harrowing penance. The mariner's tale is juxtaposed against the backdrop of a celebratory wedding feast.

p. 220 Vocabulary Skill Review
Now You Do It

Sample response:
accident: accidental; relating to an accident
education: educational; relating to education
nation: national; relating to a nation
music: musical; relating to music

Talk About It

Answers will vary. Sample response: Justin and Sam deny using your skates. Their denial of wrongdoing seemed genuine.

Write About It

Answers will vary, but the dialogue should include two or more words that have the suffix -al.

Poetry of Byron

p. 221 Before You Read
Vocabulary Practice

Sample response: 1. a. judge b. when the neighbors argued over putting up a fence

2. a. hot b. conditions of late summer
3. a. bright b. was the wrong thing to wear to the meeting

p. 222 Note-taking Guide
Sample response:
She Walks in Beauty
Subject of Poem: a woman's beauty
Description in Poem: "like the night / Of cloudless climes and starry skies"; "the nameless grace / Which waves in every raven tress"; "So soft, so calm, yet eloquent"
Speaker's Feelings: The speaker is filled with wonder at the woman's beauty and links her physical beauty with her spiritual beauty.
Apostrophe to the Ocean
Subject of Poem: the ocean
Description in Poem: "thou deep and dark blue ocean"; "Thy shores are empires"; "Dark-heaving—boundless, endless, and sublime"
Speaker's Feelings: The speaker is in awe of the immeasurable depths, power, and endurance of the ocean.
from **Don Juan**
Description in Poem: "I / Have squandered my whole summer while 'twas May"; "My days of love are over"; "All things that have been born were born to die"
Speaker's Feelings: The speaker is sad that he is aging and believes that his best days have passed.

p. 223 After You Read
Thinking About the Selection
1. **Graphic Organizer**
Sample response:
She Walks in Beauty
Comparisons: The speaker compares a woman's beauty to a cloudless, starry night.
from **Don Juan**
Comparisons: The speaker compares his youth to counterfeit, or false, treasure.
2. In *Don Juan*, the speaker says that his days of love are over, and he must now take up the good old-gentlemanly vice of avarice.

Talk About It

Answers will vary. Students should discuss the speaker's descriptions of the ocean's untamed qualities and any experiences students have had of nature's power or beauty.

The Essential Question

Answers will vary, but students should support their ideas with details from the poems.

p. 224 Vocabulary Skill Review
Now You Do It

Sample response:

1. Jerry should walk with her to the park.
2. I would like to have pizza for lunch.
3. She would behave differently with me.
4. I would walk faster.
5. You should like this flavor of ice cream.
6. They could behave well if it suited them.

Talk About It

Answers will vary, but students must form sentences with the indicated main verb and helping verb.

Write About It

Answers will vary, but poems should have at least one line that includes a main verb and a helping verb.

Poetry of Shelley

p. 225 Before You Read
Vocabulary Practice

Sample response: 1. a. tomb b. visible among the small tombstones 2. a. desire b. laugh out loud, even though he was in church 3. a. happy b. she finished her work early

p. 226 Note-taking Guide

Sample response:

Ozymandias
Words used to describe it: "cold command," "pedestal," "colossal"

Ode to the West Wind
Words used to describe it: "Destroyer and preserver," "tameless, swift and proud," "Scatter"

To a Skylark
Words used to describe it: "blithe spirit," "a star of heaven," "sprite"

p. 227 After You Read
Thinking About the Selection
1. **Graphic Organizer**
Poem: Ozymandias
Subject: ruins of an ancient statue
Speaker's Feeling About the Subject: wonder at the vast size of the statue and the completeness of its destruction

Example That Expresses Speaker's Feelings: Round the decay of that colossal wreck . . .

Ode to the West Wind
Subject: the wind and its power
Speaker's Feeling About the Subject: interested by its effects; respects its power
Example That Expresses Speaker's Feelings: Wild Spirit, which art moving everywhere

To a Skylark
Subject: a skylark
Speaker's Feeling About the Subject: praises the bird's joyous song and flight
Example That Expresses Speaker's Feelings: Teach me half the gladness that thy brain must know.

2. Answers will vary. Sample response: The subjects of "Ode to the West Wind" and "To a Skylark" are alike in that both are free spirits.

Talk About It

Answers will vary. Sample response: I think that the words show arrogance because the builder is saying that even the mightiest would look upon his works and know that they are not his equal.

The Essential Question

Answers will vary. Sample response: Shelley's poems reflect his desire to overthrow tyrants to bring in a new age of equality and justice. For example, in "Ozymandias," the monument's size, frown, sneer, and wrinkled lip, as well as the intimidating words on the pedestal, express the attempt to control others. This attempt at dominion from beyond the grave is futile because the statue lies in broken pieces. The speaker depicts Ozymandias as intimidating and controlling and describes the tyrant's monument as a "wreck." In "To a Skylark," the speaker depicts the skylark soaring, singing, and joyous—free from the difficulties of human life. The wind in "Ode to the West Wind" embodies a powerful, restless, striving force, moving everywhere in rebellion against tyrants like Ozymandias.

p. 228 Vocabulary Skill Review
Now You Do It
that: short
fuel: long
crumb: short

claim: long
pick: short
loan: long
crest: short
bite: long
hot: short

Talk About It
Students should list another short and long vowel word for each letter. Sample responses include *pat, drain, let, grease, slip, spice, sock, toad, hum,* and *tune.*

Write About It
Students' riddles should include at least one word for each long and short vowel sound. Sounds should be circled and underlined correctly.

Poetry of Keats

p. 229 Before You Read
Vocabulary Practice
Sample response: 1. a. understanding b. do an economic analysis of the country 2. a. gathered b. her real motive 3. a. overflowing b. with beach balls and floats

p. 230 Note-taking Guide
Sample response:
Speaker's Attitude: Filled with wonder and inspiration
Poem: "Fears"
Subject: The speaker's fear of dying before he has written a great deal
What the Poem Shows: The challenge of finding love and fame
Speaker's Attitude: Mournful but philosophical; thoughtful; intense
Poem: "Nightingale"
Subject: Admiration for the nightingale
What the Poem Shows: The desire to imitate the ease of the song he hears; poetic inspiration
Speaker's Attitude: Heartsick but wishful and reflective

p. 231 Before You Read
Vocabulary Practice
Sample response: 1. a. forested b. made it a popular place to stop and rest 2. a. the whole of time without an end b. The flowing river 3. a. farmlike b. gave the hikers a sense of peace

p. 232 Note-taking Guide
Sample response:
Speaker's Observations: The urn can capture a flowery tale better than his own rhyme. His interest in the scenes and the stories they tell cause him to ask questions.
Images: Pictures of men, maidens, boughs, and grass on the urn.
Speaker's Observation: The artistic beauty of the urn is unending and true in a way that the real world can never be because the real world is transitory.

p. 233 Vocabulary Builder
Still is an adverb.

p. 233 Vocabulary Builder
Mad means "behaving in a wild way."

p. 233 Vocabulary Builder
Pipes means "simple musical instruments that you blow through."

p. 234 Vocabulary Builder
Marble means "a hard white rock used for statues or buildings."

p. 234 Fluency Builder
Students should circle the exclamation point, commas, quotation marks, the dash, and the period.

p. 234 Comprehension Builder
Students should underline the last two lines of the poem.

p. 235 After You Read
Thinking About the Selection
1. **Graphic Organizer**
On First Looking into Chapman's Homer
Paraphrase: Answers will vary. Sample response: I felt like an astronomer who sees a new planet through a telescope.
Ode to a Nightingale
Paraphrase: Answers will vary. Sample response: *Forlorn* ends the joy I feel from thinking of you and makes me reflect on my own sad life.
2. Answers will vary. Sample response: "When I Have Fears That I May Cease to Be" is different from "On First Looking into Chapman's Homer" because its speaker feels only despair instead of happiness or interest in the world.

Talk About It

Answers will vary. Sample response: I think the objects that would tell people of the future the most about us are movies and television shows because they show what people of our time find entertaining.

The Essential Question

Answers will vary, but students should support their ideas with details from the poems.

p. 236 Vocabulary Skill Review
Now You Do It

Sample response:

1. As a PC user, I like a large flat-screen display.
2. She might misuse the software because of her lack of experience.
3. The playing field will be usable again when the rain stops.
4. When plastic is recycled, people can reuse it.

Talk About It

Answers will vary, but partners should use as many words from the *use* word family in their discussions.

Write About It

Answers will vary, but students' advertisements should use an example from the activity above, and should include other words from the *use* word family.

"On Making an Agreeable Marriage"
Jane Austen

from A Vindication of the
Rights of Women
Mary Wollstonecraft

p. 237 Before You Read
Vocabulary Practice

Sample response: 1. a. friendly b. always has a kind word for those around her 2. a. understanding b. declined when I missed class 3. a. not interested in b. the way her choices affected her life

p. 238 Note-taking Guide
Sample response:

Appeals to Logic: ". . . Your mistake has been one that thousands of women fall into. He was the *first* young Man who attached himself to you. That was the charm, & most powerful it is."

Appeals to Morality: ". . . I shall turn around & entreat you not to commit yourself further, & not to think of accepting him unless you really do like him. Anything is to be preferred or endured rather than marrying without Affection; and if his deficiencies of Manner &c &c strike you more than all his good qualities, if you continue to think strongly of them, give him up at once."

Appeals to Emotions: ". . . don't be frightened by the idea of his acting more strictly up to the precepts of the New Testament than others."

p. 239 Before You Read
Vocabulary Practice

Sample response: 1. a. absolution b. everyone else saw that the evidence cleared his name 2. a. made b. the building a ruin that had to be torn down 3. a. careful b. all of her belongings arranged neatly in rows

p. 240 Note-taking Guide
Sample response:

Appeals to Logic: "The conduct and manners of women, in fact, evidently prove that their minds are not in a healthy state . . ."

Appeals to Morality: ". . . their apparent inferiority with respect to bodily strength must render them in some degree dependent on men in the various relations of life; but why should it be increased by prejudices that give a sex to virtue, and confound simple truths with sensual reveries?"

Appeals to Emotions: ". . . a profound conviction that the neglected education of my fellow creatures is the grand source of misery I deplore . . ."

p. 241 Vocabulary Builder

Wollstonecraft says that she has *turned over* many books written on the subject of education.

p. 241 Vocabulary Builder

Students should write the adverb "evidently" and write the modified verb "prove."

p. 241 Comprehension Builder

Students should underline "strength and usefulness."

p. 242 Comprehension Builder

Students should circle "neglected education," "minds are not in a healthy state," "sacrificed to beauty," and "prejudices."

p. 242 Fluency Builder
Students should circle the periods, commas, and semicolons in the bracketed paragraph.

p. 243 After You Read
Thinking About the Selection
1. **Graphic Organizer**
Examples
Love/Affection: A person would prefer or endure anything else but a marriage without affection.
Money: Austen points out that the man's family is wealthy.
Respectability: Austen describes the man's "situation in life," "above all his Character," and his "strict principles, just notions, and good habits" as "of the first importance."
Importance (high, moderate, or low)
Love/Affection: high
Money: moderate
Respectability: high
2. In the excerpt from *A Vindication of the Rights of Women,* Mary Wollstonecraft compares the current state of women to flowers that are planted in soil that is too rich. Her comparison indicates that women are disregarded after their youthful beauty fades.

Talk About It
Answers will vary. Sample response: I think that the most important thing Austen said was do not marry if there is no affection.

The Essential Question
Answers will vary, but students should include the words *independence, values,* and *rebellious* in their answers and support their opinions with details from the texts.

p. 244 Vocabulary Skill Review
Now You Do It
Sample response:
1. The guards made a check of the vaults before closing the bank.
2. A pattern of red-and-white checks covered the tablecloth.
3. I wrote a check to pay for my new sweater.
4. When we finished our meal, we asked the waiter for the check.
5. She put a check next to each correct answer on the test.

Talk About It
Answers will vary. Sample response: In this sentence, *check* means "a printed piece of paper that is signed and used to pay for things."

Write About It
Answers will vary, but students' letters should include the word *check* two or more times, each use conveying a different meaning of the word.

pp. 245–246 Unit Vocabulary Review
A. **Matching**
a. **Something is authentic if:** it is done or made in the traditional or original way.
b. **Power is:** the ability or right to control people or events.
c. **Something urban is:** related to towns or cities.
d. **Artificially is:** the quality of not being real or not being made of natural things.
e. **An outcast is someone who is:** rejected by the people he or she lives among.
f. **Someone who is rebellious:** deliberately disregards authority or rules of behavior.
g. **An exotic thing:** is unusual and interesting because it is related to a foreign country.
h. **A revolution occurs when:** people change a ruler of a political system by force or violence.
i. **Something is fantastic when:** it is extremely good, attractive, or enjoyable.

B. **Word Sorting**
Noun: artificiality, outcast, power, revolution
Verb: power
Adjective: authentic, exotic, fantastic, rebellious, urban

Talk About It
Answers will vary. Sample response: The rebellious population started a revolution in the country.

Write About It
Answers will vary but should correctly use words from the word bank.

ANSWERS TO UNIT 5

Poetry of Tennyson

p. 247 Before You Read
Vocabulary Practice
Sample response: 1. a. spreading b. spread under and over the omelet and bacon 2. a. sparkling b. shone brightly in the sunlight 3. a. grooves b. made me ask him what was wrong

p. 248 Note-taking Guide
Sample response:
In Memoriam: The speaker is angry that his friend has been taken from him. The difficulty of loss can be softened by memories.
Tears, Idle Tears: The speaker is in despair about having no more time with the deceased person.
Ulysses: The speaker mourns the loss of youth and desires to seek new adventures.

p. 249 Before You Read
Vocabulary Practice
Sample response: 1. a. creates b. woolen scarves for her friends 2. a. steps b. and then jumped over the creek 3. a. thought b. on news ideas for his next book

p. 250 Note-taking Guide
Sample response:
Column 1, Row 2: She sings.
Column 1, Row 3: She weaves and views the world through a mirror.
Column 2, Row 2: She is dissatisfied.
Column 2, Row 3: She sees Sir Lancelot's reflection in the mirror.
Column 3, Row 2: The mirror cracks; the curse is upon her.
Column 3, Row 3: She goes down to the river.
Column 4, Row 2: She climbs into the boat and sings as she floats down the river toward Camelot.
Column 4, Row 3: She dies while singing; the men and women of Camelot look at her in wonder.

p. 251 Comprehension Builder
Students should circle "A curse is on her if she stay / To look down to Camelot" and label it *Why?*

p. 251 Vocabulary Builder
Students should circle "hath."

p. 252 Vocabulary Builder
Students should circle "Sang."

p. 252 Vocabulary Builder
Students should circle "sunlight." *Sunlight* means "light from the sun."

p. 253 Comprehension Builder
Students should underline "The Lady of Shalott goes down to the river. She finds a boat, unties it, and lies down in it."

p. 253 Vocabulary Builder
Students should circle "loudly," "lowly," "slowly," and "wholly."

p. 254 Vocabulary Builder
Drifts is used as a verb.

p. 255 After You Read
Thinking About the Selections
1. **Graphic Organizer**
Sample response:
"In Memoriam, A. H. H.": The speaker's feelings about a friend's death change. At first, the speaker questions the validity of accepting death as passage to an eternal state. Then he accepts that death does represent the shift to eternal life but is angry that he no longer can be with his friend. Finally, the speaker realizes that the spirit of his friend is all around him.
"Ulysses": The level of excitement in the speaker's life has changed. He had been a man who traveled the world, battled many enemies, and had great adventures. After he returned home, he became bored by the mundane business of ruling his kingdom. Now he plans to leave his kingdom to his son and return to a life of adventure.
2. Answers may vary but should include one of the following: sad, strange, despairing, regretful.

Talk About It
Answers will vary, but should include details from the poem that support students' opinions.

The Essential Question
Answers will vary, but may include the following ideas: Tennyson wanted to promote traditional values such as religion and love ("In Memoriam, A.H.H."); romance ("Lady of Shalott"); appreciation of times past or loved ones lost ("The Princess: Tears, Idle Tears"); and wisdom, hard work, honor, and strength

("Ulysses"). Students should explain their answers by including specific references to the poetry.

p. 256 Vocabulary Skill Review
Now You Do It
Sample response:
miss:
If you miss catching the 5:00 train, you can take a different train an hour later.
Devin will miss his sister when she goes to college.
present:
At present, the newspaper editor has no plans to kill the story.
LaToya is shopping for a present for her best friend.

Talk About It
Answers will vary, but students should write sentences in which they correctly use the same word in two different ways in each sentence.

Write About It
Answers will vary, but students should write jokes in which they use the multiple-meaning words appropriately.

"My Last Duchess"
Robert Browning

"Life in a Love"
Robert Browning

"Love Among the Ruins"
Robert Browning

"Sonnet 43"
Elizabeth Barrett Browning

p. 257 Before You Read
Vocabulary Practice
Sample response: 1. a. admiring b. quieted when Keisha began to play again
2. a. property brought to the marriage b. was sought after by many suitors 3. a. valuable piece b. Her large, colored diamond is

p. 258 Note-taking Guide
Sample response:
Meaning: The painting on the wall is of the Duke's late wife.
Inferences: The Duke seems to care more about owning a fine piece of art than about his wife's death.

p. 259 Vocabulary Builder
Students should circle "Frà Pandolf's." The hands are possessed.

p. 259 Comprehension Builder
The Duke says that the Duchess was too easily impressed; she liked whatever she saw.

p. 260 Vocabulary Builder
Students should circle "grew" and "gave."

p. 260 Vocabulary Builder
Cast means "to make something by pouring metal into a specially shaped container."

p. 261 Before You Read
Vocabulary Practice
Sample response: 1. a. escapes b. my uncle is humor 2. a. cross b. beyond the auditorium 3. a. strong feeling b. about her subject matter

p. 262 Note-taking Guide
"Life in a Love": Students should check **Believes in love forever.**
"Love Among the Ruins": Students should check **Believes that his love is greater than even a great civilization.**
Sonnet 43: Students should check **Believes in love forever** and **Believes in love that will continue after death.**

p. 263 After You Read
Thinking About the Selections
1. **Graphic Organizer**
Sample response:
In the Past: "our country's very capital"; "where the domed and daring palace shot its spires up"
In the Speaker's Time: "the country does not even boast a tree"; "the single little turret that remains"
2. The speaker in "Life in a Love" views love as a chase, and the speaker in "Sonnet 43" views love as passion and romance.

Talk About It
Answers will vary, but students should include details from the poem that support their opinions.

The Essential Question
Answers will vary. Sample response: The speaker in Elizabeth Barrett Browning's sonnet seems more dramatic. The speaker in the sonnet uses language such as "the depth and breadth and height / My soul can reach,"

"the ends of Being," and "I love thee with the breath, / Smiles, tears, of all my life!"

p. 264 Vocabulary Skill Review
Now You Do It
After six straight days of rain, I felt **down in the dumps.**
My older sister will always **steal the spotlight.**
Before she went on stage, her friends told her to **break a leg.**

Talk About It
Answers will vary. Students should use the idioms from the lesson to create humorous bumper stickers.

Write About It
Answers will vary. Students should use idioms from the lesson appropriately in writing radio commercials.

from Hard Times
Charles Dickens

p. 265 Before You Read
Vocabulary Practice
Sample response: 1. a. boring b. hum of the engine 2. a. pictures b. of famous people of black velvet 3. a. excited b. about going to the concert

p. 266 Note-taking Guide
Sample response:
Details That Support Purpose: Thomas Gradgrind asks students to use only the facts to define a horse; a government official wants to keep to the facts by not decorating walls or floors; a teacher who discourages imagination is named "M'Choakumchild."

p. 267 Vocabulary Builder
At his school, Mr. Gradgrind wanted to root out everything except facts.

p. 267 Vocabulary Builder
Students should circle "plain," "bare," and "monotonous."

p. 267 Vocabulary Builder
Students should circle "Don't" and "It's" and write "do not" and "it is."

p. 268 Vocabulary Builder
Mr. Gradgrind thinks that the girl's father *has no business* to call her Sissy.

p. 268 Vocabulary Builder
Memory means "the ability to remember things, places, and experiences" Students may say that the phrase "absorbed many facts" offers a clue to the meaning of *memory.*

p. 269 Vocabulary Builder
Paper is used as a verb.

p. 269 Vocabulary Builder
The visitor points out that horses never walk up and down rooms in reality.

p. 269 Comprehension Builder
Sissy wants a carpet with pictures of flowers because she loves flowers.

p. 270 Vocabulary Builder
Fancy means "imagine" or "imagination." Students should underline "it is the very opposite of *fact."*

p. 270 Vocabulary Builder
Students should circle "less" and "more."

p. 271 After You Read
Thinking About the Selections
1. **Graphic Organizer**
Sample response:
Intended Effect: to show that Gradgrind is rigid and unimaginative
Intended Message: People in power can have misguided ideas that can impose widespread damage.
2. I think the author chose the names Mr. M'Choakumchild and Mr. Gradgrind because he wanted to make fun of the teacher and the businessman and suggest that their only interests were choking the imaginations of children and grinding out graduates.

Talk About It
Answers will vary, but students should suggest that Mr. Gradgrind views fancy as the opposite of fact and that this view causes Mr. Gradgrind to favor an undimensional approach to education that ignores the rewards of developing one's imagination.

The Essential Question
Answers will vary. Sample response: Dickens would think that an education system has great influence on children, and is therefore greatly responsible for the type of adults children become. His social commentary focuses on the teachers' insistence that the children not show any individuality or creativity and

suggests that most children quickly conform to the wishes of school leaders.

p. 272 Vocabulary Skill Review
Now You Do It
dive: dove
dream: dreamed or dreamt
kneel: kneeled or knelt
wake: waked or woke

Talk About It
Answers will vary. Students should take turns making sentences by using the past-tense forms of the verbs from the lesson.

Write About It
Answers will vary. Students should write short poems that include past-tense forms of the words from the lesson.

Informational Texts: Web Sites

p. 274 Vocabulary Builder
Students should circle "novelist."

p. 274 Vocabulary Builder
Students should underline "conversational" and "curatorial."

p. 275 Vocabulary Builder
Sample response: A *virtual* tour allows people to visit a museum online rather than in person.

p. 275 Comprehension Builder
A person must have a computer with Internet access.

p. 275 Vocabulary Builder
Students should complete the sentence with one of the following: the dining room, the morning room, the back parlour, or the stairs to the first floor.

p. 276 Vocabulary Builder
Patient is used as an adjective.

p. 276 Vocabulary Builder
Jump means "change quickly from one position or idea to another."

p. 277 Vocabulary Builder
The word *this* draws attention to the word *room*.

p. 277 Vocabulary Builder
Sample response: Dickens probably *made use of* the study as a quiet place for writing.

p. 277 Comprehension Builder
Sample response: Charles Dickens had a desk that he used for writing. He probably used this desk in all the homes in which he lived from 1839 to the end of his life.

p. 278 After You Read
Thinking About the Web Site
1. You would click Opening Hours for information about the museum's hours of operation.
2. Dickens's study is on the first floor.

Reading Skill
3. The Web site will provide detailed information about the Dickens Museum and offer a virtual tour.
4. The purpose of the Andalusia brochure is to provide information about Andalusia and Flannery O'Connor's experiences while living there.

from Jane Eyre
Charlotte Brontë

p. 279 Before You Read
Vocabulary Practice
Sample response: 1. a. began b. as a result of a tossed match 2. a. thoughtful b. as he reviewed the testimony he had heard
3. a. deep thought b. helped him understand his friend's outburst

p. 280 Note-taking Guide
Sample response:
Jane Eyre
Similarities: Jane is an orphan and a student at Lowood.
Differences: Jane is brooding, has a temper, and says that she will not accept unjust treatment patiently.
Helen Burns
Similarities: Helen is a student at Lowood, and she is intelligent and thoughtful.
Differences: Helen accepts unjust treatment and even finds fault with herself.

p. 281 Vocabulary Builder
The first activities in the morning usually included getting up, dressing, and washing.

p. 281 Comprehension Builder
The girls cannot wash because the water in the pitchers is frozen.

p. 281 Vocabulary Builder
Students should circle "kindly" and "suddenly."

p. 282 Vocabulary Builder
Substance means "the most important ideas in a document, speech, or report."

p. 283 Vocabulary Builder
Students should circle "instantly" and "sharply." *Instantly* means "at once." *Sharply* means "in a sharp, strong, or painful manner."

p. 283 Vocabulary Builder
Trace is a noun.

p. 283 Vocabulary Builder
Burns comes from a place on the borders of Scotland.

p. 284 Vocabulary Builder
Miss Scatcherd dislikes Burns's faults.

p. 284 Comprehension Builder
Students should number Helen's faults as follows: 1. "I am . . . slatternly"; 2. "I seldom put, and never keep, things in order"; 3. "I am careless"; 4. "I forget rules"; 5. "I read when I should learn my lessons"; 6. "I have no method"; 7. ". . . sometimes I say, like you, I cannot bear to be subjected to systematic arrangements."

p. 285 Vocabulary Builder
Students should circle "neat," "punctual," "cross," and "cruel."

p. 286 After You Read
Thinking About the Selection
1. **Graphic Organizer**
Sample response:
Oval 2: Girls do not have enough food to eat.
Oval 3: Girls are physically abused.
Oval 4: Girls cannot wash because water is frozen.
2. Helen Burns obeys Miss Scatcherd because she wants to return good for evil, she does not want to have to leave school, and she thinks that Miss Scatcherd is right about her faults.

Talk About It
Answers will vary, but students should note that Jane is different from Helen because Jane believes that people should stand up for themselves even if the consequences may cause a problem for others, Jane allows her emotions to show, Jane does not believe in treating unkind people with kindness, and Jane views Mrs. Scatcherd as cross and cruel.

The Essential Question
Answers will vary. Sample response: Charlotte Brontë includes many details that depict the school as a place in which students are treated unfairly. Her inclusion of these details shows that she has a negative opinion of institutions that allow or promote cruelty toward children. As a popular novel, *Jane Eyre* may have helped to change the conditions at schools like Lowood by appealing to readers' sympathies.

p. 287 Vocabulary Skill Review
Now You Do It
Please p**oi**nt to that t**ow**n on the map.
The baby's favorite t**oy** is a stuffed **ow**l.
The chef began to b**oi**l the water and then turned ar**ou**nd to chop the carrots.
If you sh**ou**t, you will ann**oy** the other diners.

Talk About It
Students should take turns saying sentences that include the words from the lesson, being sure to correctly pronounce each diphthong they have learned.

Write About It
Answers will vary. Students should write poems that include words from the lesson.

"Dover Beach"
Matthew Arnold

"The Widow at Windsor"
Rudyard Kipling

"Recessional"
Rudyard Kipling

p. 288 Before You Read
Vocabulary Practice
Sample response: 1. a. calm b. until the frogs started croaking 2. a. a regular pattern b. for the entire morning 3. a. make an angry expression b. to show her concern for the problem

p. 289 Note-taking Guide
Sample response:
Dover Beach: "the turbid ebb and flow / Of human misery"; "The Sea of Faith / Was once, too, at the full"
The Widow at Windsor: "Walk wide o' the Widow at Windsor / For 'alf o' Creation she owns"; "We've brought 'er the same with the sword an' the flame."

p. 290 Before You Read
Vocabulary Practice
Sample response: 1. a. feeling guilty b. about letting the dog out without its leash
2. a. respect b. when the diver twisted high above the water 3. a. brave b. during the ambush

p. 291 Note-taking Guide
Sample response:
Stanza 1: England is powerful, but God is in control of England.
Stanza 2: Human accomplishments fade, but God's accomplishment is eternal.
Stanza 3: The power of England is fading like that of the ancient empire.
Stanza 4: The British have grown arrogant, forgetting to revere God.
Stanza 5: England has put trust in armies rather than in God.
Main Idea of Poem: Great power should be accompanied by humility, not by pride.

p. 292 After You Read
Thinking About the Selections
1. **Graphic Organizer**
Line That Appeals to Senses: Answers will vary, but should be a line of imagery from the poem.
What I Think About It: Answers will vary, but should indicate students' understanding of imagery.
2. Nineveh and Tyre are ancient cities that were once great and are no longer. When the speaker of "Recessional" says, "Lo, all our pomp of yesterday / Is one with Nineveh and Tyre," the speaker means that what we have now could all be gone someday.

Talk About It
Answers will vary, but should include details from the poem that support students' opinions.

The Essential Question
Answers will vary, but students should support their ideas with details from the poem.

p. 293 Vocabulary Skill Review
Now You Do It
The family often fed their **overweight** dog table scraps.
The **hyperactive** monkey jumped from tree to tree.
The boy who climbed the wall seemed to have **superhuman** strength.

The **ultramodern** house has high-tech features in every room.

Talk About It
Answers will vary, but students should use words from the word bank to describe a cartoon character and the situations that the character encounters.

Write About It
Hyperactive means "excessively active."
Overweight means "weighing too much."
Superhuman means "more than human."
Ultramodern means "beyond modern."

"Remembrance"
Emily Brontë

"The Darkling Thrush"
Thomas Hardy

"Ah, Are You Digging on My Grave?"
Thomas Hardy

p. 294 Before You Read
Vocabulary Practice
Sample response: 1. a. hide b. the calculation errors 2. a. thin b. after he had been sick 3. a. pushing b. his friends in the cafeteria line

p. 295 Note-taking Guide
Sample response:
Remembrance
Sadness: "All my life's bliss from thy dear life was given— / All my life's bliss is in the grave with thee."
Stanza: 5
Hope: "Then did I learn how existence could be cherished, / Strengthened and fed without the aid of joy; . . ."
Stanza: 6
The Darkling Thrush
Sadness: "The ancient pulse of germ and birth / Was shrunken hard and dry . . ."
Stanza: 2
Hope: "In a full-hearted evensong / Of joy illimited; . . ."
Stanza: 3
"Ah, Are You Digging on My Grave?"
Sadness: "No tendance of her mound can loose / Her spirit from Death's gin."
Stanza: 2
Hope: "What feeling do we ever find / To equal among human kind / A dog's fidelity!"
Stanza: 5

p. 296 After You Read
Thinking About the Selections
1. **Graphic Organizer**
Remembrance: a person whose love died 15 years previously
The Darkling Thrush: a despondent person who is cheered after hearing the thrush sing
"Ah, Are You Digging on My Grave?": a dead woman from her grave
2. Sample response: In "The Darkling Thrush," the bird brings the speaker joy and hope.

Talk About It
Answers will vary, but should include details from the poem that support students' opinions.

The Essential Question
Answers will vary, but students should support their ideas with details from the poem.

p. 297 Vocabulary Skill Review
Now You Do It
disagree: to hold an opinion different from that of someone else
disagreeable: not at all enjoyable or pleasant
agreement: an arrangement or a promise to do something

Talk About It
Answers will vary. Students should use words from the lesson to describe their reactions to school policies.

Write About It
Answers will vary. Students should use words from the lesson in a paragraph about a situation in which they came to an agreement or had a disagreement with someone.

"God's Grandeur"
Gerard Manley Hopkins

"Spring and Fall: To a Young Child"
Gerard Manley Hopkins

"To an Athlete Dying Young"
A. E. Housman

"When I Was One-and-Twenty"
A. E. Housman

p. 298 Before You Read
Vocabulary Practice
Sample response: 1. a. impressive beauty
b. of the ski lodge shocked the young couple
2. a. dirty mark b. and ruined the finish
3. a. affliction b. Crime

p. 299 Note-taking Guide
Sample response:
God's Grandeur
Beauty: "The world is charged with the grandeur of God."
Line: 1
Mortality: "Why do men then not now reck his rod?"
Line: 4
Spring and Fall: To a Young Child:
Beauty: "Leáves, like the things of man, you / With your fresh thoughts care for, can you?"
Line: 3–4
Mortality: "Sórrow's springs áre the same."
Line: 11

p. 300 Before You Read
Vocabulary Practice
Sample response: 1. a. piece of wood b. as he formed the doorway 2. a. fame b. for her decision-making skills 3. a. regret b. was that she never married

p. 301 Note-taking Guide
Sample response:
To an Athlete Dying Young
Words/Phrases: "Smart lad, to slip betimes away . . ."
Line Number: 9
When I was One-and-Twenty
Words/Phrases: "'Tis paid with sighs a plenty . . ."
Line Number: 13

p. 302 After You Read
Thinking About the Selections
1. **Graphic Organizer**
Sample response:
Line: "It is Margaret you mourn for."
Meaning: Margaret will be sad for herself.
Line: "Smart lad, to slip betimes away."
Meaning: The speaker thinks that the athlete is smart to die young.
Line: "And the name died before the man."
Meaning: People forgot about someone famous before he died.
2. In the poem "When I Was One-and-Twenty," the speaker has heard a wise man advise not to give one's heart away. The wise man means that it is unwise to fall in love.

Talk About It
Answers will vary, but should include details from the poem that support students' responses.

The Essential Question

Answers will vary. Students may express the following views: Reading Hopkins takes more time and is more complicated. Reading Hopkins aloud sounds nice because of the rhythm. Housman is more straightforward but not as rhythmic or descriptive.

p. 303 Vocabulary Skills Review
Now You Do It
beautiful: beautifully
brave: bravely
happy: happily

Talk About It

Answers will vary, but students' accounts should include at least one adverb from the lesson and may include other adverbs that end in -*ly* and -*ily* that they know.

Write About It

Answers will vary, but students' fables should include adverbs from the lesson and other adverbs that end in -*ly* and -*ily* that they know.

pp. 304–305 Unit Vocabulary Review
A. Matching
a. A paradox is a situation that seems strange because it involves two ideas or qualities that are very different.
b. To reform means to improve a system by making changes to it.
c. Progress is the process of getting better at doing something or getting closer to finishing a task.
d. An empire is a group of countries that are all controlled by one ruler or government.
e. Someone's spirit is the set of qualities that make him or her live a particular way.
f. Modernization makes something, such as a system or a building, more up-to-date.
g. A person's legacy is something that happens or exists as a result of things the person did at an earlier time.
h. Conquest is the act of gaining control by using force.
i. A commentary is a spoken description of an event, given while the event is happening.

B. Word Sorting
Answers will vary. Students should choose four of the following words: *conquest, empire, legacy, modernization, progress, reform, spirit.*

Talk About It

Answers will vary. Students should use sentences from the word bank to defend their ideas about the development of civilizations.

Write About It

Answers will vary, but students should state a logical opinion about the meaning of progress and include a discussion of a paradox that exists related to the concept of progress. Students should use as many words as possible from the word bank.

ANSWERS TO UNIT 6

Poetry of Yeats

p. 306 Before You Read
Vocabulary Practice
Sample response: 1. a. won affection b. baking cookies for the children 2. a. disorder b. the revolution 3. a. practically worthless b. Her hunger would not be satisfied by a

p. 307 Note-taking Guide
Sample response:
When You Are Old: Students should check "Aging" and "Loss."
The Lake Isle of Innisfree: Students should check "Change."
The Wild Swans at Coole: Students should check "Aging," "Loss," and "Change."
The Second Coming: Students should check "Change."
Sailing to Byzantium: Students should check "Aging" and "Loss."

p. 308 After You Read
Thinking About the Selections
1. **Graphic Organizer**
Sample response:
Animals and Creatures/Poems
a creature with a lion's body and a man's head: 2
the cricket and the linnet: 3
brilliant creatures that paddle in the cold: 1
2. The poem "When You Are Old" is addressed to a person who was loved by one man for her pilgrim soul and changing face.

Talk About It
Answers will vary. Sample response: The speaker hopes to find immortality. The speaker says that his heart is stuck to a dying animal and that he wants to take on a new form. In that new form, which will be made by goldsmiths, he will keep an emperor awake and sing to lords and ladies about the past and the future.

The Essential Question
Answers will vary, but students should support answers with details from the poem.

p. 309 Vocabulary Skill Review
Now You Do It
Sample response:
1. Achieving perfection is an impossible task.

2. The scratch on the antique table was a minor imperfection.
3. Amy accidentally turned in a(n) imperfect copy of her final paper.
4. Kisho is perfecting his Spanish skills before the trip to Spain.
5. The pieces of the puzzle fit together perfectly.

Talk About It
Answers will vary. Sample response: I want to be able to play the guitar perfectly. To begin perfecting this skill today, I must practice.

Write About It
Answers will vary. In the tale, students should describe a perfect place and include all of the words in the *perfect* word family.

Poetry of Eliot

p. 310 Before You Read
Vocabulary Practice
Sample response: 1. a. dirty b. Dad asked us to clean 2. a. dried up b. The shrub's leaves 3. a. empty b. apartment and rented it

p. 311 Note-taking Guide
Sample response:
Segment: I
Description of Scene: a cold evening at a smoggy, industrial city block
Despair: ✔
Segment: II
Description of Scene: people awakening to old morning air and beginning their dull routines
Despair: ✔
Segment: III
Description of Scene: a miserable, dream-filled night
Despair: ✔
Segment: IV
Description of Scene: repetition of daily activities, but with a small amount of hope that the cycle will be broken
Hopefulness: ✔

p. 312 Before You Read
Vocabulary Practice
Sample response: 1. a. inflexible b. continued to argue, despite the evidence 2. a. mild b. Outdoor sports are popular 3. a. the area's plants b. occurred as a result of pesticide use

p. 313 Note-taking Guide
Sample response:
Character: Magnus
Goal: to find the infant Jesus
Difficulties Encountered: weather; uncooperative camels; lack of shelter; unfriendly towns
Result: found the infant Jesus
Resolution or Lack of Resolution: The speaker could not determine whether he had witnessed birth or death.
Years Later, Continuing Problems: Because the speaker has a new spiritual consciousness, he is uneasy with the traditional beliefs of his people.

p. 314 Comprehension Builder
Students may circle two of the following: "cold coming we had"; "The ways deep"; "Such a long journey"; "The weather sharp"; "The very dead of winter."

p. 314 Vocabulary Builder
The meaning of *dead* in Eliot's poem is "the middle."

p. 314 Vocabulary Builder
Answers will vary. Sample response: ways, deep; weather, sharp; valley, wet; valley, below the snow line; and valley, smelling of vegetation

p. 315 Vocabulary Builder
Students should circle "at," "to," "of," and "on."

p. 315 Vocabulary Builder
The journey of the magi *took place* a long time ago.

p. 316 Before You Read
Vocabulary Practice
Sample response: 1. a. request b. to extend the project deadline 2. a. shaking slightly but uncontrollably b. after he was robbed 3. a. swollen b. Residents evacuated the town before

p. 317 Note-taking Guide
Sample response:
Part I: "hollow men"; "dried voices"; "shape without form"
Part II: "death's dream kingdom"; "fading star"; "rat's coat"
Part III: "cactus land"; "supplication of a dead man's hand"; "prayers to broken stone"

Part IV: "valley of dying stars"; "hollow valley"; "death's twilight kingdom"
Part V: "prickly pear"; "Falls the Shadow"; "Not with a bang but a whimper"

p. 318 After You Read
Thinking About the Selections
1. **Graphic Organizer**
Sample response:
"heard the sparrows in the gutters": hearing
"clasped the yellow soles of feet in the palms of both soiled hands": touch
"smell of steaks in passageways": smell
"the light crept up between the shutters": sight
2. In "The Hollow Men," the lips of men who awake alone form prayers instead of kisses.

Talk About It
Answers will vary. Sample response: We faced many hardships in our journey, but was the trip worth it? Yes. As I said in the poem, I would do it again. However, the trip raised a difficult question: Did we journey to celebrate a birth or a death? Answering this question is harder than was dealing with the problems we encountered along the way.

The Essential Question
Answers will vary, but students should support opinions with details from the poems.

p. 319 Vocabulary Skill Review
Now You Do It
Sample response:
Verb: laugh
Present: laughs; Gina laughs at her friend's jokes.
Past: laughed; Andrew laughed throughout the movie.
Future: will laugh; Keisha will laugh when you tell her the story.
Verb: hope
Present: hopes; Antonio hopes to go to medical school.
Past: hoped; Last season, Jackie hoped to be most valuable player.
Future: will hope; Daniel will hope for the best.

Talk About It
Answers will vary. Students should demonstrate an understanding of when to use the present, past, and future tenses of *play* and *laugh* and use each form of these verbs in a sentence.

Write About It

Answers will vary. Students' profiles should include at least four of the following verb forms: *hopes, hoped, will hope, dreams, dreamed,* and *will dream.*

"In Memory of W. B. Yeats"
W. H. Auden

"Musée des Beaux Arts"
W. H. Auden

"Carrick Revisited"
Louis MacNeice

"Not Palaces"
Stephen Spender

p. 320 Before You Read
Vocabulary Practice

Sample response: 1. a. kept apart from others b. for several days 2. a. sympathies b. victims of disasters 3. a. plots b. against the company

p. 321 Note-taking Guide

Sample response:

In Memory of W. B. Yeats
Topic/Inspiration: the death of W. B. Yeats
Theme: the power of poetry to teach joy in the human condition

Musée des Beaux Arts
Topic/Inspiration: the death of Icarus
Theme: It is the nature of life and of suffering that the world goes on, even while individuals suffer.

Carrick Revisited
Topic/Inspiration: the speaker's visit to his childhood home
Theme: the irrefutable influence of childhood experience on human character

Not Palaces
Topic/Inspiration: the function of poetry in modern life
Theme: the rejection of old artistic attitudes in favor of art that produces social change

p. 322 After You Read
Thinking About the Selection
1. **Graphic Organizer**
In Memory of W. B. Yeats: Answers will vary. Sample response: brooks, snow, wolves, forests, river, weather, Earth, dogs, seas, vineyard, deserts
Not Palaces: Answers will vary. Sample response: flower, gazelle, horizon, gardens, sun

2. In "Musée des Beaux Arts," the Old Masters were never wrong about suffering.

Talk About It

Answers will vary. Students should discuss the poem and the effects they would use in a film.

The Essential Question

Answers will vary, but students should support answers with details from the poem.

p. 323 Vocabulary Skill Review
Now You Do It

Sample response:
1. At the age of eleven, Anke is considered a preteen.
2. Kyan decided to prepay his auto insurance for a year.
3. Monica wore a helmet as a precaution against head injuries.
4. Gary will preview the film before he rents it.
5. Alberto tried not to prejudge his new math teacher.

Talk About It

Answers will vary. Sample response: As a *precaution,* movie fans may want to *preview* the film before allowing a *preteen* to see it; some movie fans will *prepay* to see the movie to make sure that they have a seat at the first showing; they will try not to *prejudge* the movie before seeing it all the way through.

Write About It

Answer will vary. Students' letters should use the words *precaution* and *preteen* to describe a specific safety hazard that should be removed from the community.

"The Lady in the Looking Glass:
A Reflection"
Virginia Woolf

from Mrs. Dalloway
Virginia Woolf

from A Room of One's Own:
from Shakespeare's Sister
Virginia Woolf

p. 324 Before You Read
Vocabulary Practice

Sample response: 1. a. filled b. after he stumbled in front of the class 2. a. scoldings b. for his poor grades 3. a. quiet b. Although she thought that explaining might help,

p. 325 Note-taking Guide
Sample response:
How she appears throughout the story: elegant, well-known and respected, mysterious and exciting
How she appears at the end of the story: old, empty, and friendless

p. 326 Before You Read
Vocabulary Practice
Sample response: 1. a. disappeared b. The magician waved her hand over the object, and it 2. a. lively b. Kristine is a popular choice for class president 3. a. permanent b. Because of its terms

p. 327 Note-taking Guide
Sample response:
Characteristics of Clarissa: She is wealthy, in her 50s, serious, like a bird, light, vivacious, very white, and stands very upright. She loves the sound of Big Ben and loves her life in London.
Characteristics of Peter: He is witty. He writes dull letters. He is remembered for his smile and his grumpiness.

p. 328 Before You Read
Vocabulary Practice
Sample response: 1. a. adventure b. as a government spy 2. a. quickly wrote b. her words as he was walking out of class 3. a. shouted b. Take out the trash

p. 329 Note-taking Guide
Sample response:
Education
William Shakespeare: William goes to school.
Judith Shakespeare: Judith learns mending and cooking at home.
Marriage
Judith Shakespeare: Judith's father arranges her marriage to a wool-stapler. She does not want to marry, so she leaves home.
Career
Judith Shakespeare: Judith tries to become an actor in London. She is rejected. The pain of this rejection leads her to take her own life.

p. 330 After You Read
Thinking About the Selections
1. **Graphic Organizer**
Cause: Judith protests marriage. Judith Shakespeare goes to the theater.

Effect: He becomes successful in the theater. Judith kills herself.
2. Mrs. Dalloway reminds her neighbor of a blue and green bird.

Talk About It
Answers will vary. Sample response: Isabella will probably be polite and offer the speaker something to drink. Isabella will probably act like an old woman who has good memories of friends whom she misses.

The Essential Question
Answers will vary, but students should support answers with details from the story.

p. 331 Vocabulary Skill Review
Now You Do It
1. Cecelia will replant her flower garden with vegetables.
2. The planter on the patio contained marigolds and zinnias.
3. We watched the workers harvest tea on the plantation.
4. Vic has to transplant the flowers from pots to the garden.
5. Doctors often implant a pacemaker to regulate the heart.

Talk About It
Partners should take turns saying sentences that contain two words from the *plant* word family and listen for correct usage.

Write About It
Answers will vary, but students should include as many words as possible from the *plant* word family in their paragraphs.

"The Lagoon"
Joseph Conrad

"Araby"
James Joyce

p. 332 Before You Read
Vocabulary Practice
Sample response: 1. a. indestructible b. but his enemies eventually defeated him 2. a. appease b. making dinner for them 3. a. large fire b. was raging out of control

p. 333 Note-taking Guide
Sample response:
Beginning Action: Arsat falls in love with Diamelen; Arsat, his brother, and Diamelen run away from the Malaysian ruler.

Climax Action: Arsat leaves his brother to die in order to save his and Diamelen's lives.
Ending Action: Diamelen dies, and Arsat goes back to face his pursuers.

p. 334 Before You Read
Vocabulary Practice
Sample response: 1. a. dimly b. the meeting date but had forgotten its time 2. a. mocked b. he went to the movie by himself 3. a. excessive pride b. by spending two hours grooming his hair every morning

p. 335 Note-taking Guide
Sample response:
Exposition: The young narrator describes the street on which he lives and then describes his friend Mangan's older sister. The narrator daydreams about Mangan's sister and follows her to school, but he never speaks to her.
Rising Action: Mangan's sister speaks to the narrator unexpectedly; the narrator promises to bring her something from *Araby* if he goes. He continues to daydream about her so much that his school work suffers. On the day of the bazaar, the narrator's uncle does not arrive home and give him money until past nine o'clock; the narrator finally arrives at the bazaar as it is closing. A young woman laughing with two young men asks whether the narrator wants to buy something; the narrator unexpectedly declines.
Climax: The narrator suddenly realizes that he has been very foolish.
Falling Action: The narrator departs from the dark and deserted hall.
Resolution: The narrator is stricken by grief and anger at his vanity and foolishness.

p. 336 Vocabulary Builder
In the first paragraph, *crush* means "a strong feeling of romantic love for someone."

p. 336 Vocabulary Builder
Students should circle "Mangan's" and underline "sister."

p. 336 Vocabulary Builder
Mangan's sister speaks to the narrator.

p. 337 Comprehension Builder
The narrator must wait because he needs money from his uncle.

p. 337 Vocabulary Builder
Students should circle "At," "in," "to," "of," "through," and the "to" that precedes "the bazaar."

p. 338 Vocabulary Builder
Piece means "something that has been produced by an artist, musician, or writer."

p. 338 Vocabulary Builder
Stalls means "booths at a market."

p. 338 Vocabulary Builder
Students should circle "one of the stalls."

p. 339 Vocabulary Builder
Students should circle "completely."

p. 339 Comprehension Builder
He feels anguished and angry.

p. 340 After You Read
Thinking About the Selections
1. **Graphic Organizer**
The Lagoon
Tuan tells Arsat that the Diamelen will be fine in the morning. false
The two men stay awake all night talking. true
Arsat feels no sorrow or shame for his brother's death. false
Araby
The speaker's uncle must be reminded to give the speaker money. true
The speaker has a difficult time selecting a gift for Mangan's sister. true
The speaker buys Mangan's sister a beautiful scarf. false
2. In "Araby," the speaker's uncle believes that "all work and no play makes Jack a dull boy."

Talk About It
Answers will vary. Sample response: Arsat's house is located in a clearing on a creek. Tuan reaches the house by climbing a ladder, which suggests that the house rests on stilts. The boatmen believe that the house is haunted because other people have abandoned it.

The Essential Question
Answers will vary, but students should support answers with details from the story.

p. 341 Vocabulary Skill Review
Now You Do It

1. That hotel is the oldest business establishment in the city.
2. The noise did not affect Felipe's enjoyment of the film.
3. Dana stepped off the sidewalk and onto the pavement.
4. After a long period of employment, Chris decided to retire.
5. With proper soil enrichment, farm production increases.

Talk About It
Lists will vary, but partners should include places that have pavement and places that provide employment, and should discuss whether both things can be found at the same place.

Write About It
Ads will vary, but students should include the words *establishment*, *enjoyment*, and *enrichment* in their ads.

"The Rocking-Horse Winner"
D. H. Lawrence

"A Shocking Accident"
Graham Greene

p. 342 Before You Read
Vocabulary Practice
Sample response: 1. a. prudent b. never criticized people in public 2. a. stubbornly b. to change her mind 3. a. weird b. amazed everyone

p. 343 Note-taking Guide
Sample response:
Box 3: Paul decides that he is lucky.
Box 4: Uncle Oscar discovers that Paul is betting on horses and winning.
Box 5: Paul secretly gives his mother five thousand pounds.
Box 6: Paul's "lucky" ability to know the winning horse begins to fade.
Box 7: Paul rides his rocking horse furiously until he knows the name of the next winner, becoming violently ill.
Box 8: Paul wins seventy thousand pounds for his mother.
Box 9: Paul dies.

p. 344 Before You Read
Vocabulary Practice
Sample response: 1. a. an anxious feeling b. as the police officer walked to her car 2. a. started b. we threw her a going-away party 3. a. inherently b. Exercising and good health

p. 345 Note-taking Guide
Sample response:
1. **How does Jerome feel about his father?** Jerome loves his father deeply.
2. **How does his father die?** A pig fell on him from a balcony.
3. **How do people react to the story?** People laugh at the story.
4. **Why is he afraid to tell Sally about how his father died?** Jerome is afraid that Sally will laugh.
5. **How does she react?** Sally is horrified, and does not laugh.
6. **How does her reaction make Jerome feel?** Jerome feels joyful.

p. 346 After You Read
Thinking About the Selection
1. Graphic Organizer
Order of Events
Box 1: 5
Box 2: 2
Box 3: 3
Box 4: 1
Box 5: 6
Box 6: 4
2. In "A Shocking Accident," Jerome's father is killed by a pig that falls off a balcony and crushes him.

Talk About It
Answers will vary. Students should find evidence from the selection that suggests the mother's guilt or innocence. Then, they should evaluate the evidence and make a judgment.

The Essential Question
Answers will vary, but students should support answers with details from the story.

p. 347 Vocabulary Skill Review
Now You Do It
Joan had no choice but to confess. She had been caught redhanded trying to leave home to visit friends without finishing her chores. At first, Joan tried to pull the wool over some-

one's eyes by saying that she had to buy a notebook. Then, Joan made the off the cuff remark that housework was not her job anyway. Ms. Moreno reminded Joan that she had to care for her younger brother as well as finish her chores. Joan called her friends and asked to take a raincheck.

Talk About It
Answers will vary. Students' descriptions should include as many of the idioms on this page as possible.

Write About It
Answers will vary. Students should write a short story that includes the idioms from this lesson.

"The Soldier"
Rupert Brooke

"Wirers"
Siegfried Sassoon

"Anthem for Doomed Youth"
Wilfred Owen

p. 348 Before You Read
Vocabulary Practice
Sample response: 1. a. frightening b. gave the children nightmares 2. a. deserted b. was boarded up and covered with vines 3. a. disappointing efforts b. The poorly written laws were

p. 349 Note-taking Guide
Sample response:
The Soldier
Central Image/Idea: A soldier's life, or dead body, is equated with England in a foreign soil.
Wirers
Central Image/Idea: A boy's life is sacrificed to mend the fence on the war front.
Anthem for Doomed Youth
Central Image/Idea: A young soldier's life can never be mourned enough.

p. 350 After You Read
Thinking About the Selections
1. Graphic Organizer
Honoring the Battlefield Dead
Bells are replaced by: the anger of the guns
Prayers are replaced by: rifles' rapid rattle
Choirs are replaced by: wailing shells and bugles

Candles are replaced by: shining eyes
Palls, or a cloths that cover coffins, are replaced by: the pallor of girls' brows
Flowers are replaced by: tender minds
2. In "The Soldier," the speaker says that if he dies on a foreign field, that corner of the field will be forever England.

Talk About It
Answers will vary. Sample response: The wiring party mends fences. When soldiers see mended fences, they can say that progress has been made. Progress of any kind helps build hope.

The Essential Question
Answers will vary, but students should support opinions with details from the poem.

p. 351 Vocabulary Skill Review
Now You Do It
Sample response:
1. Mario put a lock on his door to keep Doreen from entering his room.
2. Miriam placed a lock of her baby's hair in the scrapbook.
3. Kadeem will win the match if he gets a lock on Victor.
4. Boats on the Chicago River must pass through a series of locks.

Talk About It
Answers will vary. Sample response: The wrestler's lock and the river lock are the same because both control something. They are different because the wrestler's lock keeps something from moving, but the river lock helps something move safely.

Write About It
Answers will vary. Students' flyers should describe a new kind of lock designed to keep locks of hair in place.

"The Demon Lover"
Elizabeth Bowen

p. 352 Before You Read
Vocabulary Practice
Sample response: 1. a. ghostly b. From the abandoned house shone a 2. a. tree-dwelling b. Name one example of 3. a. opening b. was quickly repaired

p. 353 Note-taking Guide
Sample response:

Characters: Mrs. Drover

Setting: It is late afternoon in humid London; Mrs. Drover goes to retrieve a few things from her shut-up London home.

Problem: Mrs. Drover discovers a letter addressed to her from her presumed-dead fiancé of many years ago.

Event 1: Mrs. Drover reads the letter.

Event 2: Mrs. Drover remembers her old fiancé's promise and when they parted.

Event 3: Mrs. Drover recalls when she was given the news of her old fiancé's presumed death.

Event 4: Mrs. Drover feels as though she is being watched as she leaves the house.

Event 5: Mrs. Drover walks to the thoroughfare to get a taxi.

Event 6: Mrs. Drover discovers that the taxi driver is her old fiancé.

Conclusion: Mrs. Drover is trapped within the taxi as it drives off into the deserted streets.

p. 354 After You Read
Thinking About the Selection
1. Graphic Organizer

Fiancé: He does not kiss Kathleen; he holds her and looks at her; he talks without feeling; he says that he will be with her—sooner or later; her mother does not like him; a button on his clothing leaves a scar on her hand.

Letter Writer: He reminds Kathleen that today is their anniversary; he expects her to keep her promise to him; he seems to be watching her; he tells her to expect him.

Taxi Driver: The taxi driver seems to be waiting for Kathleen; he heads in the direction of her house without being asked; while she screams, he speeds off to a deserted place.

2. Kathleen Drover is afraid because she thinks the letter is a threat.

Talk About It
Answers will vary. Students should discuss their ideas for an alternative ending and support it with details described in the story.

The Essential Question
Answers will vary, but students should support answers with details from the story.

p. 355 Vocabulary Skill Review
Now You Do It
1. Antonio was ready for school, but he waited for Martin.
2. The salad tastes fresh because we just made it.
3. The choir will sound beautiful when it performs in the auditorium.
4. The new blanket felt soft and cuddly even after we washed it.
5. Michele became stronger by exercising when she walked the dog.

Talk About It
Answers will vary. Students should describe classmates with sentences that contain the indicated linking verbs.

Write About It
Answers will vary. Sample response: The math book looks clean. It smells new. When I flip the pages, the paper sounds crinkly. The book feels heavy. The paper probably tastes bitter.

"Vergissmeinicht"
Keith Douglas

"Postscript: For Gweno"
Alun Lewis

"Naming of Parts"
Henry Reed

p. 356 Before You Read
Vocabulary Practice
Sample response: 1. a. fighters b. escaped the tanks and defeated the enemy 2. a. remain b. The memory of the years we spent together 3. a. beautifully expressive b. inspired listeners to take action

p. 357 Note-taking Guide
Sample response:

"Postscript: For Gweno": the soldier's beloved

"Vergissmeinicht": Steffi, the soldier's girlfriend

"Naming of Parts": the part of a rifle and the elements of nature

p. 358 After You Read
Thinking About the Selections
1. Graphic Organizer
Lines Describing the Flowering of Spring
Box 1: "The branches / Hold in the gardens their silent, eloquent gestures."

Box 2: "The blossoms / Are fragile and motionless, never letting anyone see / Any of them using their finger."

Box 3: "And rapidly backwards and forwards / The early bees are assaulting and fumbling the flowers: / They call it easing the Spring."
2. The speaker calls death "the wild beast" and says that death "is uncaught, untamed."

Talk About It
Answers will vary. Students should develop ideas for a eulogy on the basis of the clues the speaker provides about the life and death of the soldier.

The Essential Question
Answers will vary, but students should support answers with details from the poems.

p. 359 Vocabulary Skill Review
Now You Do It
Mr. Smith cannot be a *square*—he plays in a rock band! someone who is considered boring and unfashionable
Carlos moved his game piece to the next *square*. a space on a board used for playing a game such as chess or checkers
Aneko waited for Angie by the fountain in the *square*. a large open area in the center of a town or city
The tile is a perfect *square*. a shape with four equal sides 90° angles

Talk About It
Answers will vary. Sample response: A town square should have a square shape. A town hall should be built in the center, and the building should be surrounded by trees and public benches.

Write About It
Answers will vary. Students should support their ideas with an example of someone who seemed to be a "square" but was actually an interesting or entertaining companion.

"Shooting an Elephant"
George Orwell

"No Witchcraft for Sale"
Doris Lessing

p. 360 Before You Read
Vocabulary Practice
Sample response: 1. a. control b. eventually led to independence movements 2. a. tyrannical b. The new government arrested and tried

3. a. flashy b. His gray suit was a stark contrast to her

p. 361 Note-taking Guide
Sample response:
Where it takes place: Moulmein, in Lower Burma
The problems Orwell faces: Orwell must kill an elephant that has temporarily gone wild and killed a Burmese man.
The actions he takes: Orwell kills the elephant with two thousand Burmese looking on.
His feelings and thoughts: Orwell does not want to kill the elephant because it is no longer necessary, but he has to kill the elephant in order to avoid looking like a fool to the Burmese. He also realizes that the British Imperialists are actually at the mercy of the colonized because the British can only pretend to be in control.

p. 362 Vocabulary Builder
Students should underline "the sneering yellow faces of young men that met me everywhere, the insults hooted after me when I was at a safe distance" and "stand on the street corners and jeer at Europeans."

p. 362 Comprehension Builder
Students should underline "imperialism, or the fact that Burma is a colony of Great Britain."

p. 363 Vocabulary Builder
At the top of the page, *treated* means "behaved toward someone in a particular way."

p. 363 Vocabulary Builder
Subinspector means "lower than an inspector."

p. 363 Vocabulary Builder
Answers will vary. Sample response: Students should circle and then write the following (some appear more than once): "British," group of people; "Orwell," person; "Winchester," thing.

p. 364 Vocabulary Builder
In the first bracketed paragraph, *lying* means "being in a position in which your body is flat on a surface."

p. 364 Vocabulary Builder
In the second bracketed text, *one* means "people in general, including yourself."

p. 364 Comprehension Builder

Students should underline "Orwell feels that the elephant's frenzy is over, and he won't be dangerous."

p. 365 Vocabulary Builder

Bit is a noun.

p. 365 Vocabulary Builder

He believes that he must kill the elephant.

p. 366 Vocabulary Builder

Students should underline "I did not hear the bang or feel the kick."

p. 366 Comprehension Builder

The elephant "slobbers and falls," immediately seeming to "deteriorate."

p. 366 Vocabulary Builder

The third shot knocked the remaining strength from its legs.

p. 367 Vocabulary Builder

Students should underline "him" and "they" and circle "elephant" and "Burmans."

p. 367 Vocabulary Builder

In the second bracketed paragraph, *grasped* means "completely understood a fact or an idea, especially a complicated one."

p. 368 Before You Read
Vocabulary Practice

Sample response: 1. a. energetically b. I shower after exercising 2. a. disappeared b. When her brother apologized, 3. a. playfully b. when the crowd gasped in surprise

p. 369 Note-taking Guide

Sample response:
Event: Teddy is born.
Detail: Gideon and the servants are pleased for the Farquars.
Event: Teddy is given a scooter.
Detail: Teddy frightens Gideon's young son.
Event: A tree snake spits in Teddy's eyes.
Detail: Gideon heals Teddy with an antidote from an unknown plant.
Event: The Farquars want Gideon to show a scientist the plant.
Detail: Gideon is angry and misleads them all.
Event: The relationship between the Farquars and Gideon heals.
Detail: They joke about the incident.

p. 370 Vocabulary Builder

Students should circle "great," "lingering," "admiring," "warm," and "grateful" and underline "thing," "natives," and "smile."

p. 370 Vocabulary Builder

Answers will vary. Sample response (some proper nouns appear more than once): Students should circle "Africa," "Mrs. Farquar," "Gideon," "Farquar's," "Teddy," "Little Yellow Head," "Gideon's," "God's," and "Farquars."

p. 371 Vocabulary Builder

In the first bracketed paragraph, Teddy *showed off* to Gideon's youngest son by telling him to get out of the way and racing in circles around him with the scooter.

p. 371 Comprehension Builder

Teddy speaks rudely to Gideon and says that Gideon's son is "only a black boy."

p. 371 Vocabulary Builder

Students should circle "on," "into," "with," "to," "with," and "of."

p. 372 Vocabulary Builder

The snake spat *right into* Teddy's eyes.

p. 372 Vocabulary Builder

Students should circle "her" and underline "remedies," circle "their" and underline "eyes," and circle "her" and underline "cook."

p. 372 Vocabulary Builder

Students should circle "scarcely."

p. 373 Comprehension Builder

Teddy's eyes are healed.

p. 373 Vocabulary Builder

In the bracketed paragraph, *instrument* means "something or someone that is used to getting a particular result."

p. 373 Vocabulary Builder

Plant is used as a noun.

p. 374 Vocabulary Builder

Students should circle "flustered," "pleased," and "flattered."

p. 374 Vocabulary Builder

Discomfort means "lack of comfort."

p. 374 Comprehension Builder

Students should say that Gideon is surprised, angry, and hurt.

p. 375 Vocabulary Builder
Students should circle "suddenly" and underline "decided" and circle "finally" and underline "picks up."

p. 375 Vocabulary Builder
They *made inquiries* from their laborers.

p. 375 Vocabulary Builder
Soreness means "state of having pain."

p. 376 Vocabulary Builder
Gideon would *double up* when Teddy would ask him about how he tricked everyone about the snake bite cure.

p. 377 After You Read
Thinking About the Selections
1. **Graphic Organizer**
Shooting an Elephant
Main characters: George Orwell, a British police officer; a mad elephant
Setting: Burma
No Witchcraft for Sale
Main characters: the Farquars, a white couple; Teddy, the Farquars' son; Gideon, the Farquars' African cook
2. Orwell kills the elephant in the story "Shooting an Elephant" because he does not want the Burmese people to think that he is a fool.

Talk About It
Answers will vary. Sample response: I would tell Gideon to share the plant root because it will help many people; I would tell Gideon to keep the plant root secret because the scientists only want to make money from it, and the whites already control the entire country.

The Essential Question
Answers will vary, but students should support answers with details from the story.

p. 378 Vocabulary Skill Review
Now You Do It
Sample Sentence
Box 1: The launching of the space shuttle will transfix those who see it.
Box 2: The businesswoman will transplant her family to the city in which she has taken a new job.
Box 3: The students took a transatlantic flight to London, England.

Box 4: The student completed a transaction in the admissions office.
Box 5: Living in a foreign country caused a transformation in Brian's attitude.

Talk About It
Answers will vary. Students should use the words transaction, transatlantic, and *transplant.*

Write About It
Answers will vary. Students should include the words *transfix, transform,* and *transformation* in a story about someone who has experienced an amazing transformation.

"The Train from Rhodesia"
Nadine Gordimer

"B. Wordsworth"
V. S. Naipaul

p. 379 Before You Read
Vocabulary Practice
Sample response: 1. a. quickly-sketched suggestive b. Her charcoal sketches were filled with 2. a. divided b. In biology class, we observed the worm's 3. a. waste away b. Because he was confined to bed rest

p. 380 Note-taking Guide
Sample response:
Setting (Place): a train
Details: The train pulls into a station crowded with natives selling carved wood animals.
Characters: a young woman, a man, and a native
Details: The young woman and man are newly married; the native is trying to sell his carvings.
Problems: The young woman wants to buy a carved lion but decides that it is too expensive.
Details: The husband buys the lion at a greatly reduced price, but the young woman is unexpectedly angry with him.

p. 381 Before You Read
Vocabulary Practice
Sample response: 1. a. be customers at b. our neighborhood grocery store to support local businesses 2. a. obtain the essential parts of b. the novel's plot into a few sentences 3. a. intensely b. The grieving family

p. 382 Note-taking Guide
Sample response:

What character says: B. Wordsworth says that that he is writing a great poem, one line per month. He says that the boy is a poet, too.

What character does: B. Wordsworth goes to the boy's house and asks to watch the bees. He teaches the boy the constellations and appreciation of beauty.

What others say about character: The boy says that B. Wordsworth makes the world more exciting and that he speaks and acts deliberately, as if he were experiencing things for the first time.

What character thinks: B. Wordsworth is troubled by the limitations he has encountered in life, but he is happy to have met the boy.

p. 383 After You Read
Thinking About the Selection
1. **Graphic Organizer**
B. Wordsworth: He is a poet whose ideas are valued by the speaker; he lives in Trinidad.
Man who sells wood carvings: He is a woodworker whose art is not valued by the woman on the train; he lives in South Africa.
2. In "The Train from Rhodesia," the husband buys the carved lion because he wants to make his wife happy.

Talk About It
Answers will vary. Sample response: This location was once home to B. Wordsworth, the best poet in the world. He loved bees, he loved nature, and he loved me. He taught me that life is poetry.

The Essential Question
Answers will vary, but students should support opinions with details from personal experiences.

p. 384 Vocabulary Skill Review
Now You Do It
Sample response:
Irregular Verb: shake
Present: Makoto *shakes* the jug before serving the orange juice.
Past: Last night, Jira *shook* the package, hoping to guess what was inside.
Past Participle: Karin has *shaken* the pen several times, trying to get the ink to flow.

Irregular Verb: lose
Present: Dieter *loses* an umbrella every time it rains.
Past: Alicia *lost* her new glasses yesterday.
Past Participle: Javier has *lost* his contact lenses seven times.

Talk About It
Answers will vary. Students should describe their written work by using the words *write*, *wrote*, and *written*.

Write About It
Answers will vary. Students should write a lost-and-found news story that contains at least three of the following words: *lose*, *loses*, *lost*, *shake*, *shakes*, *shook*, and *shaken*.

Poetry of Walcott

p. 385 Before You Read
Vocabulary Practice
Sample response: 1. a. ill will b. toward his brother for causing the collapse of their partnership 2. a. dimming b. of the other candidate's appeal 3. a. formally brought b. into her new position at a special ceremony

p. 386 Note-taking Guide
Sample response:
Context details: "like Boer cattle under Tory whips"; "add some color to the British theater"
Conflict in poet's mind: Walcott feels disloyal to his countrymen in light of the race riots.

p. 387 Before You Read
Vocabulary Practice
Sample response: 1. a. quiet-voiced complaint b. When he stalked out of the room, all we could hear was 2. a. extremely hot b. We spent the day inside, away from 3. a. spread out from a central point b. from his shoulder to his fingers

p. 388 Note-taking Guide
Sample response:
Detail 1: "'. . . these shadows are reprinted now on the white sand . . .'"
Detail 2: "'. . . our eyes showed dried fronds in their brown irises . . .'"
Detail 3: "'. . . ribbed corpses floated . . .'"
Detail 4: "'. . . black waiter bringing the bill.'"
Detail 5: "'. . . multiply their ruin . . .'"
Detail 6: "'. . . each man was a nation . . .'"

p. 389 After You Read
Thinking About the Selections
1. Graphic Organizer
from **Midsummer XXIII:** "tug at their chains," "bending like Boer cattle," "Tory whips," "apartheid"
from **Omeros:** "tinkling leg-iron," "chains," "the hold's iron door"
2. According to the griot in the selection from "Omeros," the corpses that had been thrown overboard floated back to the white sands of the Bight of Benin and the margin of Guinea.

Talk About It
Answers will vary. Sample response: A television reporter would present only the facts. For example, he or she might say this: "A riot broke out tonight in the alleys of Brixton. Police used water hoses to stop the rioters. People near the riot zone said that anger among the rioters increased when the police and skinheads started exchanging jokes about the rioters."

The Essential Question
Answers will vary, but students should support answers with details from the poems.

p. 390 Vocabulary Skill Review
Now You Do It
Sample response:
1. As a rule, Javier's family eats dinner at six-thirty every night.
2. When Heath saw his friends, he said, "Hey, what's up?"
3. The cake was on the house in celebration of Doug's birthday.
4. Everyone says that Mia is the spitting image of her mother.

Talk About It
Answers will vary. Students should identify people whom they might address with the query "What's up?" and discuss common responses to the question.

Write About It
Answers will vary. Students' dialogues between a diner and a server should include the idioms *as a rule, on the house,* and *spitting image.*

"Follower"
Seamus Heaney

"Two Lorries"
Seamus Heaney

"Outside History"
Eavan Boland

p. 391 Before You Read
Vocabulary Practice
Sample response: 1. a. narrow groove
b. Without a tractor, it was difficult to dig
2. a. act that causes trouble b. The noise of traffic in the street 3. a. vague ideas b. We expected that she would resign because

p. 392 Note-taking Guide
Sample response:
Follower
Images: father's shoulders, son, following behind the plow
Central Image: The son follows behind his father as he plows the field.
Two Lorries
Images: coal trucks, smoke and ashes, rain, mother, bomb
Central Image: the bus station bombing
Outside History
Images: stars, rivers, fields, pain of human suffering and death
Central Image: past and present struggle

p. 393 After You Read
Thinking About the Selections
1. Graphic Organizer
The Son as the Follower: "stumbled," "fell"; "Sometimes he rode me on his back"; "I was a nuisance, tripping, falling, yapping always."
The Father as the Follower: "keeps stumbling behind me," "will not go away"
2. According to the speaker in "Outside History," the stars are outside history and humans are always too late.

Talk About It
Answers will vary. Students should consider the topic of the poem from the point of view of the speaker's mother.

The Essential Question
Answers will vary, but students should support answers with details from the poems.

p. 394 Vocabulary Skill Review
Now You Do It
Sample response:

1. Ernesto showed good sportsmanship by shaking the winner's hand.
2. Kaida missed the sportscast of the game, but she read about it.
3. Erik wants to be a sportswriter because he loves all sports.
4. Abiba's parents attend all of her sporting events.
5. Tina worked all year to earn money for a sporty new car.

Talk About It
Answers will vary. Sample response: A *sportswriter* spends his or her day writing reports about *sporting* events for a local newspaper or television station. If the *sportswriter* cannot go to an event, he or she may cover the game by watching a *sportscast*. Some *sportswriters* may drive a *sporty* car to and from work.

Write About It
Answers will vary. Students should write a profile of someone who models sportsmanship; students should explain how this person demonstrates sportsmanship and describe what others can learn from this person's behavior.

"Come and Go"
Samuel Beckett

"That's All"
Harold Pinter

p. 395 Before You Read
Vocabulary Practice
Sample response: 1. a. held tightly b. her backpack tightly so she wouldn't drop it
2. a. shocked b. the graffiti on our playground
3. a. continue b. organizing for the benefit concert after we hired performers

p. 396 Note-taking Guide
Sample response:
The first question each woman asks: "What do you think of . . .?"
The answer each woman gives to the question: "I see little change."
Topics about which the women remain silent: the old days and of what followed them

p. 397 Before You Read
Vocabulary Practice
Sample response: 1. a. worker at the meat shop b. to wrap up two steaks 2. a. chanced b. learn that the company was hiring a new intern 3. a. normal b. was flooded by the rising river.

p. 398 Note-taking Guide
Sample response:
Who does most of the talking? Mrs. A.
Who does most of the listening and answers "yes," or "Oh yes"? Mrs. B.
Who has changed the day on which she goes to the butcher shop? the third woman
Who seems to be avoiding tea with Mrs. A? the third woman

p. 399 After You Read
Thinking About the Selections
1. **Graphic Organizer**
Come and Go
Who Talks: Ru
To Whom: Flo
About What: Box 1: Vi; **Box 4:** not speaking of the past, holding hands
That's All: a third woman
2. Just before the curtain falls in "Come and Go," Flo says that she can feel the rings.

Talk About It
Answers will vary. Sample response: I think Mrs. B. would tell Mrs. A. that the third woman visits the butcher on a different day because she wants to avoid having a silly conversation with Mrs. A. I think Mrs. B. would say this because at the end of the play, Mrs. B. seems willing to challenge what Mrs. A. says.

The Essential Question
Answers will vary, but students should support opinions with details from the story.

p. 400 Vocabulary Skill Review
Now You Do It
Sample response:
1. Sandra gave her presentation without using notes.
2. Lucas received an invitation to Jenny's birthday party.
3. The chef's demonstration made cooking look easy.

4. Diana chose children's dentistry as her specialization.

5. Tomo started a conversation with the person sitting next to him.

Talk About It

Answers will vary. Students should explain how they could prepare a demonstration of their specialization in an activity or a subject.

Write About It

Answers will vary. Sample response: Please join me in honoring my grandfather on Sunday. Listen as the mayor makes a *presentation* describing the kindness my grandfather has shown to all his neighbors. Sit and have a *conversation* with my grandfather, who very much loves to talk. I hope you will accept this *invitation*. Thank you.

"Do Not Go Gentle into That Good Night"
Dylan Thomas

"Fern Hill"
Dylan Thomas

"The Horses"
Ted Hughes

p. 401 Before You Read
Vocabulary Practice

Sample response: 1. a. mourned b. for his home when he had to move 2. a. enchanted b. watching the herd of gazelles lope past them 3. a. twisting and curving b. hike across the vast desert

p. 402 Note-taking Guide

Sample response:
Poem: "Do Not Go Gentle"
Main Idea/Writer's Message: The poet faces the approaching death of his father. He urges readers to fight death, rather than accept it.
Poem: "Fern Hill"
Main Idea/Writer's Message: The poet looks back fondly on his carefree youth and laments the loss of youth and the "chains" that the passage of time imposes.
Poem: "The Horses"
Main Idea/Writer's Message: The poet recalls an encounter with horses in nature. He celebrates the peacefulness and mystery of the experience and of nature.

p. 403 After You Read
Thinking About the Selection
1. **Graphic Organizer**
Examples of Men Who Refused to Surrender Quietly to Death
Box 1: wise men
Box 2: good men
Box 3: grave men
Box 4: wild men
2. In "Fern Hill," the speaker says that, even as a carefree child, he was at the mercy of Time.

Talk About It

Answers will vary. Sample response: To capture the scene described in "The Horses," I would produce a painting. I would use slivers of red and orange against a dark gray background to show the dawn breaking. I'd also use white paint to show the frosty ground and the frosty breath of the horses.

The Essential Question

Answers will vary, but students should support answers with details from the poems.

p. 404 Vocabulary Skill Review
Now You Do It

Sample response:
In science class, Yori examined a fish scale under a microscope. a small, flat piece of skin that covers fish and reptiles
Pedro weighs himself on the scale in the locker room. a machine for weighing people or objects
The choir warms up by singing a scale. a series of musical notes

Talk About It

Answers will vary. Students should use at least two meanings of the word *scale* in their evaluation of different types of food.

Write About It

Answers will vary. Students' evaluation of the imaginary product should include these meanings of the word *scale:* a series of musical notes and a machine for weighing people or objects.

"An Arundel Tomb"
Philip Larkin

"The Explosion"
Philip Larkin

"On the Patio"
Peter Redgrove

"Not Waving but Drowning"
Stevie Smith

p. 405 Before You Read
Vocabulary Practice
Sample response: 1. a. horizontally lying b. woman enjoyed the chance to rest and absorb the sunlight 2. a. faithfulness b. to the company earned him an award 3. a. free-spirited fun b. when the rain began

p. 406 Note-taking Guide
Sample response:
Poem: "An Arundel Tomb"
Important Symbols and Their Meanings: Symbol: The images on the tomb are unintended symbols of enduring love; Meter: Iambic tetrameter; Rhyme scheme: abbcac
Theme: Death and its effect on those who survive
Poem: "The Explosion"
Important Symbols and Their Meanings: Symbol: The unbroken eggs represent what is lost; Meter: Trochaic tetrameter; Rhyme scheme: unrhymed
Theme: Death and its effect on those who survive
Poem: "On the Patio"
Important Symbols and Their Meanings: Symbol: The thunderstorms represent the power and force of nature; the wineglass is a symbol of human attempts to capture and possess that force; Meter: Free verse; Rhyme scheme: unrhymed
Theme: The desire to possess the energy and life force of nature
Poem: "Not Waving but Drowning"
Important Symbols and Their Meanings: Symbol: The water is a symbol of the dead man's isolation; Meter: Varying meter; Rhyme scheme: *abcb*
Theme: People are often misinterpreted for an entire lifetime.

p. 407 After You Read
Thinking About the Selection
1. **Graphic Organizer**
Dead Man: I was too far out in the water. I was drowning and trying to get your attention. The cold water did not stop my heart—I was drowning and needed help. That was how life always found me—too far out and drowning.
People Around the Dead Man: Poor fellow. He was out in the water waving to us and having fun. I guess the cold water was just too much for his heart.
2. Answers will vary. Sample response: In "An Arundel Tomb," the stone figures of an earl and countess seem to say that love lasts forever.

Talk About It
Answers will vary. Sample response: The two poems are similar because they describe the effects of powerful forces—a mining blast in "The Explosion" and a thunderstorm in "On the Patio." They are different because "The Explosion" focuses on describing people before and after a deadly blast, and "On the Patio" focuses on describing the power of the thunderstorm.

The Essential Question
Answers will vary, but students should support answers with details from the poem.

p. 408 Vocabulary Skill Review
Now You Do It
1. knee; k
2. limb; b
3. hymn; n
4. lamb; b
5. knob; k
6. knit; k
7. solemn; n
8. climb; b
9. condemn; n

Talk About It
Answers will vary. Students should pronounce each word and then compose nine sentences, one for each word in the column.

Write About It
Answers will vary. Students should use at least six words featured on this page to write a poem about a quiet companion.

"Prayer"
Carol Duffy

"In the Kitchen"
Penelope Shuttle

p. 409 Before You Read
Vocabulary Practice
Sample response: 1. a. speaks b. a warning, but the other people do not hear her
2. a. gleaming b. room seemed to be lit by a thousand candles 3. a. firmly b. helped his parents rebuild their home after the tornado

p. 410 Note-taking Guide
Sample response:

Prayer
Object
Box 1: tree
Box 2: train
Box 3: grade I piano scales
Box 4: radio

Human Action that the Object Performs
Box 1: The tree sings.
Box 2: The train chants in Latin.
Box 3: The grade I piano scales console a lodger.
Box 4: The radio prays.

In the Kitchen
Object
Box 1: ironing board
Box 2: new fridge
Box 3: chair
Box 4: table
Box 5: clock
Box 6: kettle

Human Action that the Object Performs
Box 1: The ironing board gives thanks to God.
Box 2: "The new fridge hums like a maniac."
Box 3: The chair recites a prayer.
Box 4: "The table leaves no stone unturned."
Box 5: The clock casts a vote.
Box 6: The kettle is aware of the good that it does, it loves the world, and it whistles a message to the speaker.

p. 411 After You Read
Thinking About the Selection
1. **Graphic Organizer**
"In the Kitchen": jug of water, ironing board, new fridge, chair, table, clock, kettle

"Prayer": sieve, tree, train, piano scales, calling of a child's name, radio
2. In "Prayer," the sound of a distant train makes a man remember his youth.

Talk About It
Answers will vary. Students should demonstrate an understanding that the items in the speaker's kitchen provide comfort and will not be replaced any time soon.

The Essential Question
Answers will vary, but students should support answers with details from the poem.

p. 412 Vocabulary Skill Review
Now You Do It
1. Careful postoperative treatment was important to avoid infection.
2. Hoshiko decided to postdate her report because she finished it early.
3. The teacher gave a posttest to see what students had learned during the unit.
4. Claudia added a postscript to her letter because she had more news to share.

Talk About It
Answers will vary. Students should discuss postoperative care needed by a patient.

Write About It
Answers will vary. Students should use the words *posttest*, *postdate*, and *postscript* in a friendly letter describing a vocabulary test.

"A Devoted Son"
Anita Desai

p. 413 Before You Read
Vocabulary Practice
Sample response: 1. a. model b. behavior during the school field trip 2. a. agreeable b. dog was always friendly toward friends and visitors 3. a. understand b. how the other students had reached the correct answer

p. 414 Note-taking Guide
Sample response:
Character: Rakesh
Dynamic: yes
Details: At the beginning of the story, Rakesh follows the traditional path of a devoted son. Rakesh's education introduces him to modern ideas, and by the time he is established as a doctor, Rakesh ignores his father's wishes in favor of practicing new, modern medicine.

Character: Varma
Static: yes
Details: Varma remains traditional throughout the story. He does not undergo significant changes, and when his son refuses to honor his wishes regarding diet, Varma considers his son to be very disrespectful.

p. 415 After You Read
Thinking About the Selection
1. **Graphic Organizer**
Sample response:

Rakesh pleases his parents by . . . finishing college, finishing medical school, earning awards, winning a scholarship, finishing his training in India, marrying an Indian girl, working at the hospital, getting promoted, starting his own clinic.
2. Sample response: Rakesh shows his father respect by bowing and touching his father's feet.

Talk About It
Answers will vary. Sample response: I think Rakesh has a difficult choice. On the one hand, he is a doctor who saves lives. On the other hand, he is a respectful son. I think he will decide that he must sacrifice his training as a doctor and show his respect for his father by letting his father die.

The Essential Question
Answers will vary, but students should support opinions with details from the story.

p. 416 Vocabulary Skill Review
Now You Do It
1. Kasi said, "Personally, I thought the movie was dull."
2. The contents of a diary are personal.
3. Because of her outgoing personality, Daniela enjoys talking with everyone she meets.
4. Ballet dancers personify grace and flexibility.

Talk About It
Answers will vary. Students should use the words *personal* and *personally* as they distinguish private and public topics.

Write About It
Answers will vary. Students should use the words *personality* and *personify* in their self-portraits.

"Next Term, We'll Mash You
Penelope Lively

p. 417 Before You Read
Vocabulary Practice
Sample response: 1. a. unusually quiet
b. when the teacher began reading stories
2. a. making a careful judgment about b. his plan to sell products in new markets
3. a. attitude that she was better than other people b. caused her friends to disown her

p. 418 Note-taking Guide
Sample response:
Mrs. Manders's Opinions or Reactions:
Mrs. Manders likes the school's grounds and the atmosphere. She is impressed by the maid's uniform. She likes the headmaster, but she is not sure about his wife.
Mr. Manders's Opinions or Reactions:
Mr. Manders likes the atmosphere. He thinks that St. Edward's is better than two other schools. He likes the fact that "City people" send their boys to the school.
Charles's Opinions or Reactions: Charles is overwhelmed and upset by the boy's questions. He is probably afraid of being mashed by the boys. Charles is silent when his mother asks him whether he would like to attend the school.

p. 419 After You Read
Thinking About the Selection
1. **Graphic Organizer**
Oval 1: His mother worries that he may have become carsick.
Oval 2: He feels overwhelmed by the questions that the other boys ask him.
Oval 3: He feels unsteady on his feet.
Oval 4: He does not answer his mother when she asks him about attending St. Edward's.
Oval 5: His mother worries that he is pale.
2. During his visit with the other boys, Charles hears a voice that warns him, "Next term, we'll mash you. We always mash new boys."

Talk About It
Answers will vary. Students' conversations should demonstrate an understanding of Charles's point of view.

The Essential Question
Answers will vary, but students should support answers with details from the story.

p. 420 Vocabulary Skill Review
Now You Do It
1. Jamie said, "Be careful with my new stamp album; the stamps are not a dime a dozen."
2. Jan looked green with envy as she admired Christina's new video game.
3. Akio knows that he watches too much television and wants to kick the habit.
4. Lisa calls her brother a pain in the neck because he teases her all the time.

Talk About It
Answers will vary. Sample response: people sipping colas in the shade, people swimming at the local pool, people seeing movies in an air-conditioned theater, people visiting in someone's cool basement, people water-skiing on the lake

Write About It
Answers will vary. Students should write a story that explains the origin of the idiom *green with envy*. Students' stories should include the idioms *kick the habit, pain in the neck*, and *a dime a dozen*.

from **We'll Never Conquer Space**
Arthur C. Clarke

p. 421 Before You Read
Vocabulary Practice
Sample response: 1. a. unchangeable b. effects of cutting down the forests 2. a. instant b. mood change seemed strange 3. a. perplexing situation b. The last problem on the math exam

p. 422 Note-taking Guide
Sample response:
Forever Too Large: We can never abolish the space between the stars.
"Time Barrier": Nothing travels faster than light; the distance between colonies renders communication between solar systems impossible.
Independent "Colonies": Even if the speed of light is somehow surpassed, the quantity of space is too much to be conquered; colonies will be so far separated that humans will lose the bonds of "kinship and understanding."

p. 423 After You Read
Thinking About the Selection
1. **Graphic Organizer**
communication: Answers will vary. Sample response: Conversations between locations

will be impossible; by the time news reaches another location, it will be history.
travel: Answers will vary. Sample response: It will take at least five years to travel from one star to another; space colonies will need to be independent of Earth and of one another.
2. According to Clarke, the price of space exploration is time.

Talk About It
Answers will vary. Students' interviews should demonstrate an understanding that Clarke believes that technology cannot overcome some of the obstacles about travel in outer space.

The Essential Question
Answers will vary, but students should support answers with details from the essay.

p. 424 Vocabulary Skill Review
Now You Do It
1. The red dress was the perfect complement to Andrea's dark hair.
2. Mai exercises on the stationary bike in her basement.
3. Mr. Romero is the principal of the local high school.
4. Aunt Katja writes all her letter on elegant ivory stationery.
5. Casey lives by the principle of treating all people kindly.
6. Shelly received a compliment on her fine teamwork.

Talk About It
Answers will vary, but students should describe a few of their memorable experiences and include as many homophones from this page as possible in their descriptions.

Write About It
Answers will vary. Sample response: Welcome to the new school year. As your new principal, I will not be a stationary leader; I plan to walk through the building daily. I will complement your work by providing the support and materials that you need to help educate our students according to the highest principles. I believe in offering a compliment to teachers for a job well done. In fact, I have ordered special stationery for writing notes to praise teachers' efforts.

Informational Texts: Case Studies

p. 428 After You Read
Thinking About the Case Study
1. Answers will vary. Sample response: Clarke wanted rocket technology to be used to develop orbiting space stations that could send and receive radio signals.
2. Answers will vary. Sample response: Clarke concluded that although the initial cost would be great, it would still be less than other methods of replacing and running communication networks.

Reading Skill
3. The rocket would become an artificial satellite that circles the world.
4. Rockets would have to be twice as fast as those already being designed, and materials would need to be ferried up by rockets to the location where the space station would be built.

"I'm Like A Bird"
from Songbook
Nick Hornby

p. 429 Before You Read
Vocabulary Practice
Sample response: 1. a. continuous b. chatter of the people at the next table made it hard to concentrate 2. a. skeptically b. believes that trying to reduce poverty is pointless
3. a. A pleasant feeling of laziness b. spread over the child after she drank a glass of warm milk

p. 430 Note-taking Guide
Sample response:

Hornby's view of Cole Porter's music: It is better than the music that is popular today.
Hornby's thoughts about good, new songs such as "I'm Like a Bird": He enjoys playing good new songs, such as "I'm Like a Bird," repeatedly. The need to play a good song "over and over again" is "harmless." Most needs in this world are not harmless.
What Hornby is trying to "solve" in "I'm Like a Bird": He is trying to determine how the singer created a musical effect in the middle of the song.
What Hornby does with new songs twice a year: He tapes those he enjoys most and listens to them in his car.

p. 431 After You Read
Thinking About the Selection
1. **Graphic Organizer**
Statement: Nick Hornby believes that the best music was written 35 years ago.
True or False? True
Statement: He seldom listens to new music.
True or False? False
Statement: He believes that Nelly Furtado is a better singer than Cole Porter.
True or False? False
Statement: He is glad that there will always be more new songs.
True or False? True
Statement: Hornby says that it is good that pop songs do not have long lives.
True or False? True
2. Hornby describes the act of listening to the same song over and over again as a harmless need.

Talk About It
Answers will vary. Students should take a position on Dave Egger's theory and support it with examples from their own musical experiences.

The Essential Question
Answers will vary, but students should support answers with details from the essay.

p. 432 Vocabulary Skill Review
Now You Do It
Sample sentence:
Box 1: The doctor noticed changes in the cancer cells by studying them under a microscope.
Box 2: The scientists are studying the microorganism responsible for the illness.
Box 3: Lea enjoys microbiology because she is curious about things she cannot easily see.
Box 4: Shino made sure that the microphone was on before he started to speak.

Talk About It
Answers will vary. Sample response: If a *microorganism* could speak, it would probably tell me to put away the *microscope* and mind my own business. If *microorganisms* could speak, scientists who study *microbiology* might find cures to diseases more quickly because the *microorganisms* could share important information.

Write About It

Answers will vary. Students should use the words *microphone* and *micromanage* in a public service announcement targeting adults.

pp. 433–434 Unit Vocabulary Review

A. **Sentence Completion**

2. Welfare is the general health and happiness of people but not the amount of money that people have in their pockets.

3. To rebuild is to build again after something has been damaged or destroyed but not to make minor repairs.

4. A conflict is a disagreement between people, groups, or countries but not a peaceful solution to a problem.

5. Idealism is often based on standards that are difficult to achieve but not on realistic standards.

6. Something that is contemporary belongs to the present time but not to the past.

7. Consciousness is the condition of being awake and aware but not the condition of being asleep and unaware.

8. Trends are ways in which situations develop over time but not the ways in which situations change suddenly.

9. Economic growth relates to trade with other countries but not to painting or arts.

B. **Word Sorting**

Noun: conflict, consciousness, contemporary, idealism, technology, trends, welfare
Verb: conflict, rebuild
Adjective: contemporary, economic

Talk About It

Answers will vary, but students' discussions should include *technology* and as many other words as possible from the word bank.

Write About It

Answers will vary. Students should use as many words from the word bank as possible to summarize a conflict that occurs in a selection from Unit 6.

READER'S NOTEBOOK

READER'S NOTEBOOK ADAPTED VERSION

READER'S NOTEBOOK ENGLISH LEARNER'S VERSION

Learning About Etymologies

p. V9 Graphic Organizer
comb
Original language: Old English
Original meaning: toothed object
Current meaning: a thin strip of hard rubber, plastic, or metal with teeth, passed through the hair to arrange or clean it
costume
Original language: Latin
Original meaning: custom
Current meaning: the style of dress, including accessories, typical of a certain country, period, profession, and so on
guess
Original language: Middle English
Original meaning: to judge or estimate
Current meaning: to form a judgment or estimate of something without actual knowledge or enough facts for certainty
mile
Original language: Latin
Original meaning: thousand
Current meaning: a unit of linear measure equal to 5,280 feet or 1.6097 kilometers
panther
Original language: Greek
Original meaning: same as current meaning
Current meaning: a leopard; specifically, a) a black leopard b) a large or fierce leopard

p. V10 Note-taking
1. **Original meaning:** to hook or take
Current meaning: great destruction and devastation, as that resulting from hurricanes, wars, and so on
2. **Original meaning:** a storehouse
Current meaning: a publication, usually with a paper back and sometimes illustrated, that appears at regular intervals and contains stories, articles, and so on by various writers and, usually, advertisements

p. V10 Note-taking
Graphic Organizer
Sample response:
sports: home run
technology: e-mail
transportation: subway
space travel: space shuttle
medicine: HIV

p. V11 Note-taking
Sample response:
Jerome served one of our favorite dinners, spaghetti and meatballs.
Many years ago, people might take an omnibus to work, but today they would call that vehicle a bus.
We took the most direct route to Aunt Anna's house, which meant driving forty miles on the highway.
We thought we could get to shelter before the storm started, but we did not quite make it.
A few raindrops dampened our jackets.

How to Use a Dictionary

p. V12
1. The correct spelling is "dictionary."
2. The plural is formed by dropping the -y and adding -ies.
3. The word comes from Latin.
4. There are two definitions.
5. The example given is "a Spanish-English dictionary."

p. V13 My Words
Graphic Organizer
Sample response:
New Word: deliberation
Pronunciation: di lib′ər ā′shən
Part of Speech: noun
Origin: Latin
Meanings and Sample Sentence: One meaning is "the consideration and discussion of alternatives before reaching a decision." Another meaning is "carefulness or slowness." The jury's deliberation lasted several days.

New Word: pilfer
Pronunciation: pil′fər
Part of Speech: verb
Origin: Middle French
Meanings and Sample Sentence: The meaning is "to steal." The pirates planned to pilfer objects from the village.

New Word: incorrigible
Pronunciation: in kôr′ə jə bəl
Part of Speech: adjective
Origin: Latin
Meanings and Sample Sentence: The meaning is "cannot be corrected, improved, or reformed, especially because firmly established as a habit." He was an incorrigible liar.

New Word: dejection
Pronunciation: dē jek′shən
Part of Speech: noun
Origin: Latin
Meanings and Sample Sentence: One meaning is "lowness of spirits or depression." His dejection affected others around him.

New Word: elusive
Pronunciation: ē loo′siv
Part of Speech: adjective
Origin: Latin
Meanings and Sample Sentence: One meaning is "tending to escape by quickness or cunning." Another meaning is "hard to grasp or retain mentally." The detective was having problems catching the elusive criminal.

New Word: obstinate
Pronunciation: äb′stə nət
Part of Speech: adjective
Origin: Latin
Meanings and Sample Sentence: One meaning is "unreasonably determined to have one's way or stubborn." A second meaning is "resisting remedy or treatment." A third meaning is "not easily ended." The obstinate girl refused to go to the meeting.

New Word: vitality
Pronunciation: vī tal′ə tē
Part of Speech: noun
Origin: Latin
Meanings and Sample Sentence: One meaning is "vital force." A second meaning is "power to live or go on living." A third meaning is "power to endure or survive." A fourth meaning is "mental or physical vigor." Karen read about the vitality of the Irish culture.

New Word: discern
Pronunciation: di surn′, -zurn′
Part of Speech: verb
Origin: Latin
Meanings and Sample Sentence: One meaning is "to separate a thing mentally from another." A second meaning is "to perceive or recognize." I was able to discern my brother's feelings.

New Word: oppress
Pronunciation: ə pres′
Part of Speech: verb
Origin: Latin
Meanings and Sample Sentence: One meaning is "to weigh heavily on the mind or spirits." A second meaning is "to keep down by the cruel or unjust use of power." A third meaning is "to crush or trample down." The king was oppressing the villagers.

New Word: nascent
Pronunciation: nas′ənt, nā′sənt
Part of Speech: adjective
Origin: Latin
Meanings and Sample Sentence: One meaning is "coming into being or being born." A second meaning is "beginning to form or develop: said of ideas, cultures, and so on." A third meaning is "the state of an element just released from a compound and having unusual chemical activity because atoms of the element have not combined to form molecules." The new custom was in a nascent form.

Vocabulary and the SAT®

p. V19 Note-taking
Graphic Organizer
Sample response:
New Word: abrasion
How You Used Context to Understand the Word: The context actually gave a definition of the word.
New Word: girth
How You Used Context to Understand the Word: The context compared a man's girth to a round pot. This showed me that *girth* had to do with a person's size.
New Word: intimidate
How You Used Context to Understand the Word: The sentence contained a synonym for the word, and that helped me discover its meaning.

New Word: sedate
How You Used Context to Understand the Word: The other words in the description gave away the word's meaning. The person described was very anxious, but then he became very calm after he was sedated.

pp. V20–21 Practice
1. B
2. C
3. A
4. B

p. V21 Practice
1. D
2. B
3. E
4. B
5. D

Communication Guide: Diction

p. V22 Note-taking
Graphic Organizer
Sample response:
Informal: Hey! Glad you could make it!
Ornate: I fear that I will die if coffee is not immediately decanted into my nearly lifeless body.
Abstract: The mayor believes that the litter problem needs to be remedied.
Ordinary: My brother works with computers.
Down-to-Earth: Thanks for your help!
Modern/Slangy: Yeah, it's me. You wanna try some of the food on the menu?

pp. V23–V24 Note-taking
1. Students may list words or phrases such as: "welcome"; "thank you for your time"; "sir"; "ma'am"; "it's nice to meet you"; "achievements"; "this way, please."
2. Students may list words or phrases such as: "this is cool"; "hi"; "come on"; "don't get on that teacher's bad side"; "come here"; "look at this."
3. **Graphic Organizer**
1. informal; formal
2. formal; informal
3. formal; informal
4. informal; formal
5. informal; formal

4. **Graphic Organizer**
Sample response:
1.
Phrase: Hey, what's up?
Formal/Informal: informal
Phrase: Good morning. How are you?
Formal/Informal: formal
2.
Phrase: I beg your pardon. Have you seen my CD?
Formal/Informal: formal
Phrase: Hey, do you know where my CD is?
Formal/Informal: informal
3.
Phrase: Look out for that car!
Formal/Informal: informal
Phrase: Excuse me, but you may want to watch out for that approaching vehicle.
Formal/Informal: formal
4.
Phrase: It was nice speaking with you, Sophie.
Formal/Informal: formal
Phrase: Good talking to ya, Sophie.
Formal/Informal: informal
5.
Phrase: Thank you kindly for the invitation to your celebration.
Formal/Informal: formal
Phrase: Thanks for the invite!
Formal/Informal: informal